Ex Libris.
C. Squire
Coll. Merton - Oxon

WESTMINSTER COMMENTARIES
EDITED BY WALTER LOCK, D.D.
IRELAND PROFESSOR OF THE EXEGESIS
OF HOLY SCRIPTURE

THE EPISTLE
OF
ST JAMES

THE EPISTLE
OF
ST JAMES

WITH AN INTRODUCTION AND NOTES

BY

R. J. KNOWLING, D.D.

CANON OF DURHAM AND PROFESSOR OF DIVINITY
IN THE UNIVERSITY OF DURHAM

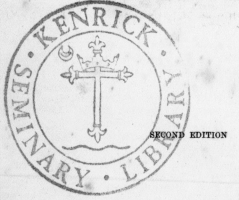

SECOND EDITION

METHUEN & CO. LTD.
36 ESSEX STREET W.C.
LONDON

First Published . . . *October 1904*
Second Edition . . . *October 1910*

PREFATORY NOTE BY THE GENERAL EDITOR

THE primary object of these Commentaries is to be exegetical, to interpret the meaning of each book of the Bible in the light of modern knowledge to English readers. The Editors will not deal, except subordinately, with questions of textual criticism or philology; but taking the English text in the Revised Version as their basis, they will aim at combining a hearty acceptance of critical principles with loyalty to the Catholic Faith.

The series will be less elementary than the Cambridge Bible for Schools, less critical than the International Critical Commentary, less didactic than the Expositor's Bible; and it is hoped that it may be of use both to theological students and to the clergy, as well as to the growing number of educated laymen and laywomen who wish to read the Bible intelligently and reverently.

Each commentary will therefore have

(i) An Introduction stating the bearing of modern criticism and research upon the historical character of the book, and drawing out the contribution which the book, as a whole, makes to the body of religious truth.

(ii) A careful paraphrase of the text with notes on the more difficult passages and, if need be, excursuses on any points of special importance either for doctrine, or ecclesiastical organisation, or spiritual life.

But the books of the Bible are so varied in character that considerable latitude is needed, as to the proportion which the various parts should hold to each other. The General Editor will therefore only endeavour to secure a general uniformity in scope and character: but the exact method adopted in each case and the final responsibility for the statements made will rest with the individual contributors.

By permission of the Delegates of the Oxford University Press and of the Syndics of the Cambridge University Press the Text used in this Series of Commentaries is the Revised Version of the Holy Scriptures.

WALTER LOCK

PREFACE

IN preparing this edition of the *Epistle of St James* I have tried to keep in view the primary objects of the Westminster Commentaries, and the various classes of readers for whom they are intended. During the passing of these pages through the press, the recent attacks upon the Epistle have received a prompt and vigorous reply from the veteran Professor, Dr Bernhard Weiss, of the University of Berlin. The force and firmness of this reply (to which frequent reference will be found) and the fact that it comes from a scholar of such eminence may well administer a rebuke to those English writers who apparently think that, in their inconsiderate objections to the traditional views of the Church, they may claim the support of every German critic of learning and status.

It is a pleasant duty to express my most grateful thanks to Dr Lock for his many and valuable suggestions, and for his ungrudging care in the revision of the proofs.

R. J. KNOWLING

Sept. 1904

NOTE TO SECOND EDITION

SINCE this Commentary was first published two important additions have been made to the literature, viz. a third edition of Prof. Mayor's volume, and a posthumous work of Dr Hort's (as far as ch. iv. 7), edited by the Master of Selwyn College (1909). A criticism of Dr Hort's work by Prof. Mayor will be found in the April and June numbers of the *Expositor* 1910.

Dr Hort in this final utterance regards 62 A.D. as the date and the writer as James the Just, head or bishop of the Church at Jerusalem, a brother of the Lord as being a son of Joseph by a former wife. This St James was not one of the Twelve, but probably became a believer by a special appearance of the Lord vouchsafed to him.

It may be added that the *Expositor*, Feb. 1907, contains an article of interest by Prof. G. Currie Martin entitled "The Epistle of St James as a Storehouse of the Sayings of Jesus." The writer regards the work before us as not strictly an Epistle at all, but as a work containing a collection of genuine Sayings of Jesus, around which other sayings gathered as time went on.

CONTENTS

INTRODUCTION

SPECIAL interest must always be felt in a book to which so many able critics assign the earliest place amongst New Testament writings, and in an author who possibly shared in the earthly life and home of our Lord. Such high claims, however, have naturally been subjected to a close examination, and often to a keen opposition, and it is not the purpose of the present Introduction to assume their validity.

I. At first sight, indeed, it might seem that nothing could be more natural than the assumption that the author of this Epistle was a Jew, and that his readers were of Jewish nationality. But as even this assumption is refused to us by some phases of recent criticism, it may be well to note a few of the grounds upon which we believe it to be justified. Thus we might lay stress upon the difficulty in interpreting the address of the letter, ch. i. 1, in a symbolical or spiritual sense (see note *in loco*); or upon the expressions 'Abraham our father,' ii. 21, 'Lord of Sabaoth,' v. 4, comp. Isaiah v. 9; upon the knowledge which the writer presupposes in his readers of the history of Job and the prophets, v. 11, 17; and of Elijah's prayer as a type of successful prayer (see note on v. 17); upon his own knowledge of Jewish formulae in the use of oaths, and of the current disposition to indulge in reckless cursing and swearing, iii. 9, v. 12; upon his employment of the word 'synagogue' for the place of meeting for worship, ii. 2[1]; upon the emphasis with which

[1] Dr Grafe, *Die Stellung und Bedeutung des Jakobusbriefes*, 1904, maintains that the word was used for religious pagan associations in Greece, but according to Schürer this was not strictly so, as the word was used rather for the yearly festal assemblies of such associations. But this usage does not alter the significance of the word by St James; see note on ii. 2.

Dr Grafe also tries to weaken the force of the expression 'Lord of Sabaoth' on the ground that it would be known to Gentile as well as to Jewish Christians. But the point is that the expression is used only by St James in the N.T. In Romans ix. 29 it is found in a quotation from Isaiah i. 9.

he refers to the Jewish Law, ii. 9–11, iv. 11, 12, and to the primary article of the Jewish Creed, ii. 19[1].

But in addition to these instances, the cumulative force of which it is difficult to ignore, we may also lay stress upon the general representation which the letter gives us of the social conditions of those for whom it was intended. It is remarkable, for example, that no reference is made to the relationship between masters and slaves. A St Peter or a St Paul, on the other hand, in addressing mixed Churches constantly dwelt upon this social relationship. It is quite true that in a Jewish-Christian document, which is in many respects akin to this Epistle of St James, the *Didache*, reference is made to the bondservant and handmaid in iv. 10, 11, i.e. in a part of the work which may carry us back to a very early date[2]. But it is evident from the context that both masters and servants are regarded as servants of the One God, and that no relationship such as that of Christian servant and heathen master is contemplated. In this connection, too, we may note the vivid picture, iv. 13, of the eager life of commerce and gain, and yet of the comparative homelessness of the traders, a life so characteristic of the Jews always, and specially of those of the Diaspora, facilitated as it was by the easy means of communication throughout the Empire in the days of the early Church[3].

[1] On the force of the expression 'do they not blaspheme?' ii. 7, as pointing most probably to unbelieving Jews blaspheming the Name of Christ, see note *in loco*.

Beyschlag draws attention to the fact that the expression 'Abraham our father,' ii. 21, is not explained in any spiritual sense as in Rom. iv. 1. See also on the possible Jewish liturgical formulae in i. 12, ii. 5, Dr Chase, *The Lord's Prayer in the Early Church*, p. 18.

[2] This document was first published in 1883, although it had been discovered in Constantinople some ten years earlier. In the first part, Ch. I–VI., in which it will be noted that most of the parallels to St James's Epistle are found (see note on p. xiv.), we have probably a series of moral instructions which were originally Jewish, but which with some additions were adopted for use in certain Jewish-Christian communities. The greater part of this portion of the work may have been in use probably in a written form as early as 70 A.D. amongst Christians (Art. 'Didache' in Hastings' *D. B.* v. pp. 444, 448, by J. V. Bartlet, and *Apostolic Age*, pp. 515, 517, by the same writer). In any case there is good reason for placing the *Didache* in its present form at the close of the first century, see Bishop of Worcester, *Church and the Ministry*, p. 417. For English readers an article on the *Didache* by Dr Harnack at the end of vol. I. of Schaff and Herzog's *Encyclopaedia of Religious Knowledge* will be of interest. Although inclined to date the document in its present form as late as 120–165 A.D., Dr Harnack allows that some of its sources are very old, and he sees in the first part, Ch. I–VI., a catechism of Jewish origin for the instruction of proselytes, which passed over into the Christian Church, and was used as an address at Baptism.

[3] See Professor Ramsay, *Expositor*, 1903, on 'Travel and Correspondence among the Early Christians.'

It is, again, remarkable that in a letter so practical, no warning is uttered against idol worship, and that no reference is made to such questions concerning it as those which agitated the Church of Corinth, or which were discussed at the Apostolic Council. No doubt it may be said that the *Didache* refers to such sins, but it is quite possible that some of its statements with regard to idolatry may be simply connected with the Old Testament[1], and it would also seem that the same document refers to heathen sins of which St James knows nothing, and that in vi. 3 the contact with heathenism is clear, cf. Acts xv. 19 (although even here the rigidity of the Jewish-Christian is emphasised in comparison with 1 Cor. x. 25)[2]. But it will be noted that in the Epistle of St James no allusion whatever is made, as is the case with other of the New Testament writings, to the former idolatries of the readers. Moreover, in this same connection we may observe that no warning is uttered against sins of impurity and fornication, as is the case in those Epistles in which intercourse of the readers with the heathen world was part and parcel of their surroundings[3]. If it is urged that here again the *Didache* takes note of sins of this character, it is evident that the list of such vices as are mentioned in that document marks a writer who had been brought into connection with the influence of Graeco-Roman civilisation.

But whilst the Epistle is distinguished by these remarkable omissions, the sins and weaknesses which the writer describes are exactly those faults which our Lord blames in His countrymen, and especially in the party of the Pharisees. And even if we consider some of the faults specified as too general in their character to belong to any one party, yet some of them are certainly characteristic of the Jewish leaders whom our Lord condemned, e.g. the excessive zeal for the outward observance of religious duties, the fondness for the office of teacher, the false wisdom, the overflowing of malice, the pride, the hypocrisy, the respect of persons. In spite

[1] Cf. e.g. 'My child, be not an augur, for it leads to idolatry,' iii. 4, and Lev. xix. 26.

[2] 'But concerning meats, bear that which thou art able; yet abstain by all means from meat sacrificed to idols; for it is the worship of dead gods' ; vi. 3.

[3] Mr Parry in his *Discussion*, p. 89, admits that this argument would be forcible if it could be shown that St James had any personal experience of the needs of his hearers. But if St James was writing, as Mr Parry thinks, more than ten or twelve years after the Apostolic Council, it would be strange that he should make no reference in his Epistle to the dangers which must have been involved in any contact between Jewish and Gentile Christians, viz. 'pollutions of idols, and fornication,' or these dangers would not have found a place in the decree of the Council.

of all his zeal and scrupulosity the 'religious' Jew had forgotten
that the first and second commandments were fulfilled in the love
of God and his neighbour, and had fallen back, as it were, upon a
fatal trust in religious privileges, in the promises made to Abraham,
a false confidence which the Baptist and our Lord had alike
condemned, and which St James was called upon still to combat.

And here we may pause to notice that one virtue upon which
St James lays stress as indispensable for teacher and taught alike is
the virtue of meekness, i. 21, iii. 13; the same virtue which is
emphasised in *Didache*, iii. 7, 'be meek, since the meek shall inherit
the earth' (Ps. xxxvii. 11; cf. Matt. v. 8)[1]. In this latter document, as in the Epistle of St James, we have the picture of a meek,
single-hearted, uncomplaining, and resigned piety. And this picture
is drawn in that part of the *Didache* which is undoubtedly the
oldest, which is marked by a Jewish tone and phraseology. If,
therefore, we find a similar type and piety portrayed in St James,
if we find similar thoughts and expressions, we may justly draw
from this similarity an argument that both writings were designed
for readers of Jewish nationality[2].

And whilst these points of contact are observable with the
Didache (some portion of which in a Judaeo-Christian form may
have been in current oral use much earlier than 70 A.D., see note
above, p xii.), it is noticeable that our Epistle may also be connected
in some thoughts and expressions with a Jewish document, dating
some fifty years *before* our Lord's Advent, the *Psalms of Solomon*[3],

[1] 'In the Palestine of the first century there was no lack of religious teaching. The Scribe was a familiar figure in Galilee as much as in Judaea; he was
to be met everywhere, in the synagogue, in the market-place, in the houses of
the rich. With him went a numerous following of attached scholars. The first
business of the Rabbi was "to raise up many disciples," and the first care of the
good Jew to "make to himself a Master." It is not without a bitter reminiscence of the religious condition of Palestine that St James of Jerusalem
counsels the members of the Christian communities to which he wrote, "Be not
many teachers, my brethren, knowing that we shall receive heavier judgment."'
Dr Swete, *Expositor*, Feb. 1903.

[2] Attention is drawn to some of these in the notes, but the following may be
given as allowed by von Soden: James iii. 3-6, 8, 9, and *Did.* ii. 4; James
iii. 14, 18, and *Did.* ii. 5; James i. 8, iv. 8, and *Did.* iv. 3; James v. 16, and
Did. iv. 14; *Hand-Commentar*, III. p. 169, 3rd edit. A similar list is given by
Mayor, and for a resemblance in the general picture of the pious Israelite drawn
in James and the *Didache*, see J. V. Bartlet's *Apostolic Age*, pp. 250 ff., and also
Hastings' *B. D.* v. p. 446.

[3] These points of resemblance will be found in the notes, but they are
referred to by Dr Moffatt in *Exp. Times*, Feb. 1902. God, in the *Psalms of
Solomon*, is especially the protector and succour of the poor and lowly as in the
Epistle; cf. also James iii. 5, and Psalms xii. 2, 3; James iii. 18, and Psalms
xii. 6; James iv. 1, and Psalms xii. 4.

although the outlook in the Epistle is less narrow, and its teaching far deeper.

This Jewish character of the Epistle is still further emphasised by the ingenious attempt of Spitta and Massebieau to discover in it merely a Jewish document Christianised by the interpolation of two or more words in i. 1 and ii. 1 ('and of the Lord Jesus Christ,' i. 1; 'our (Lord) Jesus Christ,' ii. 1[1]). This theory of interpolation is so entirely arbitrary that it is severely criticised and condemned by critics who in many other respects differ widely from each other[2]. It is quite incredible for instance that anyone who wished to pass off a Jewish work as a Christian document should have contented himself with the introduction of the two passages and of the few words mentioned above. Moreover, the phraseology of v. 7, 8, in its reference to the 'coming' or rather the 'presence' of the Lord, is unmistakably Christian, and although passages in *Enoch* are cited as parallels, yet this terminology is not to be found in them.

Spitta has certainly not proved his thesis, but he has helped to accentuate the fact that the writer of the Epistle was not only intimately acquainted with the Old Testament, and that in him the spirit of the old prophets, of an Amos or a Jeremiah, lived again, but that he was also acquainted with the Wisdom literature so well known amongst his countrymen of the Dispersion. The points of contact between St James and Ecclesiasticus have been fully illustrated by Dr Edersheim as also by Dr Zahn[3]. It is not too much to

---

[1] Spitta omits the words 'and of the Lord Jesus Christ' in i. 1, whilst Massebieau omits only 'Jesus Christ.'

[2] Amongst others by Zahn, Harnack, von Soden, Beyschlag, Belser, M‘Giffert, Adeney in *Critical Review*, July, 1896, O. Cone in Art. 'Epistle of James,' *Encycl. Bibl.*, and Sieffert in the new edition of Herzog. It is only fair to say that Spitta and Massebieau arrived at their conclusion quite independently. Mr G. A. Simcox in the *Journal of Theol. Studies*, II. July, 1901, p. 586, apparently approves of the violent method by which Spitta would get rid of the words so fatal to his thesis in ii. 1; and it is not at all surprising that the *Church Quarterly Review*, Oct. 1901, p. 8, should point out in reference to this approval that it is perfectly easy to evade and escape every difficulty, and to prove anything, if we are at liberty to treat any passage which conflicts with our own theories as a gloss.

[3] References will be found to these in the notes, but for convenience the most important are given here : James i. 5 = Ecclus. xli. 22, cf. xviii. 17, xx. 14; James i. 6, 8 = Ecclus. i. 28, ii. 12, vii. 10; James i. 9, 11 = Ecclus. i. 30, iii. 18, xxxi. 5, 9; James i. 2-4, 12 = Ecclus. i. 23, ii. 1-5; James i. 13 = Ecclus. xv. 11-20; James i. 19 = Ecclus. iv. 29; James i. 19 = Ecclus. v. 11; James ii. 1-6 = Ecclus. x. 19-24, xiii. 9; James iii. 2 = Ecclus. xix. 16; James iii. 9 = Ecclus. xvii. 3, 4; James v. 3-6 = Ecclus. xii. 10, xxix. 10; James v. 13 = Ecclus. xxxviii. 9-15. For a list see Zahn, *Einleitung*, I. 87; Edersheim in *Speaker's Commentary*, *Apocrypha*, II. 22; Plummer, *St James*, p. 72; and references in Spitta. Dr Salmon thinks (*Introd.* p. 465) that the coincidences are insufficient to prove that Ecclus. was used by St James.

say that St James is so Judaic in his language, allusions, and modes of thought that we can in many cases find exact Rabbinic parallels to his words, although we must not forget that if the result of our inquiry is to prove beyond reasonable doubt the acquaintance of St James with a widely circulated Jewish book, like Ecclesiasticus, it also illustrates in the most decisive manner the difference in spiritual standpoint between the writer of that book and the writer of the Epistle of St James.

If we turn to the Book of Wisdom it is quite possible to find many turns of thought and expression which seem to indicate an acquaintance with, and a high value of, this book by the writer of St James[1]; yet even in the Book of Wisdom, which is often regarded as in some respects the most valuable of the Apocryphal writings, we are again conscious of the same difference in spiritual standpoint noted above[2].

II. How may we account for this? The readers of the Epistle of St James are not only Jews, they are believing, i.e. Christian Jews. No one has accentuated more than Harnack the criticism that Spitta's theory, however tempting, does not cover all the facts of the case, and that some of the passages in the Epistle cannot be fairly referred to a Jewish document[3]. Amongst these he would include especially ch. i. 18, 25, 27, ii. 12, v. 7 ff., and also the use of the word 'faith' in ch. i. 3. To these we may add the phrase 'my beloved brethren,' which occurs no less than three times, ch. i. 16, 19, ii. 5, a phrase to which Spitta can find no Jewish parallel except the formal word 'brethren,' whilst St James's language would naturally emphasise the intercourse of Christians 'loving as brethren,' and amongst whom the title 'beloved brethren' was evidently in common use. But whilst we fully recognise the

---

[1] Cf. James i. 5, Wisd. viii. 21; James i. 17, Wisd. vii. 18; James i. 19, Wisd. i. 11; James ii. 6, Wisd. ii. 10, 19; James ii. 13, Wisd. vi. 6; James iv. 13–16, Wisd. v. 8–14; James v. 4–6, Wisd. ii. 12–20. See Plummer, *St James*, p. 74; Farrar, *Speaker's Commentary, Apocrypha*, I. 408; and the references in Spitta.

Both Dr B. Weiss and Dr Zahn are of opinion that the evidence is insufficient to prove that St James was acquainted with the Book of Wisdom, whilst on the other hand von Soden allows a close acquaintance both with it and with Ecclesiasticus.

[2] Another wide difference is St James's recognition of a conception wanting in the two Jewish books, that of a *personal* Messiah.

[3] Harnack rightly emphasises the fact that we have not only to note what the Epistle contains, but also what it does *not* contain, *Chron.* I. p. 490; and this is observable in an entire absence of the Rabbinical conceits and puerilities so characteristic of Rabbinical literature.

difficulty of regarding the two unmistakable Christian references (i. 1, ii. 1) as interpolations, and of believing that a writer who wished to transform a Jewish document into a Christian one would content himself with these additions[1], we should also bear in mind how much these two statements presuppose and involve. Jesus of Nazareth is the Christ; in this the writer is at one with the earliest Christian preaching; Jesus is Lord; in this the writer is at one with the earliest form of baptismal confession, 1 Cor. xii. 3. But these claims so full of significance for a Jew could scarcely have been entertained without some full and definite acquaintance with the facts upon which they were based. Further, this belief that Jesus was the Christ involved for the writer not only the acceptance of the fulfilment of the splendid prophecies of his nation in a despised and crucified blasphemer, not only the admission of certain historical facts, but an obligation to entire service and devotion (i. 1). And the writer, who thus speaks of himself in the same breath as the bondservant of God and of the Lord Jesus Christ, speaks of his readers as brethren, and not only so, but as brethren united with him not only in a common nationality but in a common faith; cf. ii. 1, 7, v. 7. In the same manner, the phrase 'the Lord of glory,' ii. 1, not only invests Jesus Christ with a Divine attribute, but carries with it a belief in the Ascension, and in the triumph over death and the grave. St Paul in an Epistle in which he emphasises his agreement with the other Apostles in the great facts of the Christian Creed, as e.g. the Resurrection, 1 Cor. xv. 1–11, takes occasion to speak of Jesus by the same title, 'the Lord of glory' (or rather 'of *the* glory,' 1 Cor. ii. 8), and it is not unreasonable to suppose that the phrase might have become a recognised title (for St Paul like St James introduces it without any explanation as an expression well known) of the Incarnate, Risen, and Ascended Lord (cf. John xvii. 5 and note *in loco*). Moreover, as St Paul introduces the title, which he only once uses, to point a significant contrast between the philosophy of the world, the wisdom which he encountered in the schools of Greek and Jew alike, and the philosophy of God, so St James introduces the same title with an immediate and very practical purpose. He would thus mark decisively and unmistakably the pettiness of all distinctions of human and social life in presence of the fact that every

---

[1] The *Sibyllines*, e.g. are no true parallels, for in these cases, as Dr Moffatt points out, interpolations were made, not to give the writings a Christian appearance and colour, but to transform them into prophecies or corroborations of Christian truth, *Historical N.T.* p. 705, 2nd edit.

Christian was enlisted in the service of One Who shared in the Divine and eternal glory. Thus the only two passages which contain direct Christian allusions help to remind us of a truth, which we should never forget, viz. that in the Epistle of St James we are dealing not with an elaborate argument, or with a philosophical treatise, but with a letter full of exhortations to meet practical needs and daily questions[1].

From the same practical standpoint the writer plainly regards the future coming of the Lord, His 'Presence,' a word which we can scarcely hesitate to refer to Christ (v. 8, 9). In view of that event men were to gain both hope and patience. And not only is the Lord standing at the door; He is amongst them, ready to heal and to save (v. 14, 15). And thus the writer delivers a counsel, specially adapted to the pressing needs of trial and persecution, whilst he would raise the daily burden of suffering and sin by recalling men to the abiding power of 'the Name,' which still conferred both forgiveness and health no less than in the earliest days of the Church's life. Christ had promised to be with His Church 'all the days,' until the consummation of the age, when He would return as Judge; and the faith of St James for things present and things to come is centred in a Divine Person, Jesus the Christ, in Whose presence there is neither rich nor poor, Who is the same Lord rich unto all who call upon Him; and that faith was not abstract or theoretical, it was not to be gauged by the number of times which its possessor named the name of Jesus, as if, as Reuss put it, his Christian convictions were a matter of arithmetic[2].

Nor is there any occasion to affirm that in the Epistle before us, and in the Sermon on the Mount, the Son of God is concealed, as it were, in the Prophet of Israel. In that Sermon it is too often forgotten that Jesus claims not only to be greater than Moses, not only to possess a supernatural power which He can impart to others, but to be the future Judge of mankind (Matt. vii. 21, 22). And so

---

[1] Nösgen has well pointed out how much the references in St James, and in the other Epistles of the N.T., to the Gospels are evidently based upon practical motives, and introduced for practical purposes; but he also shows, not only the fulness of these references, but how much they presuppose, when we consider the epistolary character of the writings in question: *Neue Jahrbücher für deutsche Theologie*, 1895.

[2] Even if there is no allusion to any of our Lord's miracles (see however note on ii. 19), the Epistle was undoubtedly written at a time when miraculous powers were still working in the Church, and these powers were the result of the Divine energy of Christ, and successfully maintained in obedience to His commands, v. 14, 15.

too, in this Epistle of St James, it is too often forgotten that while Elijah, the great prophet of the Old Testament, is 'a man of like passions with ourselves,' Jesus is the 'Lord of glory,' the arbiter of human destiny, the bestower of a Divine strength.

It is sometimes urged that there is an almost total lack of the two controlling conceptions of our Lord's teaching, 'the fatherhood of God' and 'the kingdom of God.' But surely it is enough to point out that even in this short Epistle God is spoken of twice as Father, i. 27, iii. 9, to say nothing of the expression 'Father of lights,' and that He is also represented as begetting us of His own will by the Word of truth, i. 17, 18, and that the teaching of St James presupposes the same Divine kingdom as in the Sermon on the Mount, ii. 5[1].

A further objection to the Christian character of the Epistle is often raised on the ground that no connection is traced by the writer between conversion and forgiveness and the atoning death of Christ, if indeed any reference at all can be found to the fact of His death. But even so, it must be remembered that the practical nature of the Epistle may help us to account for this. For St James, at all events, salvation is not only a new life coming from God, but it is 'the word of truth' grafted in our hearts which has the power of saving our souls; and if St James is not as explicit as St John in his doctrine of the new birth, he plainly anticipates the declaration of St Paul, 'the Spirit of life which is in Christ Jesus hath made us free from the law of sin and death.' Nor does it follow that St James knew nothing, or recognised nothing, of the validity of the atoning sacrifice made by our Lord in offering up Himself. The earliest speeches of St Peter lay stress upon repentance and conversion, but whilst undoubtedly they mention the fact, they too lay no stress upon the doctrinal significance of the death of Christ; and yet when St Paul writes to the Corinthians that Christ died for our sins according to the Scriptures (1 Cor. xv. 3), it is evident that he is not putting forward something new, but a statement in the acceptance of which both he and the earliest preachers of the Gospel were at one; he is only referring to an aspect of the death of Christ, which in his own earliest and undoubted Epistles he takes for granted as everywhere acknowledged and believed (cf. 1 Thess. v. 9, 10; Gal. i. 4). But if this Epistle

---

[1] Beyschlag, *Neutest. Theologie*, I. 344 (1891), rightly emphasises this fundamental conception common to St James and the commencement of our Lord's teaching.

speaks less of Christ by name than any other Epistle, there is no Epistle which contains so many references to our Lord's teaching, and, one might fairly say, so many echoes of His words in the Gospels. That the Epistle is permeated with doctrine similar to that of the Sermon on the Mount is admitted without hesitation by Dr Schmiedel, but he proceeds to add that the parallels are closer to the *Didache* and to *Barnabas*, and draws a distinction between St Matthew's meaning in v. 37 and James v. 12, although he admits at the same time that the latter may be quoted from St Matthew. Spitta would attempt to explain these parallels by the fact that both the Gospels and Epistles are dependent upon older Jewish documents, but it cannot be said that this theory accounts for the close resemblance between James v. 12 and Matt. v. 34, 37, James v. 2, 3 and Matt. vi. 19, and the same might be said of other instances (see further below on list of resemblances between St James and our Lord's Sermon on the Mount); and Spitta is fairly exposed to the criticism that, whilst he weakens the force of the parallels between the Epistle and the Gospels, he eagerly clutches at any supposed or remote parallel between it and Jewish writings. Thus in James ii. 5, as compared with St Matt. v. 3, St Luke vi. 20, we are assured that there is no reminiscence of the words of Jesus, whilst every possible Jewish promise in favour of the poor may be cited as a likely origin for St James's language, even passages in which there is plainly no combination of the two conceptions of 'the poor' and 'the kingdom.' It is difficult too to see why Spitta should trace all kinds of verbal parallels between James and 1 Peter, and argue from them for the dependence of the latter Epistle upon the former, whilst he refuses to draw any conclusion of dependence from the number of obvious parallels between the Sermon on the Mount and the Epistle before us.

But we may proceed further. Even if the Name of Christ was removed from the Epistle, yet His Spirit abides in it, and one might well say that if every conscious reference to any particular words of Christ on the part of the author was denied to us, the more striking becomes the connection between the teaching of the writer and the teaching of Christ, between the moral elevation of the Epistle and that of the Sermon on the Mount.

Now these references which, as we believe, the Epistle contains to the teaching of our Lord, are undoubtedly of a marked and peculiar character. They are not in any case exact quotations, although one could write in the margin of the Epistle a very considerable number of parallels, say for example with the Sermon on the Mount; they are references of such a kind as might have come from the fulness of a faithful memory, a memory retentive not merely of oral tradition but of words actually heard from the lips of Jesus. This is admitted even in quarters where we might not expect it. 'When,' wrote Renan, 'James speaks of humility, of patience, of pity, of the exaltation of the humble, of the joy which underlies tears, he seems to have retained in memory the very words of Jesus' (*L'Antéchrist*, p. 54, 3rd edition). So again he speaks of 'this little writing of James as thoroughly impregnated with a kind of evangelical perfume; as giving us sometimes a direct echo of the words of Jesus, as still retaining all the vividness of the life in Galilee' (*ubi supra*, p. 62). So too von Soden, although admitting the force of Spitta's strictures to some extent, is nevertheless constrained to acknowledge that some passages at least in the Epistle can be best explained as reminiscences of the words of Jesus.

It is commonly said, and with truth, that these reminiscences are most striking in relation to that part of our Lord's teaching which we call the Sermon on the Mount[1]. And it is important to remember that this likeness extends not merely, as in some cases, to the letter, but to a general harmony between the Epistle and those principles of His Kingdom which our Lord proclaimed from the Mount in Galilee. In the Sermon and in the Epistle the meaning of the old Law is deepened and spiritualised, and the principle of love is emphasised as its fulfilment; in each, righteousness is set forth as the doing of the Divine will in contrast to the saying 'Lord, Lord!'; in each, divided service is condemned as inadmissible; the choice cannot be God *and* the world, but God *or* the world; so too in each, God is the Father, Who gives liberally every good and perfect gift, the God Who answers prayer, Who

---

[1] The following passages may be noted : Matt. v. 3, James ii. 5 ; Matt. v. 7, James ii. 13; Matt. v. 11, 12, James i. 2; Matt. v. 9, James iii. 18; Matt. v. 22, James i. 19 ; Matt. v. 34–37, James v. 12 ; Matt. vi. 16, James ii. 15, 16 (see Mr Mayor's note p. lxxxii.); Matt. vi. 19, James v. 2; Matt. vi. 24, James iv. 4 ; Matt. vii. 1, James iv. 11, 12, v. 9; Matt. vii. 7, 8, James i. 5, iv. 3; Matt. vii. 12, James ii. 8; Matt. vii. 16, James iii. 11, 12; Matt. vii. 24, James i. 22. In addition to Mr Mayor's full and valuable list, Salmon, *Introduction*, p. 455, 5th edit., C. F. Schmid, *Biblical Theology of the N.T.* p. 365, E.T., and Zahn, *Einleitung*, I. p. 87, contain a helpful series of parallels; and instances besides those given above will be found in the notes. See also the valuable note in B. Weiss, *Einleitung in das N.T.* p. 390, 3rd edit.

delivers us from evil, Who would have men merciful as their
Father is merciful; in each, Jesus is Lord and Judge; and in each a
kingdom is revealed, in which the pure in heart draw nigh unto
God, and a blessing rests upon those who are poor as to the world,
and meek and lowly in spirit.

But it has been further maintained that there are special
likenesses not only to St Matthew but to St Luke; St Luke, it is
urged, may very probably have had access to an early tradition of
the Jewish Palestinian Church, which he follows both in the parts
peculiar to his Gospel and also in Acts i–xii. It is however very
doubtful how far these alleged points of contact justify the contention that the Epistle of St James and the Jerusalem source used by
St Luke date from the same place and the same time. There is no
difficulty in admitting a likeness between the teaching of St Luke
and that of St James, but the parallels which are cited in support
do not involve any literary dependence, and they may easily be
referred to St James's knowledge of our Lord's teaching, and to the
fact that he and St Luke would be opposing the same social
dangers[1].

The warnings e.g. against the rich, and the blessedness of men
of low estate, so strongly emphasised by our Lord, may be accounted
for by the social condition of Palestine in the days of His Ministry.
And that teaching found a place, as we know, and a prominent
place, in the Epistle of St James and in the Gospel of St Luke:
cf. Luke vi. 24; James iv. 1 ff.

Whilst then there is no reason to suppose that James iv. 14 has
any special connection with the parable of the rich man who was
not rich towards God, Luke xii. 16–21, or that any close parallel
exists between James i. 17 and Luke xi. 13, or between James iii. 1
and Luke xii. 48, there is much no doubt in the Epistle which shows
how fully St James had caught the spirit of the Lord of glory, Who
was no respecter of persons.

And may we not believe that St Luke would have gained some
knowledge of this same Divine example and its influence from
St James himself? At Jerusalem the two men had met, Acts xxi.
17, 18, and the type of piety which we find presented to us in the
earliest chapters of St Luke's Gospel is closely in accordance with

---

[1] 'Like the Epistle of James, Luke reflects the trading atmosphere of early
Palestinian Christians; the dangers presented by poverty and wealth to the
faith are vividly present to his mind,' Art. 'Sermon on the Mount' (Moffatt),
Encycl. Bibl. IV. 4379.

that presented to us in the Epistle of St James. Amongst 'the quiet in the land,' St James himself in earlier days might have found a place, and it is noticeable that in his Epistle he holds up to us a character marked by meekness and endurance.

The word, moreover, which he uses three times in his Epistle for patience and endurance is only found twice in the Gospels, and both times in our Lord's sayings as recorded by St Luke (James i. 3, 4, v. 11; Luke viii. 15, xxi. 19).

In the *Didache*, v. 2, we have a picture of the unjust judges of the poor, the advocates of the rich, from whom meekness and forbearance are far removed, not recognising Him Who made them, corrupters of the creatures of God. From such men deliverance was to be sought, for they were altogether sinful. And there may well have been many simple folk in the Christian Church who were learning, in the light of the Life of Jesus, the price which God set upon meekness and lowliness of heart, and who were striving to win their souls in patience.

Space forbids us to enter more fully into this part of our subject, but it may be observed that von Soden, in allowing that some expressions in St James are most naturally explained as reminiscences of the words of Jesus, makes reference to each of the three Synoptists; i. 5 and Luke xi. 9 = Matt. vii. 7; i. 6 and Mark xi. 23 = Matt. xxi. 21; iv. 3 and Luke xi. 10 = Matt. vii. 8; iv. 4 and Mark viii. 38 = Matt. xii. 39, xvi. 4; iv. 4 and Luke xvi. 13 = Matt. vi. 24 (*Hand-Commentar zum N.T.*, 1899, 3rd edit.). But von Soden would confine us most positively to the Synoptists; and we naturally ask if the Epistle of St James has no point of contact with the phraseology of St John. It may seem, perhaps, that P. Ewald has overstated his case in claiming references in this one short Epistle to portions of St John's Gospel, differing so widely as the conversation of our Lord with Nicodemus, and the High-priestly Prayer (*Das Hauptproblem der Evangelienfrage*, pp. 58–68, 1890). But if the pillar Apostles were so closely associated in the early Church at Jerusalem as St Paul's statement, Gal. ii. 9, undoubtedly implies, such intimacy precludes any surprise at the acquaintance of St James with what P. Ewald calls the Johannean tradition. To these points of contact between the Gospel of St John and St James's Epistle both Zahn and Mayor draw attention[1], and we may notice as the most important, James i. 17 and John iii. 3;

---

[1] Zahn, *Einleitung*, I. 88, and Mayor, *St James*, p. lxxxiv.

James i. 18 and John vi. 39, also xvii. 17; James i. 18, 25 and John viii. 31, 32; James i. 25, iv. 17 and John xiii. 17.

But the likeness between St James and the Sermon on the Mount, which may be traced as we have noted in other respects, may be further seen in the frequent employment of imagery derived from the world of nature and of mankind. And in this way again we may draw the conclusion that the writer of the Epistle, if not a hearer of our Lord, was at any rate a Jew of Palestine. The fondness of the Galilaeans for teaching by imagery and parable[1] has been often instanced in this connection, and reference may also be made to the local colouring with which the Epistle abounds.

Some of these allusions may perhaps be regarded as too general for our argument, as e.g. references to figs, oil, wine; but on the other hand it may be fairly said of others that they belong more peculiarly to Palestine, e.g. i. 11; iii. 11, 12; v. 7, 17, 18. Possibly in iii. 12 we may find a reference to the Dead Sea, and in i. 6, iii. 4, a familiarity with a port like Joppa, although we need not adopt the solution that the Epistle was written there[2]. In addition to these local allusions we have seen occasion to note the probable fondness of the author for a Palestinian writer, Jesus the son of Sirach.

III. But can we go further in our identification of the writer of this Epistle? He is a Jew, a Jew of Palestine, possibly a hearer of our Lord, or at least one who was closely acquainted with His teaching. He only styles himself 'James,' the servant of God and of the Lord Jesus Christ, and whilst this description may be said to stand in the way of positive identification, its very simplicity may at least intimate that we are dealing with some person of position and authority in the Christian community, and that this person stood in no need of any further title or higher recommendation. A forger would not have been content with such simplicity and humility. Fortunately we are able to put the matter to the test, for a spurious letter attributed to James commences thus: 'James,

---

[1] 'According to the Talmud (Neubauer, *Géog. du Talm.* 185, *Stud. Bibl.* I. 52) Galileans were noted as wandering teachers who excelled in expositions of the biblical text, couched in parabolic form,' Art. 'Sermon on the Mount,' *Encycl. Bibl.* IV. 4388.

See also the remarks in Hastings' *B. D.* vol. v. pp. 9, 10, Art. 'Sermon on the Mount,' by Votaw; Mayor, *St James*, p. xlvii.; and Carr, *Cambridge Gk. Test.* p. xlv.

[2] These local allusions are dwelt upon by various writers; e.g. Hug, Alford, Cellérier, H. Ewald, Beyschlag, Salmon, Trenkle, Plumptre, Nösgen, Feine, Farrar, Zahn, Massebieau.

bishop of Jerusalem[1].' Certainly the fact that the author does not call himself an Apostle does not in itself forbid the supposition that he may have been one (cf. 1 Thess. i. 1; Phil. i. 1), but a fictitious writer would scarcely have chosen the modest title which commences this Epistle in the endeavour to recommend his exhortations. In the same opening verse we come across the word 'greeting' (or 'wisheth joy'). No doubt it was a formal epistolary mode of address, but attention has been justly and frequently called to the similarity between this salutation and that in Acts xv. 23, contained in a circular letter issued, as we may well believe, on the motion of James of Jerusalem, to the Churches of Antioch, Syria, and Cilicia. It has of course been alleged that the same form of greeting occurs elsewhere in Acts xxiii. 26. But in this last-named instance we are dealing with an official letter written by one Roman to another, and the fact remains that no other Apostolic writer uses this formula in commencing a letter. Moreover, the coincidence marked by the use of this greeting by no means stands alone. Out of some 230 words which are found in the circular letter written after the Council, Acts xv. 23 ff., and in the speech delivered by St James at the Council, Acts xv. 13 ff., a large number recur in the short Epistle attributed to the same person. For example, in James ii. 5 we read 'men and brethren, hear,' and this form of expression occurs nowhere else in the Epistles, but it is found in Acts xv. 13; in James ii. 7 we have the remarkable phrase 'the honourable name which was called upon you,' and this phrase (Amos ix. 17) occurs nowhere else in the N.T. except in Acts xv. 17; in James i. 27 we have the exhortation to a man 'to *keep himself* unspotted from the world,' the circular letter, Acts xv. 27, closes with the words 'from which *if ye keep yourselves*, it shall be well with you[2].'

It has indeed been further urged that the description of the state of feeling in Jerusalem, and of the action taken by St James with regard to it, Acts xxi. 18 ff., corresponds fully with the tone of St James's Epistle. And if this argument does not appeal to us so strongly as that derived from the similarity of language between the Epistle and Acts xv. yet it may be fairly maintained

---

[1] So too in the *Clementines* we come across such expressions as 'James, the brother of the Lord, and bishop of bishops'; Zahn, *Einleitung*, I. p. 106.

[2] These are perhaps the most notable instances, and they are given both by Mayor and Zahn. The former writer draws attention to other coincidences, as e.g. the use of the word 'beloved' three times in St James's Epistle and its only use in Acts, in the circular letter, xv. 25, the stress laid by St James upon 'the Name' and the same stress in Acts xv. 14, and again in *v.* 26.

that both in the letter and in the history we may see the same spirit at work. For the writer of the Epistle the Mosaic Law is of binding authority, but with an attitude of sternness in this respect there is combined a recollection of the weakness of human nature, and that in many things we all stumble (iii. 2); just as in Acts (xv. 24, 25) there is consideration and forbearance for those who cannot conform to any greater burden than necessary things. In the letter there is the condemnation of the many teachers, but there is also the recollection that they too are brethren (iii. 1); just as St Paul is addressed by the same Christian and affectionate title, 'Thou seest, brother,' Acts xxi. 20. But if we are at all justified in identifying the James of Acts xv. and xxi. with the James of the Epistle we have in this James a person who possessed such influence as to preside over the Church at Jerusalem, and at least to be associated in power with Peter, and to address with authority the twelve tribes of the Dispersion.

Do we know anything further about him? It must be sufficient to say here that his early death of martyrdom precludes James the son of Zebedee from the authorship of the Epistle we are considering[1]. We may further note that when James the son of Alphaeus is mentioned, the second member of the Twelve who bears the name of James, he is always 'James the son of Alphaeus,' that in Acts xii. 17, xv. 13, xxi. 18, we have simply 'James,' and so in Gal. ii. 9, 12; and in the former of these two passages this James is actually named before Peter and John, according to the undoubtedly correct reading. This passage, Gal. ii. 9, is most significant, for the James mentioned in it as one of the pillars of the Church at Jerusalem could not be James the son of Zebedee, since he was martyred, as we have seen, by Herod Agrippa I., who died 44 A.D., and this journey of St Paul to Jerusalem in Gal. ii.

---

[1] The authorship of James the son of Zebedee has been supported in England by Mr Bassett in his Commentary on the Epistle, 1876, and two years later by a German writer, Herr Jäger. A full examination of this hypothesis will be found in Dean Plumptre's *Epistle of St James*, pp. 6–10; and Farrar's *Early Days of Christianity*, p. 267, should also be consulted. It may be mentioned that in the oldest printed editions of the Syriac Peshitto Version we find a statement that the three Catholic Epistles—James, 1 Peter, 1 John—which that Version contains, were written by the three Apostles who were witnesses of the Transfiguration. But it cannot be said that there is any MS. support for identifying the James of the Epistle with the son of Zebedee. Probably the editor of the first printed edition, Moses of Mardin, is the sole authority, misled it would seem by the earliest MSS. of the Syriac Version, which ascribed the Epistle to James the Apostle. Salmon, *Introd.* p. 469, and Plummer, *Epistle of St James*, p. 30.

took place according to the earliest chronology after that date. Nor is it probable that James the son of Alphaeus would be placed before Peter and John except upon one supposition, that *he* was James the Lord's brother, Gal. i. 19, and that that honour entitled him to the first place in the Jerusalem Church. Apart from this supposed identification we cannot say that we know anything of James the son of Alphaeus, but those who claim him as the author of the Epistle always regard this identity as a settled matter. But if James the son of Alphaeus vanishes from the New Testament after his mention in Acts i. 13 there would be nothing strange in the obscurity which he shares with the majority of the Twelve. The identification, however, which we are considering depends first of all upon the contention that 'brother' is equivalent to 'cousin.' And it may be admitted that the Hebrew word rendered 'brother' may be used to cover various degrees of relationship, but after all that can be said for this, Bishop Lightfoot's remark has not lost its force: 'It is scarcely conceivable that the cousins of any one should be commonly and indeed exclusively styled his brethren by indifferent persons; still less, that one cousin in particular should be singled out and described in this loose way, "James the Lord's brother[1]."' With this view of the meaning of the word 'brother' is closely united another, viz. the view which maintains the identification of Alphaeus with Clopas (not Cleophas as in A.V.). But if we treat the two names philologically, it would seem that they must be regarded as distinct, or that at all events their identity is unproven[2]. In the ancient Syriac Version not Clopas, but a word very different from it, Chalpai, represents Alphaeus, although it has been suggested that the Jew Chalpai might have had also a Greek name Clopas or Cleopas, according to a common custom of having two names. In this connection it may be further observed that in John xix. 25, the only passage in which Clopas occurs, it is very doubtful whether 'Mary, the wife of Clopas' is identical with our

---

[1] *Galatians*, p. 261. Sieffert points out that in the N.T. two other words are found to denote relatives and cousins, συγγενής and ἀνεψιός, Mark vi. 4, Luke i. 36, ii. 44, Col. iv. 10, not ἀδελφός, although we must remember that he is a supporter of the Helvidian view. Mayor, Art. 'Brother,' Hastings' *B. D.*, rightly draws attention to the way in which Hegesippus applies the term *cousin* of the Lord to Symeon, who succeeds James the Lord's *brother* as Bishop of Jerusalem; cf. Euseb. III. 22, and IV. 22.

[2] See in this connection Zahn, *Forschungen zur Geschichte des neutest. Kanons*, p. 343; Sieffert, 'Jakobus,' in Herzog's *Encycl.*, Heft 77, p. 574, new edit.; Schmiedel, Art. 'Clopas,' *Encycl. Bibl.* I. 851; and Art. 'Alphaeus' in Smith's *B. D.*[2]

Lord's 'mother's sister.' It is quite possible that St John mentions four women as standing at the Cross (as we find in the ancient Syriac Version), so that Mary the wife of Clopas is to be distinguished from the sister of the Lord's mother. Moreover, the expression 'wife of Clopas' might also mean in the original 'daughter of Clopas,' and in that case, as on the supposition that four women are intended John xix. 25, we should avoid the improbability that there were two sisters bearing the name Mary in the same family. It is also difficult to understand why St John should introduce into his Gospel the name Clopas at all, if he was writing for readers acquainted with the Synoptic tradition, in which Alphaeus, not Clopas, was found. But further, if Mary of Clopas is not related to Jesus, and yet is the same person as 'the mother of James the Less and of Joses,' as we gather from comparing Mark xv. 40 with John xix. 25, it follows that 'James the Less' is not identical with James the Lord's brother.

This title 'James the Less' reminds us that St Jerome, in his identification of James the Lord's brother with James the son of Alphaeus, argues that the epithet *minor* which he wrongly finds in Mark xv. 40 implies that there were only two persons, viz. the two Apostles, bearing the name of James. But the epithet in Mark xv. 40 is simply 'James the Little' which does not in itself imply comparison with only one person. We must further take into account the improbability that in the earliest days of the Church any one of the Apostles would have been known by the epithet 'the Great,' as would seem to follow from the contrast suggested by the term 'the Little[1].'

St Jerome, again, lays great stress upon Gal. i. 19 in this same attempt to identify James the Lord's brother with James the son of Alphaeus, inasmuch as James in Gal. is in his view evidently one of the Twelve. But it cannot be said that we are by any means shut up to this conclusion. For even if the words mean 'I saw no other Apostle but James' (Gal. i. 19), it does not follow that he is included of necessity among the Twelve, since the word Apostle may be used here, as it often is, in a wider sense[2]. Or the words may mean 'I saw

---

[1] St Jerome writes 'major et minor non inter tres, sed inter duos solent praebere distantiam,' *c. Helv.* xiii. See further Mayor, Art. 'Brethren of the Lord,' Hastings' *B. D.* i. p. 322, and Zahn, *Forschungen zur Geschichte des neutest. Kanons*, p. 346 ; 1900.

[2] In 1 Cor. xv. 7 James is as little distinguished from all the Apostles as Peter from the Twelve ; but in distinction from the Twelve the former title Apostle can

no other Apostle, but only James,' in which case there is no question of any inclusion of James among the Apostles, and the words in the first clause look back to Peter only. It is thus quite possible to endorse the interpretation attached to the words by Zahn and Sieffert, viz. that Paul intimates that although he saw no other Apostle, yet he had seen an illustrious personage, James the brother of the Lord.

Another consideration of no little weight is found in the fact that the brethren of the Lord are so often mentioned separately from the Twelve: cf. John ii. 12; Acts i. 13, 14; 1 Cor. ix. 5. Moreover, whilst John vii. 5 marks the unbelief of the brethren in contrast to the preceding confession of the Twelve, the same attitude of unbelief on the part of the former is plainly implied in Matt. xii. 46 (Mark iii. 31; Luke viii. 19).

But amongst these brethren there is one bearing the name of James, according to the two lists which are given in Matt. xiii. 55, Mark vi. 3, and in both cases his name stands first. We have, however, seen that it is somewhat precarious to identify 'His mother's sister,' John xix. 25, with Mary the wife of Clopas, so that *her* sons need not be meant in the James and Joses of the two Synoptic passages. It is also very noticeable that these brethren are never found with Mary of Clopas, but always in company with Mary the mother of the Lord, or with Joseph His reputed father. If we ask why the name of James stands first of the four brethren mentioned in Matthew and Mark, it seems a natural explanation that the bearer of it was the eldest of the four, and that he thus stood in a peculiarly close personal relation to our Lord, which might well account for his significant title 'the Lord's brother.'

It is sometimes urged against this that in the Acts we have two Apostles mentioned by the name of James, cf. i. 13, in the list of the Twelve, and that as, in xii. 2, one of these is put to death, it is obvious that by the name James alone, xv. 13, cf. xii. 17, the writer could only mean the other Apostle bearing that name.

But the brethren of the Lord were evidently in St Luke's view prominent persons, Acts i. 14, and, as we have already noted, the fact that James the son of Alphaeus should not be specially mentioned in the later history of the Church is not more strange in his case than in that of the other members of the Twelve. If too, as we have

only be used here in a wider sense; cf. Phil. ii. 25; Acts xiv. 4, 14. So Sieffert, 'Jakobus,' in Herzog's *Encycl.*, Heft 77, p. 578; 1900.

every reason to believe, the James of Gal. ii. 9 is the same as the James of Gal. i. 19, and the James of Gal. i. 19 cannot be the son of Alphaeus (see above), it would seem that there was a third James occupying a prominent place in Jerusalem, who was known as James simply, or as James the Lord's brother.

Now if these brethren were the sons of Joseph by a former marriage, and so half-brothers of Christ, this fact would entitle them to special regard. It may be added that their attitude in the Gospels towards our Lord has not unjustly led to the inference that they were elder brothers. We may note, e.g. a certain action and tone of authority in the manner in which the brethren are associated with the mother of our Lord, Matt. xii. 47 (cf. Mark iii. 21, 31), and so too in the notice John vii. 1–5 we have not only the *fact* of their unbelief, which might well characterise elder brethren in face of the claims of a younger man, but also their tone of command and superior wisdom.

It has indeed been thought that it is inconceivable that one who shows himself so fully acquainted with the teaching of Jesus should have been amongst the unbelievers in His claim to be the Christ, and that the writer of the Epistle must have been an actual hearer of our Lord, and an Apostle. But if the writer was a half-brother of Jesus and brought up in a house where the head of the household could be described as 'a righteous man,' Matt. i. 19 (cf. Luke i. 6, ii. 25), it is surely not surprising that even as a believer in Jesus as the Christ he should show acquaintance with that side of His teaching which is so prominent in this Epistle, in which such stress is laid upon the 'fruit of righteousness' and upon its inward growth in the prayer of 'a righteous man,' and that he should still have regard to that aspect of our Lord's teaching in relation to the Law which would impress the mind of a pious Israelite[1]. Such a man might well find that his Christian life was no real contrast to his former state, and that all that he possessed in Christ was the perfecting of what he had before. Such a man might well present a picture of a piety to which both Old and New Testament contributed, and in him we might expect to find a wise scribe, instructed unto the kingdom of heaven, and bringing out of his treasury things both new and old. This too

---

[1] 'The echoes in the Sermon on the Mount have been often noticed; but what especially concerns us to observe is how deeply St James has entered into that part of the Sermon on the Mount which we examined at the outset, the true manner of the fulfilment of the Law,' Hort, *Judaistic Christianity*, p. 151.

might well have been the case whether he had actually heard our Lord or not. For in the writer of this Epistle we are not only concerned with James the 'brother' of Jesus, but with James 'a servant of the Lord Jesus Christ,' with one who had joined the little band of the first believers (Acts i. 14), and to whom there is reason to believe that a special appearance of the Risen Lord had been vouchsafed, 1 Cor. xv. 7 (Lightfoot, *Galatians*, pp. 265, 274). 'He shall take of mine and shall show it unto you'; in that promise St James could claim a share, whether with the Twelve he remembered the words of the Lord Jesus, or whether he heard them for the first time from the lips of others[1].

Men have sometimes contrasted the conversion of St James with that of St Paul—the sudden change of the latter from the side of the Pharisees to that of the Christians with the quiet passage of the former from the service of the old Covenant to that of the new. But in each case there was hostility and unbelief, and in each case there was a conversion. And as in the case of St Paul, so too in that of St James, we naturally ask ourselves what merely human influence could have sufficed to transform the unbeliever into the bondservant of Jesus, and the stern and rigid Israelite into a follower of the despised Nazarene? 'Take upon you the yoke of the Law,' said the Rabbis, 'and you shall be free from the yoke of the world'; but here was a man trained in the observance of all legal righteousness, who had found a freedom from the bondage of the world and sin in obeying the voice of a fellow-man, Who belonged to no religious sect, and boasted of no training in the schools, the voice of One Who was both the Brother of men and their Lord: 'Take My yoke upon you, and learn of Me; for I am meek and lowly of heart; and ye shall find rest for your souls.'

As we thus picture to ourselves the position of St James, and as we study in his Epistle the further revelation of his character, we may trace in some respects at all events a likeness to the traditional view of 'James the brother of the Lord' in the well-known account of Hegesippus. There he is described as bearing the name of 'the Just' (righteous), as ever on his knees in prayer, worshipping God and asking forgiveness for the people, as converting many to Jesus as the Christ, as having no respect of persons, as looking to the coming of the Son of Man on the clouds of heaven, and as fulfilling

---

[1] See also the remarks of B. Weiss, *Neue kirchliche Zeitschrift*, June, 1904, p. 435.

in his martyr's death of patience and forgiveness the prophecy of Isaiah, 'Let us take away the Just[1].'

It may of course be said that the more we emphasise the likeness in our Epistle to features which tradition might teach us to expect in St James, the easier becomes the possibility of a fictitious writing in his name. But anyone who wished to palm off an Epistle as the work of St James the brother of the Lord would scarcely have been satisfied with the Epistle as it is; he would have placed the matter beyond doubt, so far as lay in his power. Would he not, for example, have introduced some reference to our Lord's Resurrection? St Paul most probably connects this James, as we have noted, with the Resurrection, 1 Cor. xv. 7, and the Gospel according to the Hebrews, which is regarded as one of the earliest and most reputable of the Apocryphal Gospels, claims to give us an account of Christ's appearance to him after He had risen.

IV. Objections have been, and are still, urged against this view of the authorship on the ground that the Lord's brother could not have written an Epistle in Greek. But the validity of such objections is very much lessened, if not altogether destroyed, by considerations which are increasing in weight and importance. Many years ago Professor Reuss of Strassburg met such objections by asking, 'But what do we really know of the means of culture of any particular Apostle?' We may, however, go further than this, and maintain that there is much evidence to support the belief that James the Lord's brother would be acquainted with Greek. 'The imperfect knowledge of Greek which may be assumed for the masses in Jerusalem and Lystra is decidedly less probable for Galilee and Peraea. Hellenist Jews, ignorant of Aramaic, would be found there as in Jerusalem; and the population of foreigners would be much larger. That Jesus Himself and the Apostles regularly used Aramaic is beyond question, but that Greek was also at their command is almost equally certain. There is not the slightest presumption against the use of Greek in writings purporting to emanate from the circle of the

---

[1] This passage has been recently called an 'Ebionitish ideal picture,' but still the general description may be accepted as true, and St James stands before us as one who ceased not to pray for the conversion of his people, whose sanctity gained for him the regard of his countrymen and the title of the Just, and whose bold confession of Jesus as the Christ brought upon him the penalty of death. Dr Zahn points out that the manner in which the peculiarly Christian features in St James's character are in this account less prominent than the Jewish bears upon it the stamp of truth, *Einleitung*, I. p. 73; see also Hort, *Judaistic Christianity*, p. 152; Lightfoot, *Galatians*, p. 367.

first believers. They would write as men who had used the language from boyhood, not as foreigners painfully expressing themselves in an imperfectly known idiom[1].' We may even say that the probabilities are in favour of this knowledge of Greek existing among the poor and despised rather than among the Sadducees or the Pharisees. It would seem too from the Mishna that Greek loan-words were employed for the commonest things; and from the fact that, shortly before A.D. 70, Jewish fathers were forbidden to allow their sons instruction in Greek, the inference has been fairly drawn that such instruction had been in vogue before that date[2].

If, moreover, we take into consideration the position occupied, in our belief, by St James as head of the Church at Jerusalem, constantly coming into close contact with Hellenistic Jews, we gain a further reason for the points of contact in the Epistle before us with the Sapiential books of the O.T. and the Apocrypha, although we may hesitate to go further and to find reminiscences of Stoic literature, or a dependence on the writings of Philo[3].

Moreover, there is every reason to suppose that such a man would be acquainted with the LXX translation, and that he would make use of it in writing Greek to those who knew Greek, although it is noteworthy that there are one or two passages in which the writer shows his knowledge also of the Hebrew text[4].

[1] 'Characteristics of N.T. Greek,' in *Expositor*, Jan. 1904, Professor Moulton. The same writer points out how the good Attic interjection 'behold' is used by the N.T. writers, as by St James no less than six times in his short Epistle, with a frequency quite non-Attic, because they were accustomed to the constant use of an equivalent interjection in their own tongue. And he adds that in this we have probably the furthest extent to which Semitisms went in the ordinary Greek speech or writing of men whose native tongue was Semitic.

[2] Art. 'Greece,' in Hastings' *B. D.*, by F. C. Conybeare. The date for the authority quoted in the article in relation to the last statement is questioned by Zahn, *Einleitung*, I. 43, but this makes no difference to the general argument, and Zahn adduces evidence to show that Greek was widely known in Palestine, and that it is a mistake to suppose that such knowledge was in any way confined to the upper and learned classes. Feine lays stress upon the fact that St James as head of the Church at Jerusalem would be constantly associating with Hellenistic Jews, *Der Jakobusbrief*, pp. 149, 150. See however the remarks and restrictions of Dr Buhl, Art. 'New Testament Times,' Hastings' *B. D.* v. p. 47.

[3] Dr Zahn, whilst pointing out that the instances of parallels from Philo collected by Mayor are of service for illustration, cannot find in them sufficient proof that St James was acquainted with Philo's writings. In many cases the parallels may be explained from the use on both sides of the O.T. or of Jewish tradition, and in the instances of similar imagery employed by James and Philo we have to take into account the fact that the application is often very different. Still less will Zahn admit any knowledge of Stoical literature, and in his opinion the instances adduced by Mayor of parallels with Epictetus might rather go to prove that the Stoic had read St James : *Einleitung*, I. 87 ; Feine, *Der Jakobusbrief*, p. 142.

[4] See e.g. the remarks of Zahn, *Einleitung*, I. 81, 86, and cf. James v. 20

V. But if the Epistle is written by James the brother of the Lord it is evident that the latest limit for its date is the death of this James, which probably took place, according to Josephus, in 62 A.D., and according to Hegesippus a few years later, probably in 66 A.D.[1] But in either case the destruction of Jerusalem had not as yet involved the Jews of the capital and of the Dispersion in an overwhelming calamity. No one has emphasised more strongly than Renan the fact that this calamity introduced such changes into the situation of Judaism and Christianity that one can easily distinguish between a writing subsequent to that great catastrophe and a writing contemporaneous with the third Temple. The social life depicted in the Epistle of St James fully corresponds with the state of Jerusalem before 70 A.D., with its glaring contrasts between rich and poor, and the growing insolence of the wealthy classes. If the Epistle had been written later than the year mentioned the writer could not have emphasised the social rank and riches which no longer existed; and with the loss of Jewish position and wealth, there was also involved the loss of the influence and means to persecute (*L'Antéchrist*, Introd. xii., 3rd edit.)[2].

According to a large number of commentators the picture of these social conditions represents the state of things within a few years of the destruction of Jerusalem. And no doubt so far as the social conditions alone of the Epistle before us are concerned such a date for its composition might be justified. But it would seem that these or similar conditions prevailed within the last half-century before the fall of the Jewish capital, and other considerations must also be taken into account in connection with this question of date. If the Epistle was written so late, let us suppose, as 60 A.D., to Jewish-Christian communities, it is very strange that no reference should be found in it to the conditions of relationship between these communities and their Gentile neighbours on every side of them, no reference to the question of the obligatory nature of the Mosaic Law, which caused a long-enduring friction between Jewish and Gentile Christianity. It does not really touch the question to maintain that in purely Jewish-Christian communities no such

with the Heb. of Prov. x. 12, and Sieffert, Art. 'Jakobus' in new edition of Herzog, 1900, p. 583.

[1] On the uncertainty as to the exact date see Sieffert, 'Jakobus,' in Herzog's *Realencyclopädie* (1900), p. 580; Hort, *Judaistic Christianity*, p. 148. Zahn inclines to accept the date of Hegesippus, but a full discussion of the argument in favour of Josephus will be found in Belser, *Einleitung*, 667, 668.

[2] Cf. also Mayor, p. cxx.

question could arise, for where are we to find such communities in the Diaspora of the date supposed? The entire silence of the letter as to the binding character of the Mosaic Law for all Christians certainly seems 'historically inconceivable' (as Zahn describes it), after a time when a section at least of Jewish-Christians had sought to make the observance of the Mosaic Law obligatory upon the newly-organised Gentile Churches.

But if we are justified in attaching such importance to this omission as to find in it a decisive indication of date before the Council of Jerusalem, do the circumstances portrayed in the Epistle bear out this conclusion? It is clear that the persons addressed are exposed to trials and persecutions, and that these are of two kinds, social and judicial. But if it is admitted that we are dealing with readers who are Jewish-Christians, these circumstances of trial in no way militate against an early date, and there is no occasion whatever to refer them to the organised persecutions of Domitian or Trajan. A passage in Professor Ramsay's *Church in the Roman Empire*, p. 349, is peculiarly helpful in reminding us of the possibility of legal persecution of Jew by Jew up to the year 70 A.D. (see note on ii. 6, 7). The notices in the Acts of the Apostles, brief though they are, help us to gain further intelligence as to this possibility. Immediately upon the death of St Stephen persecution breaks out against the Church, viii. 1, and the trouble spreads to Damascus and to foreign cities, ix. 2, xxvi. 10, 11. The letters from the high-priest enabled Saul to act with authority, to shut up the saints in prison, and to punish them in all the synagogues, whilst on the other hand the blood of the martyrs was thus early the seed of the Church, for they that were scattered abroad after Stephen's murder preached not only in Samaria and Judaea, but ix. 31 intimates that there were communities of believers in Galilee also, and xi. 19 enables us further to learn that Jews who accepted the word of the Christian teachers were early to be found in Antioch, as also in Cyprus and Phoenicia. There are then, it may be said, notices both in the Gospels (cf. Matt. iv. 24) and in the Acts which point to numerous Jewish residents in the land of Syria. In Syria, no less than in Galilee, the Greek language was current, and even to the time of Titus the local synagogues appear to have preserved their judicial powers. It may well be that other countries were included in the writer's thoughts[1]; but whether this

---

[1] It is of course difficult to say how much would be included by the writer in

was so or not, he evidently has ever in view his countrymen pursuing their enterprise and commerce, in some cases buying and selling and getting gain, in others eating the bread of carefulness, and tempted to murmur against God for the cruel injustice which their rich Jewish neighbours and countrymen were inflicting upon them.

And if from the earliest days of the Church's life the rich Jews figure as her persecutors, cf. Acts iv. 1, v. 17, and the high-priestly party, the wealthy Sadducees (Jos. *Ant.* XVIII. 1. 4, xx. 9. 1), take proceedings against the Apostles, it is also significant that in the days of Nero the Jews in Damascus not only numbered ten thousand, but that by that time they had obtained such influence as to cause Josephus to remark that nearly all the married women of the place had become addicted to the Jewish religion (*B. J.* II. 20. 2). Such a fact testifies to the possibilities of social bitterness and cleavage, which must have long existed in so large a Jewish community, between the Jews who accepted and the Jews who denied the claims of Jesus to be the Christ.

It is of course evident that no particular Church is addressed (a fact which may help to explain the absence of any personal references). But it is equally evident that the writer represents current conditions, and would no doubt have argued from what he saw around him in Jerusalem or its neighbourhood to the situation of Jewish-Christians elsewhere[1].

Moreover, there was a further and a more universal social evil, close at hand and all around him, against which the writer of the Epistle we are considering would no doubt have set his face like a flint. Not only was the Name of Christ blasphemed, but His Presence in the poor was forgotten.

the term Diaspora; Mayor thinks it probable that the term would be understood to refer to the original Eastern Diaspora, settled in Babylon and Mesopotamia, and extending as far as the eastern and northern borders of Palestine. But whether Asia Minor e.g. would be included would depend, as Beyschlag thinks (Meyer's *Commentar*, p. 25, 6th edit.), upon whether at the time of the composition of the letter not only individual Christians but Christian communities were to be found in that country. See also the important note in Carr, *Cambridge Greek Testament, Epistle of St James*, p. xxix.

[1] Feine, *Jakobusbrief*, p. 86, argues with considerable force and interest that the conditions described suit especially the Churches of Palestine, but that the writer under the conviction that the same dangers threatened the Churches of the Diaspora addressed the letter to them also as a circular letter of exhortation. Originally it had been a homily addressed by James to the members of the Churches close at hand, and hence the fact that the letter contains no personal allusions, and that it is not strictly systematic in arrangement.

The Gospel from the first had numbered amongst its adherents a Nicodemus, a Joseph of Arimathaea, a Joanna, and many others who ministered to our Lord of their substance, Luke viii. 2, but still its appeal would be felt most of all by the poor and simple folk, who were waiting in patient hope for the consolation of Israel. And dark days had fallen upon the poor in Palestine when the Epistle of St James was written, days in which the peasantry were distressed and the labourer oppressed in his wages[1]. It may be that social distress had been aggravated by the famine which was felt so severely in Palestine about 46–47 A.D., but Psalmist and Prophet had spoken for centuries of the wrongs of the poor[2], and our Lord's own words in the Gospels reveal to us a terrible picture of the wrong and robbery practised by the rich and the governing classes upon the needy and humble men of heart.

So far then as the social phenomena are concerned there is nothing to compel us to place the Epistle after the Apostolic Council.

Dr Zahn, who places the Council about the beginning of 52 A.D., would date the Epistle about the year 50 at the latest, before the first missionary journey of Paul and Barnabas. At this period almost all the Churches would be composed of converted Jews and Jewish proselytes[3]. In his argument Dr Zahn considers that the Acts affords many indications that a need was felt to unite these scattered communities, which all derived their origin from the mother Church at Jerusalem, by some firm and lasting bond, and that the Epistle written by St James was itself meant as a means to secure this end.

[1] Reference may be made to the graphic description in Zahn's *Skizzen aus dem Leben der alten Kirche*, pp. 42 ff., and J. V. Bartlet, *Apostolic Age*, pp. 232 ff.

[2] An interesting Rabbinical illustration of Jas. ii. 3 and the relative treatment of rich and poor is given in the *Expository Times*, April, 1904; 'B'nei Joseph on Deut. i. 19 says "*ye shall not respect persons in judgment*; when there cometh a rich man and a poor man to the Beth Din do not say to the rich man 'Sit on the seat,' whilst thou dost not lift up thine eyes on the poor man to look in his face, for then is thy judgment not a righteous judgment, and for this perverted judgment it is said *a sword cometh upon the people.*"

[3] Dr Zahn admits that there were, even before the first missionary journey, not a few Gentile Christians in the Syrian Antioch, cf. Acts xi. 20. But even if there were many hundreds, he regards them in proportion to the many myriads of Jewish-Christians, Acts xxi. 20, as only 1 : 100, and he thinks that the way in which James incidentally considers these Gentile Christians, as in the introduction of the example of the faith of the Gentile Rahab, whilst on the whole he does not take them into account, corresponds exactly to the conditions up to 50 A.D. See also J. V. Bartlet, *Apostolic Age*, p. 233, on the position of Antioch. Before the first missionary journey it would seem that the Antiochene Church was a mere 'congregation,' but in Acts xiii. 1 a new stage in its development is marked; it became 'the Church' in Antioch (Ramsay, *St Paul*, p. 64).

While the Christian Church was thus composed, and before Antioch had become a second and independent metropolis of the faith, the president of the Church of the capital would naturally hold a position of high authority throughout all the Christian Churches, and such an authority this Epistle presupposes. This authority is wielded, as we have seen, by someone who was sufficiently well known by the name James, and that, too, in spite of the frequent use of that name.

But at what precise date this position of authority was accorded to the person thus spoken of we cannot say. Dr Zahn is prepared to follow Eusebius, *H. E.* II. 1, 2, and to place the appointment of James as president of the Church of Jerusalem soon after the death of St Stephen, as early as 35 A.D.[1] At all events in Acts xii. 17 the words 'James and the brethren' would certainly seem to involve an allusion to a James who was then the head and representative of the Church in Jerusalem. James the son of Zebedee had been put to death shortly before the Passover of 44 A.D., Acts xii. 1, 2, and we have seen reason to believe that a James known as the Lord's brother, although not one of the Twelve, occupied a prominent place in the Jerusalem Church at St Paul's first visit to the Jewish capital after his conversion. After the death of James the son of Zebedee nothing was more probable than that this James, as the Lord's brother, should preside over the Church at Jerusalem ; and if this was so, we may fairly suppose that the Epistle, which in the position of authority he might fitly issue, dates between 44 and 50 A.D. It could not have been later than the latter date for reasons mentioned above.

VI. Amongst recent English writers Professor J. V. Bartlet has advocated with much force and learning a similarly early date. Viewing St James as more Jewish than St Peter in the manner of his piety, although not more attached than Peter to the Law, as the Law was esteemed by men who regarded 'the tradition of the elders,' Professor Bartlet sees in St James a representative, and in his Epistle a literary monument, of a liberal Palestinian Christianity,

[1] *Forschungen zur Geschichte des neutest. Kanons*, pp. 359, 362 ; 1900. 'James,' says Hegesippus, Euseb. *H.E.* II. 23, 'receives the Church in succession with the Apostles.' On the force of the words see Bishop of Worcester, *The Church and the Ministry*, p. 273. Dr Zahn, *u.s.* p. 361, insists that none of the Twelve Apostles could have been head of a local Church, as the Apostolic office was wider and more of a missionary character. But this is not in itself decisive, as the Church of the Metropolis could scarcely be placed on a level with a mere local Church. See further, however, the *Journal of Theological Studies*, July, 1900, pp. 535, 536.

liberal i.e. in comparison with the teaching of the legalists and Judaisers. Such a man distinguished both by his piety and by his position, and sharing with St Peter the attitude to Israel marked in such passages as Acts ii. 40, iii. 19-21, 26, v. 30-32, might well have written to his countrymen, whose needs he so fully knew, in preparation of the way of the returning Lord; and to Jews and Jewish-Christians alike he might well seem to speak in the Name of God. In the history of Israel a crisis was impending; the death of Herod, 44 A.D., was followed by a renewal of a strictly Roman government, and by the revolts under Theudas and the sons of Judas of Galilee. The bitter stress, moreover, which prevailed in social life, and the grievous recurrence of the sins condemned by the last of the prophets, Mal. iii. 5, 15, iv. 1-3, would indicate to a man like St James the approach of the Messianic kingdom, and of the Judge Who was even now at the doors. In such circumstances we can find an excellent situation for the Epistle of St James, and we can imagine that it might be sent by the hands of believing Jews, as they returned from the Passover, to other Jewish communities in Syria and in the adjacent regions[1]. But if 44 A.D. marks the *terminus a quo*, 49 (50) A.D. marks the *terminus ad quem* for the letter, since it could hardly be later, if that year saw the question of the Gentiles' position definitely raised and decided in the New Israel.

A date almost equally early is advocated still more recently by Dr Chase (Art. 'Peter,' Dr Hastings' *B. D.* III. 765). Dr Chase would hazard the conjecture that the messengers of James, Gal. ii. 12, were the bearers of his Epistle, and in this supposition he claims to find an adequate explanation of their mission[2]. In his opinion, it would be very natural that after the Council of Jerusalem

[1] At an earlier date Professor Bartlet thinks that believing Gentiles could still be ignored as simply a handful adhering to the skirts of the true Israel within Israel, *Apostolic Age*, p. 233; see also previous note on the position of Antioch, and Zahn, *Einleitung*, I. pp. 64, 72.

[2] Dr Chase does not mean that these messengers who are described as coming 'from James' represented the views of James. Perhaps in Jerusalem, as he thinks, the strong rule of the head of the Church had caused them to hide their discontent, but the spirit which they manifested at Antioch was disastrous in its effect on St Peter's conduct, and St Peter's example reacted disastrously upon the Jewish-Christians at Antioch (*u.s.* p. 765). The expression in Gal. ii. 12, 'certain came from James,' may possibly mean 'certain came from Jerusalem,' or that they were members of the Church at Jerusalem who came invested with powers from James which they abused. This was Bishop Lightfoot's view, but Dr Hort thinks that the language suggests some direct responsibility on St James's part, and that he may have sent cautions to Peter to guard against offending the susceptibilities of the Jews, a message conveyed

St James as the president of the Church there should send a letter to the Jewish converts in the Dispersion, and that he should speak of a recent trial of their faith without making any direct allusion to the cause of such trial. Two points in the Epistle are believed by Dr Chase to have an indirect reference to the temptations and anxieties of this particular time. The Epistle (1) has a special bearing upon sins of temper and speech, and these sins are specially characteristic of a keen controversial crisis. (2) In the Epistle we have a condemnation of a perversion of St Paul's doctrine of faith. St James, whilst refraining from touching on personal matters, would be anxious to reassure Jewish converts that to accept St Paul's position with regard to the Gentiles did not involve the acceptance of doctrines, which mistakenly had become associated with St Paul's name.

It must, however, be remembered that sins of speech were generally characteristic of the Jews, and that the famous passage on faith and works in the second chapter of the Epistle is variously interpreted (see further below).

But against the acceptance of the early date, suggested by the three writers named above, the prevalence of vice and worldliness which the Epistle emphasises as existing within the Christian community is still strongly urged. The picture, however, which Acts gives us of the life of the Jerusalem Church in its earliest days, is quickly marred by the selfishness and hypocrisy of Ananias and Sapphira, v. 1 ff.; there is a murmuring, even while the roll of the disciples is increasing, of the Grecian Jews against the Hebrews, vi. 1 ff.; and if we are asked to believe that the writer of the early chapters of Acts was idealising the virtues of the early community of believers, it must at least be admitted that he was singularly honest in marking such flagrant corruptions of an ideal love and holiness. And if we may refer to the Churches founded by St Paul, e.g. the Church in Corinth, which was undoubtedly very mixed in its composition, we find that within a few years of their conversion all the sins mentioned by St James were rife amongst the Corinthian converts, combined with others of a more specifically heathen character; in the Roman Church the same character depicted by St James may be seen in Romans ii. iii., and xiv.; and if it be urged that this is one of the later

by the people mentioned in Gal. ii. 12. But we cannot suppose that James would go further than this, or would sanction any violation of the Jerusalem compact.

Epistles, it must not be forgotten that in an Epistle, which is still commonly accepted as the earliest of all, 1 Thess., the Thessalonian converts, soon after their conversion, are exhorted to be at peace among themselves and to admonish the disorderly, whilst if, with some recent writers, we regard the Galatian Epistle as the earliest, it is evident that recent converts had incurred the severe rebuke and censure of St Paul.

If then we find these faults and failings in mixed Churches it may at least be urged that we should not be surprised to find them in Jewish Churches also, although we have no other example of an Epistle written to communities purely Jewish with which we can compare this Epistle of St James. But we have already seen reason to believe that the writer was placing his finger directly upon those faults, which were so notoriously characteristic of his nation, and so fatal, if continually indulged in, to the spiritual health of all who named the Name of Christ. Like the Baptist, and like One greater than the Baptist, he would warn his countrymen of the wrath to come, and his message like the message of the Baptist and of the Christ insists upon the doing of the will of God, and the exclusion of mere boastful acquiescence in an inherited privilege.

VII. But if we rightly keep in mind this practical bearing of the Epistle, then we can understand, as it seems to the present writer, the true meaning of the much controverted passage ii. 14 ff., although it is an impossible task to put into a few words the contents of a whole literature.

It is significant to note, in the first place, that St James never uses St Paul's favourite phrase 'works of the law,' and from this omission alone it would be possible to infer that he is not writing in the interests of a legal Christianity, or instituting a polemic against Paul, but rather that he is opposing a tendency characteristic of the persons whom he was addressing, and condemned alike by our Lord, the Baptist, and St Paul—cf. Matt. iii. 8, 9, vii. 21; Rom. ii. 17-24—a tendency to rest upon a faith which was a mere acquiescence of the lips, or at the best of the intellect, not a faith which worked by love: 'can *that* faith, such a faith as that,' asks St James, 'save a man?' cf. ii. 14[1]. The wise man of our Lord was he who not only hears but does His sayings, cf. Matt. vii. 21 ff., and

---

[1] It is tempting to find here, with Zahn, a reminiscence of our Lord's familiar 'Thy faith hath saved thee,' but in this passage the thought is rather eschatological, of salvation from the impending Messianic judgment.

the wise man of St James shows his works by a good life, and his wisdom is full of mercy and good works; he is not only a hearer but a doer of the word. And by these works, and not by faith only, a man is justified. Again it is significant that St James does not speak, with St Paul, of being justified by faith in Christ, and his language may well have had its roots in the Old Testament, and in our Lord's own words, Matt. xii. 37, Luke xvi. 15, xviii. 14.

It may be further noted that, at least in the passages before us, the 'faith' of St James is faith in God, a faith shared by Jew and Christian alike that God, the God of Israel, is One, ii. 19; a belief expressed in the primary article of the Jewish Creed, Deut. vi. 4-9, which every adult male in Israel repeated twice a day (Schürer, *Jewish People*, Div. ii. vol. ii. p. 84, E. T.). Here too we find that we are not dealing with the 'faith' of St Paul in his teaching on justification, and if St James had been opposing that teaching, it is inconceivable that he should have made no reference to such a passage as Rom. iv. 23-25. The picture of a Jew drawn in Rom. ii. 17 by a Jew, as also in our Lord's vehement rebukes of the scribes and Pharisees, is exactly that which forms the background of the Epistle of St James, a confident boasting of belief in God, coupled with an utter want of the spiritual and moral earnestness which should be engendered by that belief. And if the illustrations of this failure of practical belief in the simplest deeds of mercy and good works do not carry us back to our Lord's own words, Matt. xxv. 34 ff. (words also spoken in anticipation of a judgment), yet at least we cannot help seeing how thoroughly in accordance with Jewish ideas is the stress laid upon works of mercy and pity in view of the coming judgment, and the practical kind of works which St James evidently has in mind[1].

Moreover, Jewish literature affords us reason to suppose that the question of justification by faith or works may have claimed attention in the Jewish Schools, even if we cannot lay our hands upon any instance of the precise phrases 'to be justified by faith,' 'to be justified by works.' We may take for instance such a passage as that in the *Testament of Abraham*, xiii. (a document in many respects intensely Jewish, although probably in its present form the

---

[1] Cf. e.g. Tob. xii. 9, Ecclus. xxviii. 1 ff., and *Testament of Abraham*, x. B, where the soul of a woman is brought before the heavenly judge, 'and the soul said, Lord, have mercy on me. And the judge said, How shall I have mercy upon thee, when thou hadst no mercy upon thy daughter, the fruit of thy womb?' Other instances are given by Spitta, and see further commentary on ii. 14.

work of a Jewish-Christian[1]), where we read 'But if the fire approves the work of anyone, and does not seize upon it, that man is justified, and the angel of righteousness takes him, and carries him up to be saved in the lot of the just.' Or we may turn to the *Apocalypse of Baruch* and note how 'those who have been saved by their works' are elsewhere described as 'those who are justified' (ii. 7 and v. 1). Certainly in 2 Esdras we meet with passages, cf. ix. 7, xiii. 23, in which the thought of 'salvation by works' is modified by the addition of the words 'and by faith[2].' However this may be, it would certainly seem that both Baruch and Esdras help us to draw the same inference, viz. that the question of salvation by faith or works was not raised for the first time in the New Testament.

But further, if we have to look to the writings of St James and St Paul for the occurrence of the exact phrase 'to be justified by faith' or 'by works,' it may still be fairly urged that not only do both writers seem to regard these phrases as already quite familiar, but also that Jewish literature furnishes evidence that the value to be assigned to the faith of Abraham was a topic already claiming Jewish thought and attention. Thus in 1 Macc. ii. 52 we read, 'Was not Abraham found faithful in temptation, and it was imputed unto him for righteousness?' and it is noteworthy that Abraham's faith is mentioned first amongst 'the *works* of the fathers,' *ib*. 51. In Ecclesiasticus xliv. 20 we again read of Abraham 'and in temptation he was found faithful' (a repetition of the first clause in the former passage quoted). In view of such references it is quite possible that St James might have been following Jewish tradition, and that he might have found in 1 Macc. a precedent for applying the words quoted there from Gen. xv. 6 in a similar manner, viz. by finding their fulfilment in Gen. xxii. 1 ff. It may also be observed that Gen. xv. 6 was frequently commented upon by Philo, and that if we turn

---

[1] For the Christian elements in this work, probably of a Jewish-Christian writer of the second century, see *Texts and Studies*, II. 2, Cambridge, 1892, p. 50. An English translation of the Greek of both of the recensions may be found in the *Ante-Nicene Library*, additional vol., T. and T. Clark, 1897.

[2] See these and other passages quoted by Spitta, *u.s.* pp. 72, 73, 207, also by Mr Mayor, and Mr St John Thackeray, *St Paul and Jewish Thought*, p. 95. Dr Charles maintains that the doctrine of salvation by works, as it is found in *Apoc. of Baruch*, can hardly be said to exist in 2 Esdras, and he notes how in the latter book the doctrine is carefully guarded by the addition of the words mentioned above. But Mr Mayor's comments on the passages in Esdras (*Expositor*, May, 1897) should be read, and also *Speaker's Commentary*, in which 2 Esdras viii. 33 is compared with the apposite passage *Apoc. of Baruch*, xiv. 12.

from Alexandrine to Rabbinic theology, in the *Mechilta* on Exod. xiv.
31 we find the same verse expounded at length[1].

But whilst the evidence seems to show that the passage Gen. xv.
6 may have been a subject of frequent discussion, it is still urged that
the same thing cannot be said of the antithesis between faith and
works. If, however, direct evidence is not forthcoming, it is very
natural to suppose that the reconciliation of the claims of faith and
works would afford a frequent topic of discussion in the Jewish
Schools, when we bear in mind that on the one hand texts like Psalm
lxii. 12, Prov. xxiv. 12, Jer. xxxii. 19 affirmed that God's judgment would be according to a man's works, whilst on the other hand
Gen. xv. 6, Hab. ii. 4 declared that faith was reckoned for righteousness.

But it has been maintained that if St James is not directly
opposing St Paul, he is nevertheless attacking perversions of Paul's
teaching. It may, however, be fairly asked why St James in writing,
as we believe, to Jewish-Christians should be careful to guard *them*
against perversions of the teaching of Paul? They were scarcely
the persons to be influenced by, least of all to be seduced by, teaching
connected with the name of the Apostle of the Gentiles. Jülicher
(*Einleitung*, p. 143) urges that the Epistle presupposes the misuse
of Paul's teaching as to faith. But we may fairly ask what part of
that teaching? Surely not its chief part, viz. the teaching of justification by faith in Christ Jesus, for if so we are again met by the
strange circumstance that there is no reference whatever to the facts
upon which that peculiar teaching was based; cf. Rom. iv. 25, x. 9[2].
If, again, St James was trying to guard against perversions of St Paul's
teaching, it is strange that he should quote the same passage Gen.
xv. 6 which St Paul employs, Rom. iv. 1–8, and that he should
simply content himself with drawing from it his own conclusion,
without seeking to invalidate St Paul's deductions by any explanations. There would also still remain the strange fact that in
writing to Jewish-Christians on such a subject as the possible
perversions of St Paul's teaching, St James should make no reference to those 'works of law' which played so prominent a part in
St Paul's own exposition of his doctrine.

---

[1] Lightfoot, *Galatians*, p. 162, 10th edit.; Sanday and Headlam, *Romans*,
p. 105.

[2] It is noticeable that St James mentions as the object of the vaunted faith
of his converts not the fundamental fact of the Gospel, 'Thou believest that God
raised Christ from the dead,' but the fundamental axiom of the Law, 'Thou
believest that God is One.' Lightfoot, *Galatians*, p. 370.

It is of course possible, as some notable critics have maintained, that St Paul is answering perversions which might have occurred of the teaching of St James, and no doubt some points in that teaching might have been perverted by the Judaisers. When e.g. St James wrote 'whosoever shall keep the whole law and yet offend in one point, he is guilty of all,' ii. 10, what was easier than for the Judaisers to assert that St James demanded that the whole Mosaic code should be strictly observed? But apart from these possible perversions, there was nothing in the actual Epistle which St Paul could not have endorsed, although he himself was called to propound a wider and a deeper teaching, to show how God would 'justify the circumcision by faith, and the uncircumcision through faith' (Rom. iii. 30), and to point to the faith of Abraham as a type of the faith of every Christian, Rom. iv. 16–25.

It is of interest to note that a view differing from those already mentioned is adopted by Dr Zahn, *Einleitung*, I. p. 190. He considers it probable that St Paul derives the statement that Abraham was 'justified by works and hath whereof to glory,' Rom. iv. 2 (a statement which is introduced, he thinks, quite unexpectedly), not from the Old Testament, but from St James, and that whilst St Paul does not directly oppose St James's interpretation of Gen. xv. 6, he develops his own teaching as to justification by faith from the same passage, and that too much more thoroughly than he had done in his earlier Epistle, Gal. iii. 5–7.

Zahn then in adopting this view maintains strongly a connection between Rom. iv. 1 ff. and James ii. 21, 23. In this, as he himself allows, he agrees with Spitta, inasmuch as he considers that Paul writes with reference to James, although of course he differs altogether from Spitta's main position, and rightly urges that if the Epistle bearing the name of James had been merely a Jewish document, it is quite impossible to see why St Paul should have troubled to refer to the production of an unknown Jew.

VIII. But there is another reason why it is of interest to note this view of Dr Zahn's. In his exposition of it, he lays stress upon the fact that of all St Paul's writings, only Romans shows traces of the influence of St James's Epistle.

The passages upon which Dr Zahn lays *special* stress, Rom. v. 3 = James i. 2–4, Rom. vii. 23 = James iv. 1, are also emphasised by Drs Sanday and Headlam (*Romans*, p. lxxvii.) as those which bear the closest resemblance, whilst Dr Salmon (*Introd.* p. 463) regards

them with the addition of Rom. ii. 13 = James i. 22 as pointing to
a verbal similarity which is more than accidental. But it may be
fairly questioned whether these resemblances, and others of a less
striking character, may not be accounted for by remembering that
both St James and St Paul would have access to a common stock of
language in use in Christian circles, or whether they are really more
strange than many other coincidences in literature. The question
therefore of any direct literary dependence between the two documents
may be considered an open one, whether we approach it from the
point of view of an alleged identity of phraseology, or, as we have
already seen, of a controversial relationship[1].

If we turn to another N.T. book, 1 Peter, it can scarcely be said
that the evidence warrants the very confident tone of Dr Moffatt,
or that 'in spite of Beyschlag, Spitta, Schmiedel, and Zahn' it is
sufficient to affirm that the priority of 1 Peter must be allowed on
the ground that St James gives the impression of having quoted and
adapted sayings from a previous writer[2]. A different view of this
alleged priority is at all events formed by one of the ablest of recent
writers on St Peter, Dr Chase (Hastings' *B.D.* III. 788, 789), and
Dr Zahn (*Einleitung*, I. 95) has also subjected the supposed dependence of St James to a close and rigorous examination[3]. He joins
issue with the above assertion in the plainest manner, as, according
to him, it is St Peter who has softened the bold and rugged thought
of St James, and expanded his terse language. If we compare e.g.
James i. 18 with 1 Pet. i. 23 we find in St Peter what certainly
looks like an expansion of the words of St James, and, in the same
manner, the teaching of Isaiah xl. 6–8 which is only touched by
St James in i. 10 is employed far more explicitly in 1 Pet. i. 24. So
again the simpler expressions of St James in i. 21 are much more
fully given in 1 Pet. ii. 1, 2, and, in the same manner, the command

---

[1] See to the same effect Sanday and Headlam, *Romans*, p. 78, and Salmon,
Introd. p. 463.

[2] *Historical N.T.* p. 578, 2nd edit. Dr Grafe in his recent work on St
James's Epistle can only speak, p. 27, of St Peter's priority as probable.
Dr Hort and Professor Mayor agree with the Germans mentioned above, whilst
it should be remembered that Dr B. Weiss, who. is quoted on the other side,
advocates the priority of 1 Peter on the ground that it is one of the earliest
books of the N.T.

[3] Amongst the advocates of the priority of 1 Peter, we must now place Dr Bigg,
St Peter and St Jude, p. 23, 1902, *International and Critical Commentary*; but
on the other hand, and with reference to the two passages upon which most
stress is laid by Dr Bigg, see Mayor, p. xlviii., Spitta, *Der Jakobusbrief*, pp. 190,
199, and also comments above.

to resist the devil, James iv. 7, is given more explicitly and with a description of the spiritual adversary in 1 Pet. v. 8, 9.

The passage which is perhaps most often dwelt upon is the likeness between 1 Pet. i. 6, 7, and James i. 3. No doubt the fact that the phrase 'the proof of your faith' (R.V.) occurs in both is remarkable. But even if we admit that the phrase is used by both writers with the same meaning[1], the context in which it is placed is very different; in St James the thought of the writer is fixed rather upon the present, while in St Peter it is directed rather towards the future. But, without dwelling upon this, why should it be thought impossible that such a phrase should have been used by two Christian writers, who must have been at one time in each other's company (cf. Gal. i. 19) as teachers of the Christian Church, and who were also familiar with such words as those in Prov. xxvii. 21, to say nothing of other O.T. passages? In this connection it may be observed that while the similarity between James i. 3 and 1 Pet. i. 6, 7 is undoubtedly very striking both in thought and language, we may have here a reminiscence of one of the 'faithful sayings' in use among the early believers, since the language employed is to some extent the same not only in two but in three Epistles, James, 1 Peter, and Romans, cf. v. 3[2].

It has indeed been recently maintained that some points of resemblance between James and 1 Peter may be accounted for by a common spiritual atmosphere, or by nearness of time in composition. But the same writer, Dr Feine, who thus views the matter, admits that in some cases there is a literary dependence between the two writings, and that the only difficulty is to determine on which side to place the priority. He maintains e.g. that in James v. 20 and 1 Pet. iv. 8 we have an instance of an O.T. passage which had come to be used proverbially, so that neither writer gives an exact quotation, although both might make such reference to it as we find in the two Epistles. At the same time it is noticeable that St Peter uses the phrase 'to cover a multitude of sins' in a much closer connection with Prov. x. 12 than St James, whilst the latter writer may be simply employing the familiar phrase just quoted from the O.T. in a general way; cf. for instance, in this connection, Ps. xxxii. 3,

---

[1] This is doubtful, as Feine, *Der Jakobusbrief*, p. 128, and Spitta, *u.s.* p. 190, both indicate.

[2] Plummer, *Epistle of St James*, p. 59, but this must depend at least to some extent as to the previous meaning attached to the words rendered 'the proof of your faith.'

lxxxv. 2 ; Ezek. xxviii. 18 ; Ecclus. v. 6.   But, at all events, it is a
somewhat summary conclusion that James in v. 20 is necessarily
borrowing from 1 Pet. iv. 8, although this is one of the alleged
dependences which is most often cited.

Dr Bigg in his *Commentary on St Peter and St Jude*, p. 20, has
argued that the resemblances between Romans and Ephesians may
all be covered by what we may call the pulpit formulae of the time.
Why should it be thought fanciful to maintain that such a phrase as
'the proof of your faith' (or 'that which is genuine in your faith[1]')
might become a common formula, if not in the pulpit, yet at least
on the lips of the early believers in a time of trial and suffering,
such as the Epistles of James and 1 Peter both presuppose[2]?

Much has been made of the relation, or supposed relation, between
St James and the Apocalypse.   In the *Encycl. Bibl.* the writer of
'James (Epistle)' speaks of the relation as at least probable, but how
warily we should proceed is shown by his own subsequent remarks,
viz. that whilst Rev. ii. 10 is supposed by Pfleiderer to be the ground
of James i. 12, another German critic, Dr Völter, reverses the relation of the two passages.

It has been suggested that much of the language common to the
two writings may be easily accounted for by intercourse between St
James and St John as members of the Church of Jerusalem.   But if
we are not prepared to accept this solution, many points of similarity
may be fairly credited to the common fund of Christian thought
and life; the stress e.g. laid in each upon compassionate love, and
the endurance which proves itself in trial.   At all events there is
nothing in the language of the two books which may not be accounted
for quite apart from literary dependence.   It is absurd e.g. to suppose
that St James must have borrowed the thought of v. 17 from Rev.
xi. 6, and it is to be observed that von Soden refuses to admit the
probability of any literary dependence in the alleged instances
between two books of Scripture which in many respects are so widely
dissimilar.

With regard to the Epistle to the Hebrews, no literary dependence can be proved, and the most recent critic, Dr Grafe of Bonn,
frankly admits that the two examples of Abraham and Rahab,
common to Hebrews and James, had manifestly occupied a large

---

[1] See note on James i. 3.
[2] In this connection the recent remarks of B. Weiss are of interest, *Neue
kirchliche Zeitschrift*, June, 1904, p. 428.

place in the thoughts of Jewish as also of early Christian circles [1]. Pfleiderer in his new edition [2] still maintains that these two examples go to prove an acquaintance on the part of 'James' with the Epistle to the Hebrews, and he quotes in addition James iii. 18 which he regards as showing a verbal parallel with Heb. xii. 11. But it is noticeable that von Soden regards this and the other instances, not as marking any literary dependence, but as simply showing that the two writings were the product of the same spiritual atmosphere. It is, moreover, begging the question at issue to assume that James is dependent on Hebrews, as the reverse may have been the case, if there is dependence on either side.

IX. When we pass to extra-canonical writings, points of contact between our Epistle and the Epistle of St Clement of Rome are admitted by the most conservative critics, but it does not by any means follow that priority is to be claimed for St Clement. On the contrary there is much that makes for a reverse dependence. It is very difficult to believe that St Clement, as one who reverenced St Paul, would have used such expressions as 'being justified by works and not by words,' xxx. 3, cf. James ii. 14–17, 21, 24, unless he had some high authority behind him, to say nothing of the fact that the whole context in St Clement reminds us of words and expressions in St James's letter. There are also passages in St Clement's Epistle which point to attempts on his part to balance the teaching of St Paul and St James. Thus he asks, xxxi. 2, 'wherefore was our father Abraham justified? was it not because he wrought righteousness and truth through faith?' (cf. James ii. 22), whilst a little lower, xxxii. 3, he adds of the good of all time that they were justified not through themselves, or their own works, or the righteous doing which they wrought, but through God's will, and finally, xxxiv. 4, after urging the necessity of good works concludes that the Lord exhorteth us 'to believe on Him with our whole heart, and to be not idle or careless with every just work.' In this connection we may also note the significant words 'for her faith and hospitality Rahab the harlot was saved,' where the faith of Heb. ix. 31 is combined with the works of James ii. 25 [3]. And if we have solid ground for supposing that St Clement was thus acquainted with the teaching of St James, and

---

[1] Grafe, *Die Stellung und Bedeutung des Jakobusbriefes*, p. 35; 1904. See also the admirable remarks of B. Weiss, *Einleitung in das N.T.* p. 385, 3rd edit.

[2] Pfleiderer, *Urchristentum*, II. p. 541; 1902.

[3] Lightfoot, *St Clement*, II. p. 100; Zahn, *Einleitung*, I. 97; Mayor, *St James*, p. li.

that he attached such importance to it, other parallels between the two writings may fairly tell in favour of the inference that St James's Epistle was known to St Clement[1]. In some cases no doubt the similarity of language may be accounted for apart from literary dependence, as we have seen in other cases, but it is difficult to suppose that St Clement in xxxviii. 2 was not acquainted with James iii. 13, and xlvi. 5 in its interrogative form and mode of expression might well be a reminiscence of James iv. 1. It is also noticeable that St Clement lays great stress upon the sin of double-mindedness, and that he uses the same word as St James, cf. e.g. xi. 2, xxiii. 3, in which the thought of God's judgment is closely associated with this sin.

The large number of parallels between James and Hermas 'necessitates the conclusion that one of the writers is dependent on the other,' and so far there is no difficulty in agreeing with Dr O. Cone, *Encycl. Bibl.* IV. 2323.

But it is somewhat bold to add that it is not clear to which writer the priority should be assigned, and bolder still to maintain with Pfleiderer the priority of Hermas (Holtzmann thinks it 'probable'). A study of the two writers supplies the best answer to this question of priority, and it is not too much to say with Mayor and Zahn that it would be as reasonable to affirm that a modern sermon is older than its text as to maintain that the comments of Hermas are older than the parallels in St James[2]. The terse sentences of James are expanded by Hermas in a manner which cannot be said to confer upon them either freshness or strength, and if a writing is any index of a writer's character it is difficult to suppose that the personality presented to us in the Epistle of St James could be dependent upon the fantastic production of Hermas[3].

---

[1] Mr Parry, *St James*, p. 73, remarks with great force, 'St Clement is the disciple; the imitator; he refers at every point to the Apostles for example, authority, and even for the substance of his teaching; he is in no sense and in no point original or independent. On the other hand, who is this tremendous personality who speaks to the whole Church with a voice that accepts no challenge or dispute? who appeals to no authority but that of God, knows no superior but the Lord Himself, quotes examples only from the great ones of the Old Dispensation, instructs, chides, encourages, denounces with a depth, an energy, a fire, second to none in the whole range of sacred literature?'

[2] The most recent writer on St James, Dr Grafe, inclines to agree with this judgment of Dr Zahn as against Pfleiderer, *Die Stellung des Jakobusbriefes*, p. 40.

[3] The rare words common to St James and Hermas are referred to in the notes; see e.g. James ii. 6, v. 11, and the constant use of δίψυχος with its cognates in Hermas compared with its use in James as e.g. in i. 8. Dr C. Taylor, Art. in *Journal of Philology*, XVIII. pp. 297–325, on 'The Didache compared with The

Moreover, if St James had Hermas behind him, it is still more difficult to understand his omission of any definite reference to the suffering and work of the Son of God[1]. Jülicher speaks of the Epistle of St James as the least Christian book of the N.T., Christ is scarcely ever mentioned, and the picture of the Messiah has altogether disappeared; and he asks, could such a document have come to us from the days of primitive Christianity? But this difficulty is not removed, and to many minds it would rather seem to be increased, by placing the book about the same period as Hermas, or subsequent to him. It is surprising that Harnack should argue that the circumstances of persecution referred to in James ii. 6 demand a date shortly before the time of Hermas (see note *in loco*), and it is equally surprising that amongst the most recent critics Pfleiderer and Grafe should still maintain, in their endeavour to support a similar date, that technical Gnostic terms are to be found in the frequently recurring 'wisdom,' and in such words as 'sensual,' 'the wisdom that is from above,' 'perfect,' 'father of lights.' There is not one of these expressions it may be safely said which requires any such explanation (see notes in Commentary). But even the testimony of these two supporters of Gnostic influences does not always agree together, for we find that Grafe is not prepared to endorse Pfleiderer's view that in the expression 'judge of the law' in iv. 11 we have a reference to the heretic Marcion[2]. Harnack quotes Jülicher with approval in his assertion that the moral and religious state of the Christian community in St James shows such degeneration that we can scarcely credit its existence before the time of Hermas,

---

Shepherd,' gives some interesting examples, p. 320, of adaptations by Hermas from the Epistle of St James, and of the way in which Hermas was accustomed to use his materials.

[1] 'Hermas tells of the toil and suffering which the Son of God underwent to purge away the sins of His people, and of the reward which He receives in the exaltation of His human nature and in His joy at receiving His purified people into union with Himself,' Art. 'Hermas,' *Dict. of Chr. Biog.* II. 920. In *Vis.* ii. 2, 5, 8, God is said to swear by His glory and by His Son. On the Person and work of the Son the passages which should be consulted are *Sim.* v. 2. 4–6, ix. 1. 12–18, 24, 28, Dr Taylor, *Shepherd of Hermas*, p. 49; 1903.

[2] Pfleiderer, *Urchristentum*, p. 546; 1902. Pfleiderer still persists in placing the Epistle of St James far down in the second century, but the trenchant criticism of his endeavours by Professor Mayor has not been in any degree refuted : ' Would the thoroughly Hebraic tone of the Epistle...the stern censure of landowners who withheld the wages of the reapers, suit the circumstances of the Christians of Rome in that age? Where were the free labourers referred to? The latifundia of Italy were worked by slaves. The writer looks for the immediate coming of the Lord to judgment (v. 7–9). Do we find any instance of a like confident expectation in any writer of the latter half of the second century?' *Epistle of St James*, p. cxlvii.

d 2

but unfortunately the vices of worldliness and lax living censured by Hermas have been common faults in all ages of the Church, and we have already seen how quickly they gained an entrance into the circle of Christian believers.

Reference has already been made to the parallels between Philo and our Epistle, but it cannot be said that they prove any acquaintance with Philo's writings on the part of St James. In many cases, as we have noted, the likeness consists in the use of a number of common figures and imagery, and often enough this imagery is employed in a totally independent manner by the two writers. Moreover, much of this common language may be fairly explained by a mutual acquaintance not only with the Old Testament, but with the Jewish Wisdom-literature, and all the tenets of Jewish theology, as e.g. the unity of God, and the value attached to wisdom, as a gift from above to be specially sought in prayer.

It would at least seem that the greatest caution should be used in deducing a dependence upon Philo, even when his language closely reminds us of St James. Philo e.g. says, 'but as many as live in harmony with law are free' (*Quod omnis probus liber*, Mang. II. 452), cf. James i. 25, ii. 8, 12. But Philo is thinking of the Stoic view that he who follows his fancies is a slave, while he who lives in obedience to law is free; St James on the other hand has in mind a law, which is not regarded as a yoke as the O.T. law was regarded in Rabbinical literature, but which is fulfilled freely and joyfully[1].

In the Pseudo-Clementine literature we do not find perhaps so many points of contact with our Epistle as we might expect, when we consider the high and authoritative place assigned in that literature to St James of Jerusalem, the Lord's brother. But references may fairly be found to James i. 13, v. 12 (and perhaps to i. 18, ii. 19), in spite of the bold assertion of Pfleiderer that James is unknown even to the Clementines. The Ebionite tendency which, as we have seen, was attributed to St James, is said to be supported by the Clementines, but the alleged parallels rather show how widely separated St James was in his point of view from any Ebionite tendency. In *Clem. Hom.* xv. 9, e.g., we read that for all men possessions are sins[2], but there is nothing of such teaching in the Epistle of St James.

---

[1] Grafe, *Die Stellung des Jakobusbriefes*, p. 18; 1904.

[2] Zahn, *Einleitung*, I. p. 105. No parallels are examined in the case of the *Testaments of the Twelve Patriarchs* owing to the uncertainty of the date of that document.

In the same manner with regard to the alleged Essene colouring
in the teaching concerning mercy, oaths, riches, trade, the government
of the tongue, which is so much emphasised by many writers (see e.g.
Art. 'Epistle of James,' *Encycl. Bibl.* II. 2325), we must be careful not
to exaggerate such general points of contact. Thus W. Brückner[1]
would have us believe that the Epistle proceeded from a little con-
venticle of Essene Christians at Rome not earlier than 150 A.D. (in
accordance with the late date which he assigns to 1 Peter). No
doubt an Essene might have spoken much as St James has spoken
on the subjects just mentioned, but on the supposition that St James
was acquainted with the Sermon on the Mount, or with the general
spirit of our Lord's teaching, there is no need to have recourse to
Essenism. Moreover, whilst there is nothing strange in the fact
that the teaching of the Essenes and that of St James should have
some points in common, seeing that they both had their origin in
Jewish sources and in the life of a Jewish community, the stress
laid upon silence and upon poverty, to say nothing of other matters,
is unduly accentuated by the former. St James, on the other hand,
is not teaching these points as part of a religious system, but is rather
endeavouring to check special faults of his countrymen around him.

As we look back over the various points of contact existing
or supposed to exist between our Epistle and the writers we have
mentioned, we may at least conclude that in no one instance has the
literary dependence of St James been proved, even if we are not
prepared to endorse the judgment of Reuss, viz. that the numerous
cases of use of the Pauline Epistles, of the Hebrews, of Hermas, of
Philo, exist only in the imagination of the critics, and wholly over-
look the highly unique personality of the writer of this Epistle
(*Geschichte der N.T.* p. 233, 6th edit.).

X. But if the priority and the originality of the letter may be
affirmed, it is no doubt surprising that the evidence on the whole
as to its early existence and authorship is not more decisive. In the
first place, however, it may be fairly urged that in the West at all
events there may have been special reasons for the obscurity attaching to the letter and for its omission in the Muratorian Fragment.

The fact that the Epistle is addressed to Jewish-Christian circles,
and that the circumstances with which it is concerned relate to
Churches so composed, to say nothing of the fact that the writer,
whoever he was, does not claim Apostolic authority, may have con-

[1] *Die chronologische Reihenfolge*, p. 295.

tributed to this. Nor is the evidence of its use by the early fathers
so small, or so entirely wanting, as is sometimes maintained.
Tertullian's use of it is doubtful, but although Irenaeus does not
mention the Epistle, we are told from a somewhat unexpected
quarter that 'the earliest trace of an acquaintance with it is found
in Irenaeus, who refers to Abraham as "the friend of God"' (*Encycl.
Bibl.* 'Epistle of James,' II. 2326), cf. *Adv. Haer.* iv. 13, 14, and 16[1].

No doubt it is true that Origen is the first writer to refer to this
Epistle by name, and he speaks of it in one place as 'the Epistle
current as that of James,' *in Johann.* xix. 6, as if, although aware of
its currency, he was himself uncertain as to its authorship. But in
another place, *in Psal.* xxx., he speaks of James as the author without
expressing any doubt, and in the Latin translation of some of his
other works we find the term *Scriptura divina* used of the Epistle,
and that it is referred by Origen to James, who is spoken of as an
Apostle, and once definitely as James the brother of the Lord[2]. The
evidence might possibly be carried further, but it seems very arbitrary
that without any reference to the above facts Pfleiderer should still
persist in saying that Origen expressly regards the Epistle as doubtful[3]. Dr Grafe sides with Pfleiderer on equally precarious grounds.
He refers to Origen's *Commentary on Matt.* xiii. 55, in which it is
said that Jude (the brother of James) wrote a letter, while of James
it is merely said that he is mentioned in Gal. i. 19. From these
remarks Grafe concludes that Origen does not seem to have ascribed
our Epistle to James. But Origen, in the above comments on
Matthew, is speaking of the four 'brethren of Jesus' in relation to
their general bearing and character, as the whole passage shows us.
He treats e.g. at some length of the righteousness and reputation of
James, and then adds, 'And Jude, who wrote a letter of few lines,
it is true, but filled with the healthful words of heavenly grace, said
in the preface, "Jude, the servant of Jesus Christ and the brother of

---

[1] Dr Zahn considers that whilst James was probably known to Irenaeus, and
perhaps also to Hippolytus in the West, it appears to have been regarded amongst
the Greeks of the East as belonging to the most generally recognised writings. He
considers that it was undoubtedly known to Clement of Alexandria, who says, e.g.,
of Abraham, that he is found to have been expressly called the friend of God
(James ii. 23), and that the Epistle could not have been placed first amongst the
three recognised Catholic Epistles, or first amongst the seven recognised in the
West, unless it had gained an assured place of regard ; see further below, and
also for the testimony of Origen and Eusebius, Zahn, *Grundriss der Geschichte
des neutest. Kanons*, p. 21, and Plummer, *St James*, p. 21.

[2] Mayor, *St James*, p. cxlv., and Zahn, *Grundriss der Geschichte des neutest.
Kanons*, pp. 42, 56 ; 1901.

[3] Pfleiderer, *Urchristentum*, II. p. 540 ; 1902.

James."' He next passes to the other 'brethren' and says, 'with regard to Joseph and Simon we have nothing to tell: but the saying "and His sisters are they not all with us?" seems to me to signify something of their nature—they mind our things, not those of Jesus, and have no unusual portion of surpassing wisdom as Jesus has.' In a consideration of the whole passage it would seem that there is nothing to justify Dr Grafe's inference from statements which ought not to have been unduly separated from the whole context; and it must also be remembered that Grafe makes no reference whatever to the counter-testimony mentioned above.

But whatever doubts may be raised against the testimony which we have been considering, it is most significant, as Ritschl long ago pointed out (*Die Enstehung der altkatholischen Kirche*, p. 109), that the Epistle should have a place in the Syrian Peshitto, because in Syria we have specially to seek for the readers, in a country, that is, where numerous Jews dwelt, whose intercourse with Jerusalem must have been very close[1]. Further significance is added to this fact when we remember that only three of the Catholic Epistles find a place in this version, James, 1 Pet., 1 John. The other four Catholic Epistles are still excluded from the Canon of the Syrian Church. So far back as this version can be traced, the Epistle of St James is included in it, although it would appear that there is an earlier stage in the history of the Syriac Canon when none of the Catholic Epistles were included[2].

The testimony of Eusebius, like that of Origen, has been much exaggerated in its supposed bearing against the Epistle. Eusebius speaks of certain writings, and the Epistle of St James amongst them, as 'disputed,' but he does not mean that these writings were universally regarded with suspicion; on the contrary he distinctly asserts that these 'disputed' books were nevertheless familiarly known to most people although denied by some (*H. E.* III. 25. 3). Moreover, he distinctly speaks of this Epistle as Scripture in his *Commentary on the Psalms*, and as written by 'the holy Apostle[3].'

[1] With these remarks of Ritschl we may compare those of Beyschlag to the same effect in Meyer's *Commentar*, p. 22, 6th edit.

[2] Dr Sanday, *Studia Biblica*, III. p. 245; Nestle, *Textual Criticism*, p. 321, E.T.; and Carr's note, *Cambridge Greek Test.* p. xlvi. Dr O. Cone, *Encycl. Bibl.* II. 2326, refers to the admission of the Epistle in the Peshitto, as also to its acceptance by Ephrem as the work of James the Lord's brother.

[3] Zahn, *Grundriss der Geschichte des neutest. Kanons*, p. 56, 1901; and *Encycl. Bibl.* II. 2326. The Epistle with the other 'disputed' books won its way to general acceptance, and we find it accorded its rightful place in the Council of Laodicea, c. 363, and the Third Council of Carthage, 397.

If, however, the external evidence was less weighty than it is, this could not fairly counterbalance the internal evidence in favour of the early date of the Epistle and of its authorship as the work of James the brother of the Lord. Ritschl laid stress upon this consideration in the reference just given, and it has been strongly enforced by more recent writers of various schools of thought.

XI. We naturally ask for what reasons the Epistle is still so persistently attacked[1]. Some of these reasons have been already noted in the foregoing remarks, but it may be well to dwell a little more fully upon some of the most important of them in current literature. Pfleiderer in the recent new edition of his *Urchristentum* still stands out as one of the most strenuous advocates of a late date for the Epistle. He cannot allow that it belongs to the Pauline times, and he finds it equally difficult to assign it to a pre-Pauline date; the only question in his mind is how far down in the Apostolic age we can possibly place it. How late this would be from Pfleiderer's point of view we have already seen, but it is quite evident that he ignores in his anxiety for a late date very obvious difficulties which the contents of the Epistle raise. He admits e.g. that no Epistle in the N.T. is less dogmatic, and that the special contents of the Christian revelation which exist in contemporary literature are altogether wanting. This lack of dogmatic interest points in Pfleiderer's judgment, not to a time when the Church was concerned in laying firmly the foundations of its faith, but to a time when a firm foundation was already assured.

But why should this Epistle of St James be the one exception, as Pfleiderer admits, to all other literature which he considers as in any way associated with it in point of time? To this question no answer is given. Pfleiderer and Grafe with him lay great stress upon the expression iii. 6, which they connect with Orphic beliefs. And we are then asked to explain how it is conceivable that the traditional

---

It is noticeable that in the Canon of the latter Council the Catholic Epistles are placed immediately after the Acts and before the Pauline Epistles; and this is the place assigned to them in most ancient MS. versions and catalogues.

[1] Amongst older questionings as to the Epistle its rejection by Luther as 'a right strawy Epistle' demands a word. It is quite true that the preface to his translation does not now contain this statement, although it would seem that Luther himself remained firm in his rejection. Calvin refused to follow Luther and acknowledged the Epistle, and the Lutheran Church has restored it to its proper place in the N.T. 'But Luther not only started from the mistake that the Epistle was the work of James the son of Zebedee, but that every N.T. book was to conform to his standard of Apostolic teaching.' Plummer, *St James*, p. 23; Beyschlag, *Der Brief des Jakobus*, p. 22, 6th edit.

James, the brother of the Lord, the Galilaean, and the Jerusalem Zealot for the Law, could have gained such an acquaintance with the wisdom of the Orphic mysteries. But the expression 'the wheel of nature' may be fully and fairly explained without having recourse to any such needless supposition, or to an acquaintance with any such wisdom; see note below *in loco.*

Moreover, this obscure 'James,' even if he could have carried weight in his own neighbourhood, as Pfleiderer apparently supposes, must not only have been 'a great unknown,' but it is difficult to believe that when, as time went on, it was desired to bestow upon his Epistle further authority, no title should be fixed upon for its author more illustrious than that of 'James the servant of God and of the Lord Jesus Christ.' Attention has already been drawn to the recurring difficulty which meets us in this modest title. It has indeed been recently suggested by Grafe, in criticising Pfleiderer, that this title may have been assumed out of pure modesty, just as the writer of Jude calls himself 'Jude, the brother of James.' But the natural and simple explanation is that Jude could so style himself, because there could be no doubt as to the personality and authority of the brother whom he named.

Von Soden seems doubtful as to date, but he is inclined to adopt a period after the Domitian persecution, or possibly a period within the first thirty years or so of the second century. But even in von Soden's remarks we may notice that he not only admits the high value and excellent tact of our Epistle, but that he also inclines to account for the opening words by supposing the existence of some kind of affinity between the unknown author and the head of the Church at Jerusalem. In this connection we naturally pass to von Soden's own hypothesis of the origin of St James's Epistle. He regards this unknown writer as a Jewish-Christian, fully acquainted with Jewish literature and thought, and anxious to help to rectify by his letter the improprieties existing in the Christian circles known to him. For this purpose he calls chiefly to his aid reminiscences of his own Jewish period, while in ch. i. and ii. there are also reminiscences of Jewish and Christian influences. Thus, out of the whole Epistle, only i. 2–4, 12, 18, 21, ii. 1, 5, 8, 14–26, iv. 1–6, 10, remain as the writer's own, all the rest is of Jewish origin. Two sections, iii. 1–18, iv. 11–v. 6, are complete in themselves, and have no point of agreement with Christian ideas or writings (*Hand-Commentar*, 3rd edit. p. 176). In all this von

Soden, who, as we have seen, dismisses Spitta's hypothesis, adopts one no less arbitrary. No one has pointed this out more clearly than Grafe[1], as also the unlikelihood that a man of such marked culture as 'James' should issue such an extraordinary compilation as that which this hypothesis demands. It is e.g. very difficult to suppose that in a perfectly coherent section such as ii. 1–13, those verses 1, 5, 8, are to be ruled out as foreign elements.

Not less arbitrary than von Soden's is Harnack's description of the Epistle. It is, according to his account of it, wanting in all arrangement, it is a disconnected collection of prophecies, exhortations, instructions; the images follow each other in a kind of kaleidoscope; it is full of paradoxes from beginning to end; in some parts it reads like the very words of Jesus, deep and profound, in others it breathes the spirit of the old prophets; now it is written in the style of classical Greek, now in the style of a theological combatant. But in spite of all this it exhibits, like certain Old Testament prophetical books, a marked unity amidst so much diversity. The writer of all these different addresses originally composed them in no way with a view to the connection in which they are now found. He wrote about 125 A.D., and then, after his death, these addresses were edited, and finally published under the name of James at the end of the second or the beginning of the third century (*Chron.* I. 487).

But in the first place this account of the letter is as paradoxical as its contents are affirmed to be, since it attributes to the same document both unity and the utter want of it. In the second place we have to imagine some teacher of the second century who combines within himself all that Harnack requires; the unknown teacher is described as a powerful personality, bringing out of his treasures the old and the new, and deriving his homiletical addresses not less from Jewish adages than from the discourses of Jesus and the wisdom of the Greeks. He must indeed have been a wonderful personage who united in himself all the varying and often dissimilar elements of culture which Harnack's hypothesis demands. Once more, Harnack entirely fails to account for the ascription of the letter to 'James the servant of God and of the Lord Jesus Christ' (see further below).

Jülicher speaks more positively than von Soden for a late date, viz. 125–150 A.D., while he admits that there is much in the letter

---

[1] *Die Stellung des Jakobusbriefes*, p. 45, and for further criticisms see *Encycl. Bibl.* II. 2325, and *Theologische Rundschau*, I. 1901.

which points to James 'the first bishop of Jerusalem' as the author. But when Jülicher, following Pfleiderer, proceeds to describe the Epistle of St James as the least Christian document in the N.T. and asks how such a writing could have been a product of primitive Christianity, we may fairly answer, how could such a document have been a product of any later period? (*Einleitung*, p. 143). The more we prove the absence of Christian phraseology or allusions, the more difficult does it become to suppose that a writer, who had behind him the Gospels, as Jülicher admits, would have contented himself with such scanty references to the Person and Work of the Lord. St Clement of Rome writes his letter to Corinth at the close of the first century. He too appeals like 'James' to the Old Testament examples of piety and endurance, but he refers in the same breath, and ever and again, to the blood of the Lord as the means of redemption; he refers definitely to the words of the Lord Jesus, and he speaks definitely of the same Lord as being made the firstfruits of the resurrection when God raised Him from the dead. We have already seen how Hermas, writing later, and it would seem in a document which clearly belongs to the same Roman Church, makes repeated references to the work of the Son of God.

But it may be further noted that while von Soden is inclined to regard Rome as the place of composition, Jülicher inclines against the claims of Rome, and expresses himself as entirely in the dark[1], while both critics are united in condemning the theory of Harnack, viz. that in the case of the Epistle bearing the name of James, and in the Epistles bearing the names of St Peter and St Jude, the name of an Apostle was interpolated in the opening words of the address to give prestige and authority to the writing. It is sufficient to remark as against this hypothesis that at least one other Catholic Epistle, the First Epistle of St John, was accepted by the Church without the recommendation of any name at all[2]. And the more we emphasise the desire of the Church to bestow authority upon the document, the more inexplicable becomes its contentment with interpolating the simple title 'James.'

The most recent German critic of the Epistle of St James is

---

[1] Grafe and others fix upon Rome because they assume that a likeness of spirit exists between the Epistle of James on the one hand, and Hebrews, the Pastoral Epistles, Clement of Rome, Hermas on the other, and that therefore all these writings were composed in the same place.

[2] Dr Sanday, *Inspiration*, p. 381, and to the same effect von Soden, *Hand-Commentar*, III. (2nd part), p. 176, 3rd edit.

Dr Grafe, of Bonn[1]. His work has gained the high praise of Schürer, and some references have already been made to it.

Dr Grafe does his best to minimise any indications of Jewish Christianity in the readers of the Epistle, and we have seen how he deals with the word 'synagogue,' and the expression 'Lord of hosts' (p. xi.). He is also at pains to minimise any references to our Lord, and even in v. 7 he declines to say whether 'the coming of the Lord' refers to God or to Christ. One would have thought that the phraseology in v. 7 and 8 was 'unmistakably Christian,' 'the coming,' i.e. 'the presence of the Lord,' as Dr O. Cone frankly admits, *Encycl. Bibl.* II. 2325. Grafe asks how the name 'James' became attached to the Epistle, and he cannot get away from some association in the choice with James, the brother of the Lord, the head of the Church at Jerusalem. The other personages bearing the name of James cannot be considered, because they so quickly vanish out of the history. It is not so inconceivable, however, that a later writer should prefix the name 'James' to his letter, since his strong moral spirit had a certain affinity to that of the famous James. But in what this affinity could consist it is somewhat difficult to see when Dr Grafe tells us in the same breath that the letter is in no way animated by a Jewish or Jewish-Christian spirit. It can scarcely be affirmed that such a spirit was wanting in the illustrious James of Jerusalem, rather was it one of his chief characteristics. In this writer, according to Grafe, we have a man who does his best to warn his fellow-Christians at a time when the Church was becoming a Catholic Church against growing worldliness and laxity, and throughout his writing he breathes the spirit of Jesus, Who demanded of His disciples not the saying 'Lord, Lord,' but the doing of His will. And so although the writer preaches to us nothing of the work of salvation wrought by Christ, and has no word to say as to the significance of the blood of Jesus, his Epistle still edifies the Church to-day.

But if this is to be taken as an account of the writer's object, it is difficult to see why such a short Epistle full of earnest exhortation should not have met a practical need of the Christian life in the first century no less than in the second. In every age the Church has had need to 'remember still the words, and from whence they came, "Not he that repeateth the name, but he that doeth the will."'

[1] *Die Stellung und Bedeutung des Jakobusbriefes, in der Entwickelung des Urchristentums;* 1904.

Grafe would place the Epistle possibly as late as the second or third decade of the second century, and he would do so mainly because he holds that Hebrews, Clement of Rome, the Pastoral Epistles, and Hermas, are all the product of the same spiritual atmosphere. This conclusion cannot be said to be very satisfactory or illuminating, although it is a short and easy way of getting rid of difficulties raised by evidence of priority or of dependence.

We cannot pass from Dr Grafe's name without noting that his statements have received a prompt reply from the veteran B. Weiss in the *Neue kirchliche Zeitschrift* for May and June, 1904. Dr Weiss points out how frequently the expressions used in our Epistle can only be explained of unbelieving Jews, e.g. ii. 7 (cf. v. 3, 5). In this connection he lays stress upon the concrete relations of life which the letter presupposes, upon the peculiar faults which it blames, upon its vivid representation, so true to our knowledge of the social life of Palestine, of the strife between the rich and the poor, and he further shows that the judgment-seats, ii. 6, are not those of Gentile but of Jewish courts. As in his *Introduction to the N.T.* Dr Weiss strongly defends the address, i. 1, against any symbolical interpretation, and he urges the unfairness of supposing that we have no knowledge of any Jewish-Christian communities in the Diaspora, and that no such communities existed, in face of such a statement as 1 Cor. ix. 5, according to which Peter and the other Apostles and the brethren of the Lord made missionary journeys, in which it is absurd to suppose that their own countrymen were neglected.

In dwelling upon the Christology of the Epistle Dr Weiss rightly emphasises how much is presupposed in ii. 1, and how arbitrary it is of Dr Grafe to insist upon retaining this passage as against Spitta, whilst at the same time he refuses to refer v. 7 to Christ as the Judge. The force of such passages as i. 18, 25, is also dwelt upon, and Dr Weiss rightly refuses to depreciate the Christianity of a writer who could so express himself.

Other references to these valuable articles will be found elsewhere, and it must be sufficient to add that they present us with an admirable summary of the reasons for attributing a very early date to the Epistle before us [1].

The objection that 'a simple Galilaean' could not have shown such a knowledge of Greek as the author manifests is fairly met by Dr Weiss, and attention is drawn to the fact that the love

[1] The reply of Dr Weiss may now be obtained in a cheap and separate form.

of imagery and the moral pathos so characteristic of the Epistle may well have been derived from a close acquaintance with those prophetical books which every pious Jew knew so well.

The honour in which James the brother of the Lord was held on all sides might well have inspired the hope that a letter from him would impress even unbelievers of status amongst his fellow-countrymen. But this points, as Dr Weiss urges, to an early date, when Christianity was threatened not by Gentile but by Jewish authorities, and this date is confirmed by the fact that the Epistle shows no trace of the questions which arose when Gentile and Jewish Christians were brought into immediate contact.

But one further objection is common to all the adverse critics whose writings we have been considering. They all urge a second-century date for the Epistle of St James on the ground that the author, whoever he may have been, represents Christianity as a *nova lex*, a new law. It is difficult to understand the exact point of this objection, which is so persistently urged, and it is altogether mis-leading to assert that Christianity here appears quite in the second-century manner as a law, 'the perfect law,' i.e. the fulfilment of Judaism.

It would be more true to say that it does nothing of the kind. In chap. i. 25, cf. ii. 8, 12, the perfect law is not contrasted with Judaism as a religion, but the Jewish-Christian readers, to whom St James was addressing himself, are reminded of the royal law, the law of love, the fulfilment and not the abrogation of the Mosaic code (cf. Matt. xxii. 40, vii. 12; Rom. xiii. 8–10; and notes in commentary on James i. 25, ii. 12). The conception of the 'new law' in the so-called Epistle of Barnabas ii. 6, is quite different, as the context shows; it is opposed to the Mosaic law, which is regarded as antiquated, with its offerings and ceremonies. No doubt Justin Martyr, *Dial. c. Tryph.* xi. (cf. Hermas, *Sim.* v. 6. 3), speaks of a 'new law,' but the sense in which he employs the expression differs again from the language of St James; for the Mosaic law is declared to be abrogated, Christ Himself being given to us as the eternal and perfect law. Harnack alleges as a special point against the pre-Pauline authorship of the Epistle that the writer, when he speaks of law, never means the Mosaic law in the concrete, but a law which he had 'distilled' for himself. But what evidence of this do we derive from the Epistle? If a conception of law which regards the Decalogue, and the religious and moral contents of law as alone essential, is a 'distillation' of law, then we may fairly ask if the same conception may not be found in St Paul, nay in our Lord's own teaching; and if so, why not in the teaching of St James? (see further note in commentary on 'the perfect law,' James i. 25)[1].

But if there is no need to transfer to the second century St James's conception of law, the same remark may be made with regard to his treatment of faith and works.

Something has already been said as to the practical bearing of St James's remarks, in proof that his opposition is probably not to Paulinism, but to a Jewish acceptance of faith as purely intellectual, and to an antinomianism which might at any time invade the Church, and which St Paul, nay our Lord Himself, rebuked and condemned. Jülicher, however, insists that such a discussion of faith and works in relation to salvation could not have found any place before the time of St Paul's wide activity. But if St James's Epistle is not a document of primitive Christianity, then we are not in a position to say whether such a discussion could find any place or not, for we have no other writing of this early period to help us to an answer, since St Paul's earliest Epistles were addressed not to Jewish, but to mixed Churches. It is therefore difficult to see from what source Jülicher could obtain the information which would justify his assertion, and we have already seen that there is some reason to suppose that such a discussion might well have found a place in the Jewish schools before St Paul's day.

But Jülicher is not content with such arguments in proof of his theory that the Epistle before us dates from the second century. He characterises the attempt to assign it the earliest place in the New Testament as still more laughable than the attempt (that of B. Weiss and Kühl, amongst others) to place 1 Pet. before St Paul's writings. But we may be pardoned for thinking that it would be still more ridiculous for an unknown writer to attempt to pass himself off as James of Jerusalem, without making the slightest effort to claim the title of Apostle or Elder, or in any way of a leader of the Church, and to address from his obscurity an Epistle to the twelve tribes of the Dispersion. It has well been pointed out by Zahn that whilst the hostile critics differ amongst themselves as to the date of the Epistle, they nevertheless agree in one particular, viz. that the author wished that his writing should be taken for the work of the illustrious James, the head of the Jerusalem Church. But, if so, it is strange, as we have already seen, that no attempt is made by this

[1] See further Weiss, *Neue kirchliche Zeitschrift*, May, 1904, p. 417.

unknown writer to assert his assumed dignity in an unmistakable manner.

A further consideration may be fairly urged in view of this second-century theory. Any endeavour to assign the Epistle of James to such a late date is directly at issue with another phase of modern criticism, upon which we have already commented, that which is represented by Spitta and Massebieau. An Epistle cannot be a document of the second century, it cannot come to us from the reign of Hadrian, or even later, with nothing to indicate Jewish Christianity either in writer or readers, and at the same time be a product of the Judaism of the first century B.C. with nothing Christian in the writer or in those to whom the letter was addressed.

In contradistinction to these two extremes an endeavour has been made in the above pages to show that the Epistle bearing the name of St James is a document which comes to us from a very early date in the history of the Christian Church, and that it cannot at all events be placed after the death of James the Just, the brother of the Lord. Any theory which dates the Epistle after that event raises greater difficulties, not only as to authorship, but as to doctrinal and social questions, than those which it purports to remove.

Note on 'the Brethren' of the Lord.

XII.   Of the different views as to the exact relationship between our Lord and His 'brethren,' that which regards the latter as the sons of Joseph by a former marriage has much in its favour. This view cannot be said to be inconsistent with the language of the New Testament, and in some degree it affords a good explanation of it. The attitude e.g. of the 'brethren' towards our Lord is certainly that of elders to one younger in years, see above p. xxx. The fact, moreover, that our Lord commits His mother to St John and not to the 'brethren' is more easily accounted for, if we suppose, with good reason, that Salome was the sister of the Virgin mother, and that St John was thus the Virgin's nephew. A nephew might well be preferred to stepsons on the natural ground of closer relationship, to say nothing of the unbelief of the latter at the time of the Crucifixion. Professor Mayor who holds strongly the Helvidian view, viz. that the 'brethren' were the sons of Joseph and Mary, is also careful to point out how easily even in that case St John might have been preferred in the Saviour's choice of His mother's earthly home[1]. Mr Mayor supposes that

---

[1] Art. 'Brethren of the Lord,' Hastings' *B. D.* i. 324. Dr Zahn, who holds with Mayor the Helvidian view, considers that the preference of St John is accounted for not on the ground of relationship, but because of the unbelief of the 'brethren.'

our Lord's 'brethren,' that is to say, in his view, the *younger* sons
of Joseph and Mary, were very probably married men with their own
homes, and much more likely is it that if the 'brethren' were the stepsons
of Joseph, and thus *older* than Jesus, they would have their own separate
households. Moreover, this latter view gives a perfectly adequate account
of the employment of the word 'brethren' in the Gospels, for if Joseph
could be regarded popularly as the father of Jesus, it was not unnatural
that the sons of Joseph should be regarded popularly as His brethren, and
it must not be forgotten that the Virgin herself gives the title 'thy father'
to Joseph, Luke ii. 48, although she knew the whole secret of the Lord's
Birth. Moreover, the half-brothers of Jesus might well have been called
ἀδελφοί (although if cousins, there was no reason why they should not have
been called ἀνεψιοί), just as in the O.T. we find the twelve patriarchs
so called, although born of different mothers.

But this Epiphanian view, which we are now considering, can appeal
also to the voice of tradition, and that too to tradition probably reaching
back to the middle of the second century. It is no doubt quite true that
the earlier sources of the tradition known to us are derived from two
apocryphal books referred to by Origen, *Comm. in Matth.* xiii. 55, viz.
the Gospel of Peter, and the *Protevangelium Jacobi* (this latter book being
the oldest and apparently the most influential of the apocryphal Gospels)[1].
It would seem that Origen favoured this view himself, that the 'brothers' of
Jesus were sons of Joseph by a former wife, and if Epiphanius mainly
derived his information from Hegesippus (as Bishop Lightfoot urges),
then the testimony of the latter may also be cited for the Epiphanian view,
that is to say, the testimony of an early writer dating from Palestine about
160 A.D. and himself a Hebrew Christian. But on the other hand it must
be remembered that Dr Zahn thinks it 'more than improbable' that
Hegesippus shared the view afterwards associated with the name of
Epiphanius, and he points out that in all the fragments of Hegesippus
which he cites there is no evidence that the terms brother, cousin, uncle's
son, grandson, are used in any but their natural sense. Quite apart,
however, from the testimony of Hegesippus, it would seem that the
Epiphanian view may at least claim the sanction of early tradition, a
tradition which by no means necessarily has its base in a false asceticism,
or in a depreciation of married life[2]. And if we cannot say, with Lightfoot,
that this view prevailed chiefly in Palestine, where such depreciatory views
of the married state were not so acceptable as elsewhere in the Church,

---

[1] This is the opinion of Dr Zahn, who regards this apocryphal Gospel as the
oldest document containing the view advocated by Epiphanius. Dr Zahn
apparently quite admits that the same view may have been held by Justin
Martyr, but that he was influenced by the apocryphal Gospel just mentioned:
Forschungen zur Geschichte des neutest. Kanons, p. 308; 1900.

[2] It is of interest to note that Ephrem, although he maintains elsewhere the
virginity of Mary, in the Armenian Version of his Commentary on Acts i. 13
plainly regards James and Jude as sons of Joseph: J. Rendel Harris, *Four Lectures
on the Western Text*, p. 37.

K.   *e*

Epiphanius, it should be noted, claims to give us as his authority 'the traditions of the Jews.'

A writer in the *Guardian*, June 7, 1899, after stating very strongly his objection to a view based upon apocryphal Gospels, which places us 'in the region of pure romance' (Zahn speaks of 'the legendary theory'), admits at the same time that the Hieronymian and Helvidian views are open to greater objections, and that it might even be necessary to fall back upon the Epiphanian if there was no other alternative to these three views. He therefore argues with great force for a modification of the Hieronymian theory, and represents James the brother of the Lord, and James the son of Alphaeus, as the same person, being the cousin of Jesus on the *paternal* side, while on the Hieronymian view he was a cousin on the *maternal* side. He believes that the only difficulty is to be found in the fact that we are obliged to make the word for 'brother' mean 'cousin.' But some objections to the identification of the two terms, especially in the present instance, have been already mentioned, see p. xxvii., and no adequate reason has yet been alleged as to why the Evangelists did not use the word ἀνεψιοί if they meant 'cousins[1].' This modification of the Hieronymian view also finds favour with Canon Meyrick in his able discussion of the whole question in Dr Smith's *B. D.* II.[2] p. 1516, and he calls it the Hegesippian theory, whilst the writer in the *Guardian* prefers to call it the historical tradition of Hegesippus. But it may be fairly said that the passages in Hegesippus are open to a very different interpretation, and it seems strange that the theory associated above with his name should have obtained no hold in the Church if Hegesippus, in Canon Meyrick's words, is our earliest witness, being born about the year 100, and if his means of information, as a Palestinian converted Jew, were thus infinitely superior to those of others.

The Hieronymian view, to which reference has just been made, owes its origin to St Jerome[2]. But it must always remain a serious obstacle to its acceptance that until the days of its author it never seems to have occurred to anyone; indeed St Jerome never attempts to claim any traditional support for it[3], and even he himself is inconsistent in his own want

---

[1] See also Zahn, *Forschungen zur Geschichte der neutest. Kanons*, p. 360, and Farrar, *Early Days of Christianity*, pp. 273, 274.

[2] Dr Plummer in a most interesting note, *St James*, p. 30, points out that Dr Döllinger in earlier days supported the identification of James of Alphaeus with James the Lord's brother, but in June, 1877, he told Dr Plummer that he regarded his former opinion as mistaken, and that he was convinced that the Apostle James of Alphaeus was to be distinguished from James the Lord's brother. The Eastern Church, he added, had always distinguished the two, and he considered that their identification in the West was due to the influence of St Jerome.

[3] Dr Zahn examines at length, *u. s.* pp. 235, 320, the attempt to claim Hegesippus as a supporter of this view, but not only would it be strange that Hegesippus should advocate a view of which there is no trace in literature until 383 A.D. but he names James the first bishop of the Church of Jerusalem as the 'brother of the Lord,' and his successor Symeon as the 'cousin of the Lord.' Cf. Eus. *H. E.* II. 23, and IV. 22. 4. Could Hegesippus have written thus, asks Dr Plummer, if James was really a cousin?

of adherence to it (Lightfoot, *Galatians*, p. 260). Moreover, whatever may be said of other theories, this theory at all events avowedly had for its object the assertion of the virginity of Mary[1].

Of this Hieronymian view, or rather of a modification of it, Mr Meyrick (see *u. s.*) has been the most conspicuous defender. But we have already seen how difficult it is to substantiate one of his main arguments, viz. that Alphaeus and Cleophas are the same name (see p. xxvii. above). It may also be urged that if on the Hieronymian view we identify James the son of Alphaeus with James the brother of the Lord, it is very difficult to account for St John's statement that even His brethren did not believe on Him, vii. 5, since in that case one of the 'brethren' and possibly two others were already Apostles; and if the writer of the Epistle of St James was an Apostle, as the theory before us also supposes, we are not only at a loss to account for the absence of any claim in the Epistle to Apostolic authorship, but also for any hesitation as to the reception of the letter by the Church if there was any valid ground for regarding it as of Apostolic authorship.

In favour of the Helvidian view, i.e. the view advocated by Helvidius about A.D. 380, the earliest reference is made to the testimony of Tertullian, who plainly regarded the 'brethren' as uterine brothers of Jesus, *Adv. Marc.* iv. 19; *De Carne Christi*, 7; *De Monogam.* 8.

But it can scarcely be said that the Helvidian view gained any wide adherence in the Church, although Zahn would claim for it the support not only of Bonosus and Jovinianus, who seem to have used it for controversial purposes, but also of Victorinus of Pettaw. St Jerome, however, although not prepared to deny the testimony of Tertullian, questions the validity of the attempt to claim Victorinus as an adherent of Helvidius. Additional support for the Helvidian view is also found in the tenets of the sect called the Antidicomarianites, i.e. adversaries of Mary, Epiphan. *Haer.* lxxix., who were contemporary with Helvidius and Bonosus. This sect adopted the Helvidian view, and thus claimed to cut away the ground from the Collyridian superstition, which paid honour to Mary as the Virgin.

In modern days a number of distinguished names may no doubt be quoted in favour of this Helvidian view, e.g. Alford, Edersheim, Farrar, Mayor, Plummer, and amongst German writers, B. Weiss, Meyer, Beyschlag, Sieffert, Zahn. But it must in all fairness be acknowledged that so far as the interpretation of the language of Scripture is concerned we are not shut up of necessity to the Helvidian view, nor is the use of the term 'firstborn' so 'obvious' as it seems to the writer (Dr O. Cone) of the Art. 'James' in the *Encycl. Biblica*. Of the three (or four) views put forward we prefer to adopt with Bishop Lightfoot the Epiphanian view, not only because of its probable antiquity, but also because, without any depreciation of marriage, it answers to our feelings of reverence and reserve in relation to the Virgin mother of the Lord[2].

[1] See also Mayor, Art. 'Brethren,' *u.s.* p. 322.
[2] Amongst the more recent literature bearing on the subject we may mention the valuable articles 'Brethren of the Lord,' 'James,' and 'Mary,' by

XIII. *Modern Criticism and the Epistle of St James.*

In the preceding pages we have already dealt to some extent with recent literature connected with this Epistle. For convenience, in our further treatment of the subject, it may be well to divide the various writers with whom we are concerned into three groups : (1) those who accept a very early date for the Epistle, (2) those who prefer a later date, although still regarding James the Lord's brother, or James the son of Alphaeus, as the author, (3) those who place the Epistle at the end of the first, or in the second century, and *ipso facto* refer it to some unknown writer.

It has been said of the first view that in this country it has always been a favourite (Moffatt's *Historical N. T.* p. 577). But, with the frequent assumption that German criticism is altogether hostile to conservative views of date and authorship, it is entirely forgotten that some very distinguished names in German theological literature may be quoted in favour of the view in question, e.g. Neander, Ritschl, Lechler, Mangold, Beyschlag, and amongst living scholars B. Weiss, Zahn, Nösgen and Belser. In face of such testimony it is very puzzling to know why Harnack should tell us that the advocates of an early date, which would place the Epistle in the Apostolic age, are becoming more and more disregarded (*Chron.* I. p. 486).

It is no doubt true to say that since Alford this early date has been advocated by many English scholars, but it is surely somewhat arbitrary to affirm that 'there is little pith or moment' (Moffatt, *u. s.* p. 577) in a theory supported, not only by the names to which we have already referred, but also by Plumptre, Mayor, Chase, Fulford, Carr, Pullan, and Bartlet.

We must also not forget that many English scholars find a place in our second group, e.g. Hort, Salmon, Sanday, Farrar, Bennett, Parry (Plummer is undecided between the two early dates), and that in Germany Feine and Sieffert are in accordance with them. These writers would apparently date the Epistle within a short distance of the death of James the Lord's brother. The Romanist

Professor Mayor in Dr Hastings' *B. D.*; the lengthy and important examination of the different theories by Dr Zahn, *Forschungen zur Geschichte des neutest. Kanons*, pp. 225–363 (1900); Sieffert, Art. ' Jakobus ' in the 3rd edition of Herzog's *Realencyclopädie* ; and the treatment of the question by Mr Goudge, 1 *Corinthians*, in the Westminster Commentaries.

writer Trenkle adopts the same date, but he agrees with his fellow-Romanists Schegg and Belser in regarding James the son of Alphaeus as the author, and in identifying him with James the Lord's brother.

Those who thus adopt an intermediary date do not get rid of considerable difficulties. If it is allowed that the controversy as to the obligation of the Mosaic Law had cooled down, and that there was no need to refer to it, we must not forget that it is one thing to omit a reference to a subject of a controversial character, but another thing to write throughout as if the controversy had never occurred. St Paul in the Epistle to the Ephesians, which could not be far removed from the intermediary date for our Epistle, cannot forget the controversy, although no doubt he looks back upon it as upon a battle already won. But in St James there is no hint that the controversy had ever taken place, and it is difficult to believe that if he was writing at the date supposed he should have omitted to take any notice of the new relationship established between Jew and Gentile, and of the changed conditions thus involved.

Another difficulty in the way of this intermediary date is the assumption that the Epistle presupposes a later and not a very early stage of Christian development, and that its conceptions represent the results of a considerable period of Christian activity and thought. But if we turn to 1 Thess., a letter addressed to a mixed Church, we find that in its pages a very considerable stage of Christian growth and doctrine has been reached ; and yet the Epistle was written much closer to the earliest date demanded for the Epistle of St James than to the intermediary date required by the view which we are considering. How much e.g. of Christian teaching is contained and presupposed in such words as these, 'remembering without ceasing your work of faith and labour of love and patience of hope in our Lord Jesus Christ, before our God and Father,' 1 Thess. i. 3.

Moreover, on the theory that St James was writing in the early sixties, it becomes very difficult, as we have already maintained, to explain his position with regard to St Paul in the famous passage ii. 14-26. If St James is not opposing St Paul, but some perversion of St Paul's teaching, we must remember that from the time of Gal. ii. 1-10 St James would have had some definite knowledge of St Paul's teaching, and if in his Epistle he is opposing perversions of that teaching, he does so in a most extraordinary manner, as he makes no effort to explain St Paul's true position, which he must have known. We have already expressed the opinion that any direct polemic is out of the question, but the explanation of the passage ii. 14–26 becomes much more easy on the supposition of a very early date[1], and in the belief that St James and St Paul were evidently concerned with very different meanings of 'faith' and 'works,' when the former was writing the Epistle which bears his name, and the latter was writing his Epistle to the Romans[2].

Some of the views characteristic of the third group of critics have been already discussed, and those who desire a further criticism of Pfleiderer, Jülicher, Harnack, von Soden, will find it in the two editions of Professor Mayor's invaluable work.

More recently these German critics have been supported by the American writers McGiffert, Bacon, O. Cone, and in England by Dr Moffatt.

But there are variations in date amongst the American as amongst the German writers, and the same unsatisfactory solutions of the difficulties of the letter. Dr Cone e.g. thinks it far more probable that the writing is the product of the second century than of the Apostolic age, *Encycl. Bibl.* II. 2326; McGiffert inclines to the belief that the letter was written before the end of the first century by some Jewish-Christian 'to whom Paul meant no more than any other travelling Apostle or Evangelist' (*Apostolic Age*, p. 584). But this latter date brings the Epistle perilously near the date of the Epistle of St Clement of Rome (a document which in spite of some recent objections we are fully justified in placing within a few years of the close of the first century), in which St Clement could write from Rome to the Corinthians and bid them to take up the Epistle of the blessed Apostle Paul (*Cor.* xlvii. 1). But if the conclusions which we have previously affirmed are correct, it is difficult to suppose that St Clement would have balanced the teaching of some unknown and obscure writer against the teaching of 'the blessed Apostle' (see page xlix.). In one point, however,

---

[1] An article appeared in the *Expository Times*, April, 1903, by the Rev. T. A. Gurney, who makes another recent advocate of the intermediary date. But it is interesting to note that his paper produced a reply in the same magazine for June in which Mrs Margaret Gibson inclines strongly to the very early date for the Epistle, and for its priority to Romans and 1 Peter.

[2] The point is very clearly drawn out by Ménégoz in *Die Rechtfertigungslehre nach Paulus und nach Jakobus* (translated from the French), 1903.

we can heartily agree with McGiffert as against his two fellow-countrymen, viz. in the belief that the Epistle bearing the name of James was not written in Rome.

The most recent German writer on the Epistle of St James is Dr Grafe, of Bonn. References will be found to his work in the preceding pages, and as it has gained the high praise of Schürer some little time has been spent upon it. But the reply of B. Weiss in the *Neue kirchliche Zeitschrift*, May and June, 1904, should also be studied (see above p. lxi.).

There is, however, one point on which Dr Grafe and the most extreme advocates of a later date for St James are in agreement with those who advocate the earlier dates mentioned above, viz. in their rejection of the theory proposed by Spitta and Massebieau as to the origin of the Epistle. This ingenious theory fails to commend itself to writers who are in many respects far removed from each other's standpoint. Thus in Germany, Harnack and Zahn, in America McGiffert and Cone, in France Ménégoz, in Holland van Manen, in England Mayor and Moffatt, all agree in this rejection (see also p. xv.)[1].

It would be an easy, although a somewhat profitless task, to show how the various German writers who advocate a late date for the Epistle contradict one another in points of detail.

But it is more important to observe how signally this third group of critics fail to explain why the title 'James' should have been bestowed upon the author or reviser of the letter, or why the reference to persecutions should be taken to mean the organised persecutions of the Roman power, or why the mention of elders of the Church should indicate a late date of ecclesiastical development, or why words and phrases capable of a simple explanation should be supposed to contain a reference to the tenets of Gnosticism or to the Orphic mysteries, or why the absence of references to the facts of the Life of our Lord should be more intelligible in the middle of the second than in the middle of the first century.

On the other hand it may be fairly urged that there is much in recent literature which makes a helpful contribution to the many varied questions connected with this Epistle.

Thus e.g. it has enabled us to realise more fully the Jewish background and allusions of the letter on the one hand, and its

---

[1] Dr Moffatt, while rejecting Spitta's theory on the whole, still regards the words 'our Jesus Christ' as a gloss: *Historical N. T.* p. 706, 2nd edit.

definite Christian tone and teaching on the other ; it has reminded
us that the social persecutions to which reference is made may be
fairly regarded as Jewish in their character, as inflicted by Jews
upon Jews ; it has furnished us with a valuable and fresh proof from
the papyri of the widespread knowledge of the Greek language, and
of the likelihood of the possession of such knowledge by St James ;
it has shown us this Epistle standing as it were between pre-
Christian and Jewish literature on the one hand, and the post-
Apostolic Christian writings on the other[1], occupying a position
unique in the commanding personality of its author, and in the
originality and weightiness of its contents[2].

XIV. *Modern Life, and some Aspects of the Teaching of St James.*

It is customary to speak of the practical morality of St James,
and to note this as one of the chief characteristics of his Epistle.
What is the bearing of this practical tone upon our modern social
surroundings? A very close one ; and this closeness may be seen
to be none the less important whilst we fully recognise at the same
time the social conditions in which St James actually wrote.

We have already described (Introd. p. xxxiv.) the nature of these
conditions, and there is no difficulty in supposing that St James
from his position in the metropolis knew what was going on in the
various Churches of Palestine and Syria, and that the peculiar

---

[1] Dr Eric Haupt, in a review of Spitta's book which has attracted much
attention, *Studien und Kritiken*, 1896, confesses himself at a loss about our
Epistle. He cannot agree with Spitta, although he is much inclined to do so,
nor can he adopt the early and pre-Pauline date for the letter which he had
formerly advocated. His reason is that some of the expressions cannot, in his
opinion, be ascribed to St James, the Lord's brother. Amongst these he notices
the whole of *v.* 6 in ch. iii. and such phrases as ' the engrafted word,' and ' the
wheel of nature.' To these expressions special attention is directed in the notes
of this commentary, as also to others upon which Dr Haupt dwells, e.g. ' the
face of his birth,' 'variation,' and 'shadow cast by turning.' Feine, *Jakobusbrief*,
p. 142, well points out how many of the *hapax legomena* in St James, so far as
the N.T. is concerned, are found also in the LXX, and he gives us a list of some
fifteen words which may be thus explained.

[2] Amongst the older commentaries which have been found useful in preparation those of Schneckenburger, Kern, Theile, Schegg, Cellérier, Gebser (valuable
patristic references), and of Euthymius Zigabenus, may be mentioned. The practical lessons of the Epistle are well drawn out in Dr Dale's *Epistle of St James* ;
in a series of articles by Dr S. Cox in the *Expositor*, I. p. 65, IV. p. 441, 4th
series ; by Mr Adderley in his *Notes for General Readers* ; by Ethel Romanes,
Meditations on the Epistle of St James, 1903 ; and by R. Kögel, *Der Brief des
Jakobus in fünfundzwanzig Predigten ausgelegt*, 2nd edit. 1901. The Bishop
of Ripon's *Wisdom of James the Just* contains many striking and interesting
illustrations.

Jewish sins which St James condemns could scarcely fail to appear wherever Jewish communities were formed or existed[1].

With St James's knowledge of his countrymen and of the social life of the Jewish capital it is no wonder that he speaks in tones of indignation against the rich and their misuse of wealth, and the words which describe the estimation of poverty and riches current amongst the Hebrew people in the days of Jesus may be employed no less forcibly of the social environment of St James. 'There came to exist among them what has been called a "genius for hatred" of the rich. "Woe unto you," says the Book of Enoch, "who heap up silver and gold and say, We are growing rich and possess all we desire." "Your riches shall not remain for you, but shall suddenly disappear; because you have gained all unjustly, and you yourselves shall receive greater damnation" (*Enoch*, xcvii. 8 ff.)': Professor Peabody, *Jesus Christ and the Social Question*, p. 206.

But it may be doubted whether this writer does not go too far in describing St James's language as that of unsparing attack and bitter irony and of positive indictment against the prosperous as sinners. It may be rather said that his remarks on the teaching of Jesus are singularly applicable to the teaching of St James : 'The desire of the nation should be turned altogether away from the thought of wealth as a sign of piety, or of poverty as a sign of divine disfavour. ......There is but one supreme end for the life of rich and poor alike —the service of the kingdom; and there is but one fundamental decision for all to make—the decision whether they will serve God or Mammon' (*u. s.* pp. 207, 221). The truth is that St James like his Lord refuses to lay down any social plan, or to draw up any definite programme, or to say a word to alter the existing conditions of society by any violent or revolutionary scheme[2].

But if it be correct to say that the Gospel takes what is best in *socialism* and *individualism* alike, this is also a correct estimation of the social teaching of St James. No one is more sensible of the evils arising from respect of persons, and of the hollowness of a faith

---

[1] Zahn, *Skizzen aus dem Leben der alten Kirche*, pp. 44, 45.

[2] 'Jesus laid down no social programme for the suppression of poverty and distress, if by programme we mean a set of definitely prescribed regulations. With economical conditions and contemporary circumstances He did not interfere. Had He become entangled in them, had He given laws which were ever so salutary for Palestine, what would He have gained by it? They would have served the needs of a day, and to-morrow would have been antiquated. To the Gospel they would have been a burden and a source of confusion'—Harnack, *What is Christianity?* p. 97; and Zahn, *u. s.* pp. 50–58.

claiming reality without the love which is 'life's only sign'; no one is more keenly alive to the need of embracing rich and poor alike in a common brotherhood; but no one is less 'careless of the single life'; philanthropy does not exhaust 'religion'; the 'religious' man must fulfil, it is true, the royal law of love, ii. 8, but he must not forget the virtues which concern so intimately his own inmost life; love, for example, cannot survive the loss of purity, for impurity is selfishness. St James no less than St Peter would have us honour all men, and that honour must be extended even to those who provoke us and stir our anger, since in each fellow-mortal we see not merely a man taken from the same common clay, but a man made in the image of God, iii. 9.

Again, it is noticeable that whilst St James is not writing to Churches in which organisation was unknown, whilst he is not writing to fellow-countrymen who were unacquainted with organised charity and practical relief[1], he lays stress upon personal service as due from all alike within the Christian community[2]; and here again St James catches the spirit of his Master, for He too in His relations with the poor teaches us the method and the blessing of individualised charity : 'it is difficult to overestimate the significance of the fact that in the relation of Jesus to the poor He deals almost exclusively with individuals.'

The socialism then of St James is a Christian socialism, not only because it regards men's social instincts in the light of 'the faith of our Lord Jesus Christ,' but also because it takes account of each man's worth, of each man's responsibility, in the sight of God. The Christian life is not only social, it is personal; the Christian is to visit the fatherless and widow, but he is also to keep himself unspotted from the world. In days when men are tempted to think lightly of what are sometimes called the self-regarding virtues, it is well to remember that both St James and St Paul enforce this same practical combination, and that the earliest Epistle of St Paul, like this Epistle of St James, lays the same stress upon social morality and personal purity ; Christians were to support the weak, and to be long-suffering

---

[1] 'The Hebrew race, throughout its entire history, has been endowed with a peculiar sense of responsibility for its weaker brethren, and in modern life is excelled by no element in any community in thoroughness and munificence of organised charity,' Peabody, *u. s.* p. 228.

[2] On the importance of this factor of personal service see the remarks of President Roosevelt, *Contemporary Review*, Nov. 1902; and on the danger of losing it if social settlements become nothing more than 'centres of organisation,' see Mr C. F. Masterman's Essay in *The Heart of the Empire*, 1901.

towards all men, but each one of them was to know how to possess
himself of his own vessel in sanctification and honour, 1 Thess. iv.
3–8.

But, further, the socialism of St James is a Christian socialism,
not only because it would have us act in the spirit of Christ, but
because it would have us remember Christian, supernatural motives,
and because it appeals at every turn to a supernatural life.   The
wisdom which men are to seek is derived not from man, but from
God ; it is gained by prayer ; it is not of the earth, earthy, but from
above, iii. 17 ; not only the poor, but the rich are to seek the honour
which cometh from God only, i. 9, cf. ii. 5 ; endurance of temptation
is to be rewarded not by earthly success, but by the crown of life
promised to those who are lovers not of themselves but of God ; by
the word of truth we are begotten to a new and divine life, and the
salvation of our souls is wrought by this engrafted word ; pure
'religion' is to consist in the visitation of the fatherless and the widow,
but the 'religion' of the Christian is not exhausted by the practice
of morality, it is a religion which binds us to a Person, 'our God and
Father.'

'There is a vastly prevalent idea,' says a recent writer in a widely
read journal, 'that the chief good thing in connection with religion
is "Christian work," this distinctly lessens any interest in religion,
being really a mere patting of religion on the back on the score of
its philanthropic appendages[1].'   But, however this may be, one thing
is certain that the Epistle of St James, while it insists so strongly
upon practical Christianity, never allows us to forget that religion
is the root, of which morality and philanthropy are the fruit, and that
Christian work is the outcome of faith and prayer.   Moreover, the
exhortation to the simplest duties of brotherhood, ii. 1, is based upon
words which remind us irresistibly of the grace and the beauty of
Him, Who although rich, yet for our sakes became poor, 2 Cor. viii.
9 ; the entire surrender of self which God demands is to be gained,
and can only be gained, by fresh bestowals of a supernatural gift,
'He giveth more grace,' iv. 6 ; far above the reference to any earthly
tribunal ranks the appeal to the one Judge and Lawgiver, iv. 12 ;
God rules the world, not chance ; a will, a Divine will directs the affairs
of men, the will of the Lord and Father, iii. 9, iv. 13 ; the motive to
patience lies in the recollection of the future coming of the Judge—
an appeal to that side of the teaching of Jesus, in which modern

---

[1] *Hibbert Journal*, Jan. 1900, p. 245.

socialism only sees an attempt of the Christian Church to cajole the
poor into contentedness with the poverty and sufferings of this
present evil world[1]—the Judge standeth at the door, the coming of
the Lord draweth nigh, v. 8, 9.   Whatever else criticism may effect
it cannot rob the Epistle of the appeals to these supernatural
elements ; they are bound up with it, they are apparent throughout
it ; their constraining power is involved from first to last ; the
presence of God, the love of God, the judgment of God; these three
thoughts are to pervade and sanctify all human life, in its seasons of
crisis and peril, but no less in the daily round and common task;
trial is to be welcomed and rewarded, selfishness is to be expelled,
and murmurings are to cease, v. 9 ; the inequalities of life, its poverty
and wealth, its joys and sorrows alike, are to be viewed in the leading and in the light of God; and lo! the crooked will be made smooth,
and the rough places plain; 'is any suffering? let him pray; is any
cheerful? let him sing praise' ; 'give what Thou wilt, without Thee
we are poor ; and with Thee rich, take what Thou wilt away.'

And in these three characteristic thoughts of St James we may
further see the foundation and strength of the virtue which is also so
characteristic of him, the virtue of patience.   If St John may be called
the Apostle of Love, and St Peter the Apostle of Hope, St James
may be called the Apostle of Patience.   He would have us learn
patience in temptation, in good works, under provocation, in persecution, in waiting still upon God.   And here again he has a word
of exhortation to which a modern world might well give heed.   St
James's outlook was very different from our own, but whether we are
studying the world of nature, or the world of history, we have need of
this same virtue of patience.   The words of Bishop Butler have certainly
not diminished, but have rather gained in strength since he wrote
them, and they may still be of use to those who are tempted to wonder
that if Christianity comes from God, its progress should be so slow:
'Men are impatient, and for precipitating things, but the Author of
Nature appears deliberate, accomplishing His natural ends by slow,
successive steps.'   Or we turn to the world of history, and even
where we can only see a part of His ways, we may learn a lesson of
faith and trust that God's own patience will also have its perfect
work : 'Small as our subject was (the history of Cyprus and Armenia)
it was a part of that which touches all, the world's government and

---

[1] See the valuable paper on the 'Social Teaching of Jesus,' Dr Stalker,
Expositor, Feb. 1902.

the long patience of Providence. "And I said, It is mine own infirmity, but I will remember the years of the right hand of the Most Highest."' Bishop Stubbs, *Lectures on Mediaeval and Modern History*, p. 207 (see also on ch. v. 7, in commentary).

There are many other ways in which the stern and practical words of St James have a special message for our own day, and some attempt has been made to show this in the notes on the text.

We can scarcely fail, for example, to see how he would rebuke the common tendency to throw the blame of sinful action or moral failure upon our circumstances, our heredity, our weakness of mind or body, upon anything or anyone except ourselves. And so here, as elsewhere, we may mark the practical character of St James's teaching. He deals with temptation not merely as a philosopher, but after the manner of one of the old prophets, a preacher of righteousness. At the same time he gives us what we may perhaps call the first attempt at an analysis of temptation as a Christian moralist would view it; outward circumstances alone cannot become an incentive to sin, unless there is in the man's own heart, in the man himself, some irregular, uncontrolled desire, his own lust, as St James calls it, by which he is enticed to a love altogether alien from the love of God (see notes on i. 13).

Or, again, we may see how in an intellectual age, in an age which boasts itself in 'the irresistible maturing of the general mind,' St James would recall men to the knowledge that true wisdom is first of all pure; not primarily intellectual, or metaphysical, but spiritual and moral. And if we ask from what source St James derived these qualities of wisdom, it is not unreasonable, in view of his Christian experience, to answer from the life of Christ, 'Learn of Me; for I am meek and lowly of heart.' Our Lord had spoken of a wisdom revealed to those who had taken upon them His yoke, and so St James could speak of the 'meekness of wisdom.' Our Lord had spoken of a vision of God which was granted to the pure in heart, and so St James could speak of a Divine wisdom which was not sensual or earthly, but first of all pure. Our Lord had spoken of the peacemakers as the sons of God, and so for St James the wisdom of the Christian was pure, then peaceable. Our Lord had warned men against a divided heart, 'Ye cannot serve God and Mammon,' He had condemned the religious teachers of the day as hypocrites, and so St James exhorts to the possession of a wisdom free from doubtfulness and hypocrisy. Our Lord had called him

a wise man who heard His words and did them, and so St James in
answer to the question 'Who is wise and understanding among you?'
makes answer, 'Let him show by his good life his works in meekness
of wisdom.'

And this same question and answer of St James may be of further
and wider import in our own day, when we are so repeatedly told that
the lives of professing Christians, of those who are hearers only and
not doers of the word, present the greatest obstacle to the spread of
Christianity, when the faith of our Lord Jesus Christ is tested by its
power to guide and influence human conduct. A few months before
the war broke out with Russia the leader of the Progressive party
in Japan, speaking to a society of young men in the capital, maintained that the new education had left the moral evils of Japan
untouched, and that development had been intellectual, not moral.
'But,' he added, 'the efforts which Christians are making to supply
to the country a high standard of conduct are welcomed by all right-
thinking people. As you read your Bible you may think that it is
out of date. The words it contains may so appear. But the noble
life which it holds up to admiration is something which will never be
out of date, however much the world may progress. Live and
preach this life, and you will supply to the nation just what it wants
at the present juncture.' It is no wonder that the attitude of Japan
towards Christianity is stated to be one of keen and yet respectful
sympathy, and what men are chiefly looking for in Japan, as
everywhere, is the evidence of Christianity in conduct. And in this
Epistle of St James we may hear from end to end not only the
bracing call of duty, but the call to go on to perfection: 'ye shall be
perfect, as your heavenly Father is perfect.' We have been well
reminded that the word 'perfect' occurs more frequently in this
short Epistle than in any other book of the New Testament; before
the Christian there is set the standard of a 'perfect law' and the
character of a 'perfect man.'

With this ideal before him, we cannot wonder at the indignant
protest of St James against the servile fawning upon the rich and
the studied disregard of the poor, a protest loud and deep against
the temper of mind which prompts men to estimate everything not
by moral but by material wealth and worth, a temper which injures
rich and poor alike, engendering intolerable arrogancy in the one,
and envious dissatisfaction in the other. In the manifestation of
this temper men become not only judges, but judges 'with evil

thoughts,' ii. 4; in this respect of persons they cannot preserve the faith of our Lord Jesus Christ, of Whom even His enemies witnessed that He 'regarded not the person of men.'

We see further how this same disposition of mind leads men to take a wrong estimate not merely of their relationship to their fellow-men, but of their relationship to God, how the passionate pursuit of pleasure and gain overrides the claims of God and banishes the thought of God; and those who best know the sorts and conditions of life characteristic of our great cities also know that in the love of money and the restless craving for amusement the moral and spiritual energies are exhausted, and that covetousness is idolatry, whether the lust of impurity banishes the vision of God, or the greed of gain rules the heart and mind. We may be sure that in days characterised not always by high thinking, but in every grade of life by much talking, St James would point us not merely to the moralist who regards speech as of silver, and silence as golden, but to the judgment of a greater than any moralist, of One before Whom we must one day be made manifest and stand to be judged, 'By thy words thou shalt be justified, and by thy words thou shalt be condemned'; he would remind us that however widely man has been enabled to replenish the earth and subdue it, however loudly he may boast of his increasing knowledge of himself, of his moral and mental powers, one little member of the human body, the tongue, is still untamed; and if St Paul bids men to speak the truth because of their membership one of another in the One Lord, St James would warn them against hasty judgments and intemperate speech by the constant reminder of their brotherhood in Christ.

In that word 'brother,' so often repeated, St James declares himself 'a man of like passions,' v. 17, with those whom he would help to save, and in its utterance mercy rejoiceth against judgment.

St James in his love of man and of nature has recently been compared in some striking words to St Francis of Assisi, whilst his sternness and insistence on the moral law suggest a comparison with another great teacher of Italy, Savonarola (Bartlet, *Apostolic Age*, p. 248[1]).

But the Epistle of St James presents not only, as we might expect, points of likeness to the lives of great Christian teachers of

[1] Dean Plumptre sees in Macarius of Egypt, in Thomas à Kempis, in Bishop Wilson the same ideal of life, the aim at the wisdom which is from above, pure, peaceable, and carrying with it the persuasive power of gentleness, *St James*, p. 34.

a later date, it is in itself an *Imitatio Christi*. The tenderness, and yet the severity of St James, his sympathy with nature and with man, and yet his hatred and denunciation of man's sin, his sense of man's supreme dignity, and yet of his entire dependence upon God, as we note all this in the pages of St James are we not reminded of the human life of Him in Whom St James had learnt to see his Master and his Lord?

But the Master and Lord of men was also their servant, 'I am amongst you as he that serveth' (Luke xxii. 27), and for St James the Christian life is a life of service; in his opening sentence he proclaims himself as the bondservant of Jesus Christ, 'the greatest servant in the world,' as Lacordaire was wont to call Him; his closing exhortation bids a man to be ready to do a service for his brother-man which most resembles the work of Him Who came to seek and to save; he is the servant of Christ; but as such he is also 'servus servorum Dei,' of men made in the image of God.

EPISTLE OF ST JAMES.

Contents of the Epistle.

It is not easy to make an analysis of the contents of this Epistle, and the varied nature of the attempts to do so may be seen by a comparison of the elaborate table of Cellérier, *L'Épître de St Jaques*, pp. xxiii–v. (1850), with the few lines given to the subject in more recent Commentaries. The terseness and abruptness which characterise parts of the letter sometimes seem to lend countenance to the view that we are dealing with what was originally a homily, full of earnest exhortation to newness and perfection of life, and of wholesome warning against worldliness and degeneracy. This view that the Epistle was in the first instance a homily, delivered perhaps primarily to the Jerusalem Church and then circulated in its present form amongst the Churches of the Jewish Diaspora (Sieffert speaks of it as a circular pastoral letter), is held to account for the want of close systematic construction in the letter. Harnack, indeed, would see in the Epistle not one homily but a collection of homilies, but even if we admit the lack of continuous argument, there seems to be no need for such an elaborate hypothesis.

But those who adopt an earlier date for the compilation of the Epistle also justly lay stress upon the moral advice and hortatory form of its pages, as contrasted with some of the more dogmatic of the New Testament books, and they see in it, as noted above (see Introd. p. xxxiv.), references not only to the duties of daily Christian life, but also to the special features of a life lived amidst the religious, social and commercial surroundings of the Jewish Diaspora, in the first half of the first Christian century. And this consideration may help us to see that the writing before us is not merely an 'Epistle,' not merely a piece of literature containing a purely ideal address and dealing with nothing but general questions; it is rather characterised by some, at least, of the personal and intimate relationships of a 'letter'; it treats of special circumstances, and by no means of vague generalities, it is not the product of art and of man's device, but of stern and actual experiences of life (on the distinction between an 'Epistle' and a 'letter,' see Deissmann's Art. 'Epistolary Literature,' *Encycl. Bibl.* II.)[1].

It is of course quite possible that one of the most marked features in the writer's style of repeating a leading word of a sentence, or one allied to it, in the sentence which succeeds, may also have influenced not only the

---

[1] In his valuable and suggestive *Jesus Christ and the Social Question*, Professor Peabody is perhaps also open to the charge of forgetting that the strong denunciations of St James were prompted by the special social conditions around him, pp. 197 ff.

emphasis or definiteness of the writing, but also the sequence of the writer's thoughts. But however this may be, the main subjects and divisions of the Epistle may perhaps be paraphrased as follows in their practical bearing[1].

CHAPTER I.

1—12. Trials (temptations) from without, to be received with joy. In the proof, the testing which they bring, patience (endurance) is worked out, i.e. completed, and in that working out, perfection is gained. But this perfection cannot be attained to without wisdom, and wisdom cannot be attained to without faith; lacking faith a man does not endure, he has no stedfastness, but is unstable in all his ways. This joy, this exulting in trial, may be the lot of rich and poor alike: for the latter learns that having nothing he is, nevertheless, an heir of the kingdom of God; the former learns that while earthly riches cannot last, endurance of trial brings the true riches, blessedness and the crown of life. **13—15.** Temptation from within. While the Christian should rejoice in trial, i.e. the external circumstances of temptation, the inner side of temptation must not be referred by a common but fatal mistake to God; for as God, who is absolute goodness, cannot be tempted by evil, He tempts no man to sin. The tempter is the man's own lust, and lust begets sin, and sin when it has reached maturity brings forth death. **16—18.** The mistake of regarding God as a tempter is enforced from the positive side. God is light, with Him is no darkness at all; God is the same, He changes not; and so, while man's wilful and fitful desires result in sin and death, the Divine will begets men, not for death, but for life by the Word of truth, the instrument of a new birth. The Divine purpose sees in those who are thus begotten, not the whole of a new creation, but the firstfruits of it; in us as Christians God makes manifest to the world what He desires that all men should become. **19—21.** What is to be our attitude towards this Word of God, by which we are thus born again to newness of life? For the reception of this Divine Word we must prepare to be ready hearers, and refrain from hasty speaking and unruly passion; all that is impure and malicious must be stript off; we must be clothed instead with meekness. **22—25.** But receptivity must be succeeded by activity, and hearing by doing; unlike a man who looks at his face in a mirror, and with a glance is gone, forgetting what he looked like, it is needful for us to stoop down and gaze into the heavenly mirror, the perfect law of liberty, and to make that law our bounden duty and service; thus we shall be blessed in our doing. **26.** A man may seem to be 'religious,' he may observe the outward ceremonial and the ordinances of 'religion,' but if he offends in his tongue, his religion is vain. **27.** With God and the Father—the God of the fatherless, and the defender of the cause of the widow—the ritual which is pure and undefiled is the imitation of His own mercy, and the endeavour to walk in love, with watchful care against the evil world.

---

[1] For a recent attempt to trace a poetical structure in this Epistle and in that of St Jude see the *Journal of Theol. Studies*, July, 1904.

I.   JAMES, a [1]servant of God and of the Lord Jesus Christ, to the twelve tribes which are of the Dispersion, [2]greeting.

> [1] Gr. *bondservant.*   [2] Gr. *wisheth joy.*

I. 1. *James.* See Introd. p. xxiv. *a servant.* So A. and R.V., but the latter in marg. *bondservant* (Greek); the same word is used Phil. i. 1, Jude 1 (cf. Philem. 1), without any official or additional title. The phrase 'a servant of God' might well have been derived by St James from the O.T., where the same or a similar title is applied to the prophets from Amos onwards. But in the first recorded hymn of the assembled Church, the Apostles and their company had prayed to God as His bondservants (Acts iv. 29, the same word in Gk.), and in that little company St James may well have been present. And as on that occasion, so here, the expression carries with it the consciousness of absolute dependence, and the conviction that the will of God was the only rule of life for every member of His Church; for those in authority, as for those under authority. The simplicity of the title stands out in marked contrast to the way in which men of the world lay claim in their correspondence to the current titles of honour and distinction (see also iii. 1 and the comment of Euthymius Zigabenus *in loco*). This humility, by which the writer disclaims any desire to emphasise his knowledge of Christ 'after the flesh,' is a proof not only of the genuineness of the letter, but also of the real greatness of St James, since he is not concerned to assert himself as 'the brother of the Lord'; see further Introd. p. xxx.

and of the Lord Jesus Christ. If the Greek word here used for 'Lord,' a word so frequently found in the LXX for Jehovah, does not in itself assert in this passage the divinity of Jesus Christ, yet its associations would be unmistakable; it cannot denote in this place a mere earthly Master, the obligation of service to Christ being conjoined with that of service to God, as equally binding and imperative. Moreover, the word is used by St James in this Epistle with reference both to God and to Christ. This union of the service of God and of Christ thus expressed by the same word of absolute submission is found only in this passage in the N.T., but there is nothing strange in this fact, for if the phrase 'a servant of God,' Tit. i. 1, and 'a servant of Christ,' Gal. i. 10, could be interchanged, it is difficult to see why they should not be conjoined. We may further note that the human name Jesus is here associated with the official name Christ in this, probably the earliest book in the N.T., and that the Messianic title is thus recognised not only by a Jew, but by a Jew who had known, as we believe, the earthly home of this same Jesus Who was made both Lord and Christ[1].

to the twelve tribes which are of the Dispersion. Cf. Psalm cxlvii. 2

---

[1] Spitta maintains that the words under discussion are an interpolation, because in this connection they are unique, and he would omit them altogether; 'a short and easy method' of dealing with an inconvenient passage, but see Introd. to this Epistle, **p. xv.**

(LXX); 2 Macc. i. 27; John vii. 35; 1 Pet. i. 1. In *Psalms of Solomon*, viii. 33, 34, we read: 'O God, turn thy mercy upon us and have compassion upon us. Gather together the dispersed of Israel with mercy and lovingkindness.' The R.V. takes 'the Dispersion' as a technical term used of the Jews outside the Holy Land, dispersed amongst foreign nations, a point missed in A.V.

It is difficult to suppose that the words under discussion are employed by the writer symbolically or figuratively, or to regard them as parallel with such passages as 1 Pet. ii. 9, Rev. vii. 4, xxi. 12. Here we are dealing with the address of a practical, matter-of-fact letter, concerned throughout with the concrete relations of social life, and it may be fairly urged that whilst Jewish-Christians might be spoken of as banished or exiled from their heavenly home, such a separation would scarcely be expressed by the *technical term* 'Dispersion.' That such a technical term would lie ready to the hand of the writer is plain enough, but there is no need to connect its use with such passages as Gen. ix. 19, or to say that the word as used by St James is an imitation of 1 Pet. i. 1, and that the local designation added there is omitted here, the term 'Dispersion' being thus used of Christians scattered over a world to which they did not belong. All such explanations seem rather to beg the question at issue (see further Introd. p. xxxv.).

The expression of belief in an undivided Israel, 'the twelve tribes,' is intensely Jewish, and may be compared with Acts xxvi. 7; cf. also 1 Esdras vii. 8; *Orac. Sibyll.* ii. 170; *Apoc. of Baruch*, lxxxiv. 3; 'and truly I know that, behold, all we in the twelve tribes are bound by one chain, inasmuch as we are born from one father,' *ibid.* lxxviii. 4. The advocates of the early date of the Epistle maintain that the address in St James, couched in this Jewish form, points to a very early period, when no special name was as yet given to the Christian believers in Israel, and when the hope was still cherished that the whole people would believe in the Christ; to a period when those who believed in Him had not yet broken away from the connecting bands of the synagogue. The writer in his prophetic words of warning and reproof is then not forgetful even of his unbelieving countrymen, amongst some of whom he might perhaps anticipate that his letter would find its way. And if St James of Jerusalem is the writer, his character and influence, and his devotion to the Law, might well justify such an anticipation.

the Dispersion. The term 'Diaspora' was of course a wide one, and it is possible to give it here a wide inclusion if we regard the Epistle as 'sent forth with believing Jews, as they returned from the Passover any time between 44 and 49 A.D.,' and St James might well suppose that the conditions and temptations of Jewish communities would be much of the same character everywhere (*v.* Bartlet, *Apostolic Age*, p. 233). But at the same time there is much to be said for the view which regards Syria, and more especially perhaps the southern parts of it, as the primary destination of the letter. See further Introd. p. xxxv. Josephus, *B. J.* vii. 3. 3, speaks of Syria as the country most largely mingled with the Jewish race, on account of its nearness to Palestine, and of Antioch the capital this was

2   Count it all joy, my brethren, when ye fall into mani-

specially the case, whilst in other cities also the Jewish inhabitants were counted by thousands: Schürer, *Jewish People*, Div. II. vol. II. p. 225, E.T.

greeting, R.V. marg. *wisheth joy*, thus expressing the full force of the Greek, and showing too how the word 'joy' is probably taken up by the writer in the sentences which follow in a way characteristic of him (see for other instances p. 9). Precisely the same formula of epistolary greeting is found in the encyclical letter, which may well have emanated from James, Acts xv. 23 (a coincidence pointed out by Bengel), but it is not employed elsewhere by the N.T. writers; though it occurs in the letter of Lysias to Felix, Acts xxiii. 26. It frequently finds a place in the Books of the Maccabees, where it is used by Gentiles to Jews and by Jews to Gentiles; twice in the LXX it is an equivalent for the Hebrew salutation 'Peace,' Isaiah xlviii. 22, lvii. 21, and in the Syriac version of this Epistle it is rendered by the same word of salutation. There is certainly nothing strange in its use here, for it could be used by a Jewish high-priest, 1 Macc. xii. 6, and by Palestinian Jews in addressing their brethren in Egypt, 2 Macc. i. 10; and 2 John 10, 11, points to its early adoption in Christian circles. On the other hand, there is force in the consideration that the employment of this simple formula indicates an early date, for otherwise the fuller Christian salutations of other Epistles might have found a place here. Zahn gives some interesting examples of its use in the papyri (*Einleitung*, I. 55).

2. *Count it all joy.* Sometimes rendered 'pure joy,' i.e. nothing but joy, *merum gaudium* (Wetstein); sometimes as expressing the highest degree, the maximum of joy (Beza, Grotius). Possibly the words may mean '*every kind* of joy' (Bengel), so as to balance exactly '*manifold* temptations.' 'Joy,' i.e. cause for or ground of joy: cf. Luke ii. 10; 2 Cor. i. 15, W.H.; see R.V. marg. With the words before us cf. 1 Pet. i. 6, 7, iv. 13.

count, i.e. consider; the Greek verb is not in the present, but in the aorist tense, with reference that is to each single temptation as it occurs.

my brethren. As in the LXX, so in the N.T. the word was used of brother, neighbour, member of the same nation, but also in the latter of fellow-Christians, members of the same spiritual community, Acts ix. 30; 1 Cor. i. 1. The frequent recurrence of the word in this Epistle shows not only the stress laid by St James upon this national and religious bond, but also the affection and humility of the writer; it may also in this context be in itself an exhortation to manliness and courage; St James calls them not children, but brethren.

when ye fall into. The form of the word in the original denotes a falling into, so as to be encompassed and surrounded by (the trials are 'manifold'), and it is used in classical Greek as here with the idea of falling into sufferings and calamities; so in 2 Macc. vi. 13 the word is used of Israel falling into troubles which are the chastening of God, and in 2 Macc. x. 4, of falling into persecutions inflicted upon Israel by the heathen nations. The word may here denote not only the external nature of the temptation, in contrast

3 fold [1]temptations; knowing that the proof of your faith

¹ Or, *trials*

to *v.* 13, but also its unexpectedness.

temptations, R.V. marg. *trials*; cf. 1 Pet. i. 6, *v.* 13, below, and see especially Ecclus. ii. 1 ff. : 'My son, if thou come to serve the Lord, prepare thy soul for temptation. Set thy heart aright, and constantly endure, and make not haste in time of trouble....Whatsoever is brought upon thee take cheerfully, and be patient when thou art changed to a low estate. For gold is tried in the fire, and acceptable men in the furnace of adversity.' The word is used in a general sense of proving, trial (cf. Ecclus. xxvii. 5, 7), and also of adversity, affliction sent to prove or test a man's character; cf. our word *trial.* 'Said Rab, Never should a man bring himself into the hands of temptation; for behold David, king of Israel, brought himself into the hands of temptation, and stumbled: he said, Examine me, O Lord, and *prove* me' (Sanhedrin 107*a*): *Sayings of the Jewish Fathers* (Taylor), p. 127, 2nd edit.

In the verse before us the word may be used of outward persecutions (cf. ii. 6, 7, v. 4–6; 1 Thess. ii. 14), which the Jewish believers suffered from their unbelieving countrymen, and if the word is restricted to this meaning, the expression 'manifold' may refer to the varied sufferings which the Christians experienced in different cities. But *v.* 10 would seem to indicate that riches no less than poverty might be a 'trial.' The rendering 'manifold' is given by A.V. here and in 1 Pet. i. 6, iv. 10, and so by R.V. (also in Heb. ii. 4): elsewhere rendered 'divers,' i.e. of divers sorts; cf. 3 Macc.

ii. 6; *Psalms of Solomon*, iv. 3; Matt. iv. 23. And in this manner the word might include both the trials of external conditions and the allurements to evil.

An attempt has been recently made to show that the latter is the dominant idea of the word here, as in *vv.* 12–14, and that all allusion to external persecution is 'merely incidental.' But even if this could be urged of such a passage as ii. 6, it could scarcely be said of *v.* 10 (see *in loco*), not to mention the tragic issue involved in *v.* 6.

3. *knowing.* Only in this confidence of knowledge could St James exhort his believing countrymen to rejoice in trial; otherwise his greeting 'joy to you' would have sounded like a mockery, as also his exhortation 'count it all joy.' But the manifold suffering of these Jewish Christians was a proving, a testing of faith, a discipline of character, which would bring with it something higher than happiness, even *blessedness*, i. 12; something superior to riches, the heirship of a kingdom, ii. 5.

The hostility of the world or the synagogue might ridicule the Christian life as madness and its hopes as vanity, but St James, if he had not heard the counsel spoken by the lips of Christ, had caught the spirit of his Master's teaching:—Rejoice (the same word in the Greek) and be exceeding glad; persecutions for My sake bring blessedness and enduring reward; cf. Matt. v. 10–12.

the proof of your faith. The word translated by R.V. 'proof,' and so also in 1 Pet. i. 7, occurs only in these two passages in the N.T. (cf.

4 worketh patience. And let patience have *its* perfect work, that ye may be perfect and entire, lacking in nothing.

Hermas, *Vis.* iv. 3). It is taken by many commentators (e.g. by Zahn) to mean instrument or means of proving, and these means would be the manifold temptations just mentioned. Thus in Rom. v. 4, where St Paul says 'knowing that tribulation worketh patience,' we have really what St James says. Others would render the word here as = *exploratio, probatio*, in an active sense, i.e. the trying, proving, testing. But a fresh and illuminative rendering has lately been given to the word by Dr Deissmann (*Neue Bibelstudien*, p. 86, see also E.T.). It would seem that the Greek word for 'proof' is not a substantive but an adjective, in support of which statement Deissmann adduces many instances from the papyri, where the word is used in the sense of valid, genuine, and so of articles of gold, as of the worth of ornaments in a bride's dowry, etc. He would therefore render the phrase here, as in 1 Pet., 'that which is genuine in your faith'; cf. 2 Cor. viii. 8, and Luther's translation, *euer glaube, so er rechtschaffen ist*, i.e. 'your faith, so it be true, genuine,' etc. (It is highly probable that the Greek commentator Oecumenius took the word as an adj.[1])

This early mention of and prominence given to *faith* is rightly regarded as an indication that St James was not likely to depreciate its proper use; see further *v.* 6. 'In the Epistle of St James "faith" is twice applied to prayer (i. 6, v. 15), where it means faith that God will

grant what is prayed for. Twice it means "Christian faith" (so here and in ii. 1). In the controversial passage, ii. 14–26, where faith is contrasted with works, the faith intended is "faith in God."......Faith with St James is more often the faith which is common to Jew and Christian; even when it is Christian faith, it stops short of the Christian enthusiasm': see *The Meaning of Faith in the N.T.* (Sanday and Headlam, *Romans*, p. 31).

worketh, lit. 'works out' (Lat. *efficere*).

patience, rather 'endurance,' with not merely a passive but an active side; 'a noble word,' Trench calls it; 'it does not mark merely the endurance...but the *brave* patience (*perseverantia*) with which the Christian contends against the various hindrances, persecutions, and temptations that befall him in his conflict with the inward and outward world,' *Synonyms*, II. 3; see too *Speaker's Commentary* on 2 Cor. vi. 4: 'perseverantia quod majus est quam patientia' (Theile): cf. Matt. x. 22, xxiv. 13.

4. *have its perfect work*, i.e. have its full effect, attain its end, according to the derivation of the word; see further below.

perfect and entire. Both adjectives are used in the LXX in a moral and religious sense, the first of Noah in Gen. vi. 9, and Ecclus. xliv. 17, and the second of the knowledge of God, which is 'perfect righteousness,' Wisd. xv. 3, and of 'perfect piety,'

---

[1] Zahn, whilst accepting Deissmann's solution for 1 Pet., prefers his own rendering as given above for the passage before us, but Deissmann's translation makes excellent sense in both places (see further *Expository Times*, June, 1901).

4 Macc. xv. 17. The first adj. is variously employed, but always with reference to the idea of the attainment of an 'end,' the meaning of the noun from which it is derived ; so of full-grown men in a physical sense, so too in an ethical and spiritual sense, 1 Cor. ii. 6; Phil. iii. 15; Col. i. 28, etc.: cf. its use of religious growth, LXX 1 Chron. xxv. 8, where the teachers (the 'perfect') are set over against the scholars. The second adj. according to its derivation would mean that which is whole and entire in all its parts, complete ; so the cognate noun denotes physical wholeness, both in the O. and N.T., Isaiah i. 6; Acts iii. 16. But, as in the case of the former adj., the transition was easily made to the meaning of mental and moral entireness ; see instances above, and in the N.T., 1 Thess. v. 23. We may thus fairly say that in the 'perfect' character no grace is merely in its weak imperfect beginnings, but all have reached a certain ripeness and maturity, whilst in the 'entire' character no grace which ought to be in a Christian man is wanting; so Trench, *Synonyms*, I. xxii., and Hastings' *B.D.* III. Art. 'Perfection.' The first adj. with its cognate words is used in the LXX as in classical Greek with reference to sacrifices, and also of the priests by Philo, and the second adj. in a similar way by Philo, both of priests and sacrifices, but not so in LXX. On this account some commentators think that the term may be introduced here owing to this sacrificial import, and with the thought that Christians should present themselves as perfect sacrifices to God (compare the language in *v.* 18), but it can scarcely be said that there is any definite hint of this in the text. It is of interest also to note that this word

'perfect' is found more frequently in this Epistle than in any other N.T. book. The whole level of life seems lifted even in these early days of the Church's history, and if we ask the reason, the best answer has been found in the reminder that the Sermon on the Mount with its call to perfection (Matt. v. 48) had intervened between the Old Testament and the New.

lacking in nothing, i.e. in no respect lacking this perfectness and completeness, although in many things we all stumble, cf. iii. 2. Only One can be strictly called 'perfect,' whilst we are encouraged to aim at perfection, even as children ever setting before them, and striving to attain to, the likeness of their Father.

On the stages of Christian growth here, and their resemblance to Rom. v. 4, see Mayor, pp. 35, 178. The rendering above in *v.* 3 would require a somewhat different, but no less valuable order. 'That which is genuine in your faith' produces endurance ; thus Moses endured because by faith he saw Him who is invisible, Heb. xi. 27, and this endurance, if abiding and lasting, has for its result a Christian character thorough and complete.

If men who have worked amongst the poor can tell us that this Epistle with its demand for what is practical in our religion has a special message for our own day (see *Introduction* to Mr Adderley's *St James*), it is significant that the writer places in its forefront 'that which is genuine in your faith' as the source and sustainer of an endurance capable of bearing not only the tribulation and persecution, which may arise because of the Word, but also the daily toil and labour, the daily trials of the Christian life.

5   But if any of you lacketh wisdom, let him ask of God,
who giveth to all liberally and upbraideth not; and it

5. (*lacking* etc.)...*But if any of you lacketh.* The R.V. rendering of the participle in the previous verse enables us to note another characteristic of St James already mentioned in *v.* 2, viz. his method of passing from one paragraph or sentence to another by the repetition of a word; cf. *vv.* 6, 13, 14, 24, ii. 2, iii. 2, 4, 8, iv. 8, 11, v. 8, 17 (a usage also noted as frequent in Plato).

wisdom. St James does not refer merely to practical wisdom in meeting the various 'trials' of daily life, although he knew how necessary that was in the circumstances of those around him; but he assigns this high place to wisdom as he had learnt to know it not only in the Book of Wisdom, in Ecclesiasticus, in Proverbs, but in men 'full of the Holy Ghost and wisdom,' Acts vi. 3, as he may have seen it in Him, 'a greater than Solomon' (cf. 1 Kings iii. 9–12), Who is described as 'filled with wisdom,' Luke ii. 40. Beyschlag speaks of it as, in the thought of St James, that gift of God which makes a man ready for every good work (see further on iii. 15–17), as not essentially different from that which is called in a parallel passage the gift of the Holy Spirit, Luke xi. 13, although he adds, in his last edition, Mayor's words: 'the prayer for wisdom takes a more definitely Christian form in St Paul's prayer for the Spirit'; cf. Col. i. 9; Ephes. i. 17. It is because we do not possess this Divine gift of wisdom that our modern life lacks dignity, force, consistency, while its possession would

transfigure life, showing us what it is, and how to make the best of it: see Dale's practical comments, *Epistle of James*, p. 12.

Spitta refers to Wisd. ix. 6, where the word 'perfect' is used in close connection with the possession of 'wisdom,' but although the collocation of the two words is striking, 'for though a man be never so perfect among the children of men, yet if thy wisdom be not with him, he shall be nothing regarded,' it may be fairly urged that the exhortation to pray for wisdom was so natural in the province of the religious life that it need not be referred to the passage cited; nothing indeed was more likely than that St James should introduce such an exhortation in view of the special circumstances of his readers without any recurrence in thought or word to this one particular passage.

let him ask of God. Cf. Matt. vii. 7 (Luke xxi. 15). For the prayer to God for wisdom cf. Prov. ii. 6; Ecclus. i. 10; Wisdom vii. 7, ix. 4; also 1 Kings iii. 5–15, iv. 29–34. Two of the leading words of St James are found together in *Epist. of Barnabas*, xxi. 5, 'And may God, Who is Lord of the whole world, give you wisdom...patience[1].'

who giveth to all, not only to a Solomon. Cf. Matt. vii. 11: the words may be taken in a wider sense to refer not only to the gift of wisdom, but to all the good gifts of God; 'giveth,' i.e. giveth continually.

liberally. So A. and R.V.; cf. A. and R.V. in 2 Cor. viii. 2, ix. 11, and

---

[1] An interesting illustration from Plato, *Legg.* III. (687 E), is given in the *Journal of Theol. Studies,* vol. II. p. 432.

6 shall be given him. But let him ask in faith, nothing
doubting : for he that doubteth is like the surge of the

R.V. in Rom. xii. 8, in each case
simplicity or *singleness* in margin.
The Greek use of the adverb would
rather justify the rendering *simply*,
and this rendering fits in better
with the following description 'and
upbraideth not,' the gift being un-
conditional, and without any of the
imperfections which stain human
gifts. The rendering *liberally* for
the adverb seems to have arisen
from the fact that 'simplicity,' dis-
interestedness in giving, is nearly
allied to liberality (Vulg. *affluenter*).
The cognate adj. = lit. without folds,
and so of that which is single, simple ;
cf. Sanday and Headlam's *Romans*,
p. 357, and the description of Issachar
as the 'simple' man, *Test. xii. Patr.*

and upbraideth not, i.e. in contrast to the behaviour of men (as
perhaps is further indicated in *v.* 10
and v. 9), who cast favours bestowed
in one's teeth. Cf. Ecclus. xx. 15,
xli. 22. Others take the word to
mean that God does not reject or
repel men, or treat them abusively,
whilst others again would take the
word in the most general sense to
mean that God does not upbraid
with any kind of reproach, although
we are so unworthy to make any
request of Him; but see Mark xvi.
14.

and it shall be given him. Matt.
vii. 7 ; Luke vi. 38. A reminiscence
of the words of Jesus.

6. *But let him ask in faith.* To
St James also, says Bengel, faith is
prora et puppis, prow and stern.
With the whole of the verse, cf.
Ecclus. i. 28, ii. 12, vii. 10, and
xxxiii. 2, xxxv. 16, 17 ; 'faith,' trust
in God that the request will be
granted according to His will : cf.

Mark xi. 22 ff., and the expression
v. 15, 'the prayer of faith.' The influence of the whole passage on
Hermas is very marked, cf. *Mand.* ix.
6, 7 ; *Sim.* v. 4, 3. In this verse we
again note the writer's characteristic
of 'catching up' a preceding verb.

nothing doubting. The 'wavering'
of A.V., so Tynd., may have been
introduced on account of the word
'wave' following. In Matt. xxi. 21,
although not so found in profane
writers, the word is used in the sense of
doubting, hesitating; so too in Mark
xi. 23, Rom. iv. 20, xiv. 23 (Jude 22,
R.V.) as the opposite of faith: this
practical doubting which shows that
a man is divided between God and
the world St James reproves elsewhere, cf. ii. 4, iv. 3, 4.

the surge of the sea, the Greek
word suggesting size and extension
(often in the LXX) as compared with
the usual word for 'wave'—the violent agitation of the sea; only once
elsewhere in N.T., Luke viii. 24, of
the tempest on the Lake of Gennes-
aret. Such a storm St James might
often have seen ; see also note on
iii. 4. The same noun in its metaphorical use also denotes 'storm'
rather than 'wave' (see Dean of
Westminster on *Ephes.* iv. 14).

driven by the wind and tossed, in
A.V. 'with' for 'by.' The first participle in the Greek may perhaps
have been coined by the writer, since
it does not occur in the LXX or
classical Greek, although a verb
very similar in form is found in the
latter. St James seems to have had
a special liking for verbs with the
particular termination of the verb
before us.

tossed, only here in the N.T. but

7 sea driven by the wind and tossed.   For let not that man
8 think [1]that he shall receive anything of the Lord ; a
doubleminded man, unstable in all his ways.

[1] Or, *that a doubleminded man, unstable in all his ways, shall receive
anything of the Lord.*

used by Philo of water agitated by
winds, so by Dio Cass. of the surge
of the sea tossed to and fro, and by
Dio Chrys. of the demos, compared
to a sea agitated by the wind. This
second participle is apparently employed to strengthen the first as a
stronger expression, and there is no
need to regard the former word as
denoting external, and the latter
internal agitation (Bengel).   The
Divine wisdom cannot dwell in a
mind thus tossed hither and thither,
and never continuing in one stay.
The verb in the text is referred to
two derivations, (1) a noun meaning
a bellows or fan used with reference
to kindling a flame (or to cooling
with a fan), and (2) a noun denoting
the rapid movement of wind or waves,
etc. (used also of a storm), a derivation which is undoubtedly the more
probable; cf. the word Eu-ripus (from
the same deriv.), where, so it was
said, the tide ebbed and flowed seven
times a day ; hence used proverbially
of an unstable, wavering man, as by
Aeschines and Aristotle, and here by
St James.   With this verse cf. Ephes.
iv. 13, 14, where the 'perfect' are
contrasted with children 'tossed to
and fro' by every wind of teaching.

7. *For let not that man think.*
The 'for' is perhaps best taken as
giving the reason for the exhortation
'let him ask in faith.' 'Faith does
not think,' says Bengel truly; 'fides
non opinatur.' The verb for 'think,'
seldom found in the Greek of the

N.T. (John xxi. 25 ; Phil. i. 17), expresses a judgment which has feeling
rather than thought for its ground
(Grimm-Thayer), 'fancy'; 'that man,'
the whole expression in the Greek
would seem to indicate something
of contempt.

the Lord, usually taken as referring
to God the Father, and possibly the
context which is concerned with the
gifts of God in answer to prayer demands this, but, on the other hand,
it would certainly seem that in v.
14, 15, Christ is thought of as answering 'the prayer of faith,' and it may
be so here.

8. *a doubleminded man, unstable in all his ways,* in apposition
to 'that man' (see Mayor, Weiss).
A.V. inserts 'is' before 'a doubleminded man' with all other E.V.
and Vulg., but the connection with
the former clause is quite plain as
above. W.H. and R.V. marg. render:
'For let not that man think that a
doubleminded man etc. shall receive
anything of the Lord[1].'

doubleminded. The man is regarded as having two minds, the one
set on God, the other on the world
(cf. iv. 8), and so the character is entirely opposed to the single-hearted
and entire devotion claimed by
Christ, Matt. xxii. 37. In modern
life the career and character of
a 'doubleminded' man has been
forcibly portrayed in Arthur
Clough's famous poem *Dipsychus,*
and more than one recent writer

[1] So far as textual authorities are concerned, it may be noted that B and the
Syriac support the rendering adopted in the text.

9　　But let the brother of low degree glory in his high

has emphasised 'doublemindedness' as a characteristically modern fault. But 'that which is genuine in our faith' can save us from it; therefore let a man pray 'in faith': 'St James does not charge us with hypocrisy, with pretending to a goodness we do not possess, or with feigning a desire for goodness we do not feel. He simply charges us with vacillation, with inconsistent aims and desires....Alas! we ask for decision itself with an undecided heart, not expecting, not altogether wishing to receive, a full and immediate answer to our prayer.' Dr S. Cox, *Expositor*, III. 40, 4th series.

The actual Greek word here used may possibly have been coined by St James, as it does not occur in the N.T. except in his Epistle, and not at all in LXX, although we may compare with the thought expressed by it Ps. xii. 3 (lit. 'a heart and a heart'), Ecclus. i. 28, *Book of Enoch*, xci. 4 (cf. Taylor, *Sayings of the Jewish Fathers*, p. 148, who finds a possible reference here to Prov. xxi. 8, and see Rabbi Tanchuma on Deut. xxvi. 17, 'Let not those who wish to pray to God have two hearts, one directed to Him and one to something else').

But it is noteworthy that in *Didache*, iv. 4 (cf. ii. 4 and v. 1 where 'doubleness of heart' is mentioned amongst the sins of the 'way of death') we have a strikingly similar compound word, not found in LXX or in classical Greek, 'Thou shalt not doubt whether a thing shall be or not be,' i.e. whether thy prayer shall be granted or no; cf. *Barn.* xix. 5 (and see Introd. for the similarity between the language of the *Didache* and this Epistle). In early Christian literature the word became very common; it was used e.g. some 40 times by Hermas (cf. *Mand.* ix. 4 ff. in connection with the present passage); Clem. Rom. *Cor.* xi. 2, xxiii. 3; *Const. Apost.* vii. 11. Sanday and Headlam, *Romans*, p. 115, have some important remarks on this early Christian use of the expression.

unstable. The Greek word does not occur in the N.T. except in this Epistle, cf. iii. 8 (but see note on the reading); and with this expression 2 Pet. ii. 14 may also be compared. It is found in LXX, Isaiah liv. 11. In classical Greek it often occurs, and it is employed by Polybius of fickle men. St James in his frequent use of the Apocrypha may have been thinking of Ecclus. ii. 12, 'Woe be...to the sinner that goeth two ways!' lit. 'upon two ways,' where however the words seem to refer not so much to uncertainty as to want of decision, and to the attempt to keep in with both sides.

in all his ways, taken quite generally as in Hebrew of a man's way of life, habits, actions; cf. Ps. xci. 11; Prov. iii. 6; Jer. xvi. 17.

9. *But let the brother;* 'but' retained by R.V. may be used to introduce a piece of advice in sequence to that already given, or to contrast the confident exultation of the Christian with the indecision of the faithless doubter. The word 'brother' should be taken quite generally (W.H. bracket the article before it) as applying to both classes, the rich and those of low degree, for both should be taken literally. Would there not be in the Christian Church rich men like Joseph of Arimathaea, Nicodemus, Zacchaeus? We can scarcely suppose that there

10 estate : and the rich, in that he is made low : because as

were no well-to-do adherents of a religion which had attracted a Barnabas and a John Mark.

of low degree. Cf. Luke i. 52. In the LXX the word is used in some cases of those literally poor, e.g. 1 Sam. xviii. 23, Prov. xxx. 14, Isaiah xxxii. 7, but the word came to signify very frequently the 'poor' in the spirit of resignation and humility, as in the Psalms, Prov. iii. 34, Ecclus. xiii. 20, *Book of Enoch*, xxv. 4, cviii. 7–9, as contrasted with the selfish and proud, 'the rich'; see on iv. 4 and cf. *Psalms of Solomon*, ii. 35, iv. 28, xvii. 46, Luke i. 51, 52, and Introd. p. xxxvi., on the social cleavage between the rich and the poor in Jewish life.

glory in. So R.V. here and elsewhere; cf. Rom. ii. 17 etc. The word is a favourite with St Paul, but it is only used elsewhere in the N.T. in this passage and in iv. 16, generally in a good sense. It is also frequent in the LXX, and with the present passage the following may be compared : 1 Sam. ii. 10 (not in Hebrew), Jer. ix. 23, Ecclus. i. 11, ix. 16, x. 22, and in the N.T. especially Rom. v. 3. The construction 'glory in' is not found in classical Greek, but it is frequent in LXX and N.T.; cf. also *Psalms of Solomon*, xvii. 1.

his high estate, lit. 'in his height.' Cf. Luke i. 52. For the metaphorical use of the word cf. Job v. 11, 1 Macc. i. 40 (Ecclus. xi. 1), and a similar use is also found in classical Greek.

The 'high estate' includes both the present and the future dignity of the Christian, his heirship to the kingdom (ii. 5), and the glory which cometh from the only God (John v. 44). The believer in Christ could 'take joyfully' the want or loss of earthly possessions, knowing that he had his true self for a better and abiding possession, Heb. x. 34, cf. Luke xxi. 19[1]. On the reference of the words to the Christian's exaltations and spiritual wealth in this present life, it is of interest to compare the remarks of Ritschl on the same passage, *Justification and Reconciliation*, pp. 458, 505, E.T.

In *Psalms of Solomon*, xvii. 7, the writer, speaking apparently of the Sadducees who preferred a worldly kingdom to the kingdom of God, says 'they preferred a kingdom to that which was their excellency,' where for 'excellency' the same Greek noun is used as here. The words truly represent what St James saw all around him; the rich unbelieving Jews making choice of the things seen and temporal, in preference to a kingdom which was righteousness, peace, joy in the Holy Ghost.

10. *and the rich, in that he is made low.* Are we to understand this of a rich Christian, or of a non-Christian? By most commentators the former view is adopted as above, but on the other hand it is maintained that the whole context is against this interpretation, inasmuch as the

---

[1] Spitta maintains that the exhortation to 'glorying' is introduced quite unexpectedly, and that the thought is so strange that it can only be accounted for because the writer has before him Jer. ix. 23. But if we compare this verse with *vv.* 2, 12, we see that the dominant thought throughout is that of the right relation of the Christian to 'trials.' At the same time the passage in Jer. may well have suggested some of the language.

entire section i. 2–12 is concerned
with the 'trials' of Christians,
amongst which the prosperity of
some Christians could find no place;
but prosperity and riches might be
a temptation no less than poverty
and misfortune (1 Tim. vi. 9; Matt.
xiii. 22). It is further urged that in
v. 11 it is said that the rich man, not
his wealth, shall fade away, and that
this could only be said of one who is
opposed to the *Christian* brother of
low estate, whilst it is quite arbitrary
to introduce a distinction between
the 'rich man' *qua* rich and *qua*
Christian, for if this had been in
his thoughts St James would have
written 'so also shall his riches fade
away.' But it is quite possible that
in *v.* 11 St James uses the words 'the
rich man' of the rich *qua* rich, as
the immediate context may imply
(see below), and that in *v.* 10 he is
enforcing a warning common to the
teaching of the prophets and to that
of our Lord and His Apostles, not
only against the misuse of riches, but
as to their transitory nature; cf.
Matt. vi. 19; Luke xii. 15–21; 1 Cor.
vii. 30, 31. In Ecclus. xiii. 3, to
which reference is sometimes made,
the context shows that it is the rich
man, not *qua* rich, but *qua* unjust,
who is censured; and so in this
Epistle where the rich are spoken
of, as in ii. 7, v. 1–6, the context shows
that they are condemned for their
arrogance and extortion. But in so
far as the rich man failed to glory in
that he was made low, in so far that
is as he failed to become one of the
'little ones,' great in the kingdom
of God, Luke ix. 48, and one of 'the
chief, who served,' Luke xxii. 26, he
knew nothing and had gained nothing
of the true riches committed to his
trust when the Name of Christ was
called upon him. As a Christian,

the rich man would possess *ipso
facto* 'the high estate' which his poor
Christian brother enjoyed, but he
must be prepared to take the lowest
place in the kingdom, and to enter
into the joy of a Lord, who, though
rich, became poor (Zahn, *Einleitung,*
I. p. 70). It is of course a possible
view that St James had in mind the
sufferings to which Christians, both
rich and poor, might be exposed from
their unbelieving fellow-countrymen,
and that his words were meant to
strengthen rich and poor alike, if
the former were tempted by the
loss of their wealth, or the latter
by the chance of bettering their
fortunes, to renounce their Christian
faith. But whilst this thought
may be fairly associated with the
passage, the words, as we have
already seen above, need not be
so limited. Or we may take the
words 'in that he is made low'
to refer to the trials which would
come to a rich man, if by some
sudden stroke of fortune he suddenly
found himself poor in this world's
goods. Certainly Ecclus. ii. 4, 5
quoted above in *v.* 2 might seem to
support this view, and it is noticeable that *vv.* 1 and 12 of the same
chapter afford very probable points
of contact with *vv.* 2 and 8 of this
first chapter of St James.

Those who would limit the words
under discussion to non-Christians
are obliged to regard the language
with reference to the rich as ironical,
since the verb to be applied with 'the
rich' can only be the same as that
which is used with 'the poor.' This
is sometimes supported by our Lord's
use of irony in such words as Matt.
vi. 2, 5, 16; the only thing in which
the rich can boast is in the certainty
of his being brought low, or in his
humiliation at the coming judgment.

11 the flower of the grass he shall pass away. For the sun
ariseth with the scorching wind, and withereth the grass ;
and the flower thereof falleth, and the grace of the fashion
of it perisheth : so also shall the rich man fade away in his
goings.

But this is not a very satisfactory
account of the word 'humiliation'
here, nor is it demanded, as is sometimes urged, by the immediate
context.

*because as the flower of the grass
he shall pass away.* Cf. 1 Pet. i. 24
where the words of Isaiah xl. 6 are
quoted more fully; see also Ps.
xxxvii. 2 ; Job xiv. 2 ; Ecclus. xiv.
17, 18.

The writer is here asserting a
general truth, cf. 1 Cor. vii. 31, and
not introducing a special threat
against the rich, although the bear-
ings of such a truth might more
easily be forgotten by the rich. In
accepting the 'humiliation' of a
Christian, the rich man would receive
from God 'according to the riches
of His glory' an exaltation divine
and lasting (Matt. xxiii. 12); for
all *human* glory was doomed to pass
away (cf. LXX of Isaiah xl. 6).

11. *For the sun ariseth.* So R.V.,
omitting 'no sooner' of the A.V.,
words not found in the Greek, and
not needed. The tense (aorist) of
the verb and of the three following
verbs depicts the events as actually
before the eyes and yet as past 'in
the very moment of describing them.'
Others take this tense of the verb
as implying what usually happens
in all such cases; hence the term
'usitative' or 'gnomic' aorist[1]. The
four verbs thus succeeding each
other present a pictorial vividness

characteristic of the writer ; cf. with
this passage 1 Pet. i. 24 ; Isaiah xl.
7 in LXX.

ariseth, a verb constantly used
in LXX of the sun arising; cf. with
the language of the text Jonah iv. 8.

with the scorching wind, but A.V.
takes the word as signifying the
heat, the burning heat of the sun.
In the rendering of R.V. it is, however, often found in LXX ; cf. Hos. xii.
1 ; Ezek. xvii. 10; Jonah iv. 8; and it is
so taken by some in Matt. xx. 12;
Luke xii. 55. On the other hand,
Isaiah xlix. 10, Ecclus. xviii. 16,
and the N.T. places cited above, are
sometimes held to justify rendering
of A.V., since the destruction is
effected by the sun itself, and not
by the 'heat' as distinguished from
the sun; cf. Ecclus. xliii. 3. The
latter translation also points more
emphatically to one of the local traits
with which this short Epistle abounds
(see Introd. p. xxiv.), the sirocco or
the scorching S.E. wind of Palestine
(although no doubt by either rendering the excessive heat of an Eastern
sun might be vividly depicted).
Mayor inclines to this latter rendering from the fact that the article
is found with the Greek word under
dispute, cf. R.V. 'with *the* scorching
wind,' and see as above Jonah iv. 8.

falleth. Cf. Isaiah xl. 7. The verb
so translated as in A. and R.V. of the
N.T. expresses the actual falling off
of the flower, as of the petals from the

---

[1] On the use of this tense both in classical examples and in the N.T. it may
be of interest to refer to Burton, *New Testament Moods and Tenses*, p. 21.

12   Blessed is the man that endureth temptation: for when
he hath been approved, he shall receive the crown of life,

calyx; the same verb is found in
Isaiah xxviii. 1, 4, rather in the sense
of decaying, withering; cf. Job xiv. 2.

the grace of the fashion of it;
'the grace,' cf. the cognate adj. in
Ecclus. xxiv. 14 of a fair olive-
tree ; only twice in N.T. but often in
LXX, and also in *Psalms of Solomon*,
ii. 21, xvii. 47.

of the fashion, lit. 'of its countenance,' i.e. of its outward appearance, cf. Ps. civ. 30; Luke xii. 56;
Matt. xvi. 3; also of the outward
appearance of inanimate things, cf.
the Latin *facies*; not merely as a
Hebrew pleonasm, although the word
may be said to be used Hebraisti-
cally.

the rich man, i.e. *qua* rich; see
above.

fade away, only here in N.T., a
word probably suggested by preceding simile, cf. its use of withering
roses, Wisd. ii. 8; Job xv. 30. A
similar metaphorical use of the word
in relation to boastfulness in riches
is found in Philo, *De vict.* p. 855 A,
and with this use cf.*Apoc. of Baruch*,
lxxxii. 7, where of the Gentiles we
read: 'and we meditate on the beauty
of their gracefulness, though they
have to do with pollutions, but as
grass that withers will they fade
away.' In the same passage we have
other parallels to St James's imagery
elsewhere in this Epistle : the Gentiles will be 'as vapour,' 'as sunshine
will they pass away,' *ibid. vv.* 3, 6.

in his goings. So R.V. because the
word is different from that translated
'ways' in *v.* 8 (although sometimes
the two words are regarded as synonyms, cf. Prov. ii. 9).
This word may either express
quite literally the journeyings, cf. **iv.**

13, Luke xiii. 22, or perhaps the
projects and adventures of a man in
the pursuit of wealth. The plural
may indicate the troublesome and
varied nature of the man's various
engagements. The attempts to sub-
stitute other words which might
mean 'in his gettings' or 'in his
property' are not warranted by any
sufficient evidence.

12. *Blessed is the man.* Cf. v. 11;
1 Pet. iii. 14, iv. 14. This teaching
as it were by beatitudes may remind
us of our Lord's own teaching in the
Sermon on the Mount, but the same
mode of expression is frequent in
the O.T., as in the Psalms, and so
too in Ecclus.

If we regard both rich and poor
of the preceding verses as those
tried by temptation, the blessing
may of course be taken as meant for
both; each has been put to the
proof, and for each there is the
crown of life; thus the verse closes
the paragraph from *v.* 2. On the
other hand, those who hold that the
rich previously referred to are not
members of the Christian Church
take the blessing as of the poor only.

Spitta would understand the words
of the rich man, who is 'blessed'
because he preserves himself safely
amidst his severe testing, and he
quotes a striking passage from
Ecclus. xxxi. (LXX, xxxiv.) 8 ff.,
'Blessed is the rich that is found
without blemish, and hath not gone
after gold. Who is he ? and we will
call him blessed; for wonderful
things hath he done among his people.
Who hath been tried thereby, and
found perfect ? then let him glory.'
The same writer also quotes from
Midr. Shemoth r. par. 31, where

the rich who is tested, and shows himself open-handed towards the poor, is said to enjoy his gold in this world, and to keep his capital for the world to come.

But it may be fairly held that there is no occasion to confine the thought here to the rich, and Spitta's limitation seems only to be warranted by a misunderstanding of the previous verses.

that endureth temptation, not merely who falls into it, *v.* 2, or suffers it. The active side of the virtue of patience (cf. *v.* 3) is here clear enough. But the endeavour is maintained not in the man's own strength, in self-righteousness, or Stoical self-sufficiency, but in the love which waxeth not cold, Matt. xxiv. 12, 13; see also below.

when he hath been approved, not simply 'when he is tried' as in A.V.: the trial has been made and the result has been favourable. In all other passages of the N.T. the word is rendered 'approved' in A.V. as in R.V. For its use in the N.T. see Rom. xiv. 18, xvi. 10, 2 Tim. ii. 15, and for the cognate noun Rom. v. 4, Phil. ii. 22, and for the cognate negative adjective, in a bad sense, 2 Tim. iii. 8, Tit. i. 16, 1 Cor. ix. 27, 2 Cor. xiii. 7. The word has been sometimes taken here as referring to the testing of athletes for the games (cf. the possible metaphorical use of the negative adj. in 1 Cor. ix. 27, and see also below), but both the positive and negative adjectives are used strictly of metals and coins, tested and proved or the reverse (cf. in O.T. Gen. xxiii. 16; 2 Chron. ix. 17), and here the words might easily be extended in a wider sense to the proving or testing of character.

With these words Resch compares those of Tertullian, *De Bapt.* c. 20,

where he cites apparently as a saying of the Lord, 'No one untempted shall attain to the heavenly kingdom,' *Agrapha,* p. 187, and in view of Luke xxii. 28, 29, some such saying may well have been in vogue, although it may have been merely proverbial and not actually derived from Christ (see the comments of Mr Ropes, *Die Sprüche Jesu,* p. 124).

the crown of life. It is doubtful whether there is any reference in this expression to the prizes of the arena. It must be remembered that amongst the Jews a crown or a diadem was used to signify a special honour, or as a representation of the highest happiness and prosperity: cf. Ps. xxi. 3, lxxxix. 39; Prov. iv. 9; Ezek. xxi. 26; Zech. vi. 11, 14. Amongst the Rabbis too we find such sayings as the following: 'There are three crowns: the crown of Thorah, and the crown of Priesthood, and the crown of Royalty (Ex. xxv. 10, xxx. 1, 3, xxv. 23, 24); but the crown of a good name mounts above them (Eccl. vii. 1),' Taylor, *Sayings of the Jewish Fathers,* iv. 19 (cf. vi. 5), pp. 72, 101, 2nd edit.

At the same time in some of the N.T. passages, as e.g. 1 Cor. ix. 25 2 Tim. iv. 8, and see ii. 5 above, the reference to the games seems unmistakable, and the same conclusion is derived from the consideration of the imagery in such passages as Wisd. iv. 2, 4 Macc. xvii. 15, and Philo, *Legg. All.* ii. 26, M. p. 86, where he speaks of a beautiful and glorious crown different from that of any festival assembly of men, and employs the word used of the festival of the Olympian games.

The question has been raised as to whether the notion here is that of sovereignty or of victory, but the mention of a kingdom in ii. 5, and

K.

some of the passages cited above in
O.T., together with 2 Sam. xii. 30,
1 Chron. xx. 2, might well lead us to
regard the former thought as prominent here, whilst it may be admitted that in the closest parallels of the
N.T., e.g. 1 Pet. v. 4, 2 Tim. iv. 8, Rev.
ii. 10, the leading idea is rather that
of victory[1].

A further question arises as to
whether the expression refers only
to the future life, or to the present
life also: if we compare ii. 5, such
expressions as 'rich in faith' and
'heirs of the kingdom' indicate a life
which is at all events commenced
for the Christian, cf. Rom. v. 17, and
of which he is already in possession
at least in germ (cf. also Ritschl,
Justification and Reconciliation, p.
500, E.T.). 'The crown which consists
in life eternal' is the rendering
adopted by Mayor (and so to the
same effect Beyschlag); cf. 1 John ii.
25.

As the undoubted source of the
passage before us Spitta (and so von
Soden) points to Zech. vi. 14, and it
is certainly noteworthy that the LXX
of that verse reads, 'The crown shall
be to those who endure,' etc., the
noun and verb being identical with
those in the verse of St James. But
it must be remembered that the
Hebrew text is quite different, and
that Spitta's attempt to discount this
fact is not very successful, whilst a
passage like Wisd. v. 16 also presents
a very close parallel; and the imagery
was very common: cf. Ecclus. xv.
6; Wisd. iv. 2; Ps. viii. 5; and *Aristeas*,
63. 8.

which the Lord promised. So A.
and R.V., but in the latter 'the Lord'
is printed in italics, indicating that
no such subject is expressed in the
Greek, according to the reading
adopted by W.H. and Weiss. If we
are justified in taking 'the Lord,' *v.* 7,
to apply to Christ, or if the verse
before us is an unrecorded saying of
Jesus, we are of course justified in
inserting 'the Lord,' i.e. Christ, as
the subject here. On the other hand,
ii. 5 seems rather to point to 'God'
as the subject, and so also does
the fact that so many of the O.T.
promises are made to those who love
God (this is the view adopted by
Zahn and Beyschlag, no less than
von Soden, and the same subject of
the verb is found in the Syriac
Version and in the Vulg.).

to them that love him. Cf. Rom.
viii. 28; 1 Cor. ii. 9; 2 Tim. iv. 8. In
the O.T. the phrase was very frequent: cf. Ps. xcvii. 10, cxlv. 20, and
also see Ecclus. i. 18, xxxi. 16;
Tob. xiii. 14, xiv. 7; 1 Macc. iv. 33;
Psalms of Solomon, iv. 7, vi. 9,
x. 4, xiv. 1; and *Book of Enoch,*
cviii. 8.

'Amor parit patientiam,' writes
Bengel in his comment on this verse,
'Love begets patience (endurance)';
the love of God is the motive power
which works patience, and patience
strengthens the conviction that 'all
things work together for good'
(Rom. viii. 28) for those in whom
that love is being perfected.

There is some reason for supposing
that in this verse we have an *Agraphon* of our Lord, i.e. a saying of his
unrecorded in our Canonical Gospels.
That such sayings were current we
learn from Acts xx. 28, and in the
Acta Philippi we read, 'Blessed
is he who hath his raiment white,
for it is he who receiveth the crown

---

[1] On the word 'crown' as distinguished from the word 'diadem,' a distinction
apparently emphasised too much by Trench, see Mayor *in loco*.

13 which *the Lord* promised to them that love him. Let no
man say when he is tempted, I am tempted ¹of God : for

[1] Gr. *from.*

of joy.' Many English scholars regard
the words in this light, and Resch,
Agrapha, p. 253, argues at length for
this same view. He points out, e.g.,
(1) the non-existence of any corresponding promise in relation to the
word 'crown' in the O.T. ; (2) the
coincidence of several N.T. passages,
1 Cor. ix. 25, 1 Pet. v. 4, Apoc. ii. 10,
iii. 11, 2 Tim. ii. 5, iv. 8, and the
striking parallel in *Acta Philippi*
with reference to the crown; (3) the
phrase used in 2 Tim. iv. 8 which
closely resembles that in James i.
12 ; cf. ii. 5.

On the other hand, it is urged
that this recurring phrase 'to those
that love Him' must not be referred
to a word of the Lord, but perhaps
to some liturgical formula, or some
current mode of expression, and
that the imagery of a crown as the
reward of victory was too common
and too frequently in vogue to
justify Resch's conclusions (Ropes,
Die Sprüche Jesu, p. 38).

13. A serious question arises as
to whether the verb translated
'tempted' is to be taken in the same
sense as the cognate noun rendered
'trials' in *v.* 2, and 'temptations'
in *v.* 12, R.V.

Probably from the close connection
of the words, and from the writer's
characteristic of taking up, as it
were, a word from a preceding
word, both noun and verb are used
with reference to each other, but in
vv. 2 and 12 the noun signifies rather
the objective circumstances of the
temptation, while the verb in *v.* 13
relates to the subjective yielding of
the man to enticement.

I am tempted of God. Cf. Ecclesiasticus xv. 11, 12, 20, 'Say not thou,
It is through the Lord that I fell
away : for thou oughtest not to do
the things that he hateth. Say not
thou, He hath caused me to err : for
he hath no need of the sinful man....
He hath commanded no man to do
wickedly, neither hath he given any
man license to sin.'

In the original the words 'of God'
stand first, emphatically. Probably
the Greek preposition would be better
rendered 'from God' as in R.V.
marg., for it signifies the remoter
rather than the immediate agent.
The man would scarcely dare to
stamp God as the immediate tempter,
but, as in the passage of Ecclesiasticus quoted, he might be seduced
by the praise of the ungodly to a
fall which he would attribute to God.
In one sense no doubt 'temptations'
have their origin from God ; He
ordains them (cf. Gen. xxii. 1 ff.), but
He also overrules them, and He
'will with the temptation make also
the way of escape,' R.V. 1 Cor. x. 13,
i.e. the way suitable for each temptation.

There is no occasion to find a
reference here to any definite philosophical teaching, such as that of the
Pharisees or Essenes, still less to that
of Simon Magus, or to that of the
Gnostics. The words do but give
expression to the inclination so con-
genial to man to shift the blame by
some or any means from himself to
God ; cf. Gen. iii. 12 ; Prov. xxx. 8, 9.
So too in *Psalms of Solomon*, v. 8,
we read, 'Make not thy hand heavy
upon us, that we sin not by reason of

God [1]cannot be tempted with [2]evil, and he himself
14 tempteth no man : but each man is [3]tempted, when he is

> [1] Or, *is untried in evil*   [2] Gr. *evil things.*
> [3] Or, *tempted by his own lust, being drawn away* by it, *and enticed*

our sore necessity'; and Philo refutes the idea that Moses in his teaching had given occasion to the falsehood that God compelled men to sin, as some impious persons affirm (Philo, *Quod deter. pot.* 177 D).

The same human tendency may be amply illustrated from classical literature, as e.g. *Iliad*, XIX. 86, where Agamemnon excuses his injustice towards Achilles by saying, 'I am not to blame, but Jove and Fate,' although from other passages it would seem that the ancients themselves regarded such assertions as rash and impious: cf. Aesch. *Agam.* 1474, where Clytemnestra tries to throw her guilt on the evil genius of the family, and the Chorus refuse the plea.

cannot be tempted; one word in the original, a word not found in LXX or N.T. Very similar phrases are used in relation to God by Philo, Plutarch, M. Antoninus. God in His absolute purity is 'untemptable of evil'; man is tempted by his own lust.

In marg. R.V. we have the rendering 'is untried in evil,' i.e. is unversed in, has no experience of evil (or, evil things), but although the word may be so rendered, it seems best to take it as above.

The active sense 'God does not tempt to evil' is now generally abandoned, as it would reduce the words which follow to mere tautology.

evil. R.V. marg. 'evil things'; but there is no occasion to restrict the words, in accordance with some interpreters, to the evils of affliction or persecution. The whole context

seems to imply that moral evil is meant.

Resch (*Agrapha*, p. 233) quotes an interesting passage, *Clem. Hom.* iii. 35, which correctly interpreted runs, 'But to those who think that God tempteth, as the Scriptures say, He (i.e. Christ) saith, The Evil One is the tempter,' and in these latter words he would see another unrecorded saying of our Lord. But it is quite possible that the writer cited may have had in mind the passage before us in St James, or some reminiscence of our Lord's words, Matt. v. 37, xiii. 19, 25.

and he himself tempteth no man. So R.V. with emphatic rendering of the pronoun; in A.V. simply 'he.'

14. *but each man;* contrast marked in these words. There is a tempting—not from God, but from a man's own lust (although Mayor marks the opposition differently, see *in loco*).

The words as rendered in R.V. emphasise not merely the universality of temptation as in A.V. but rather its special peculiarity in the case of each individual man.

is tempted, when he is drawn away by his own lust, and enticed, R.V. (and so A.V. with exception noted below); see marg. 'is tempted by his own lust, being drawn away (by it) and enticed.'

Dr Plummer urges that both in A. and R.V. the punctuation and order of the words are faulty; both verbs belong to 'by his own lust,' and 'the metaphor is not seduction from the right road, but alluring out of security into danger.' The Greek participle rendered 'drawn away'

15 drawn away by his own lust, and enticed.　Then the lust,

should thus rather be 'drawn out,' like game from a covert or fish from a hiding nook into some place exposed to nets and hooks ; and so the man is represented as drawn out from his security, which is effected by his own desire ('his own,' i.e. emphatically in contrast to God, *v.* 13) enticing him as with a bait. Both the participles might be transferred from their literal use in application to hunting or fishing to a metaphorical use of alluring to sensual sin, and thus desire entices the man from his self-restraint as with the wiles of a harlot, a metaphor maintained by the words which follow, 'conceived,' 'beareth,' 'bringeth forth'; cf. 2 Pet. ii. 14, 18, where the same verb is found, and Philo, *Quod omn. prob. lib.* 22, 'driven by passion or *enticed* by pleasure' (see further Mayor's note and its strictures).　So again in *Testaments of the Twelve Patriarchs,* Jos. 2, Joseph says of Potiphar's wife, 'she pressed and drew me on to fornication,' where the same verb is employed as in St James, although compounded with another preposition.　The drawing out cannot have the force of drawing out as to the shore of a fish caught, as in Herod. II. 70, for this would demand that the enticing should precede the capture, whereas the Greek gives the reverse order, but possibly this must not be pressed, as the words may be given, not in the order of action, but in the order of thought (see Carr's note).　The latter verb is used only twice elsewhere in N.T., cf. 2 Pet. ii. 14, 18, and not at all in LXX, and the former five times in LXX in different senses, also in 3 Macc. ii. 23.

by his own lust, R.V., the Greek preposition implying direct personal agency.　In this connection we may compare *Sayings of the Jewish Fathers,* v. 4, 'with ten temptations was Abraham tempted,' not 'God did tempt Abraham,' cf. James i. 13; see Dr Taylor, p. 130, and also his comment on the expression before us, *l.c.,* 'the evil *nature* seduces a man in this world, etc., cf. Sukkah 52 *b.*'　With this again compare the famous passage, *Apocalypse of Baruch,* liv. 19, where, after speaking of Adam's fall and its results, the writer adds, 'Adam is therefore not the cause (i.e. of spiritual bliss or torment) save only of his own soul, but each one of us has been the Adam of his own soul.'　'The real force of this verse,' writes Dr Charles, 'is that a man's guilt and sin are not derived from Adam, but are due to his own action.　The evil impulse does not constitute guilt or sin unless man obeys it.　As the Talmudists say, it was placed in man to be overcome.'

In the present day this assertion of St James strikes at the root of all attempts to shift the blame and responsibility of wrong-doing from ourselves to outward circumstances, to the working of natural laws, to the bias of inherited tendencies.　And the consciences of mankind ratify the plain and direct indictment of St James, if such words as repentance, remorse, and sin are to retain any force and meaning.　'He speaks of sin, of salvation, of redemption, and conversion, as if these things were realities.　He asks me, What does M. Renan make of sin? "Ah well, I suppose I suppress it,"' Amiel, *Journal Intime,* E.T., I. lxvi.　If, indeed, it had been possible, men would long

> when it hath conceived, beareth sin : and the sin, when it
> 16 is fullgrown, bringeth forth death. Be not deceived, my

ago have 'suppressed' both the fact and the sense of sin, and the most popular interpreters of the deepest voices of humanity, the poets and the dramatists, not of one age but of all times, do but repeat, more or less distinctly, the confession of the Hebrew Psalmist, 'I acknowledge my transgressions, and my sin is ever before me'; see Plummer, p. 91, on this bearing of the teaching of St James, and the various testimonies quoted by Maclear, *Introduction to the Creeds*, p. 250, and by Mozley in his famous Essay on *Original Sin asserted by Philosophers and Poets* in 'Essays and Papers,' p. 148.

15. *the lust.* So R.V. (translating the article), *the* lust, as if personified.

when it hath conceived, beareth. Cf. the constant Hebrew expression, Gen. iv. 1, 17, xxx. 17, etc., rendered by the LXX as here in St James. The same metaphor is continued: lust is united with the man's will, which has been ensnared by her, and the offspring of the union is sin, 'sin' in general, without the article in the Greek. 'Beareth,' R.V., as in distinction from the other Greek word rendered 'bringeth forth' below.

and the sin. So R.V. because the article is here expressed in the Greek, i.e. the particular sin resulting from the unresisted temptation of the individual man. Mayor, however, regards the article as simply taking up the same preceding noun; see above, *v.* 4.

when it is fullgrown, thus continuing the metaphor (A.V. with Tyndale 'finished'). Sin all along had carried in itself the germ of death, and so when it has come to maturity, death is the result, unless

the power of sin is previously broken by a higher power of life. There is no need to suppose that the purpose of the verse is to furnish any technical instruction as to the origin and scope of sin, but rather to show us how temptation could not come from God, since its fruit was so terrible.

bringeth forth. It is doubtful how far we need press the reference of the verb to any monstrous or unusual births, as do some commentators; the word occurs again in *v.* 18, and although not found in LXX may be illustrated from its mention in 4 Macc. xv. 17; see further Lightfoot, *Revision of N.T.* p. 77, and *Didache*, iii. 2, 3, for somewhat similar metaphorical language.

English readers will compare Milton's allegory, *Par. Lost*, II. 745–814 (so Alford, Plumptre, Farrar), in which Satan by his own evil lust begat sin, and then by an incestuous union with sin, death results.

death. Cf. Rom. vi. 23; *Didache*, v. 1; used here in all its undefined terror, not merely of bodily death, although that might well be included as so often the issue of vice and transgression, but rather of spiritual death, as in contrast to the life bestowed by God on those who love Him. There is no need to define it as eternal death, since a soul, if converted, may be saved 'out of death,' v. 20.

16. *Be not deceived;* a warning against the suspicion cast upon God's character, cf. 13, but a warning tempered and softened in its earnestness by the affectionate 'my beloved brethren.' The words refer not only to what precedes, but also to what follows, inasmuch as the leading

17 beloved brethren.　Every good ¹gift and every perfect
boon is from above, coming down from the Father of

¹ Or, *giving*

thought is to guard against any
representation of God which would
make Him, the source of all good, the
source of temptation to sin; cf. for
similar formulae, 1 Cor. vi. 9, xv. 33;
Gal. vi. 7; 1 John iii. 7.

17. *Every good gift and every
perfect boon.* It is difficult to distinguish between the two nouns in
English, but it is well to remember
that a contemporary writer like Philo
has made a special distinction between
them, inasmuch as the latter noun is
much stronger than the former, and
contains the idea of greatness and
perfection which is lacking in the
former; Philo, *De Cherub.* 25; and
so *De Leg. Alleg.* iii. 70, where he
applies to the latter noun the same
epithet 'perfect' as in the Greek of
the verse before us. See Lightfoot,
Revision of N.T. p. 77. This being
so, 'boon,' Lat. *bonum*, is perhaps
the best rendering we can get.
Beyschlag, without however referring
to Philo, sees an advance in the
latter noun upon the former, inasmuch as the latter expresses something greater, and he compares the
way in which it is employed Rom.
v. 16 as a free gift (see also Sanday
and Headlam, *Romans, l.c.*). In both
nouns he sees the thought of something given, and therefore not derived from the man himself, in
contrast to *v.* 14. Others distinguish
the two nouns by describing the
former as the act of giving, and the
latter the thing given, and *largitio*,
donatio are quoted as the equi-
valents of the former, *donum ipsum*,
munus, as of the latter. It is
doubtful how far the whole verse
can be compared with John vi. 32;

we should rather illustrate it by Matt.
vii. 11, Luke xi. 13.

Evidently there is a marked contrast intended between God as the
source of all good and as, in the false
conception of *v.* 13, a tempter to evil,
and this is sufficient for the practical
purpose of the writer. Jewish
theology emphatically asserted that
only good things were bestowed by
God. Thus Philo asserts, *De Conf.
Ling.* p. 346 c, that God is only the
cause of good things, and see also
for a similar confession Tob. iv. 19;
Wisd. i. 13; Ecclus. xxxix. 33. The
words of St James seem to have
been a kind of proverbial saying
among the Jews; see *Exp. Times*,
April, 1904.

It is of further interest to note
that the words form a hexameter
line, and that they may possibly be
a quotation from some unknown
Greek poet (so among recent writers
von Soden, Spitta, and Mayor).
Beyschlag however attributes the
rhythm to chance, following some
of the other commentators. A
similar explanation may be given of
Heb. xii. 13, where Bishop Westcott
remarks that the commonly received
reading forms an accidental hexameter. Others again have seen in
the words a fragment of some early
Christian hymn, or even, although it
cannot be said with much support,
an unrecorded saying of the Lord.

is from above, i.e. from heaven
as the dwelling-place of God, cf. Acts
xiv. 17 (xxvi. 13); John xix. 11,
iii. 31; or the words perhaps are more
properly explained by what follows;
cf. iv. 1.

coming down. So R.V., W.H.,

lights, with whom can be no variation, neither shadow

Vulg. (von Soden, Mayor), separating the verb copula from the participle. But others refer to iii. 15 and take the verb and participle together as = 'comes down,' and they have apparently the support of the Syriac Version and of the older interpreters. It may however be fairly alleged against this view that it makes 'from above' less connected, and, one might almost say, superfluous. The words thus combined may further imply that these good and perfect gifts come down from heaven to earth in a constant stream, giving this force to the present participle.

the Father of lights. The title suggested primarily, it may be, the thought that God was the creator of light, of the luminaries, the stars and heavenly bodies, and their ruler and upholder: cf. Gen. i. 14; Jer. iv. 23, xxxi. 35; Ps. cxxxvi. 7; *Apoc. of Baruch,* liv. 13; *Book of Enoch,* lxxv. 1–3; Ecclus. xliii. 1–10 (cf. Job xxxviii. 28). In Job xxxviii. 7, the two expressions 'morning stars' and 'sons of God' appear as 'two parallel conceptions,' but here apparently a reference may fairly be found to the Jewish conception that the heavenly bodies were the angels or hosts of God (in LXX 'sons of God' is translated 'angels'). This exact expression 'Father of lights' is not successfully paralleled by Spitta, and he admits that both of his main instances are unsatisfactory, since in the one the expression is only found in the text adopted by Ceriani of *Apoc. of Moses,* xxxvi., and in the other the expression 'Father of light,' which he cites from the *Testament of Abraham,* vii., is only found in the later recension, and is there applied not to God but to the

angel of light. But the language of Philo may be compared with the thought expressed here by St James, as he regards God not only as light but as the archetype of every other light, and constantly interchanges the words 'father' and 'creator' of all things.

But we must not suppose that St James would thus limit the thought of God as the Father of lights. If it be said that the immediate context appears so to limit it, it may be fairly urged that the subsequent words carry us on to the thought of God as the source of all spiritual and moral light; cf. 1 John i. 5 and marginal references in R.V. The writer of the Book of Wisdom had spoken of Wisdom as the brightness of the everlasting light, as being more beautiful than the sun; being compared with the light she is found before it, Wisd. vii. 25–29. And St James would not only remind his readers that if the lights of heaven, sun, moon, and stars, brought such blessing to men, how much more He Who made them; but he would again enforce the truth that if God was the source of all light, then we cannot refer sin to Him, the darkness which blinds the eyes of the soul and of the understanding.

can be. So R.V. (but A.V. simply 'is'), i.e. it is not possible in His nature, cf. Gal. iii. 28, 'there is no room for, no place for,' negativing not the fact only but the possibility (Lightfoot), although it is doubtful how far we can always press this idea of impossibility in the word.

no variation, neither shadow that is cast by turning. The first noun, not found elsewhere in N.T. (but cf.

LXX, 2 Kings ix. 20), is translated 'variation,' not 'variableness,' by the Revisers, for it expresses actual change, not the abstract quality. The noun in question has the sense of variation from a set course or rule, and in fact it might be used of change or difference quite generally, e.g. of the changes of the seasons, or of the difference between beauty and deformity. Mayor takes the word here of the contrast between the natural sun, changing its position in the sky from hour to hour and month to month, and the eternal source of all light (see further below).

neither shadow, etc. The words thus rendered in R.V. have been taken to refer to the shadow cast by the daily and yearly apparent revolutions of the sun. But it is quite possible to take the noun translated 'turning' in the sense of change in general, not, that is, of the heavenly movements as in LXX, Deut. xxxiii. 14, Job xxxvii. 33, and specially cf. Wisd. vii. 18, but as it is used frequently in Philo, to contrast the changeableness of all that is created with the immutability of the Creator (see instances of this use of the word in Philo given by Mayor and Schneckenburger as expressing *inconstantia naturae*). If we adopt this meaning, the word rendered 'shadow' may be taken as referring us back to the thought of God as 'the Father of lights' upon whom (carrying on the imagery) no change in this lower world can cast a shadow. So Mayor would render 'overshadowing of mutability,' and takes the whole passage to mean that God is alike incapable of change in His own nature (παραλλαγή) and incapable of being changed by the action of others (ἀποσκίασμα). Or

we may take the noun rendered 'turning' as a qualitative genitive, and render 'shadow of change' as = changing shadow, i.e. an overshadowing which changes the face of the sun; but this rendering would not in any way interfere with the interpretation of the passage given above.

The rendering in A.V. 'shadow of turning' is no doubt ambiguous, and it might be taken as expressing the Old Latin *modicum obumbrationis*, as if the first Greek noun was = shade, trace, small amount. This meaning certainly makes good sense, but it is very doubtful how far it can be applied to the rare Greek noun here employed. Oecumenius and Theophylact both take the word in this sense here; and if we cannot follow them in this, their preceding words emphasise the general meaning of the passage already adopted, 'for He Himself crieth by the prophet, "I am the Lord, I change not,"' Mal. iii. 6.

Spitta refers the terms under discussion to the stars, their changes in place and the times of their setting and rising: cf. Job xxv. 5; also Ecclus. xvii. 31, xxvii. 11; *Enoch*, xviii. 15, and lxxiii. 3, lxxiv. 4. Such passages may help to show us that the language of St James and the contrast which he institutes would not be foreign to Jewish thought, and that there is no need to take his words here as technical astronomical terms. In Wisd. vii. 18 we have a striking approach to the very words of St James, where the writer speaks of 'the alterations of the turning of the sun,' lit. 'the changes of the solstices,' the two terms being nearly identical with those in St James, and also of 'the changes of

18 that is cast by turning. Of his own will he brought
us forth by the word of truth, that we should be a kind of
firstfruits of his creatures.

seasons' (see *Speaker's Commentary*[1]).

We read in his biography that these words 'with whom can be no variation' etc. were constantly upon the lips of one of the most eminent of modern scientific men, James Clerk Maxwell. But it was not merely upon the thought of the immutability of God as contrasted with the mutability of phenomena that James Clerk Maxwell rested his highest hopes in life and in his last hours on earth—a Theist might have found satisfaction in dwelling upon the same contrast—but it was upon the thought (as his biography further teaches us) of a Father of lights, revealed in His Son, the giver of the true light, the light of life and the light of the world.

18. *Of his own will.* In contradistinction to *v.* 13 and to the notion that God could be a tempter of men. His will is shown not by tempting them but by conferring upon them the power of a new birth. The will of man could be perverted, and his lust could bear sin, and sin death, but God's will could not be perverted or changed from its purpose, and His action in accordance with the purpose is shown us in the statement which follows.

he brought us forth by the word of truth. Sin brought forth death (the same word is used in *v.* 15), God, the Father of lights, could only beget life. 'Us,' i.e. not us as men,

but us as Christians (see further below), born not of the will of the flesh, nor of the will of man, but of God (John i. 13). With these words Ephes. i. 13, 1 Pet. i. 23 and *v.* 3, John iii. 7, 1 John iv. 7, should be compared, and whilst to the expression 'the word of truth' we cannot attach the high personal sense which we find attaching to the Word in John i. 1, yet we cannot forget that our Lord (John xvii. 17–19) speaks of 'the word' which is truth, that by it the disciples are to be sanctified, and that it might be justly called 'at once the element in which the Christian lives and the spring of his life' (Westcott on John viii. 31). Others however take the words as simply referring to the Gospel, because it has for its contents the truth revealed to us from God.

In his desire to eliminate everything specifically Christian from the Epistle, Spitta has contended that reference in this verse is made by the writer not to the Christian new birth, but to the natural creation by God in Genesis i. 26. It is no doubt true that the phrase 'word of truth' may be paralleled from the Psalms, e.g. cxix. 43, 160, but this does not in the slightest degree involve the exclusion of any Christian sense in the phrase before us, especially in face of the frequent parallels in the New Testament, with which we may compare in part iii. 14, v. 19, in this same Epistle. Moreover, if the

---

[1] On the use of the words as technical astronomical terms Carr's notes in *Cambridge Greek Testament* may be consulted. The latter noun translated 'shadow that is cast by turning' is not found elsewhere in Greek, although a cognate noun is found in Plutarch and a cognate verb in Plato.

phrase is referred to the creative word and act of God, it is difficult to see why this creative 'word' should be styled here 'the word of truth' (see further below, on the context).

A further and thoughtful attempt however has been recently made to find in this phrase 'word of truth' particular reference to the creation of man 'according to our image and likeness,' God's creation of man being the result of this purpose, enforcing the truth about man, revealing man's true nature and life[1]. And so too 'the implanted word is to be regarded as the same active principle which St James has thus already named as used in creation, but it is no longer the external fact of creation declaring the truth about human nature, it is now represented as an active principle within the man which has the power of saving him, and this can be nothing else than the new principle of life, given in Christ Jesus.' In this way the expression 'the truth' in iii. 14 and v. 19 is related to 'truth' of i. 18, as the ideal of regenerated human life is to the ideal of created human life. But as against this view there is much to be said for the interpretation of the phrase 'word of truth' adopted above (and see further on the expression 'firstfruits of his creatures').

that we should be a kind of firstfruits. As Israel, Jer. ii. 3, could be spoken of as 'holiness to the Lord, and the firstfruits of His increase,' and as Philo could speak of Israel as the firstfruits of the whole human race (see reference in Wetstein *in loco*),

so St James might well see in the Christian Church, although a small part of his nation, the firstfruits destined to include not only Israel (i. 1), but the residue of men, the ingathering of the Gentiles into the Kingdom of Christ; cf. the words of St James, Acts xv. 16–18. For the employment of the same noun elsewhere in a specifically Christian sense see 2 Thess. ii. 13; Rom. viii. 23, xvi. 5; 1 Cor. xv. 20; Rev. xiv. 4.

a kind of, because the term is used with a metaphorical meaning. So Calvin comments on the words in the original: we are in a certain measure the firstfruits.

of his creatures. The same word is found Wisd. ix. 2, xiii. 5, xiv. 11, Ecclus. xxxviii. 34, 3 Macc. v. 11, and also in one significant passage Ecclus. xxxvi. 20 (15), where it is apparently used of the Israelites. The word as employed here may be interpreted in the widest sense, as the language of St James quoted above from Acts xv. indicates, 'the residue of men, all the Gentiles upon whom my Name is called'; cf. also Mark xvi. 15; Rom. viii. 20, 21; Col. i. 23; the Christian Church, the spiritual Israel, being the firstfruits of the new creation. Spitta here again would refer the whole phrase to the lordship of man over creation, but, as we have seen, St James is speaking figuratively, and there can be little doubt that he had in mind the O.T. conception of the offering of the firstfruits to God (cf. Exod. xxii. 29; Deut. xviii. 4, xxvi. 2), and that the Jewish-Christian Church is conceived of as the firstfruits of the world which should be won to Christ.

---

[1] Parry, *St James*, pp. 20 ff. Amongst other recent writers Mr Fulford in his Commentary also takes 'the word of truth' of the Divine fiat which brought about the creation of man, and refers to Dr Hort's *Judaistic Christianity*, p. 151, as perhaps indicating a somewhat similar view.

19   ¹Ye know *this,* my beloved brethren.   But let every
20 man be swift to hear, slow to speak, slow to wrath : for
the wrath of man worketh not the righteousness of God.

¹ Or, *Know ye*

But if so, there is no need to confine
this reference with Spitta to the
relationship of man to the other
creatures, since the offering in
question is always concerned with
the relationship of man to God; and
even if the word 'firstfruits' could
be used of those 'first in honour,' the
whole verse is marked by Christian
phraseology, and the expression 'the
word of truth' is sufficient, according
to the view taken above, to exclude
any limitation to the natural creation.

19.   *Ye know this...But,* R.V.

If we follow R.V. with Wycl., and
so Westcott and Hort, we may explain :

ye know this, viz. all that I have
said as to the goodness of God and
His favourable kindness towards us.
But be not content with theoretical
knowledge; those begotten of the
Word should be swift to hear, slow
to speak, etc. The 'wherefore' of
A.V. might easily have been substituted for 'ye know' in the original,
so as to make the verse follow closely
from the preceding, 'but' being
omitted¹.

my beloved brethren. Cf. *v.* 2, and
for the full phrase as here i. 16, ii. 5 ;
1 Cor. xv. 58. The note of warning
deepens the note of affection.

swift to hear. With these words
we may compare various similar injunctions in the Jewish Sapiential
books, and esp. Ecclus. v. 11, 'be
swift to hear,...and with deliber-
ateness (or, forbearance) give answer'
(see too iv. 29, xx. 7), and Taylor,

Sayings of the Jewish Fathers,
p. 25, 2nd edit. The two clauses
'swift to hear, slow to speak,' may be
connected with the attitude of the
man towards 'the word of truth,'
the attitude which should be recep-
tive rather than critical.

slow to wrath. With this we
may compare Eccles. vii. 9, 'be not
hasty in thy spirit to be angry,' and
see also Taylor, *u. s.* pp. 64, 90, 101.
The wrath denotes the angry, resent-
ful temper, showing itself not only
in grumbling against God in the face
of trial or temptation, but also in
fanatical and overbearing speech,
the opposite of the meekness of
v. 21; comp. esp. iii. 13, and the
sequence in *v.* 14.

20. *for the wrath of man worketh not the righteousness of God :*
cf. Rom. xii. 18-20. In view of the
early date of the Epistle (see Introduction), we cannot find here any
reference to the state of righteousness before God in a Pauline sense,
nor is there any strict connection
with the passage so often associated
with the words 'unrighteous anger
shall not be justified' (the better
reading), Ecclus. i. 22.

To work the righteousness of God
means to do what God wills, that
which is right in His sight : cf. Matt.
vi. 33; Acts iv. 19; and for the
phrase 'to work righteousness'
cf. Acts x. 35; Heb. xi. 33; Rom. ii.
10 (2 Cor. vii. 10); so we have the
opposite phrase ii. 9; Matt. vii. 23;
and so too 1 Macc. ix. 23.

¹ The Greek MSS. vary here between two words, the one expressing *ye know,*
the other *wherefore.*

21 Wherefore putting away all filthiness and overflowing of
¹wickedness, receive with meekness the ²implanted word,

¹ Or, *malice*   ² Or, *inborn*

of man. Without laying any stress upon the word used here for 'man' in the original, it would certainly seem that a contrast is marked between human and Divine, as if man by his fitful passion could expect to work the righteousness of Him Who is 'righteous in all His ways.' On the other hand St James would emphasise the fact that it is the work of the Christian, of one begotten of the word of truth, to carry out God's righteousness on earth. We cannot limit the reference of the verse to the Jewish zeal and fanaticism in making proselytes, or in maltreating fellow-countrymen who had accepted the Messiah, although no doubt St James would have endorsed St Paul's words, Rom. x. 2, 'they have a zeal for God but not according to knowledge.' There is much indeed in the history not only of the Jewish Church in the days of St James, but also of the Christian Church in each succeeding century, which reads as a sad commentary upon the truth here stated so decisively. And St James and his fellow-Christians had seen in the Cross of Christ the infinite distance which separates the judgment of human passion from the judgment of Him Who judgeth righteously; and that shameful travesty of justice in the condemnation of their Lord had shown them what the 'wrath of man' could do in its attempt to work 'the righteousness of God (see a Sermon on this text by E. De Pressensé, *The Mystery of Suffering and other Discourses*, p. 184).

21. *putting away*, aorist participle, because 'the previous putting off is the condition of the subsequent reception.'

Cf. for the phraseology and thought, Ephes. iv. 25; 1 Pet. ii. 1; Heb. xii. 1.

all filthiness and overflowing of wickedness, R.V. The A.V. translation 'superfluity of naughtiness' according to modern usage would seem to indicate that a certain amount of naughtiness was good. The word 'filthiness' apparently continues the previous metaphor taken from the putting off of clothes: see e.g. Isai. lxiv. 6, Zech. iii. 4, and in the N.T. 1 Pet. iii. 21, Col. iii. 8, Ephes. iv. 25; and cf. ii. 2, below. *receive*, not merely 'hear' (cf. Luke viii. 13; Acts viii. 14, xvii. 11; 1 Thess. ii. 13), and *with meekness*, because that which is opposed to meekness, wrath, is first 'put away,' R.V.

A further question arises as to whether 'filthiness' is to be taken alone, or with 'malice,' as the other noun rendered 'overflowing.' The latter seems best, as the context is not concerned with uncleanness in general, or with the special sin of impurity, as perhaps in iv. 4, 8, but with 'filthiness' as connected with 'malice.'

Or perhaps it may be best to give the conjunction an explanatory force, and to render 'all defilement caused by the overflowing malice of the heart.' The rendering 'overflowing' is justified by the meaning attached to the same noun elsewhere in the N.T., cf. Rom. v. 17; 2 Cor. viii. 2, x. 15; but there is something to be said for the rendering 'what is left over' (cf. the cognate noun, Mark viii. 8), i.e. of old inherited faults which remain even in those who are

22 which is able to save your souls.   But be ye doers of the

born again, i. 18, with special reference here to the old Jewish sins of
his countrymen which St James
rebukes in other parts of his Epistle;
cf. Introd. p. xiii.[1]

wickedness, but 'malice' R.V.
marg., and so other E. Versions,
'malice' or 'maliciousness': cf. Rom.
i. 29; Ephes. iv. 31; Col. iii. 8; Tit.
iii. 3; 1 Pet. ii. 1 (margin).

This meaning fits in well with the
context, whilst 'wickedness' is too
general, and 'naughtiness' in its
modern use too restricted to the
faults of children, although Latimer
and Shakespeare employ it as
= wickedness. In classical Greek
the word translated 'malice' is often
used for vice in general, but it is
evident that it cannot be so employed
in the N.T. since it appears as one
vice amongst many, see refs. above.
Lightfoot takes it of the evil, vicious
habit of mind, Trench, *Synonyms*, I.
41; but for a full understanding of
the word see Mayor *in loco*, and
Grimm-Thayer, *Synonyms*.

the implanted word. 'The word'
is identical with 'the word of truth,'
v. 18. It may perhaps seem strange
at first sight that Christians are
bidden to receive a 'word' which
has already been implanted; and so
it is sometimes explained that 'the
word' which is the agent of the new
birth must ever be received anew
that the new life may be retained
and progress. The same objection
may of course be equally raised
against rendering the adjective
'innate' as in Wisd. xii. 10; and so
some writers regard 'implanted' as
expressing a constant quality of 'the

word,' i.e. 'whose property it is to
root itself like a seed in the heart';
cf. Matt. xiii. 21–23, xv. 13. But for
a further examination of the deeper
meaning of the phrase see also below.

which is able to save your souls.
It is remarkable that this language
is addressed to those who had been
already described as begotten by the
word of truth, so that salvation is
regarded by the writer as in a sense
still in the future, although it may
be also a present possession: cf.
1 Thess. v. 23. '*Able*,' *magna effi-
cacia*, Bengel; with the language
cf. John v. 24; Rom. i. 16.

The same expression 'able to
save' is used below, iv. 13, of God, so
that as the same Divine power is
here ascribed to 'the implanted
word' it has been well observed that
'the word' so described is scarcely
distinguishable from the indwelling
Christ. And this teaching would be
very natural on the part of a Jew
like St James, when we remember
how often in Jewish thought 'the
word' suggested the closest intimate
relation between the substance and
the agent of revelation: cf. Art.
'Logos,' Hastings' *B. D.*

your souls. St James might
have written 'you,' the personal pronoun simply, but he uses what has
sometimes been described as a Hebraism, although in view of his
solemn language in v. 20 it is much
more likely that here also he is
emphasising the thought of a salvation with eternal issues: cf. our
Lord's words in Matt. x. 28, xvi. 26.

22. *be ye*. So R.V. and A.V.
Sometimes the verb in the original

---

[1] Zahn, *Einleitung*, I. 68, amongst recent writers may be noted as a strong
advocate for this rendering.

23 word, and not hearers only, deluding your own selves. For
if any one is a hearer of the word, and not a doer, he is
like unto a man beholding ¹his natural face in a mirror :

¹ Gr. *the face of his birth.*

has been pressed to mean 'become
doers' as of a process continually
going on, representing true Christian
practice as a matter of growth, but
here, as so often, it is best to take it
as meaning 'show yourselves in
action as being.' If in the previous
verse we see a reference to the
parable of the Sower, we recall how
the same parable vividly marked the
distinction here emphasised by St
James between hearing and doing,
and it is significant that in St Luke's
narrative our Lord's declaration,
'My mother and my brethren are
those which hear the word of God
and do it,' Luke viii. 21, follows
closely upon the interpretation of
the parable of the Sower.

But in any case we have in this
verse what may well be a reminiscence of the teaching of Jesus:
cf. Matt. vii. 21, 24 ff.; Luke vi. 46
(John viii. 31, xiii. 17); and a leading
characteristic of the teaching of
St James is the stress laid upon
practice and conduct, cf. ii. 14–20.
Indeed the word translated 'doers'
is itself a characteristic word of the
Epistle, in which it occurs no less
than four times, and only once elsewhere in the N.T. in the same sense,
Rom. ii. 13 (see also for the same
phrase 1 Macc. ii. 67).

and not hearers only. It seems
best to join the adverb closely with
the noun, 'be not such as are hearers
merely.' The Jewish Rabbis were
themselves wont to emphasise this
warning against hearing and learning without practising; see e.g.
Taylor, *Sayings of the Jewish
Fathers,* p. 91 (cf. p. 25):

'There are four characters in
college-goers. He that goes and
does not practise, the reward of
going is in his hand; he that
practises and does not go, the reward
of practice is in his hand; he that
goes and practises is pious; he that
goes not and does not practise is
wicked.' In the first character we
have St James's 'hearer of the word,
in the second the 'doer of the word,'
the third character combining the
two, and the last being neither.

It is very possible that both St
James and St Paul, Rom. ii. 13, had
in mind the besetting sin of their
countrymen to rest satisfied with
the hearing of the Law and its exposition in the synagogues : cf. Acts
xv. 21; Rom. ii. 17. The word
translated 'hearers' is found three
times in this Epistle, *vv.* 23, 25, and
only once elsewhere in the N.T.,
Rom. ii. 13, and it is of interest to
note that it is used with its cognate
verb in classical Greek of attending
a discourse or lecture.

deluding your own selves, R.V.
Other E.VV. render 'deceiving.' In
N.T. only elsewhere in Col. ii. 4.
The word is properly used of de-
ception by fallacious reasoning, but
also of deceiving or deluding generally, as often in LXX, Gen. xxix. 25 ;
Lam. i. 19. In *Psalms of Sol.* iv.
14 the same verb is also found, 'he
deceiveth with his words,' and twice
in the same Psalm, *vv.* 12, 25, the
cognate noun is used of deceit and
craftiness. In *v.* 26 St James explains its meaning.

23. *like unto a man.* There
seems no occasion to emphasise, as

24 for he beholdeth himself, and goeth away, and straightway

some writers have done, the word in the Greek for 'man'; it may be used quite generally as in *vv*. 8, 12.

beholding, used often of considering attentively, both in LXX and N.T., but here rather in contrast to the continuous gaze of *v*. 25.

his natural face, lit. 'the face of his birth.' The words have been very differently interpreted. On the one hand, the noun rendering 'birth' has been taken to denote fleeting, earthly existence; cf. Judith xii. 18, 20; Wisd. vii. 5; *Psalms of Solomon*, iii. 11; and in this case a contrast could be drawn between the reflexion in the mirror of the natural face, the face belonging to this transitory life, and the reflexion in the Word of the true ideal of human character. But on the other hand, the same expression has been taken to refer to the man's true individuality, to his creation in the image of God (cf. iii. 9) and to the clause which follows, 'for he beheld himself'; and then a contrast is drawn between a man beholding in each case his true self, but in the former case only momentarily, as he listens to God's Word and forgets it, in the latter case fixedly, as he contemplates and never loses sight of the ideal self revealed in the perfect law. But although this latter rendering has given occasion to some beautiful thoughts[1], yet the former is to be preferred because of the usual meaning of the word translated 'birth,' cf. its use in iii. 6, below. It is also noticeable that in Philo we have examples of its employment to express the seen and temporal as

contrasted with the unseen and eternal.

in a mirror. For the use of the same word figuratively a few instances may be cited, Wisd. vii. 26; Ecclus. xii. 11; and in the N.T., 1 Cor. xiii. 12 (2 Cor. iii. 18). The same figurative use is frequent in Philo. The mirrors of the ancients were metallic, made most frequently of an alloy of copper and tin, although there were mirrors of silver, and mention is made of mirrors of gold; Art. 'Mirror,' Hastings' *B.D.* vol. III.

24. *for he beholdeth himself*, more precisely 'he beheld himself.' On the tense (aorist) see note *v*. 11 above. We may note again a favourite characteristic of the writer in taking up, as it were, a word just employed: 'beholding...beholdeth'; cf. *v*. 4.

and goeth away, more precisely 'has gone away,' the tense (perfect) denoting the suddenness of the action and also the permanence of the result.

and straightway forgetteth, more precisely 'forgat'; here also we have a permanent state expressed, but the writer uses the aorist to emphasise the act itself as immediate and sudden.

25. *but he that looketh*. The verb used denotes more even than the verb for 'beholding,' which may have the meaning of looking or considering attentively. It expresses that one stoops to a thing in order to look at it, to stoop and look into, and so to look carefully into, or our desire to know anything; cf. John xx. 5, 'and stooping and looking in, he seeth the linen clothes lying,' and so

---

[1] Reference may be made to Adderley's *St James*, p. 35, and to the substance given of the remarks in the Bishop of Oxford's Sermon 'The Virtue of Self-assertion in the Life of the Intellect' (*Faculties and Difficulties*, Longmans).

25 forgetteth what manner of man he was. But he that
looketh into the perfect law, the *law* of liberty, and *so*

in *v.* 11, 'as she wept, she stooped
and looked into the tomb.' In the
LXX, the word occurs Cant. ii. 9;
Ecclus. xiv. 23, xxi. 23. In the
Oxyrhynchus Papyri, 2nd cent. A.D.,
an instance is found of the same
verb in the same sense of 'looking
down' from an upper room into the
street below, *Expositor*, Dec. 1903,
Dr Moulton's notes from the Papyri.

*the perfect law, the law of
liberty*, R.V., thus expressing the
reiteration which is demanded by
the original.

As a pious Jew St James would
have known of the willing obedience
with which each true Israelite would
have rejoiced to keep the law; cf.
Psalm cxix. 32, 111, 159. So too
Philo, *Quod omnis probus liber sit*,
871 A, in a striking passage speaks
of men who are governed by anger
or desire or any other passion as
altogether slaves, whilst as many as
live in accordance with Divine law
are free men. The same thought is
emphasised still more precisely in
Sayings of the Fathers, vi. 2 (cf.
iii. 8): 'And the tables were the
work of God, and the writing was
the writing of God, graven upon the
tables,' Exod. xxxii. 16; read not
Charuth, graven, but Cheruth, freedom, for thou wilt find no freeman
but him who is occupied in learning
of Thorah.' But if the Epistle of
St James is no mere Jewish document, the words before us may well
be referred to a higher source than
that of Psalmist or Rabbi.

This Law is 'perfect,' not only
because it may be contrasted with
the burden and yoke of the Law in
its Pharisaic observance, but because
it completes and realises the object

and meaning of the Mosaic law, Matt.
v. 17, cf. Jer. xxxi. 33; because it
sums up all commandments in the
one command and principle of love:
'he that loveth his neighbour hath
fulfilled the law,' cf. Rom. xiii. 8 ff.;
Gal. vi. 2. 'The law of liberty' has
been called one of the paradoxes of
St James, because it is of the essence
of law to impose prohibition and
restraint. But the law of love which
St James identifies, ii. 8, 12, with
the law of liberty is a law of constraint rather than of restraint; it
imposes it is true a bounden duty
and service, but it inspires a motive
which makes the burden light; in its
fulfilment men become sons of their
Father in heaven, Matt. v. 45, they
delight in the law of God: 'Only
love, and do what thou wilt.'

Our Lord Himself, cf. John viii.
31 ff., had contrasted the slavery of
sin with the freedom of sons which
He as the Son conferred, the freedom
which resulted from abiding in His
word, and St James may well have
been acquainted with this or similar
teaching.

There is no need to find in this
expression 'the new law' of the
second century, i.e. Christianity as
opposed to Judaism (see Introduction, p. lxii.), although of course it may
be most truly maintained that this
Epistle teaches us how one great
truth of Judaism, viz. the truth of
law, found its expansion in Christianity, just as the truth of *the
kingdom*, mentioned in every Jewish
prayer, found its real and spiritual
meaning in the universal Christian
Prayer: 'Thy kingdom come.'

and so continueth, i.e. continues
to look, in contrast to the man who

K.

continueth, being not a hearer that forgetteth, but a doer
26 that worketh, this man shall be blessed in his doing. If
any man [1]thinketh himself to be religious, while he

[1] Or, *seemeth to be*

takes a glance and is off (see above).
A.V. renders 'continueth *therein*,'
i.e. in the law of liberty, but this is
not in the Greek, although the
earnest gaze results in adherence to
the bidding of the Law; cf. for the
phraseology John viii. 31, but this
reference is connected rather with
A.V. than with the rendering of
R.V.

*being not a hearer that forgetteth,
but a doer that worketh*, R.V. The
two clauses are thus symmetrical in
translation, as they stand in the
original. Literally 'a hearer of forgetfulness,' which may be explained
as a Hebraistic idiom, or simply as due
to the vividness of phraseology common to Oriental languages. The
word translated 'forgetfulness' occurs
only once elsewhere, Ecclus. xi.
27, and it may therefore be a further
indication that that book was known
to St James. *A doer that worketh*,
literally 'a doer of work,' emphasising
the thought of habitual activity.

blessed. With this beatitude we
naturally compare Psalm i. 1, 2; and
our Lord's own words as to the
blessedness and happiness of doing,
Luke xi. 28; John xiii. 17. His
own promulgation of the new law of
His Kingdom had also commenced
with a series of blessings, Matt. v.
3 ff., and 'to look into that law and
to continue in it was to share the
beatitudes with which it opened.'

in his doing. The blessing comes
not only upon patience and endurance (i. 12, v. 11, 7), but it is found
also in the exercise of daily duty.

in his doing, R.V., not 'his deed'

as A.V. as if of an accomplished
work. The noun here refers to his
obedience rendered to the Law; it is
only found elsewhere in Ecclus. xix.
20 (li. 19), in a passage which affords
a somewhat close parallel to the
thought of St James: 'All wisdom
is fear of the Lord, and in all wisdom
there is doing of the law.'

26. *If any man thinketh himself*, i.e. supposes, fancies. The
rendering of A.V. and R.V. marg.
'seemeth to be' is misleading; it is
not the hypocrite, but the self-de-
ceived, of whom St James is writing,
as the context shows. For the verb
and its meaning here, cf. 1 Cor. iii. 18,
x. 12, xiv. 37; Gal. vi. 3.

religious. So A. and R.V. The
adj. is only found here in N.T., and
nowhere in LXX, but the cognate
noun rendered in this and the following verse 'religion' also occurs in
Acts xxvi. 5; Col. ii. 18. This cognate noun is found twice and the
cognate verb twice in LXX; Wisdom
xi. 15, xiv. 16, 18, 27; and in each
case with reference to superstition
and the service of false gods; and if
this does not indicate that the words
were generally used in a bad sense,
it indicates that they might easily
degenerate into a use which was
more concerned with the form than
with the essence of piety.

In Josephus the noun is used of
the public worship of God, of religion
in its external aspect, cf. e.g. *Ant.*
IX. 13. 3, and *B. J.* VII. 3. 3; and this
is apparently its meaning in the N.T.,
whilst by Philo it is directly contrasted with the piety and holiness

bridleth not his tongue but deceiveth his heart, this man's
27 religion is vain.　Pure religion and undefiled before our

which claims to be such on the score
of divers washings and costly offerings.　The renderings 'religion' and
'religious' in our translation may be
illustrated by the use of the word
'religion' in Milton, *Par. Lost*, I. 372,
where he describes some of the
heathen idolatries as 'adorned with
gay *religions*, full of pomp and gold,'
and in Shakespeare, *As You Like It*,
v. 4. 166, we read 'where meeting with
an old *religious* man,' i.e. belonging
to a religious order, and so making
an outward profession of religion
(Skeat, *Glossary*).　See further Trench,
Syn. I. p. 196; Hatch, *Essays in Biblical Greek*, p. 55.　There is no reason
to see in the word a reference to the
lustral observances of Jews or Jewish-
Christians, a view derived, it would
seem, from the close connection in
the text between 'religion' and the
two adjectives 'pure' and 'undefiled.'
But at the same time we must not
forget that St James is writing to
men who were still observing the
Jewish ceremonial law, and so, in the
spirit of the O.T. prophets, he warns
them that no such observances would
be acceptable with God, if breaches
of the law of love in word or deed
were committed.　Cf. Titus i. 15,
and see further on *v.* 27.

*while he bridleth not his tongue
but deceiveth his heart*, all forming
the protasis; the words look back to
v. 19 and forward to iii. 1–18.

bridleth.　The verb only here and
in iii. 2 in the N.T., but found in
later Greek, and similar metaphorical expressions with reference to the
mouth are of frequent occurrence in
classical writers and so too in Philo.
But in early Christian writers the
same verb may be very strikingly

illustrated from Hermas, *Mand.* xii.
1: 'For clothed with this desire (the
good and holy) thou shalt hate the
evil desire, and shalt *bridle* and
direct it as thou wilt.'　With the
language of St James we may compare Ps. xxxii. 9, xxxix. 1, cxli. 3.

deceiveth his heart; generally
taken as equivalent to 'deluding
your own selves' in 22 *supra.*
But in the latter passage the verb
employed might refer merely to an
error of the understanding, whilst
here the whole expression emphasises
the moral nature of the error; 'the
heart' would be a natural expression
for St James, as throughout the Bible
the word is used of the moral
character to denote the seat and
centre of personal life.

vain, used frequently in the O.T. of
heathen deities and their worship
(cf. Acts xiv. 15), and perhaps here
with the thought of a 'religion' as
unprofitable in its nature as that
associated with the idols of the
Gentiles.　The adjective is also used
of faith, 1 Cor. xv. 17, when useless
and unprofitable: cf. also Matt. xv. 8;
Tit. iii. 9.

27.　*Pure religion and undefiled*,
in contrast to a 'religion' which values
too highly lustrations and external
cleansing.　The adjectives are often
found together as in Hermas, *Mand.*
ii. 7; *Sim.* v. 7. 1; so too in Philo.　An
attempt has been made to distinguish
between the two adjectives, as referring the former to the outward, the
latter to the inward, but it is very
doubtful whether such a distinction
can be maintained.　In Hermas in
the first quoted passage, 'that thine
own repentance and that of thy
household may be found to be sincere,

God and Father is this, to visit the fatherless and widows
in their affliction, *and* to keep himself unspotted from the
world.

and thy heart pure and undefiled,'
the two adjectives are used together
of the heart, and in the second of the
flesh, although the context shows
that the cognate noun of the latter
adjective may be used of the spirit
as much as of the flesh. The distinction is sometimes drawn by regarding
the former adjective as relating to
others, and the latter to the man
himself (Wetstein). In classical
Greek both words are also employed
in an ethical sense.

before, i.e. in His judgment, He
being the judge. Cf. Rom. ii. 13;
Gal. iii. 11; 1 Pet. ii. 20.

our God, R.V., giving the force of
the article which ought to be retained
in the original before 'God.'

Father. Cf. Psalm lxviii. 5, cxlvi. 9
(see below, iii. 9).

It has been thoughtfully suggested
that the two following clauses may
balance the two titles: before our
Father=to visit the fatherless and
widows; before God=to keep himself
unspotted from the world. 'A
father of the fatherless, and a judge
of the widows is God in his holy
habitation,' Ps. lxviii. 5.

to visit. Cf. Matt. xxv. 36, 43.
The same verb is used in Ecclus.
vii. 35 (cf. Jer. xxiii. 2), in the same
sense, and almost always in classical
lit. of visiting the sick; in modern
Greek, also with the meaning of
'visiting.'

the fatherless and widows. The
combination is found only here in the
N.T. but it is frequent in the O.T. as
a kind of proverbial expression for
those most in need of help and
sympathy; cf. also Ecclus. iv. 10,

xxxv. (xxxii.) 14; 2 Macc. iii. 10,
viii. 28. In the former of the two
passages in Ecclus. God Himself
is represented as not despising the
supplication of the fatherless and
widows, and in the latter the man
who is as a father unto the fatherless,
and a husband unto their mother, is
described as being 'the son of the
Most High.' The same verb is used
by Hermas, *Mand.* viii. 10, where the
servant of God is bidden to minister
to widows, to *visit* the orphans and
the needy, and so too by Polycarp,
Phil. vi. 1, in exhorting the presbyter
to *visit* all the sick, not neglecting
the widow or the orphan. In one of
the earliest scenes of Church life
widows have a place in the daily
ministration, Acts vi. 1, and with all
its limitations the picture stands
in marked contrast to that of the
outwardly 'religious' Pharisees devouring widows' houses, Matt. xxiii.
19. For notice of the special care bestowed by the early Christians upon
the widows and orphans see Uhlhorn,
Charity in the Ancient Church,
E.T., 45, 90, 184, 321, 323, 361,
384.

The early Church could never
forget that in His care for the widow
and the orphan the Incarnate God
had 'visited' His people, Luke vii.
11–16.

in their affliction, to mark the
necessity and the aim of visiting.
Upon the comfort of mourners in
their affliction the Law and tradition
laid great stress, and it was said that
there was a special gate in the
Temple, the entrance for mourners,
that all who met them might dis-

charge this duty of love ; Edersheim, *Jewish Social Life*, p. 172.

In the consideration of this passage we must always remember that St James is not herein affirming, as we sometimes hear, these offices to be the sum total, nor yet the great essentials, of true religion, but 'declares them to be the body (the θρησκεία) of which godliness, or the love of God, is the informing soul,' Trench, *Syn.* I. pp. 196 ff., and cf. Coleridge, *Aids to Reflection*, Aph. xxiii., and also above on the word 'religion.'

to keep himself. As in the earliest Epistle of St Paul, 1 Thess., so here, while the duties of Christian social life are enforced, the obligation of personal moral purity is never forgotten. There was indeed a Divine presence to be seen in the charities which heal and soothe and bless, and in men who were made in the image of God (iii. 9), but a clearer vision still was for

'The soul pure-eyed that, wisdom led, E'en now His blessed face shall see.' Cf. Introduction, p. lxxiv. The language of St Paul, 1 Tim. v. 22, at once suggests itself as a parallel; but a closer parallel to the thought and context in St James may perhaps be found in the language of St John, if we adopt the R.V. marg., 'He that is begotten of God *keepeth himself* (same words in the original), and that wicked one toucheth him not,' 1 John v. 18. It is noteworthy that a very similar phrase 'to keep yourselves' occurs in the circular letter, Acts xv. 29, which may well have been drawn up by St James.

unspotted. Here again the language may have been suggested by the Jewish ritual; in 1 Pet. i. 19, the same adjective is used of a lamb described as 'without blemish and

without spot'; the former adjective, although sometimes used of persons, being frequently applied in LXX to the sacrifices of the Law. The same two adjectives are also found in 2 Pet. iii. 14, and the word in the text occurs again in 1 Tim. vi. 14 (in LXX (Sym.) Job xv. 15). In Hermas, *Mand.* viii. we find a lengthy insistence upon personal purity and social activity in the Christian life, which may well have been suggested by this verse in St James.

from the world. Cf. 2 Pet. ii. 20. The word used by St James here and in iv. 4 is the same as is used in Wisdom, cf. vii. 17, xi. 17, and also by the Greek philosophers, of the world as a universe of order, and it is noticeable that the only time the word occurs in St Paul's addresses in Acts is in his address before the philosophers of Athens, xvii. 24, in speaking of 'God who made the world.' But this 'order,' as the word means, might be considered without any direct connection with God, and so apart from Him, as concerned entirely with the sphere of human life, and thus not only as apart from God, but as separated from Him, an order which has become disorder, because no longer the expression of God's will, but of a thousand different wills fighting for the mastery, and so the scene of 'confusion and every vile deed,' iii. 16; see below on iv. 4, Westcott, Add. Note on John i. 10, and Mayor, *St James*, comment on 'the World,' p. 210.

The use of the word by St James in these two passages is fully accounted for by its similar employ. ment elsewhere in the N.T.; it is frequent in St John, and we may also have recourse to parallels of some little interest from the *Book of Enoch*, in which the righteous

are described as those who have
hated and despised this world of
unrighteousness, and have hated all
its works and ways, xlviii. 7; who
loved God, and loved neither gold
nor silver nor any of the goods of
the world, whose spirits were found
pure, so that they should bless His
name, cviii. 8.

Dr Moffatt (*Hibbert Journal*, Jan.
1904) speaks of 'the felicitous anticipation of James i. 27,' in a passage
in which Zarathustra (*Yasna*, xxxiv.

1–2, 5) asks, 'What is your Kingdom,
O Mazda?' It is no ritual or
material splendour but charity—'to
care for your poor in their suffering,'
and also, from a sense of gratitude,
to consecrate one's soul and body to
God and to God's purposes. Yet
this Zoroastrian religion, as the same
writer reminds us, however much it
might possess in some respects a
finer spirit, was burdened with
superstitions and fettered by ceremonial purity and externalism.

CHAPTER II.

1—4. The consideration of religion in its external aspect leads naturally
to the warning against the worldly spirit which in its respect of persons entered even their assemblies for worship. By preferences ostentatiously shown
to the rich the divided heart is again made manifest; they were receiving
from men in place of the glory which cometh from the Lord of glory; they
were not judging righteous judgment, their judgment was determined by
appearances. **5—7.** How different the judgment of God Himself! He
had chosen not the rich but the poor, for the poor of this world are rich in
faith, while the rich of this world oppress and wrong, and blaspheme the
Name of Christ. **8—13.** If, however, this regard for the rich is actuated
by a desire to fulfil the royal law of love, embracing rich and poor alike, ye
do well; but if you are prompted not by love but by respect of persons, for
the rich because they are rich, the law is broken equally as if your
neighbour had been injured by the wrong of adultery or murder: for the
Law is one and the Lawgiver is one; the Law is the expression of one will,
the will of a Father Who is love. All our words and deeds will be judged
by a law of the spirit, not of the letter, a law of liberty, a law which takes
cognisance not merely of external acts, but of temper and motive. To
have no mercy for the poor is to be condemned by this law, for mercy is
the law of Him Who is merciful; and yet, since it is a law of liberty,
God accepts what is done in a merciful spirit, and thus mercy rejoiceth
against judgment. **14.** But someone may be thinking, will not faith,
no less than mercy, cause us to rejoice in the judgment of God? but
the question is what kind of faith? certainly not a faith without works[1].

---

[1] Or the connection may be somewhat differently expressed, 'At this point
James imagines the man of orthodox belief but disobedient life, turning to
defend himself with the plea that there is more than one way of pleasing God.
One he urges is strong in "faith," another in "works." Let each cultivate his
own talent, without insisting that his neighbour should possess it likewise, on
the principle of live and let live.' J. V. Bartlet, *Apostolic Age*, p. 241.

15—20. A homely, practical test applied; to express a wish that a brother or a sister should be warmed or clothed without an effort for their benefit, what shall it profit? so a faith which is mere assent to the first article of the Creed is no profit to anyone; unless it is translated into action it remains profession without practice; such a 'faith' is in some sort shared even by the demons, nay, upon them it exerts a certain effect, it makes them shudder with fear. 21—26. But the faith of Abraham, yea the faith of Rahab, how different from this useless barren thing! these examples prove that a faith worthy of the name is an active principle; faith wrought with, energised with works, and by works faith was perfected.

II. My brethren, [1]hold not the faith of our Lord Jesus

[1] Or, *do ye, in accepting persons, hold the faith...glory?*

II. 1. *My brethren;* very appropriate here, after the duties of the Christian brotherhood and of true religion which have just been urged, and in view of the following exhortation to brotherly kindness.

hold not the faith, in R.V., but in marg. 'do ye, in accepting persons, hold the faith etc.?' so W.H. and some of the older commentators. But the imperative best suits the immediate context; the 'for' e.g. in *v.* 2 is not so easily explained if the previous words are interrogative. Moreover, the interrogative word in the original, although not always found in questions presupposing a negative answer would be used to imply that the questioner, although inclined to believe a thing true could scarcely credit it, whereas here the 'respect of persons' is admitted, *v.* 6.

the faith of our Lord Jesus Christ, objective, i.e. the faith which has our Lord for its object; cf. Mark xi. 22, Acts iii. 16, for a similar use of the genitive. If we cannot say positively that the expression 'faith of Jesus' in the N.T. never means the faith which Jesus gives, but always the faith directed towards Him as its object, there can be no doubt that the latter signification is the more usual. See further Introd. p. xv.

the Lord of glory. So R. and A.V., and it seems best to adopt this rendering. For the expression cf. Acts vii. 2; John i. 14; 1 Cor. ii. 8; Ephes. i. 17. The same title is also found no less than some nine times in the *Book of Enoch,* so that it may fairly be considered as a not unlikely expression from a Jewish writer. The majority of moderns render 'our glorious Lord Jesus Christ,' regarding the genitive as qualitative, but Bengel's suggestion to take the genitive 'the glory' as in apposition, and to render 'the faith of our Lord Jesus Christ who is the glory,' has commended itself to others[1].

Our Lord speaks of Himself as 'the Truth,' 'the Life'; and in John xvii. 5 we read, 'And now, O Father, glorify me with Thine own self with the glory which I had with Thee before the world was'; cf. St Paul's remarkable expression 'the Father of the glory,' Ephes. i. 17. The rendering therefore which Bengel suggested must at least command attention. It is urged indeed that the passages which he cites are

[1] So Mayor, and earlier Bassett; Plummer too inclines to this view.

2 Christ, *the Lord* of glory, with respect of persons.　For if

insufficient in proof—Luke ii. 32;
Ephes. i. 17; 1 Pet. iv. 14; Isaiah xl.
5—but other passages may be added
to them, e.g. John xvii. 5, 22; Rom.
ix. 4; 2 Pet. i. 17; and it is noteworthy that the term (the) 'glory'
would seem to be employed as an
equivalent for Immanuel; cf. the LXX
use of the same noun for the Shekinah, and Dr Taylor's *Sayings of the
Jewish Fathers*, pp. 43, 44, 2nd edit.
Deficiency of proof may perhaps be
more fairly alleged against the passages 2 Cor. iv. 4, Col. i. 27, 1 Tim. i.
11, cited to support another rendering 'the faith of (in) the glory of our
Lord Jesus Christ,' the rendering of
the Syriac and Vulgate[1], but the
phrase 'faith in the glory' would be
a very strange one.

It has been recently maintained
that the words under discussion
should be rendered 'our Lord Jesus
Christ, our glory,' and that this
rendering best suits the context[2].
In this interpretation the words
would correspond with the phrase
'the implanted word.' The Lord
Jesus, the Son of Man, is in a
true sense, it is urged, the glory of
man, and especially the glory of
Christians, and the active principle
referred to in the phrase 'the implanted word' is in fact the communication of the life of the risen Son of
Man, Ascended Lord of all human
life, and revealer in His own Person
and Character of its duties and
destinies.　But this rendering, suggestive as it is, requires first of all
that the genitive of the personal
pronoun should be taken with both
the words qualifying the personal

name, '*our* Lord,' '*our* glory,' which
hardly seems quite natural, and in
the second place it can scarcely be
considered necessary in view of the
many passages cited above and of the
Jewish usage which some of them at
all events support.

The bold assertion that the words
'Jesus Christ' are interpolated is
fully met by pointing out that if the
text had at first stood simply 'the
Lord of glory' no Christian interpo-
lator would have broken up these
words, and inserted between them
the name of Jesus Christ: he would
rather have inserted 'Jesus Christ'
before or after the Jewish phrase
'the Lord of glory,' and we should
have had 'the faith of Jesus Christ
our Lord of glory,' or 'the faith of the
Lord of glory, Jesus Christ.' In this
passage the difficulty of the text as
it stands becomes no small proof
of its originality; but see further
Introd. p. xv.

It has been said that the phrase
'the Lord of glory' is the one express
Christological phrase of the Epistle,
but whilst this is so, it must not be
forgotten that it has been also said
that such a phrase involves a belief
in the Resurrection and Ascension
and even in the Divinity of Christ.

with respect of persons.　The
noun, here in the plural to intimate
the various ways in which partiality
might show itself, is derived from
the Hebrew phrase to accept, or
rather, to raise the face, used in the
LXX generally in a good, although
sometimes in a bad sense. But in
the N.T. the noun with its compounds (*v.* 9) is always used in the

---

[1] Zahn has recently supported this rendering, *Einleitung*, I. 108.
[2] Parry, *St James*, pp. 24, 36.

there come into your ¹synagogue a man with a gold ring, in

¹ Or, *assembly*

latter sense, of the partiality which has respect to mere outward circumstances and not to intrinsic merit; cf. Rom. ii. 11; Ephes. vi. 9; Col. iii. 25; Acts x. 34; 1 Pet. i. 17; and Lightfoot's note on Gal. ii. 6. The Hebrew phrase was sometimes varied in the original, as in N.T., Jude *v.* 16, on which the remarks of Ryle and James, *Psalms of Solomon*, ii. 19, should be consulted. Twice in *Apoc. of Baruch* God is spoken of as One Who is no respecter of persons, xiii. 7, xliv. 4; cf. *Jubilees*, v. 15; and in *Sayings of the Jewish Fathers*, iv. 31, He is described as a Judge with Whom there is no respect of persons.

It may be also noted that this same phrase to accept the face or the person occurs in *Didache*, iv. 3, 'thou shalt not show respect of persons in rebuking for transgressions'; and it is closely followed by the expression of another characteristic thought of this Epistle, 'thou shalt not be of two minds,' etc. On the connection between the *Didache* and this Epistle of St James see Introd. pp. xii., xiv.

A suggestion has sometimes been made that the words before us, whether in any way related to John xvii. 1, 5, or not, remind us involuntarily of the saying in John v. 44, 'How can ye believe, which receive glory one of another, and the glory that cometh from the only God ye seek not?' At least we may admit that here as there a marked contrast is made between the regard for earthly glory and substance, and the seeking after the glory which comes from Him Who is 'the glory.' In 'the glory as of the Only-begotten of the Father,' as in the Father Himself,

there could be no respect of persons, and St James may well have known how even the enemies of Jesus acknowledged in this respect at least His likeness to God; cf. Matt. xxii. 16; Mark xii. 14; Luke xx. 21.

2. *For if there come into.* The scene here so vividly depicted may often have presented itself to the eyes of St James, and there is no occasion to suppose that it was derived from the language of Ecclus. xi. 2–6 (cf. x. 22–24) as has recently been maintained. The aorist in the original may perhaps be best explained by the characteristic of St James to express by it that which is constantly recurring as one definite past fact; cf. i. 11, 24.

your synagogue, R.V. text: 'assembly,' marg.

If too much may sometimes have been made of this word as a decisive argument for the early date of the Epistle and its address to Jewish readers, it must remain a significant fact that this is the only place in the N.T. in which the word 'synagogue' is used instead of the usual word 'church' for assemblies, which evidently claim to be gathered for Christian worship. Even if it is to be maintained that some of the congregations to which the Epistle was addressed might be called 'churches' and not 'synagogues,' stress might still be laid upon the naturalness of the expression from St James writing from Jerusalem, with his own Palestinian experiences before him.

Great importance has been attached to the fact that Hermas and others have used the same word 'synagogue' of Christian assemblies, but it must not be forgotten, (1) that whilst this

fine clothing, and there come in also a poor man in vile

may be admitted, there is also evidence of the use of the word as a specifically Jewish-Christian word, since Epiphanius, *Haer.* xxx. 18, refers to Jewish-Christians of Palestine who were wont to speak of their assembly as a 'synagogue' and not 'a church' (συναγωγή, not ἐκκλησία), and that in the *Testaments of the Twelve Patriarchs* the term 'synagogue' although applied to churches of the Gentiles is introduced to give a Jewish colouring to the work; (2) that St James does not hesitate to use the word 'church' where he is speaking of the 'church' as a body, cf. v. 14, and the fact that he uses another word in the description of a single incident like that in the text, where the whole context points not to the act of assembling but to the *place of assembly*, suggests that we are still on Jewish soil or in its neighbourhood[1]. See further Introd. p. xi.

your synagogue. The pronoun seems to forbid the supposition that a synagogue of *Jews* could be meant, and St James would scarcely have blamed Christians for the manner in which different classes of people were treated in a *Jewish* synagogue, nor in the latter would Christians have been able to assign the places to the worshippers. At the same time it is evident that this Jewish-Christian assembly is open to non-Christians.

with a gold ring, or as the adj. might perhaps be rendered 'golden-ringed'; for this custom of adorning the fingers with a number of rings many illustrations are cited by Wetstein and other commentators; cf. Lucian, *Tim.* 20; *Nigrin.* 21; Pliny, *N.H.* xxxiii. 6; Martial, v. 11; Juvenal, vii. 139, etc. Familiar passages illustrate the wearing of the ring amongst the Jews for ornament, or favour: cf. Gen. xxxviii. 18, 25, xli. 42; Isaiah iii. 21; Luke xv. 22; and they would no doubt imitate in many respects the fashion of the period. It is interesting to note that while in *Const. Apost.* i. 3, a warning is uttered against the wearing of rings by Christians, Clement of Alexandria makes an exception of the ring amongst articles of luxury forbidden to Christians, because of its use for the purpose of sealing.

in fine clothing. Cf. Luke xxiii. 11; Acts x. 30; 2 Macc. viii. 35: and Philo, M. 2, p. 56. The Vulgate in this passage, as also in Acts x. 30, Apoc. xv. 6, renders the adjective employed here in the Greek by the Latin *candidus*, white, because it was often used of brilliant and glistering whiteness. In this passage this colour would be in marked contrast with the soiled clothing of the poor, and it was also the colour usually worn amongst the Jews, the finest white garments being adopted by the rich.

and there come in also. The entrance of each is vividly depicted as actually taking place before their eyes.

in vile clothing. Cf. Zech. iii. 4; Apoc. xxii. 11; and for a good in-

---

[1] Amongst recent German literature Feine's note, p. 85, *Der Jakobusbrief,* should be consulted as against Harnack. See also Hort, *Judaistic Christianity,* p. 150; whilst Sanday, *Inspiration,* p. 346, speaks of the description of the Church as a 'synagogue' in which it is assumed that all the members are not Christians as 'the most significant proof that the Epistle really belongs to the Apostolic age'; see Introd. p. xi. The same point is well illustrated by Dr Chase, *The Lord's Prayer in the Early Church,* p. 2.

3 clothing ; and ye have regard to him that weareth the fine
clothing, and say, Sit thou here in a good place ; and ye say
to the poor man, Stand thou there, or sit under my foot-

stance of a similar use of the word
of sordid clothing, see Josephus,
Ant. VII. 11. 3. Here in opposition
and contrast to the fine clothing of
the rich.

It would seem from the whole
description that both rich and poor
are not Christians ; if they had been
members of the Church they would
already have had their places in the
assembly, and there would have been
no need for places to be assigned to
them. Verse 6 makes this view
conclusive as regards the rich. St
James would have seen in the action
of those same rich a matter for still
further reprobation, if they had been
guilty of oppressing poor fellow-
Christians. Moreover, the expression '*your* synagogue' points to the
same view. In 1 Cor. xiv. 22, 23, it
is evident that non-Christians came
into the Christian assemblies, and in
the circumstances of the Jewish
Diaspora it was only probable that
non-Christians should enter the assemblies of their Christian fellow-
countrymen to see and to hear.

3. *and ye have regard.* The verb
means to look upon, but it is often
used of looking upon with favour
(1 Kings viii. 28; Ps. xxiv. 16; Ecclesiast. xi. 12; Luke i. 48, etc.),
frequently in a good sense, as of
God looking upon man with pity,
but the state of mind is determined
by the context, as here of looking
upon with admiration. All eyes are
turned to the entrance of the rich.

*to him that weareth the fine
clothing;* a graphic touch : note the
repetition of the phrase, only the
outward and the perishing attract-
ing attention. The noun 'clothing'

which occurs no less than three
times in this passage, is uniformly
rendered in R.V. by the same word
'clothing,' whereas in A.V. it receives three different renderings.
This is quite misleading and is
rightly noticed by Lightfoot, *On a
Fresh Revision,* etc. p. 39.

A sharp contrast is evidently
marked in the words which follow,
a contrast emphasised more pointedly in R.V. by the omission of the
second 'here': sit—stand; here—
there; in a good place—under my
footstool. See also Introd. p. xxxvii.

in a good place. There is reason
for this translation from the employment elsewhere of a somewhat
similar Greek expression for a good
place. The word here is an adverb,
and might in itself imply either
honourably or comfortably. Aelian,
V. H. II. 13, Alciph. *Ep.* III. 20, use
the cognate adjective to express a
good place in a theatre (Field).

Stand thou there, or (if you prefer
to sit) *sit,* etc.; emphasising still more
the contempt for the poor. In this
text W.H. read simply 'stand, or
sit there etc.,' marking sharply the
contrast with the preceding 'sit.'

under my footstool, i.e. on the
floor close to my footstool. The
passage is noted as the only one in
the Bible in which the word is used
literally (Hastings' *B. D.*).

The practices which our Lord
condemned in the Jewish assemblies,
Matt. xxiii. 6, seem to have passed
into the Christian Church, and to
have fostered the same Pharisaical
pride and haughtiness; Edersheim's
Jewish Social Life, p. 263. How
keenly the opposition between this

4 stool; [1]are ye not divided [2]in your own mind, and become
5 judges with evil thoughts? Hearken, my beloved brethren;

[1] Or, *do ye not make distinctions*   [2] Or, *among yourselves*

spirit and the spirit of true Christian
brotherhood and the honour of all
men, in public worship, is often felt
in modern days by shrewd observers
may be seen by the remarks of
W. Macready in his letter quoted
in Pollock's *Life* of the actor.

4. *are ye not divided in your own
mind*. So R.V. text, divided as
it were between profession and
practice, between the profession of
Christian equality and the deference
to rank and wealth, and so becoming
amenable to that sin of doublemindedness which this letter so
sharply rebukes, i. 8. But when we
remember how often the verb is
used in the N.T. to enforce the
opposite of faith and belief—Matt.
xxi. 21; Mark xi. 23; Acts x. 20;
Rom. iv. 20, xiv. 23 (Jude *v.* 22
probably)—there is much to be said
for the rendering 'did ye not doubt
in yourselves?' The context speaks
of faith in Jesus Christ, and this
faith they were not keeping whole
and entire; He was not for them
'the Lord of glory,' Who regarded
not the person of man, whilst they
drew such distinctions between rich
and poor. In adopting this view it
must be remembered that in i. 6
the participle of the same verb is
found, 'let him ask in faith nothing
doubting,' and as there it was a
question of undivided faith in God,
so here it is a question of undivided
faith in the Lord Jesus. See note
on i. 6.

Moreover, this rendering makes
the verb though passive in form
retain the force of the middle voice
in accordance with Matt. xxi. 21;
Mark xi. 23; Rom. iv. 20. This

usage of the verb in the N.T. seems
in itself to forbid the active rendering 'are ye not partial?' A.V., to say
nothing of the ambiguous word
'partial' in its modern employment.
The R.V. marg. renders 'do ye not
make distinctions among yourselves,'
but here again the Greek may well
be interpreted otherwise, and it may
be fairly urged that, although this
rendering makes perfectly good
sense, there does not seem to be
much force in such a query, since it
is so obvious from the preceding
words that distinctions had been
already drawn.

The sense of the passage would of
course be materially altered if we
rendered with some authorities the
whole of the two clauses as stating
a fact: 'ye did not hesitate about
making these distinctions, and thus
ye became evil judges.'

W.H. read the sentence in marg.
as a statement of fact, but as they
omit the negative (ού) the sense is
not really affected: 'ye are divided...
and have become' etc.

judges with evil thoughts. The
genitive is one of quality: cf. i. 25;
Luke xviii. 6. By so acting, by thus
despising the poor and deferring to
the rich, they became wrong-con-
sidering judges, judges with evil
thoughts, or the words may possibly
refer to their thoughts of doubt and
unbelief, which thus possessed them.
The word for 'thoughts' generally
refers to bad, perverse thoughts,
both in N.T. and LXX. In the latter
it appears to be used most frequently
of the thoughts of sinners, as in
several passages in the Psalms, and
Isaiah lix. 7; Jer. iv. 14; 1 Macc. ii.

did not God choose them that are poor as to the world *to
be* rich in faith, and heirs of the kingdom which he promised

63; and cf. in N.T. Matt. xv. 19;
Luke v. 22; Rom. i. 21. The same
proneness to usurp the office of
judge is censured in iv. 11.

5. *Hearken,* placed first as a
demand for attention, in the desire
to show the folly of their thoughts
and behaviour. It has been called
one of the rousing words of St James:
cf. i. 16, iv. 13.

my beloved brethren. Cf. i. 16, 19,
for a similar affectionateness of tone
in pressing home a warning as a
question.

choose. The verb is used of God's
choice of the Israelites, Acts xiii. 17,
and here of the choice of Christians;
cf. Mark xiii. 20, and especially
1 Cor. i. 27 ff., a passage often compared with the language of St James
before us.

poor as to the world, R.V., i.e.
in earthly goods, or 'poor to the
world,' i.e. in the judgment of the
world: cf. Acts vii. 20, 2 Cor. x. 4,
for a similar use of the dative.
The former perhaps better emphasises the contrast between the
poverty of earthly goods and the
true riches. For 'the poor' and
the Jewish social life of the time see
Introd. pp. xxxvi. ff.

Such passages as 1 Sam. ii. 8, and
the constant reference to the care of
the poor and needy by God in the
O.T. prophets, in the apocryphal
books, and in contemporary literature, e.g. *Psalms of Solomon,* v. 13,
xv. 2, are relied upon by those who
can see in the Epistle nothing but
a Jewish document. But our Lord's
own words, Luke vi. 20, might well

suggest the language in this passage
(see further below), and St James
had before him the life of Christ, Who
became one of the poor, and the life
of His followers, who were for the
most part poor men. It is interesting to note that the term 'Ebionite'
adopted by a sect of Jewish-Christians, towards the close of the first
century, was chosen by them because
in thus calling themselves the 'poor'
they claimed to strive to follow the
Master's precept, Matt. x. 9; Acts iv.
34; cf. Epiph. *Haer.* xxx. 17.

to be rich, thus taking the adj.
'rich' not in apposition to 'the poor'
but as an oblique predicate after the
verb[1].

in faith. The prep. is not instrumental, but expressing the sphere
in which they are regarded as rich:
cf. 1 Tim. i. 2, vi. 18. We may note
here, as above in i. 6, the stress laid
upon faith by St James. The same
kind of contrast between outward
poverty and inward spiritual riches
may be abundantly illustrated; cf.
e.g. *Testaments of the Twelve Patriarchs,* Gad 7, where the poor who
gives thanks in all things to the Lord
is said to be enriched with all things.
But our Lord's own teaching had
emphasised the thought that there
were higher and truer riches than
the abundance of wealth, Luke xii.
21; Matt. vi. 19. Plato too could
speak of the wise man as the rich
man, and Philo could speak of the
true wealth laid up in heaven by
wisdom and holiness. The Rabbis
spoke of a man as rich or poor in the
Law ('dives in lege, pauper in lege,'

---

[1] So Mayor and Beyschlag.

6 to them that love him ? But ye have dishonoured the

Wetstein), but no exact parallel is found for the expression in St James.

heirs of the kingdom. The language would be natural upon the lips of a Jew, since he associated the thought of inheritance, originally applied to the Holy Land, with the possession of all the Messianic blessings, Isaiah lx. 21, lxi. 7, and these blessings would be enjoyed through a King and in a kingdom ; cf. *Psalms of Solomon*, xvii. 4–6, 23–51. In one of the earlier of these Psalms, xii. 8, we have language very similar to that of St James in this passage : 'and let the saints of the Lord inherit the promises of the Lord,' the first instance perhaps in which the expression 'the promises of the Lord' is found in extant Jewish literature to sum up the assurances of the Messianic redemption (so Ryle and James's edition, p. 106). But when we remember how our Lord had openly spoken of the kingdom of heaven as the possession of the poor and of those persecuted for righteousness' sake, Matt. v. 3, 10 ; how He had cheered His disciples with the good pleasure of the Father to give the kingdom to the little flock, Luke xii. 31, 32 ; how He had closed His ministry with the solemn promise of a kingdom, the inheritance of the blessed ones of His Father, Matt. xxv. 34, it does not seem improbable that such teaching would gain currency amongst His followers, and that St James should be acquainted with it.

which he promised. The same verb occurs in i. 12. It is used in classical Greek of voluntary offers, and so is fitly used here and elsewhere in the N.T. of the Divine promises ; and twice in the *Psalms*

of Solomon, vii. 9, xvii. 6, the promises of God (see also above).

to them that love him. See above on i. 12, where we have the same phrase. In the preceding passage the promise consists in the crown of life. Here too it may be noted that the *Psalms of Solomon* speak of life, xiv. 6, 7, as an inheritance in the Messianic consummation : sinners have for their inheritance darkness and destruction, 'but the saints of the Lord shall inherit life in gladness.' Such words remind us of the question asked of our Lord by the rich young man, Matt. xix. 16, and in our Lord's answer 'if thou wilt enter into life keep the commandments' we may see an intimation that 'life' like 'the kingdom' is not only a future but a present possession for those who obey God.

The words further remind us that St James does not wish us to suppose that the destitution of poverty is in itself a virtuous condition, or the possession of riches a vicious one ; he would have said with St Paul 'that all things work together for good to those who love God,' whether they be rich or poor. But St James, as we have had occasion to note, was guarding against a flagrant form of a sin common in every age, and grossly so in his own, 'respect of persons,' and forgetfulness of the judgment of Him Who regarded not the rich more than the poor, for they were all the work of His hands : Job xxxiv. 19 ; *Psalms of Solomon*, v. 13, 14 ; Introd. p. xxxvii. At the same time none had spoken more emphatically of the danger of riches than Christ in so far as they led men to set their heart, their love upon them and not upon God ; Matt. xiii. 22 ; Mark x. 23.

poor man. Do not the rich oppress you, and themselves
7 drag you before the judgement-seats? Do not they blas-

The poor, it might be fairly said, have
more opportunities of trusting not
in wealth but in providence, and of
practising the virtues which keep
men close to the life of Christ, but
still it must be never forgotten that
'opportunities are not virtues, and
poverty is not salvation.'

6. *But ye*, in strong contrast to
God, who had chosen the poor, *have
dishonoured the poor man*, R.V.
The rendering 'despised,' A.V. (which
seems to be given to no less than
seven different Greek verbs), does not
represent the force of the original.
The same Greek verb is found in
Ecclus. x. 23, 'it is not meet to
dishonour the poor man that hath
understanding,' and also in Prov. xiv.
21 (cf. xxii. 22), 'he that dishonoureth
the poor sinneth,' language to which
St James's words afford a close
parallel.

The aorist may refer to the particular case just mentioned (so
perhaps the sing. is used in this
verse, 'the poor man,' R.V.), or it
may be an instance of what is called
the gnomic aorist; see above on i. 11.

Do not the rich oppress you? i.e.
the rich Jews, their own fellow-
countrymen, these very men to
whom they paid such servile deference. If St James had meant rich
Christians he surely would not have
refrained from pointing out the
glaring contrast between their bearing towards the poor and their
Christian calling. For the verb
rendered 'oppress' and its use here
a striking parallel is afforded by
Wisd. ii. 10 (cf. 19), 'let us oppress
the poor righteous man.' The verb

is frequently used in the LXX of the
oppression of the poor and needy:
cf. Amos iv. 1; Zech. vii. 10; Jer. vii.
6; *Psalms of Solomon*, xvii. 46.
There could have been no question of
rich Jews if the city and the temple
had fallen, as such a reference could
not have been consistent with the
social conditions.

and themselves. So R.V., emphasising the fact that these very men to
whom they pay court do not hesitate
to employ violence; cf. Acts viii. 3, of
Saul it is said that 'haling men and
women he committed them to prison.'

drag. The verb is used elsewhere
in N.T. of dragging with force, as in
classical Greek; cf. Acts xxi. 30.

the judgement-seats; here Jewish
tribunals, certainly not Christian.
The word might include Gentile
tribunals; cf. 1 Cor. vi. 2 (in the LXX
it is used of a Jewish place of judgment, *Hist of Sus.* v. 49). There is
however no reason to think of
Roman tribunals and so to argue
that the letter could not have been
composed before Domitian or Trajan.
'James wrote to Jews, who were not
governed solely by Roman law, but
who, down to A.D. 70, administered
justice to a certain extent among
themselves, according to their own
sacred law, even in Roman cities of
the Eastern provinces. Of course
the most serious penalties, and
especially death, were beyond the
independent Jewish jurisdiction; but
still much suffering could be legally
inflicted by Jews on other Jews,
unless the victims possessed the
Roman citizenship' (Ramsay, *C.R.E.*
p. 349)[1]. The oppression would in-

---

[1] Cf. Schürer, *Jewish People*, II. 1, 185, E.T.; and see also Zahn, *Einleitung*,
I. 63, 70.

pheme the honourable name [1]by the which ye are called?

[1] Gr. *which was called upon you.*

clude both social and legal persecution, and we can well suppose how
bitter and aggravating it would be:
see Introd. p. xxxv.

7. *do not they blaspheme?* (perhaps 'is it not they who?' marking
the pronoun which is here emphatically repeated). If we remember
that it is 'the rich' who are thus said
to blaspheme, it is much more natural
to see here again rich, unbelieving
Jews. Not only is blasphemy frequently mentioned in specific connection with the Jews, Acts xiii. 45,
xviii. 6, xxvi. 11 (cf. 1 Tim. i. 13), and
their hostility to the Christian faith,
but rich Jews led the early opposition
to the Apostles; cf. Acts iv. 1–3, v.
17, xiii. 50. It is quite conceivable
that their blasphemy might be
uttered in the Jewish law-courts, or
that it would intensify the hostility
of a Jewish judge to find that the
accused belonged to the hated sect
of the Nazarenes. But the utterances
of the blasphemy need not refer to
judicial courts at all, and certainly
not to trials before Roman tribunals.
On the other hand, the words cannot
be explained to mean that Christ
is blasphemed by the evil deeds of
Jews or Gentiles; this thought would
be expressed by the passive and not
the active of the verb, and if by the
latter it could be signified in so
many words, as Eusebius, *H.E.* v. 1,
speaks of those who blaspheme the
Way by their mode of life.

the honourable name, i.e. of Christ.
As He is called the Good Shepherd,
John x. 11, so here He bears,
according to the Greek, the good,
the beautiful Name; cf. Ps. cxliii. 3,
where the same adjective is used of
the Name of God; the Name of Christ
came to be specially spoken of as *the*
Name, Acts v. 41. Whether it was
in existence or not, it is not likely
that the name 'Christian' can be
here meant, since Jewish opponents
would not be likely to use in obloquy
a title so closely connected with their
dearest hopes: moreover, they could
scarcely be said to blaspheme a title
such as this, or 'the poor' or
'brethren.' At the same time it may
be noted that St James as a Jew
would not be likely to associate
blasphemy with any name less than
a Divine Name, and just as the Jews
regarded punishment as following
upon profanation of *the Name,* i.e. of
Jehovah (*Sayings of the Jewish
Fathers,* pp. 66, 88), so it is significant that St James speaks here of
profaning the Name of Christ.

by the which ye are called, but in
R.V. marg. the rendering of the
Greek 'which was called upon you,'
i.e. in Baptism, Acts ii. 38, viii. 16, x.
48. The phrase is taken from the
O.T., where it is frequently said of Israel that the Name of God was named
upon them, Deut. xxviii. 10; 2 Chron.
vi. 33, vii. 14; Jer. xiv. 9; Amos ix. 12;
and such a phrase implies a declaration of dedication to the service of
God. So Christians are dedicated to
Christ in Baptism; cf. Hermas, *Sim.*
viii. 6. 4, where the same phrase is
used of those who had been baptised
into the Christian Church[1]. It is

---

[1] In this connection, and for this view, Heitmüller's recent treatise, *Im
Namen Jesu,* p. 92 (1903), may be consulted.

8 Howbeit if ye fulfil the royal law, according to the scripture, Thou shalt love thy neighbour as thyself, ye do well:

evident that His Name, and not that of Jehovah, is here meant, in spite of attempts to prove that the latter is intended, for the Name is said to be called 'upon *you*,' not 'upon them,' so that no reference can be made to a God acknowledged by both classes alike. It is therefore nothing to the point to quote, with Spitta, passages from *Enoch*, e.g. xliv. 8, in which the rich are said to trust in riches, to forget the Most High, and to commit blasphemy and unrighteousness.

In the N.T. this phrase is only once used elsewhere, and there in words quoted by St James; cf. Acts xv. 17.

8. *Howbeit if*, R.V., thus expressing the Greek particle which A.V. does not notice. St James is supposing that his readers may justify their action by referring to the law of love of neighbours and enemies alike; and in so far as they keep that law from good motives they did well, but if they respected the rich merely for their riches, they sinned.

fulfil, i.e. by avoiding any respect of persons, and thus showing love and honour to all alike; a similar phrase only in Rom. ii. 27.

according to the scripture; best taken as referring simply to the passage in Lev. xix. 18, quoted here from LXX. It is unnatural to take the words closely with 'fulfil,' as if to show that there is a fulfilment of the law in its Scriptural meaning and sense.

the royal law, perhaps so called as being the supreme law; all other laws are contained in it: cf. Mark xii. 28; Rom. xiii. 8; Gal. v. 14. But others take it to mean that this law is so called because given by God, the King Supreme, or by Christ, Matt. xxii. 37, to Whom Christians belong, and Whose Name has been called upon them. In either case we may see how closely St James approaches to the teaching of our Lord. To explain the epithet as meaning that this law is valid also for kings, or as indicating a royal way, direct and plain, is scarcely satisfactory. But St James may well mean a law which is a law for kings and not for slaves; the heirs of the kingdom, ii. 5, are not in bondage to any man, for they had been made free; let them therefore act not as those subject to fear, but as those who are themselves kings, who would then be ashamed to respect persons by cringing to the rich or dishonouring the poor. This or a somewhat similar meaning may be enforced by two passages from St Clement of Alexandria, *Strom.* vi. 164, vii. 73, in which he speaks of those who do not actively love and benefit their neighbours as not being 'royal,' and also of the 'royal' road, by which those of royal descent travel, as consisting in justice done not from fear or constraint but by free choice. In a striking passage, *De creat. princ.* 4, Mang. II. 364, Philo also uses the expression 'a royal road' to signify the way and mode of life befitting a king[1].

ye do well. It is again noteworthy

---

[1] Cf. 1 Pet. ii. 9 (Exod. xix. 6). Both Mayor and Zahn (*Einleitung*, I. 82) regard this view as making excellent sense. A strikingly similar use of the adjective in connection with law is found in pseudo-Plato, *Minos*, 317 c. Its use is frequent in the LXX; cf. 4 Macc. xiv. 2.

9 but if ye have respect of persons, ye commit sin, being
10 convicted by the law as transgressors. For whosoever
shall keep the whole law, and yet stumble in one *point*,

that a similar phrase occurs at the
close of the circular letter, Acts xv.
29. At the same time it will be
noted that the words also occur elsewhere in the N.T., cf. 2 Pet. i. 19;
they are found too in 1 Macc. xii.
18, 22, 2 Macc. ii. 16, and in classical
authors.

9. *but if ye have respect of
persons.* Closely preceding the law
of love in Lev. xix. 18 we read, *v.*
15, 'ye shall do no unrighteousness
in judgment ; thou shalt not respect
the person of the poor, nor honour
the person of the mighty' (cf. Deut.
xvi. 19), and St James may well have
had such a charge in mind, especially
as below, *v.* 4, we have another
parallel to the language of Lev. xix.
9, 13.

ye commit sin, a strong phrase,
lit. ye work sin : cf. i. 20; Acts x. 35;
Heb. xi. 33, etc.; and in LXX, Ps. v. 5,
xiv. 2; Zeph. ii. 3, etc.

being convicted by the law. Here as
elsewhere in the N.T. (and probably
so in the O.T. instances) the verb is
best translated 'convicted,' not 'convinced.' In John viii. 46 (cf. xvi. 8)
it is evident that its force and
meaning are thus properly brought
out; cf. Jude *v.* 15; Tit. i. 9 (Hastings'
B.D., 'Convince'). The law may
refer to the law of love, the royal
law, or it may refer to the law
cited above from Lev. xix. 15, but

either law would obviously be violated by respect of persons.

as transgressors. The word would
be fitly used here, as lit. it meant
those who overpassed or stepped over
a line, and so those who violated a
code or law: cf. Rom. ii. 25, 27, iv. 15,
and see Ecclus. x. 19, xix. 24;
2 Macc. vii. 2 ; 3 Macc. vii. 12, etc.[1]

10. *shall keep the whole law.*
Here the context points a reference
to the whole Mosaic Law,—shall keep
the Law as a whole.

and yet stumble in one point,
R.V. The verb is rendered 'offend'
here and in iii. 2 by A.V., which also
has 'fall' for the verb in 2 Pet. i. 10.
But in Rom. xi. 11 A.V. has
'stumbled' (cf. for the use of the
same verb Deut. vii. 25, in LXX).
The A.V. rendering 'offend' is
connected with the Lat. *offendere*,
to strike against; see further Art.
'Offence,' Hastings' *B.D.*

in one point. This is better than
to render 'in one law,' although
this would be quite admissible in the
original (Grimm-Thayer gives both
renderings). For a similar phrase
with reference to the law a parallel
may be found in 4 Macc. v. 17, 18.
St James is laying down a general
principle, the truth of which he
proves by what follows; and thus
'the respect of persons' which he
has condemned is shown to be a

---

[1] It is an interesting suggestion that the phrase 'a transgressor of the law,'
which thus occurs both in Paul and James, may have been borrowed by them
from the remarkable addition to Luke vi. 4, given in Codex D, where precisely
the same phrase occurs : 'On the same day, seeing a certain man working on
the Sabbath, He saith to him, "O man, if thou knowest what thou art doing,
thou art blessed ; but if thou knowest not, thou art accursed, and *a transgressor
of the law*." ' (Cf. Plummer's *St James*, p. 56, and Resch, *Agrapha*, p. 189.)

11 he is become guilty of all. For he that said, Do not
commit adultery, said also, Do not kill. Now if thou dost
not commit adultery, but killest, thou art become a trans-
12 gressor of the law. So speak ye, and so do, as men that

violation not of one law only, but of
all laws. Various illustrations have
been given of similar teaching among
the Rabbis; cf. two sayings of
R. Jochanan, *Sabbath*, fol. 70. 2,
'But if a man does all things, but
omits one, he is guilty of each and
all,' and *Pesikta*, 'Everyone who
says I take upon myself the whole
law except one word, he has despised the word of the Lord and
made all His commandments vain';
so also *Bemidbar Rab.* ix. on Numb.
v. 14, 'our teacher has taught us how
adulterers and adulteresses trans-
gress the Ten Commandments.' On
the other hand all kinds of extra-
vagances seem to have found their
way into Rabbinical pages, as e.g.
that the Sabbath weighs against all
precepts; if a man keep that, he has
kept all: *Shemoth Rabb.* 25. With
the principle laid down by St James
we may compare our Lord's own
teaching, Matt. v. 19 (Rom. xiv. 23).

he is become guilty of all, i.e. liable
to be convicted of transgressing all
the commandments. For the word
rendered 'guilty' see 1 Cor. xi. 27,
and in LXX, Isaiah liv. 17, 1 Macc.
xiv. 45, also found in *Psalms of
Solomon*, iv. 2.

It is quite possible that this
teaching of St James might have
been perverted by the Judaisers,
and that they might have appealed
to him as insisting on the observance
of the whole Mosaic Law, and placing circumcision etc. on the same
level as the violation of great moral

precepts, and this perversion may
be in the minds of St James and the
other Apostles in their protest, Acts
xv. 24.

11. *For he that said*, i.e. God, with
a solemn reference to Exod. iii. 14.
But see also Parry, *St James*, p. 32,
where the possible reference to the
words of the Lord Jesus is mentioned.

Do not commit adultery, etc. The
best reason for the introduction here
of these two commandments may
be found in the fact that they are
placed first amongst those which
relate generally to our duty towards
our neighbour, and that they are the
most weighty of such; or possibly it
was felt that the injunction against
adultery, the destruction of family
life, might fitly follow upon the
injunction to honour one's parents
(*Encycl. Bibl.* I. 1050), or there may
well have been some traditional
order varying from that in the
Hebrew of the Pentateuch. For
a similar order see also Luke xviii.
20; Rom. xiii. 9; and LXX, Exod. xx.
Cod. 13, and Deut. v. 17–19; Philo,
M. 2, p. 189.

a transgressor of the law. A law
is the expression of the will of him
who ordains it, so that he who
violates the law in any particular
sins against the same will, and
therefore becomes a transgressor of
the whole law. St Augustine was
so exercised as to the meaning of
this passage that he wrote specially
upon it to St Jerome (*Epist.* 167)[1].
He maintains that as all other com-

---

[1] 'Intermingling many remarks about the Stoics, who taught that all sins
are equal, and that whoever possesses one virtue possesses all.' For English
readers Dr Plummer *in loco* gives a good account of St Augustine's letter.

13 are to be judged by a law of liberty. For judgement *is* without mercy to him that hath shewed no mercy : mercy glorieth against judgement.

mandments hang upon the law of love to God and to man, he who sins against love is guilty of violating all the commandments, for no one sins without breaking this law of love; murder, adultery, theft, covetousness, all violate it; but love worketh no ill to his neighbour, love therefore is the fulfilment of the law. Thus not only is each law the expression of one will, but the whole law may be so regarded.

12. *So speak ye, and so do.* The repetition of the adverb emphasises the earnest exhortation of the writer, and the laying stress upon word and deed alike is characteristic of him: cf. i. 26, iii. 1 ff., ii. 2 ff.

as men that are to be judged, R.V., lit. 'as those about to be judged,' the verb in the original used in classical and Biblical Greek of things which will come to pass by fixed necessity or by Divine appointment: cf. Matt. xxv. 31; 2 Cor. v. 10. In anticipation of the final judgment, judge yourselves by the same law day by day. Vulg. renders *incipientes judicari,* 'beginning to be judged.'

by a law of liberty. See note on i. 25.

13. *For judgement is without mercy,* lit. 'the judgment is merciless'; 'the judgment,' i.e. of God. Our Lord's teaching, Matt. v. 7, vii. 1, xviii. 28 etc., naturally occurs to the mind, and may be said to give the key to our verse. In the O.T. parallels may be found, cf. esp. Ecclus. xxviii. 2 (although for this passage reference should be made to the strictures of Dr Edersheim in the *Speaker's Commentary*), Tob. iv. 7–12. In the *Testaments of the Twelve Patriarchs,* Zab. 8, we read:

And do you, my children, have compassion in mercy towards every man, that the Lord also out of compassion may have mercy upon thee; for God also in the last days sends his compassion upon the earth, and where he finds a compassionate heart there he makes his dwelling, for in proportion as a man feels compassion towards his neighbour, the Lord has compassion upon him.' And with this compare also, 'Every time that thou art merciful, God will be merciful to thee, and if thou art not merciful God will not show mercy to thee' (Jer. Babha Q. viii. 10), or again, 'To whom is sin pardoned ? to him who forgiveth injury' (Rosh Hash. 17 *a*).

to him that hath shewed no mercy. The phrase to show or do mercy was quite common in the LXX, and there seems no reason to suppose that St James had in mind Luke x. 36.

mercy glorieth against judgement. So R.V., which makes the force and terseness of the words more emphatic by the omission of any connecting particle. The verb which stands first, also for emphasis, brings mercy before us as if in a vivid and strong personality. The sentence no doubt means that the mercy shown by the merciful, as in contrast to him who shows no mercy, enables him to stand in the judgment which otherwise would overwhelm him; so mercy is full of glad confidence and knows no fear in view of the hour of judgment ('tanquam victrici insultat').

For the verb see iii. 14; Rom. xi. 18; and in LXX, Jer. xxvii. (l.) 11, 38; Zech. x. 12. (The Syriac has 'ye shall be exalted by mercy over judgment.')

14   What doth it profit, my brethren, if a man say he hath
15 faith, but have not works? can that faith save him? If a

But the form of the sentence as given in R.V. asserts a universal truth, and the mercy of God is represented as 'glorying against' a judgment which may seem to be merciless, Matt. ix. 13; Hos. vi. 6: 'earthly power doth then show likest God's, when mercy seasons justice,' Shakespeare, *Merchant of Venice*, iv. 1. In the *Speaker's Commentary* on Wisd. ix. 1, a striking passage of the Talmud is referred to, which gives the story of Rabbi Ishmael ben Elishah, who, entering into the Holy of Holies, saw the Lord of Sabaoth sitting on a throne, and prayed: 'May it please Thee to cause Thy mercy to subdue Thy anger; may it be revealed above Thy other attributes; and mayest Thou deal with Thy children according to the quality of mercy.' And it seemed as though God was pleased at the prayer. 'Berakhoth,' p. 7. 1. In the same comment a traditional saying of Mohammed's is given: 'When God created the creation He wrote a book which is near Him upon the sovran throne, and what is written is this: *Verily my compassion over-cometh my wrath.*'

14. For the paragraph that follows see Introd. p. xli.

The whole of it may be closely connected with the thought of the judgment, and of that which alone will stand in the judgment, and save from the judgment; the 'works' carry us back to the 'mercy' of *v.* 13, and the 'save him' to the judgment of *vv.* 12, 13.

The 'faith' which admits respect of persons and disregards the poor must be quite incompatible with the faith which is centred on Jesus

Christ, Who although the Lord of glory regarded the person of the least of those brothers and sisters whom St James had in mind, *v.* 15; cf. Matt. xxv. 40. There are no doubt passages in Jewish literature (see Introd. p. xlii.) in which faith and works are contrasted, in which calling upon the Lord is regarded as securing safety in the Messianic judgment, *Psalms of Sol.* vi. 2, but St James had before his mind the words of a greater than any human teacher, Who had taught men that saying, Lord, Lord, was valueless in comparison with doing the will of the Father, Who had warned men that 'in that day' many would fail, in spite of their pretentious claims to gain recognition from the Judge.

What doth it profit? R.V. In the original, the words may be almost colloquial, and somewhat more abrupt (as A.V. indicates). In the N.T. the phrase recurs in 1 Cor. xv. 32; cf. Job xv. 3; Ecclus. xli. 14; Matt. xvi. 26; 1 Cor. xiii. 3.

my brethren. The expression emphasises not only tenderness and sympathy of the writer, but also the fact that he is thinking here of the faith of Christians; cf. *v.* 15.

if a man say. The phrase is not 'if a man has faith,' so that stress may perhaps be laid upon 'say,' and if so we may explain that as in what follows mere empty words are contrasted with needful deeds, so an inoperative faith can only testify to itself by saying, not by doing.

faith. On the place of faith in questions similar to those raised by St James, which were apparently occupying the Jewish schools, see Introd. p. xli. St James in writing

16 brother or sister be naked, and in lack of daily food, and

to Jewish-Christians might well use the word with reference not only to the fundamental doctrine of the Jewish Creed, cf. *v.* 19, but also with reference to specific Christian doctrine. But it could not at all events be a mere theoretical or intellectual faith in which we ought to pray, i. 6, in which the poor are rich, ii. 5, and which cannot coexist with 'respect of persons.'

can that faith save him? R.V., i.e. such faith as this (article before the noun in the original). But others take the article not as having the force of a demonstrative pronoun, but as simply referring to that which has been already mentioned, 'if a man say that he has faith.'

save him, i.e. in the final judgment; cf. *v.* 13. See also note on i. 21.

15. *If,* R.V. The worthlessness of a faith without works is compared with a pity which consists in mere words without corresponding deeds, and this connection is brought out by the omission of the conjunction 'but' retained by A.V. at the beginning of the verse; if the conjunction is read, we should simply have a parallel case of the difference between profession and reality, and not an illustration of the principle stated in the preceding verse.

brother or sister, reminding them of their relationship in Christ, and of the claims made upon them through their union in Him; cf. i. 2.

Such a scene may have actually passed before St James's notice, or he may according to his wont be enforcing his teaching by some vivid and imaginary picture.

naked. The word is used both in Biblical and classical Greek of those ill-clad, as well as of those literally

naked (cf. *nudus* in Latin); here perhaps the context *v.* 16 may point to the former meaning. In the O.T. the phraseology of Job xxxi. 19, 20, Isaiah lviii. 7 recurs to the mind in connection with the picture given by St James. In the latter passage the prophet describes the fulfilment of the true fast acceptable to God, viz. by works of mercy, in feeding the hungry and clothing the naked. A striking passage, *Testaments of the Twelve Patriarchs,* Zab. 7, affords a similarity in its phraseology, but a contrast in its contents, to the picture here drawn by St James: 'I saw a man in distress naked in the winter, and being moved with compassion towards him I stole a garment out of my house secretly and gave it to him. And do you, my children, have compassion upon all without distinction, and give to each with a good heart of that which God gives to you. But if ye have nothing on occasion to give to the needy, sympathise with him in heartfelt compassion.' So *ibid.* Iss. 7, 'With every sufferer I sighed, and gave my bread to the poor; I eat not alone.'

Both our Lord's words, Matt. xxv. 36, 43, and the solemn scene of the Last Judgment may well have been present to the mind of St James, especially when we remember that his thoughts were dwelling upon mercy and judgment.

in lack of. Cf. i. 4, 5, where the same Greek is so translated. A.V. follows Tyndale.

daily food; better *of the day's supply of food,* indicating more sharply the indigence which failed to obtain a supply for even a single day. So in Dion. Hal. *Ant.* viii. 41, we have the picture of a wretched

one of you say unto them, Go in peace, be ye warmed and
filled ; and yet ye give them not the things needful to the

man who from his own wealth cannot procure provision for even a
single day (Wetstein). The rendering *needful*, *necessary*, adopted by
von Soden, is too general for the
thought which the word would emphasise. Reference may also be
made to Nestle's Art. 'Lord's Prayer,'
Encycl. Bibl. III. 2820[1].

16. *and one of you say;* quite
generally, and not to be limited as
if spoken only by those who thought
faith sufficient for salvation; lit.
'some one from among you.' The
words may help to mark the fact that
the person represented as speaking is
thought of as belonging to the circle
of believers. Cf. 1 John iii. 17, 18.

Go in peace; Judg. xviii. 6; Acts
xvi. 36 (2 Kings v. 19); cf. Tobit x.
13. This and the following verbs may
be used in contempt or in mockery
and insult, although we are not
bound to suppose that James would
have pictured Christians as so utterly hard-hearted and impervious
to pity; the expressions are rather
formulae of good wishes and well-
meaning, but merely phrases and
nothing more, phrases which amount-
ed to a cold and selfish rejection,
although couched in words which
sounded warm and considerate;
St James was a master of irony.

be ye warmed and filled. So A.
and R.V., corresponding to the two
above-mentioned wants and needs,
v. 15. If the verbs are thus con-
strued as in the passive (cf. Job
xxxi. 20; Hag. i. 6), they express as
it were a command, issued in the
haste to be rid of this troublesome

brother, or perhaps a wish that the
poor might be clothed and fed, although it is no doubt possible to
take them as in the middle voice
and to render 'warm yourselves,
feed yourselves.'

In either case the point of comparison with what follows about
faith and works is marked if we
remember that the words doubtless
expressed advice excellent in sound,
but that there was no corresponding
effort to make it effectual.

It has been well said that there
is plenty of this 'be ye warmed'
now-a-days, plenty of theoretical and
excellent advice, but no corresponding effort to translate theory into
practice, if trouble or effort of any
real kind is involved.

filled, in earlier Greek of feeding
or fattening animals with fodder,
in comedy and in colloquial Greek
of men feasting or eating; in N.T.
always of eating or satisfying with
food, without the earlier associations;
cf. Matt. v. 6; Mark vii. 27, 28; so
in LXX and modern Greek (Ken-
nedy).

and yet ye give them not; second
person plural, perhaps from the
preceding 'of you' also in the plural,
or because the plural is often used
after an indefinite singular; in thus
generalising his words St James
would remind his readers that the
poor and needy belonged to the
Church, that they were the brethren
of all.

the things needful. Only here in
N.T., but used in classical writings;
in 3 Macc. vi. 30 the word is used of

---

[1] Dr Chase makes the interesting suggestion that we have here a reminiscence
of the petition for 'the bread of the day' in the Lord's Prayer, and in the words
'the things needful to the body' a very early comment on the scope of that
petition, *The Lord's Prayer in the Early Church*, p. 48.

17 body ; what doth it profit? Even so faith, if it have not
18 works, is dead in itself. ¹Yea, a man will say, Thou hast
  faith, and I have works : shew me thy faith apart from *thy*
19 works, and I by my works will shew thee *my* faith. Thou
  believest that ²God is one ; thou doest well : the ³devils

---

¹ Or, *But some one will say*   ² Some ancient authorities read *there is one God.*
³ Gr. *demons.*

---

things needful for feasting; here the
food and raiment referred to; cf.
1 Tim. vi. 8.

what doth it profit? repeated
perhaps for emphasis, and to arrest
attention.

17. *Even so faith...is dead in itself,*
R.V. The A.V. 'dead being alone'
does not express the true significance
of the Greek. Such faith may be
present like the corpse of a man, but
it has no life, it is inwardly dead as
well as outwardly inoperative.

18. *Yea, a man will say,* R.V.,
and in marg., *but some one will say.*
Often explained as marking even
more definitely the introduction of
an objector (cf. Rom. xi. 19 ; 1 Cor.
xv. 35), who maintains that both
faith and works represent forms of
pure religion each of which may be
acceptable with God. But if this
was the force of the words the
objector would naturally say to
St James, 'I have faith and thou
hast works,' instead of saying as in
the text, 'thou hast faith and I have
works.'

Another suggested explanation is
that a note of interrogation should
be placed after the first clause which
would then read 'hast *thou* faith ?'
'thou who thus speakest so slight-
ingly of it?' and then this objector
is answered in the following words
'but at any rate I have works,' and
he is called upon to show the faith
to which he lays claim in the question 'hast *thou* faith?' In this view

the objector is the same person
who is signified in *v.* 14 as saying
that he has faith and not works.

But on the other hand it is urged
that no objector is introduced, but
that the writer puts himself into the
background, or in accordance with
the dramatic vividness of the letter,
as we sometimes avail ourselves of
a similar turn of speech, supposes
another to speak, 'Nay (or, Yea), one
may say,' etc.—faith without works
has been shown to be profitless; but
it is possible to go even further
than this and maintain that even its
very existence stands in need of
proof.

apart from. The meaning is made
much plainer by this rendering here
and *vv.* 20, 26. The same may be said
of several other passages where the
R.V. translates the same adverb in
a similar manner ; see e.g. John xv.
5 ; Rom. iii. 21, 28, iv. 6; Ephes. ii. 12;
Heb. xi. 40. A.V. reads in the marg.
'by thy works'; but this is not well
supported, and if retained must be
taken of course ironically. It is also
to be noted that the personal pro-
nouns are omitted in R.V. text,
although retained in italics in the
English, 'apart from *thy* works, and
I by my works will show thee *my*
faith.'

19. *Thou believest that God is
one,* R.V. text, in marg. 'there is
one God' as A.V. The former rendering seems best as expressing the
primary article of the Jewish Creed ;

20 also believe, and shudder. But wilt thou know, O vain

cf. Deut. vi. 4; Mark xii. 29; and also Hermas, *Mand.* i. 1, 'First of all believe that God is one' (Dr Taylor's edit. *in loco*, S.P.C.K. 1903). In the MSS. there is considerable variation in the order of the words, but in some of the most important the word for 'one' stands first, apparently so indicating that the unity of God is the chief point to be emphasised. For Christians too, 'I believe in one God,' is the first truth of revealed religion, and it stands first in the Nicene Creed; cf. 1 Cor. viii. 6; Ephes. iv. 6.

On the primary and vital importance attached by the Jew to this declaration of belief, see Taylor, *Sayings of the Jewish Fathers,* pp. 38, 116, and cf. Philo, *Leg. ad C. M.* 2, p. 562. Thus, e.g., 'Whosoever prolongs the utterance of the word One (Deut. vi. 4) shall have his days and years prolonged to him' (Berakhoth, f. 13 *b*); so too Josephus, *Ant.* III. 5, remarks that the First Word teaches that God is One. Of the famous Rabbi Akiba it is related that when undergoing the extreme tortures of a martyr's death he began reciting his last prayer, and as he reached the closing word in the distinguishing formula of the O.T. religion, 'Hear, O Israel, the Lord thy God is *one*,' he yielded up his breath. His tormentors were amazed at his constancy, and it is no wonder that in Jewish legend a voice from heaven was heard, 'Blessed art thou, for thy soul and the word One left thy body together' (Edersheim's *History of the Jewish Nation,* p. 220).

In writing to Jewish-Christians there is nothing strange in the fact that St James should thus refer to a belief which was the great pride and confidence of the Jew, and should thus rebuke a reliance on mere orthodoxy. If it is urged that it is impossible to suppose that amongst Jewish-Christians monotheism would be referred to as a prominent article of their specific Christian belief, we may well ask whether the same article would form among *Gentile* Christians a more significant tenet of *Christian* belief. It is best to take the words as uttered by the same interlocutor as in *v.* 18, and they are introduced to show that the existence of 'faith' without 'works' is not only reproveable, but that even if it exists, so far from being a possession which confers a blessing, it may be productive of a reverse result. The construction in the original seems to show that reference is made to the mere acceptance of an intellectual belief, and not to a belief denoting loyalty and trust.

By some editors, as by W.H., the words are pointed interrogatively, 'Thou believest that there is one God?' well and good.

thou doest well. So far, so well; not necessarily an ironical phrase (cf. *v.* 8, Mark xii. 32), but the context, with its sarcasm in the words 'believe' and 'shudder,' may point to an ironical meaning here.

the devils also believe. The word in the original is rendered in R.V. marg. 'demons.' In classical Greek the word might be used of spiritual beings who were inferior to God and yet superior to men, and that too in both a bad and good sense; cf. Acts xvii. 18. In the LXX the word is used generally for the demons regarded as deities of the heathen, and in support of this meaning here it is urged that such demons would know well that there was only one true God and that they were no true deities. But it is best to take the word in its usual N.T. sense of evil spirits subjected to Satan who enter into and possess men; and thus we may connect this passage with the passages in the Gospels which tell us not only of the belief but also of the terror of the demons, in the presence of the Son of God: Mark v. 7; Matt. viii. 29; Luke iv. 41 (cf. Acts xix. 15); see further Introd. p. xviii. According to some statements of later Jewish theology the fallen angels and the daughters of men begat giants from whose souls the spirits went forth to destroy without incurring condemnation until the great judgment over the fallen angels and the godless, *Enoch*, xv. 9–12, xvi. 1; cf. *Book of Jubilees*, x. 5[1].

shudder. This belief in the existence of one true God only begets fear and trembling and a horrible dread. The word is properly to bristle, to stiffen, as of the hair standing on end, Job iv. 15, but also used to express awe or terror in a high degree, Dan. vii. 15; 4 Macc. xiv. 9, xvii. 7. It is used in classical writers exactly as above in Job, so by Hesiod and Plutarch. *The Testament of Abraham*, xvi. affords a striking instance of this employment of the word; 'Michael said to Death: Come hither, the Lord of creation, the immortal King calls thee, and Death when he heard *shuddered...* and came in great fear and stood before the invisible Father, *shud-*

dering and groaning and trembling.' Josephus using the cognate verbal adjective speaks of 'the dreadful name of God,' *B. J.* v. 10. 3; and the same word is found on a papyrus of the fourth century A.D. in which a demon is invoked 'by the dreadful names,' Deissmann, *Bible Studies*, p. 288, E.T. What an impression this verse of St James made upon early Christian literature is seen by the reference to it in Justin Martyr, *Trypho*, xlix., where he speaks of even the demons 'shuddering' at Christ; in Clem. Alex. *Strom.* v. p. 724, where the demons and a company of gods are said 'to shudder at' and fear God; in Lactantius, *De Ira*, 23, where earth and heaven and sea and the infernal realms 'shudder at' God, the King and Creator of all.

The word may well refer to the demons in the narratives of the Gospels and their fear of immediate torments—they cried out.

St James does not work out the comparison between the 'faith' of the demons and that which he is considering, but he says enough to show that the fruit of the faith of the demons is only fear, they are not urged by their belief in God to trust or service or thanks, their knowledge of God's existence and presence does not influence them to enter into a right relationship with Him; so too for the Christian a bare faith, a mere acknowledgment of the truth of the first article of the Creed, leads to nothing and profits nothing. At the same time it is of course quite possible that St James may intend

---

[1] A striking parallel to the thought expressed in Matt. viii. 29, 'to torment us before the time.' Thus in *Enoch*, xvi. 1, we read, 'in the days of murder and of destruction and of the death of the giants when the spirits have gone forth from the souls of their flesh, in order to destroy without incurring judgment—thus will they destroy until the day when the great consummation of the great world be consummated over the watchers and the godless.'

21 man, that faith apart from works is barren? Was not

his reference to the 'faith' of the demons to show that 'belief' could exist without being of such a kind as to save, v. 14; or that as the demons tremble at the thought of judgment to come, so for the Christian a mere intellectual belief will result in fear and trembling and nothing more—a poor result indeed!

It may be fairly said that if St James had in mind St Paul's doctrine of justification it would be a strange way to meet it with the argument before us—the Pauline conception of justifying faith had its object, not in the unity of God, but in Christ, His Death and Resurrection.

20. A third ground of support for this view of the uselessness of faith without works. The question may be referred to the interlocutor of the previous verses, or St James may speak again from this point in his own name.

wilt thou know? lit. dost thou wish to know? the question is best taken as expressing a correction, or perhaps to arrest attention, or introduce a new argument (cf. 2 Cor. viii. 1), at the same time perhaps intimating a certain perversity or reluctance on the part of the person addressed; on the part of the questioner the words express both confidence, 'dost thou wish for a decisive proof?' and at the same time indignation.

O vain man; in LXX the adjective is used of worthless persons, and of vain, worthless words; here of a man who makes great claims to the possession of faith and yet is void of all that follows from a true

faith, like the Latin *vanus.* The word is often taken as an equivalent of *Raca,* Matt. v. 22 (in the Syriac it is simply *debilis*), and if so it is a proof that the early Christians did not regard themselves bound to keep the Sermon on the Mount in the letter, whilst they would of course guard against the spirit of hatred.

O, sometimes of admonition, but more frequently of reproof.

that faith apart from works is barren? On 'apart from' see above, v. 18. *Barren,* lit. idle (without work), doing nothing[1]; and this meaning is most frequent in the N.T., but in 2 Pet. i. 8 the word is rendered 'barren' in A.V. It is often used of things from which no profit is derived, although they should be productive, cf. Wisd. xiv. 5 so here faith without works is described as unproductive. Possibly the word may have here the meaning of idle, i.e. shunning the work which it ought to perform. It is suggested that there may be a play on words, 'apart from works'—'without work' (von Soden).

It is also urged with much plausibility that James is not maintaining that an inoperative faith produces no works (for this would need no proof), but no salvation, and such a faith could not save, cf. v. 14, and thus in this sense he describes this 'faith' as barren.

Such a thought may well have been connected with the word, but primarily the context seems to connect it with deeds and actions.

21. The example first chosen was at once the most familiar and the most authoritative; Rom. iv. 1; Gal.

---

[1] This is the best supported reading. 'Dead' A.V. might easily have been introduced for conformity with 17 and 26.

Abraham our father justified by works, in that he offered

iii. 6; Heb. xi. 17; and especially in relation to the present passages, 1 Macc. ii. 52; Ecclus. xliv. 20; Wisd. x. 5; *Book of Jubilees*, xvii–xix.

Abraham our father. The title at least suggests that the readers were Jews; Introd. pp. xi., xii.; cf. Matt. iii. 9; *Sayings of the Jewish Fathers*, v. 4. 9, where the same title is thrice given to Abraham. The thought of Abraham as 'the father of believers' is specifically Pauline. The form of the question as given in the original would seem to indicate that an anti-Pauline polemic could not have been intended; if so, it would have been necessary to prove as against Rom. iv. that Abraham was justified by works, whereas here this is taken for granted even by opponents.

justified. The simplest plan is to consider this much discussed term in the light of the usage of the verb 'to justify' in the O.T. and other Jewish literature. This is the usage which, we may well believe, would have been present to the mind of a man like St James, and which would be likely to commend itself to the intelligence of his Jewish readers. Considered from this point of view it would seem that the word in the O.T., LXX, and Apocr. does not mean 'to *make* righteous,' any more than it does in classical usage, but to declare, or to show to be righteous. It may be further said to have a forensic or judicial sense in that it is used of declaring righteous by the recognition of a man's innocence or his absolution from guilt; cf. Deut. xxv. 1; 1 Kings viii. 32. The same force and meaning attach to the verb in other Jewish literature; cf. Wisdom vi. 10, 'they that keep holiness shall be judged holy,' i.e. shall

be regarded as holy; cf. also Exod. xxiii. 7; Ecclus. xiii. 22; xlii. 2 (2 Esdras iv. 18, xii. 7). In the *Psalms of Solomon* the verb frequently occurs, but with the meaning of 'to vindicate as just' the character of God; so too in 2 Esdras x. 16, *Apoc. Baruch*, lxxviii. 5 (cf. Ps. li. 4), the same application of the verb is found. The form of the verb in Greek might seem at first sight to require the meaning 'to make righteous,' as in the case of verbs of similar ending, 'to make blind,' 'to make golden.' But it is to be noticed that this *efficient* signification belongs to this class of verbs when they are derived from an adjective with a *physical* meaning, and not, as in the case before us, from an adjective with a *moral* meaning.

When we turn to the N.T. we find that the meaning of the verb is still determined to a large extent by its employment in the LXX. As instances we may take Matt. xii. 37, 'for by thy words thou shalt be justified and by thy words thou shalt be condemned' (cf. Deut. xxv. 1; 2 Chron. vi. 23); or Luke vii. 29, 'they justified God,' i.e. acknowledged, or declared God to be righteous; and for similar undoubted uses of the verb in the same sense as is advocated above we may instance Matt. xi. 19; Luke vii. 35, x. 29, xvi. 15, xviii. 14; Rom. ii. 13 (marg. R.V. 'accounted righteous'); 1 Tim. iii. 16 (the apparent exception in the use of the verb by T.R. in Rev. xxii. 11 is rectified in the proper reading). Whether St James has in view the future judgment, when sentence will be passed by God upon a man's conduct as a whole, or whether he views the two instances which he adduces in relation only to

22 up Isaac his son upon the altar ?   ¹Thou seest that faith

¹ Or, *Seest thou...perfect ?*

their immediate effect, the meaning of the verb is still the same; i.e. 'was not Abraham declared, or shown to be righteous?' (see further Hastings' *B. D.*, Art. 'Justification'; Sanday and Headlam, *Romans*, detached note on i. 17 ; and Beyschlag in Meyer's *Commentary* on the passage before us).

by works. The context confines the phrase to one specific act, but the plural is used as signifying the category which is here under consideration—'faith'...'works'; cf. for the construction Matt. xii. 37. Others take it as including those other works of faithful Abraham, which reached their highest point in the sacrifice of Isaac.

in that he offered up, causal participle; the word is used of presenting as a priestly act, cf. Isaiah lvii. 6; Heb. vii. 27, xiii. 15 ; 1 Pet. ii. 5 ; and sometimes with the words 'upon the altar' added, e.g. Gen. viii. 20 ; Lev. xiv. 20 ; 2 Chron. xxix. 27, etc. With the language here cf. Gen. xxii. 9. The word here employed for 'altar' is not found in classical writers, but it is used in LXX, Philo, Josephus. In the LXX it is characteristically the altar of God, although sometimes used of idol altars. For the word see Westcott, *Hebrews*, p. 453, and for the word for *offering up* cf. the same writer on Heb. vii. 27. The phrase here may mean simply to bring as an offering to the altar.

Isaac his son; Isaac named to show and to emphasise the greatness of the sacrifice. St James may here be following a current Jewish view contained in the remarkable passage 1 Macc. ii. 52, 'was not Abraham found faithful in temptation, and it was reckoned to him for righteousness?' as in Gen. xxii. nothing is said of the justification of Abraham, whilst in Gen. xv. 6 his belief in the Divine promise of a countless seed is reckoned for righteousness (see below on *v.* 23). But there are expressions in Gen. xxii., e.g. *vv.* 12, 16, 18, which may well be regarded as a 'justification' of Abraham before God, although as in the case of Rahab no verbal declaration of his being justified is needed (see below also in *v.* 23). Here again it has been well pointed out that the passage is evidently not concerned with justification as in Rom. iv. 5, where God is spoken of as justifying the ungodly by something which the man has not in himself, but with the simple pre-Pauline sense of the word, a declaration of what the man actually is : 'he that doeth righteousness is righteous.' Such usage is neither Pauline nor anti-Pauline; but rather stands outside any conscious relation to the teaching of St Paul. What St James is concerned to show is that the faith of Abraham is no mere barren profession, but an active principle, as against the perversions of the Rabbis and the religious externalism of the Pharisees.

22. *Thou seest*, R.V., better perhaps than a question as in marg. and A.V. Either reading makes good sense. If the question form is retained it is quite in accordance with the stirring lively manner of the whole paragraph. But if R.V. text is retained, the words form an answer to the preceding verse, and the positive assertion here and in *v.* 24 follows naturally upon the 'wilt thou

wrought with his works, and by works was faith made
23 perfect; and the scripture was fulfilled which saith, And

know?' of *v.* 20. This very plainly
shows that St James had no intention
of depreciating the faith of Abraham
which was testified to alike by Scripture and by tradition. Neither faith
nor works alone justified Abraham
but the cooperation of the two; this
is the point upon which St James
insists.

Thou seest that, R.V., not 'how' as
in A.V. It is not to the method as
A.V. might suggest but to the fact
of the cooperation that attention is
called.

wrought with, rather, 'was all
along cooperating with, imperf. tense,
'cooperabatur' Vulg. The verb occurs not only in the N.T. and LXX,
but in two instances in *Test. of the
xii. Patriarchs,* Iss. 3, Gad 4[1].

In *v.* 21 a belief without works was
characterised as 'idle,' i.e. doing no
work, because it could not save; so
here the thought is emphasised that
the belief of Abraham is not idle, inactive, but active for his justification
(in the original the two words *idle,
without works......wrought with,
worked with* are contrasted).

*and by works was faith made
perfect;* cf. i. 3, 15. It has well been
urged that on the one hand St James
cannot mean that the previously imperfect faith is perfected by works,
as by something added to it from
without, since faith is the motive of
works; nor on the other hand can
he mean that faith is already perfected before works, and merely
shows itself by works; but that since

Abraham's faith in God and his active
obedience went hand in hand, the
former was strengthened by each
new test to which it was exposed in
the exercise of the latter, until in
the final test of obedience in the
offering of Isaac, and in the endurance of that 'trial,' it attained
its due perfection (Beyschlag)[2].

23. *and the scripture was fulfilled;* cf. Gen. XV. 6, LXX. The *fulfilment*
lay in the fact that in Abraham's
offering up of Isaac there was the
supreme act of a faith, which had
at first been imperfect; cf. Gen. XV. 8,
'And he said, O Lord God, whereby
shall I know that I shall inherit it?'
This sacrifice of Isaac had apparently
been connected already in Jewish
thought with Gen. XV. 6, in 1 Macc.
ii. 52. St Paul in using the same
quotation in Rom. iv. 2 places it in
connection with the birth and not
with the sacrifice of Isaac, Rom. iv.
16–22, as in the original passage in
Genesis. St Paul also uses the same
passage in apparent contradiction to
St James, when he writes Rom. iv. 2,
'For if Abraham was justified by
works, he hath whereof to glory; but
not toward God.' But St James no
less than St Paul would have condemned 'a boasting' on the part of
those who claimed to be justified by
works, Rom. iv. 2, and St James no
less than St Paul would not have reckoned a faith for righteousness which
was the mere barren profession of
orthodoxy, in the way that the mere
citation of Gen. XV. 6 was apparently

---

[1] The other reading, in some MSS., the present tense, was probably introduced
for conformity with the present 'seest.'
[2] Bengel's words are to be noted, 'Abraham returned from the sacrifice much
more perfect in faith than he had approached it.'

Abraham believed God, and it was reckoned unto him for
24 righteousness ; and he was called the friend of God. Ye

often employed amongst the Jews,
but a faith in which a man waxed
strong and gave glory to God, being
fully assured that what He had promised He was able also to perform:
Rom. iv. 21; see also Introd. p. xlv.

believed God, not simply believed
that God existed, as a mere intellectual tenet; cf. *v.* 19 (Abraham's
faith led him not simply *credere
Deum* but *credere Deo*).

*and it was reckoned unto him for
righteousness.* The same phrase is
found in Psal. cvi. 31 of the zeal of
Phinehas, and also, as we have seen,
in 1 Macc. ii. 52 of the faithfulness of
Abraham under temptation; see also
the references to *Book of Jubilees*
below. The translation 'reckoned'
gives correctly the force of the verb
which is often used in LXX to express
what is equivalent to, having the like
force and weight as something mentioned. The word 'righteousness'
is used as it is used by our Lord in
the Sermon on the Mount, Matt. v.
20, and by St John, 1 John iii. 7.

St James may well have known
of the ten temptations of Abraham
which are mentioned in Jewish tradition (cf. Numb. xiv. 22), but it
cannot be said that such knowledge
is certainly intimated in our text,
although according to one list, and
that the most general, of these temptations the sacrifice of Isaac as the
supreme test stood tenth and last.

It is however worth noting that
twice in the *Book of Jubilees* Abraham is described as faithful, and of
an enduring spirit at the close of the
description of his ten temptations,
and that it is further said that he
was called, as a result of this proba-
tion, the friend of God (see ch. xvii.
and xix.), and was so designated on
the heavenly tablets. Further, in
this same *Book of Jubilees* (ch. xxx.),
Simeon and Levi are praised for
their slaughter of the Shechemites,
Gen. xxxiv., and of this action it is
said that 'it was reckoned to them
for righteousness,' and Levi is described as written, like Abraham, on
the heavenly tablets, as a righteous
man and a friend of God. If therefore Jewish tradition laid stress upon
the faith of Abraham (see above, and
Lightfoot, *Gal.* p. 162) there is also
evidence that it was not forgetful
of the actions of Abraham, and St
James might well say that Gen. xv.
6 was *fulfilled* in a faith which was
not merely a belief of the intellect, but
which worked by love, a faith made
perfect by the self-sacrifice of love in
obedience to a higher love; cf. 'with
ten temptations was Abraham our
father tempted, and he withstood
them all: to show *how great was
the love of Abraham our father*';
see *Sayings of the Jewish Fathers,*
v. 4.

and he was called, etc. The words
do not of course belong to the quotation, but they are added to the
argument, as if the speaker would
add 'and on this account he was
called,' etc. The verb translated
'called,' has sometimes been taken
to indicate here prestige, recognition
by others, as e.g. in Luke i. 32, 76.

the friend of God. The title is
not found in Genesis, either Heb. or
LXX, but in 2 Chron. xx. 7, Isaiah
xli. 8, and LXX of Dan. iii. 35 we
have a word, which is used to
denote a more intimate relationship than the ordinary word for
companion, translated by 'friend'
in A. and R.V. (Vulg. *amicus*), with
reference to Abraham's relationship

see that by works a man is justified, and not only by faith.

to God; in LXX 'thy beloved,' 2 Chron. xx. 7, Dan. *u.s.*; 'whom I loved,' Isaiah xli. 8.

But in Gen. xviii. 17, 'Shall I hide from Abraham?' etc., the LXX add after 'from Abraham' the words 'my son,' and this verse is quoted by Philo in one place as if it so ran. Yet in another place Philo in quoting the same passage has 'from Abraham my friend.' It would therefore seem likely that this latter title was a familiar one amongst Jews; cf. *Book of Jubilees*, xix. 9 (xxx. 20, 21), where Abraham is said to be inscribed in the heavenly tablets as a friend of God[1]. It is also plain that the title is to be explained as of one 'whom God loved,' not as one 'who loved God.' In Wisdom vii. 27 it is likely enough that the writer is using the expression 'friends of God' in the same manner as it is used by Plato, *Legg.* IV. 8, and other philosophers, and by Philo, *Frag.* ii. p. 652, where he writes that every wise man is a friend of God (cf. *Sayings of the Jewish Fathers*, vi. 1, where of the man busied in the Law it is said that 'he is called friend, beloved: loves God, loves mankind'). In Clem. Rom. the phrase is found twice, *Cor.* x. 1, xvii. 2, and once in Iren. *Adv. Haer.* iv. 16. 2, where in each place the reference is probably to this passage in St James; Jerome also, on Judith viii. 22, uses the same expression of Abraham, how he was made the friend of God. The familiar use of this same title in the East has often been commented on, and a striking instance of its employment is given by Dean Stanley in connection with the visit of the present King, Edward VII, then Prince of

Wales, to the Shrine of Abraham, *Jewish Church*, I. 430.

A valuable note on 'The Friend of God' by the German writer Dr Nestle will be found in the *Expository Times*, Oct. 1903.

24. *Ye see that by works a man is justified;* 'ye see,' best taken as indic. (and not imper. or interrogative), as affirming a conclusion from the previous argument; the plural is used because no longer is any 'vain man' addressed as an opponent, but the Christian brethren.

If the exact phrases 'to be justified by works' or 'by faith' are not found previous to St James and St Paul, yet there are passages in Jewish or Jewish-Christian literature which may suggest that such language was in use. With regard to the doctrine of justification by works, a notable passage meets us in *The Testament of Abraham*, xiii.: 'After death the archangel tests men's works by fire, and if the fire burns up a man's work, the angel of judgment carries him away to the place of sinners; but if the fire does not touch his work, then he is justified, and the angel of righteousness carries him to be saved in the lot of the just.' So too in a remarkable passage in 2 Esdras ix. 7, a passage possibly dating some quarter of a century or so before the birth of Christ, we find that a man is described as able to be saved 'by his works or by the faith with which he believed' (although elsewhere, xiii. 7, salvation appears to depend on works and faith combined). And in the *Apocalypse of Baruch*, representing the standpoint of orthodox Judaism in the first

---

[1] The words 'my friend' or 'thy friend' (i.e. God's) occur again and again in the Jewish-Christian *Testament of Abraham*.

25 And in like manner was not also Rahab the harlot justified

century of our era, the righteous are represented as saved by their works, li. 7, as justified by the law, li. 3, and righteousness is described as 'by the law,' lxvii. 6[1].

But with this close connection between works and the righteousness of the law, which is so characteristic of *Baruch*, it may be justly held that St Paul would be at home, whilst on the other hand St James, although no doubt familiar with the teaching, seems to have had something much more simple in mind. He is not thinking of the works of the law as such; in other words he is not writing 'in the interests of Judaism but of morality'; and St Paul no less than St James could speak of a 'faith working through love,' Gal. v. 6; 'these words bridge over the gulf,' writes Bishop Lightfoot, 'which seems to separate the language of St Paul and St James. Both assert a principle of practical energy, as opposed to a barren inactive theory' (cf. also St Paul's language, Rom. ii. 13 and 17 ff.).

is justified (cf. *v.* 21), i.e. is declared or accounted righteous.

and not only by faith, R.V. The stress is on the word 'only.' St James by no means denies the value of faith, as we have seen throughout, nor could he with Gen. xv. 6 before him have refused to recognise it; nor does he deny that faith contributes to justification; but it must be a right faith, not a faith apart from works, but a faith combined with works, as in 2 Esdras xiii. 23, 'God will guard those who have works and faith in the Most Mighty.'

Nor is there any contradiction between this passage and Rom. iii. 28 for St James is speaking here of works, and not of 'works of the law' as St Paul there; St James is considering faith as concerned with the recognition or practical denial of one God, St Paul is considering it as the highest motive-principle of the spiritual life[2].

25. *And in like manner*, R.V. Not contrasting the second example with that of Abraham, but showing that equally in this case justification was the result of works and not only of faith. The further connecting 'also' indicates an advance in the argument by the production of a still more decisive proof; cf. *v.* 21.

Rahab the harlot. There is no occasion to take the word in other than its ordinary sense, although not only Josephus, *Ant.* v. 1. 2, 7, describes her as an inn-keeper, but St Chrysostom and other writers, as e.g. Grotius, have tried to give a milder interpretation to the word (Lightfoot, *Clement of Rome*, App. p. 413).

Not only is a woman named belonging to an alien race, but a weak and erring woman (*mulieris criminosae, mulieris alienigenae*, Bede; see also Ambrose on Psalm xxxvii. 3). And although the same law prevailed in her case as in Abraham's, viz. that of justification by works, yet St James may well have chosen her, both as a woman and as an alien, as affording the most telling illustration of the breadth of the law in question. No doubt in Jewish tradition Rahab was highly celebrated. She was one

---

[1] *Apocalypse of Baruch*, lxx., lxxxi., and pp. 26, 31, edit. Dr Charles.
[2] Cf. Dr Charles, *u.s.* p. 26, and Lightfoot, *Galatians*, p. 164, on 'The faith of Abraham.'

by works, in that she received the messengers, and sent

of the four great beauties, classed
with Sarah, Abigail, Esther; according to one tradition she became the
wife of Joshua, according to another
the ancestress of eight prophets and
ten priests, Huldah the prophetess
being ranked amongst her descend-
ants, *Megillah*, 6. 14. 1. Moreover,
the incident referred to here by
St James had a place also in Jewish
literature, as e.g. where Rahab prays
for forgiveness for three sins because
she can name three good works, in
that she had let down the spies at
her own risk by a *cord* through the
window, on the *wall*, *Mechilta* on
Exod. xviii. 1. All this may fairly
help to show that St James might
easily have selected a person so
celebrated, and there is certainly
no need to suppose that the writer
of our Epistle must have borrowed from Heb. xi. 31. In this
latter passage she is also described
as 'Rahab the harlot,' and as there
the title seems to magnify the
triumph of faith, so here the addition magnifies its working by
marking the distance between a
sinful woman and the father of the
faithful. It is not therefore necessary to suppose that St James has
chosen Rahab to be an illustration
for Gentile Christians, who might
possibly read his circular letter,
while Abraham is chosen as an
illustration appealing to Jewish
Christians. In his selection of this
particular illustration it is quite
possible that we may see an indication of the Jewish and Rabbinical
training of the writer, who thus like
the Jewish doctors introduces the
name of a famous woman to show
that the woman shared in the same
conditions as those required from

the man; Philo, e.g., mentions in
connection with Abraham the strange
illustration of Tamar as also striving
after nobility (*De nobilitate*, p. 108 E).

justified by works, i.e. shown to
be righteous; see above on *v.* 21.
Rahab appealed to her 'works,'
Joshua ii. 12, and the force of her
appeal was recognised, Joshua vi.
17, 25; so Josephus, *Ant.* v. 1. 7,
refers Rahab's safety to her good
deed. She too had heard of 'the
works of the Lord,' Josh. ii. 9–11,
and this hearing was no mere acquiescence that such a powerful God
existed, cf. *v.* 19 above, but begat
a faith and a conviction (cf. Heb. xi.
31) that He was God in heaven
above and on earth beneath, and
that what He had promised to do
He would also perform; like Abraham Rahab too 'believed God,' and
there is no contradiction when
Heb. xi. 31 refers the same action
as is mentioned here to Rahab's
faith, for it is said that by faith she
'perished not with them that were
disobedient,' i.e. her faith prompted
her to right action, to an obedient
recognition of the claims of God.
Moreover, in the passage before us,
v. 26 would imply that faith also
was present in Rahab, and that that
faith was not inactive. It is interesting to note how Rahab's faith in
the God of Israel led to the mercy
and kindness towards her neighbours
upon which St James has so insisted;
cf. ii. 13, iii. 17, and LXX, Josh. ii.
12, 14.

in that she received the mes-
sengers. The verb is only used elsewhere in the N.T. by St Luke, and
in each case as here with the idea of
receiving as a guest: cf. Luke x. 38,
xix. 6; Acts xvii. 7; cf. LXX, Tob. vii.

26 them out another way?   For as the body apart from the
    spirit is dead, even so faith apart from works is dead.

8; Judith xiii. 13. It is sometimes
held that the idea of receiving
secretly is contained in the word,
but it is not necessarily so, although
it might be implied from the circumstances as here; in Heb. xi. 31
the simple verb is employed in the
sense of receiving. In Heb. xi. 31
the messengers are called spies as in
Josh. ii. 1, and in two or three MSS.
and Versions of St James they are
so called, but evidently the alteration has been made to accord with
the other passages named.

sent them; rather 'thrust them
out,' signifying the hastiness of the
act: cf. John ii. 15; Acts ix. 40,
xvi. 37. The word may also be
introduced not only to portray the
action with characteristic vividness,
but the zeal of Rahab and the
danger connected with it. But it
is of course quite possible that the
verb may be used with the same
simple significance as in Mark v. 40;
Matt. ix. 25.

another way, i.e. than that by
which they had come, where danger
lay, Josh. ii. 15, 16, 22.

26. *For as the body apart from
the spirit.* On the rendering 'apart'
see ii. 18, 20 above. The comparison
at first seems strange, as one would
have expected that the comparison
would be inverted and that works
would correspond to the body and
faith to the spirit (cf. Heb. ix. 14,
where we read of 'dead works').
But St James is combating the faith
which was a mere profession, a mere
external thing; and this could only
be moved and quickened into something better by works, which might

here be fairly identified with the
animating principle, the love from
which they sprang. Others have suggested that 'spirit' should be translated 'breath,' as if the words meant
that as a body is dead without any
animating breath, so is faith which
does not pass into action. But
though the word is so used in
Gen. vi. 17, Psalm cxlvi. 4, etc., it is
maintained that its N.T. usage would
not altogether warrant this interpretation (cf. however 2 Thess. ii. 8;
Rev. xiii. 15); on the other hand,
St James does not use the word
elsewhere, and we must also remember his familiarity with O.T.
phraseology. Still more recently a
word signifying 'movement' has
been suggested as a conjectural
reading instead of 'spirit,' but even
if such a reading could be supported,
the sense would not be improved,
for a body 'without movement' is
not necessarily dead, since it might
be asleep or benumbed.

Perhaps, however, it is better on
the whole not to press the particular
members of the comparison, as if
the writer compared body and faith
on the one hand with spirit and
works on the other, but the relation
which exists between body and spirit
is compared with that between faith
and works; if body and spirit are
separated death results, and so if
faith is separated from works it has
no life, it is 'dead in itself.' The
particle 'for' at the beginning of the
verse is retained by R.V. as in A.V.,
but omitted by W.H. The abruptness of its omission would be quite
characteristic of the writer.

CHAPTER III.

1, 2. Another evil characteristic of the Judaism of his day and against which St James warns his brother Christians is the desire to become teachers, without facing with any seriousness the tremendous responsibilities involved. In many things all err, but in nothing more than in speech; to be free from error in this respect would be a test of perfection and a mastery of self. **3—6.** As the horse is controlled by the little bridle in his mouth, as the great ships are turned by a small rudder, so the man who has command of his tongue controls, it is true, a little member, but one which is strong enough to affect his whole nature. Like a spark which inflames a whole forest, so the tongue can set on fire the whole round of human life; amongst our members it constitutes as it were a world of unrighteousness, set on fire by Gehenna. **7—12.** Every kind of animal man has been able to tame, but the tongue is untameable, a restless evil full of deadly poison. And yet with this same tongue we bless God, and we curse men made in the image of God; herein is a grave moral inconsistency, and nature rebukes it on every side; can a vine yield figs? like root like fruit. **13, 14.** If you would be teachers be wise, and the proof of true wisdom, like the proof of true 'religion,' is found in a man's conduct, and in each case meekness is required; for with bitter jealousy and faction in the heart, a man is not helping the truth but is exalting himself. **15, 16.** This means a false wisdom, a wisdom of the flesh, of the world, of the devil, from below, not from above; and this envying and strife issue in confusion and every vile deed. **17, 18.** Contrast with this pretentious wisdom the true wisdom of God; it is first of all pure, because its own object is God, not the gratification of passion and wrath, and so it is peaceable, gently reasonable, persuasive, winning its way because of mercy and good works, without partiality in its favours, with singleness of motive and aim; and those who thus sow in peace, those who possessing the true wisdom make for peace, will have as their reward a harvest of righteousness.

III. Be not many teachers, my brethren, knowing that we

III. 1. *Be not many teachers,* R.V., i.e. Rabbis. A.V. 'masters,' which formerly = teachers (cf. Mal. ii. 12); cf. Hastings' *D.B.,* 'Master.' 'Do not become many (of you) teachers' is perhaps best. The excessive eagerness to gain the office of teacher or rather Rabbi may be connected with the same excessive estimation of mere external orthodoxy above moral practice. In i. 19, 26, the danger had been referred to, and the author now proceeds to enlarge upon it in estimating the various sins which

threatened the common life of the Christian brotherhood. Perhaps it may be fairly said that nowhere was the separation of faith and works likely to be more frequent or more offensive than in that arising from vain and empty speech on the part of men who, while claiming to be instructors of the foolish, 'say and do not.' It should also be borne in mind that the writer had just been speaking of some glaring evils connected with the religious life of the 'assembly,' ii. 2, and it is therefore

2 shall receive ¹heavier judgement.   For in many things we

¹ Gr. *greater.*

reasonable to suppose that the discussion of a further and a kindred evil would follow, an evil rife in the Jewish synagogues, the eagerness to be called of men Rabbi. If we regard them from this point of view the words may become a testimony to the early date of the Epistle, and to the likelihood that the writer not only had Jewish-Christians in mind, but also our Lord's words in Matt. xxiii. 8, or some similar warning. Jewish literature itself contains passages in which, whilst the excessive honour paid to the Rabbi is recorded, there is also evidence that the warning of St James was not out of place: the fear of the Rabbi was sometimes placed on a level with the fear of God; the scholar who controverts his Rab is as if he controverted the Shekinah; he who engages in strife with his Rab is as if he engaged in strife with the Shekinah; but Abtalion said, 'Ye wise, be guarded in your words; perchance ye may incur the debt of exile, and be exiled to the place of evil waters; and the disciples that come after you may drink and die, and the Name of Heaven be profaned' (*Sayings of the Jewish Fathers,* Dr Taylor, cf. pp. 14, 19, and 71)¹. The picture of the ideal representative of the study of wisdom is drawn for us in Ecclus. xxxix. 1–11, and the honour with which such study was rewarded: cf. *Testaments of the xii. Patriarchs,* Levi 13,

where the man who teaches and practises wisdom is described as a sharer in the throne of the king. 'Teachers' are mentioned early in the Church, and the title may have passed into it from its earlier Jewish use: cf. Acts xiii. 1; 1 Cor. xii. 28; Eph. iv. 11; *Didache,* xiii. 2, xv. 1.

we shall receive heavier judgement, R.V., and in A.V. marg. 'judgment.' The word translated 'judgment' is in itself a neutral word, but it is used for the most part in the N.T. to express an adverse judgment: cf. Mark xii. 40; Luke xx. 47. In these two passages in the Gospels the form of the phrase is very similar to that employed here by St James, and we may have again as it were an echo in the Epistle of our Lord's words. There is of course no need to find here any more than in Rom. xiii. 2, or in 1 Cor. xi. 29, any reference to eternal punishment. The graver the responsibility as a teacher, the heavier the judgment incurred before God, i.e. in comparison with those who were only hearers². Although St James associates himself with other teachers as one of themselves, and although his exhortation is marked by the affectionate recollection that he was writing to his brethren, yet the severer aspect of the subject is not forgotten, and here as in ii. 12, 13, v. 9, 12, the sterner issues of judgment follow upon failure in duty. In this verse the Vulgate apparently

¹ See further Edersheim, *Jewish Social Life,* pp. 127, 137, for the high estimation in which both Rabbis and teachers in schools were regarded, and Weber, *Jüdische Theologie,* pp. 125 ff.

² The *Century Bible* (Bennett) refers to Portia's words, 'I can easier teach twenty what were good to be done, than be one of the twenty to follow mine own teaching,' *Merchant of Venice,* Act i. 2.

all stumble. If any stumbleth not in word, the same is
3 **a perfect man, able to bridle the whole body also. Now if**
we put the horses' bridles into their mouths, that they may

as an emendation reads the second person instead of the first person plural.

2. *For in many things we all stumble*, R.V.; cf. ii. 10. The verb has sometimes been taken to denote the lesser sins, the weaknesses of daily life, since the Apostle in his humility of mind does not hesitate to acknowledge such offences in himself. But it is not necessary to press this, and we have here probably a truth witnessed to not only in heathen literature, but in the O.T. and other Jewish writings : cf. 1 Kings viii. 46 ; Prov. x. 19, xx. 9 ; Eccles. v. 1, vii. 20. Reference may be further made to such passages as 2 Esdras viii. 35, 'For in truth there is no man among them that be born but he hath dealt wickedly.' Taking the words thus generally, the writer means that as in any case we are guilty of so many stumbles it is specially inadvisable to strive ambitiously to enter upon such a province as that of teaching, in which it was most of all difficult to keep free from guilt. That the Jews were themselves aware of this danger is plainly seen : 'Simeon his son (i.e. of Gamaliel I.) said, All my days I have grown up amongst the wise and have not found ought good for a man but silence ; not learning but doing is the groundwork ; and whoso multiplies words occasions sin.' So too R. Akiba could write 'a fence to wisdom is silence,' *Sayings of the Jewish Fathers*, i. 17, and iii. 20.

If any stumbleth not in word, i.e. not only the word of teaching and exhortation, but in the sense of i. 19 ; cf. *vv.* 9, 10, of speech in general. In Ecclus. xix. 16 we read 'and who is he that hath not sinned with his tongue ?'

a perfect man. See note on i. 4. The same word was used of Abraham, *Book of Jubilees*, xxiii. 10 ; of Noah, Gen. vi. 9, vii. 1, Ecclus. xliv. 17, where he is called 'perfect and righteous'; of Moses, Philo, *Leg. Alleg.* i. 23 (Mang. I. 83). Here the man may be described as perfect inasmuch as he has accomplished the most difficult moral task. Bishop Westcott after pointing out that the full-grown man is 'perfect' as compared with the child, the disciplined Christian is 'perfect' as compared with the uninstructed convert, adds that 'there is also an ideal completeness answering to man's constitution in his power of self-control, James iii. 2, in his love for his fellows, Matt. v. 48,' *Hebrews*, p. 135.

able to bridle the whole body also. See i. 26. The verb suggests the succeeding comparison, quite in the author's characteristic manner; *able* etc. because he who has accomplished the most difficult task can accomplish all others, i.e. can bridle all other members of his body since he has bridled his tongue; cf. *v.* 6, where the tongue is mentioned 'among our members.' Other interpretations, which would regard the words 'the whole body' as=*tota vita*, the whole life, or=the company of believers, are quite beside the mark.

3. *Now if we put......obey us*, etc. In R.V. these words mark the protasis, and then follows the apodosis *we turn about......also* : 'if we put the bridle into the horses' mouths to make them obey us, by so doing we

4 obey us, we turn about their whole body also. Behold, the
ships also, though they are so great, and are driven by
rough winds, are yet turned about by a very small rudder,

obtain the obedience not of their
head only, but of their whole body;
in the same manner, he who can rule
his tongue can rule his whole self.'
In some such way as this the meaning
of the writer may be fairly expressed,
and there is no need to make the
whole verse into the protasis and
then to suppose an aposiopesis (i.e.
a breaking off of the sentence as in
Luke xix. 42; Mark vii. 11; Acts
xxiii. 9), as if the writer would say
'now if......and so rule their whole
body'—so we must also do the same,
i.e. place a bridle upon our tongues
and so morally control our whole
body. Such an aposiopesis does not
seem at all natural, and the instances
cited above are certainly not similar
to the supposed instance in the
passage under consideration. The
reading of A.V.(with which cf. *vv.* 4, 5)
undoubtedly makes very good sense,
'Behold, in horses we use the bit for
the purpose of making them obey,
and thus control their whole body,'
but not only MS. authority but also
its difficulty would seem to decide
for the reading in R.V.[1]

the horses' bridles, etc., R.V. This
rendering follows the connection of
the Greek words, but in all other
E.V. we have 'the horses' mouths':
cf. Psalm xxxii. 9, 'bridles'; in A.V.
'bits' (Vulg. *frena*). R.V. is more
natural as taking up the word of the
preceding verse 'to bridle.' The
noun rendered 'bridle' is used especially for the bit of a bridle, but
sometimes also for a bridle or rein.

A very similar phrase to that here
used occurs in Aelian, *Var. Hist.*
IX. 16, and for the thought see further
next verse, and cf. Soph. *Antig.* 483.

Philo speaks of the easy way in
which the horse, the most spirited of
animals, is led when bridled, *De
Mundi Opif.* p. 19 E.

4. *Behold.* The word perhaps
marks little more than a vivid transition, but its frequent use in this
short Epistle (cf. *v.* 6, v. 4, 7, 9, 11)
is characteristic of a Hebrew writer
familiar with the O.T., where a word
of the same meaning so often commences a sentence.

also, or perhaps 'even.' It is
simpler perhaps to regard this verse
as continuing the thought, and not
introducing a fresh comparison, although it is sometimes maintained
that in *v.* 3 the writer by the imagery
of the bridle in the mouth points to
the tongue as the member which the
teacher ought to control, whilst here
and in *vv.* 5, 6, he points rather to
the terribly destructive power of the
tongue, and to the destructive might
of the small over the great.

so great, opposed to 'a very small
rudder.' For the general imagery
cf. *Enoch,* ci. 4, 'And see ye not the
sailors of the ships, how their ships
are tossed to and fro by the waves,
and are shaken by the winds, and
are in sore trouble?'

rough winds, R.V.; 'fierce,' A.V.,
so Tynd. (seems applicable rather to
persons and as if the word had an
ethical meaning). Vulg. has *validi,*

---

[1] In this verse the reading of A.V. is strongly supported by Mayor, but R.V.
can refer to W.H., and amongst recent commentators to von Soden and
Beyschlag.

5 whither the impulse of the steersman willeth. So the

'strong winds.' For the adj. as applied to winds parallels may be found in Aelian, *De Animal.* v. 13, IX. 14, and possibly in LXX, Prov. xxvii. 16, but the meaning there is doubtful. The difficulty of 'turning about' the ships is thus indicated by their greatness and by the kind of winds necessary to turn them; and so the might of the small rudder is doubly emphasised.

are yet turned about. St James in his characteristic manner takes up the same verb as he used in *v.* 3; cf. i. 13, 14, ii. 14, 16, 21, 25.

rudder, R.V., and so generally here. In A.V. 'helm,' so Tynd., but in Acts xxvii. 40 'rudder' as here. The helm, although properly only the handle of the rudder, was often used as in poetry for the whole.

the impulse of the steersman. The word translated 'impulse' is often found in classical Greek of the impulse or eagerness to do a thing, so too in Stoic phraseology of the movements of the mind. Probably in the only other passage in which the word occurs in the N.T., Acts xiv. 5, it should be similarly taken of impulse or eagerness to assault, not of the assault itself, as it is clear that this did not actually take place. So here it signifies the desire or eagerness of the steersman. Others however would take it of something external, of the pressure of the hand on the tiller, on the ground that it is only by this external pressure that the steersman actually 'turns about' the ship. For the former meaning see especially Trench, *Synonyms*, II. p. 162. In A.V. the word is altogether omitted. It is possible to take the word 'impulse' as referring both to the external and internal (as Corn.

à Lapide appears to have taken it).

the steersman, R.V.; in A.V. with Genev., so Tynd., Cranm., Rhem., 'governor,' which meant in its primary sense the pilot or steersman of a ship. In the two passages where 'rudder' occurs Wycl. has 'governayle.'

In the original the word for 'steersman' is not the word used specially for the professional steersman, but simply a participle 'he who directs,' indicating that anyone who has command of the rudder can influence the movement of the ship. So in Philo the same verb is used of directing a ship.

With regard to the imagery of the verse, the two figures of the horse and the ship and of their control by the bit and the helm are found closely combined by Philo, *De Agricult.* 15 (Mang. I. 311); so too in *Flaccum*, 5 (Mang. II. 521); cf. passage in Soph. above, *Antig.* 332ff.; Plutarch *De Poet. aud.* p. 33; and Theoph. Simoc. *Ep.* 70. In the last-named passage the bridle and whip in the one comparison, and the sail and anchor in the other, are likened to the means taken to direct the tongue by speech or by silence.

In this connection reference may be made to a passage in Arist. *Quaest. mech.* 5, wherein the writer speaks of the rudder, which is small but has such great power that by its little helm and by the gentle pressure of one man the great bulk of the ship can be moved (cf. Lucret. IV. 899).

5. The tongue is a small member, the rudder is a very small part of the ship, but as the latter controls the whole vessel, so the tongue though small can control the whole nature of the man. The epithet 'little'

tongue also is a little member, and boasteth great things.
Behold, ¹how much wood is kindled by how small a fire !
6 And the tongue is ²a fire : ³the world of iniquity among

---

¹ Or, *how great a forest
is among our members that which &c.
is among our members that which &c.*

² Or, *a fire, that world of iniquity : the tongue*

³ Or, *that world of iniquity, the tongue,*

---

refers back to the preceding 'very small rudder.'

boasteth great things; not meant to express an empty boast, as the whole passage is intended to emphasise the reality of the power possessed by the tongue. The tongue though 'little' boasteth 'great' things —the contrast is again marked. If the expression is read as two words in the original, as in R.V. and W.H., the verb is only found here in the N.T. It does not occur at all in the LXX. But as one word it is found four times in the LXX, of haughtiness of character and bearing; cf. Psalms xii. 3, lxxiii. 8, 9.

how much wood is kindled by how small a fire! R.V. text. This rendering, or the marg. *how great a forest* etc., gives a better and clearer meaning to the original word than 'matter,' A.V., for the latter term as probably used here by our translators must be regarded as archaic. Bacon advises to 'take away the *matter*' of seditions, 'for if there be *fuell* prepared, it is hard to tell whence the spark shall come that shall set it on fire,' *Essay* 15 (Skeat, 'Glossary of Bible Words'); in Ecclus. xxviii. 10 the word 'matter' is similarly used, 'as the matter (i.e. fuel) of the fire is, so it burneth,' A.V., although it is of course possible that the word may be used to denote materials of any kind (cf. the Latin *materia* which primarily = timber). The rendering 'matter' is also liable to be mistaken for one of the deri-

vative meanings of the original Greek word, viz. the subject-matter of an argument or discussion. On the whole it seems best to retain the primary sense of the original noun and to translate it 'forest' with R.V. marg. The vivid and graphic imagery of the fire consuming the forest is quite characteristic of St James, and it may have been suggested by such passages as Psal. lxxxii. 14 ; Isaiah ix. 18, x. 16–18 ; Zech. xii. 6 (cf. also *Psalms of Sol.* xii. 2 ; *Apoc. of Baruch,* xxxvi. 10, xxxvii.). The contrast between the smallness of a spark and the greatness of the conflagration which it caused was common both in Jewish literature (cf. its use in Philo) and in classical, both Greek and Latin : cf. e.g. Phokylides, 144, 'from a spark a vast wood is set on fire.' According to the reading adopted both by R.V. and W.H. the same word is rendered in this verse in two different ways, 'how great,' 'how small,' but the change in meaning is determined by the context, and, like the Latin word *quantus,* the Greek word may have both meanings. The Vulg. translates 'how great' in each place, but the verb 'kindles' shows that the smallness of the fire in its beginning is referred to, and not the greatness of it in its ultimate spread.

6. The two punctuations should be carefully noted. If we render 'the tongue is a fire, a (that) world of iniquity,' so A.V. and R.V. marg., the expression 'world of iniquity'

may be taken to mean the sum total of iniquity. The passage often quoted in support of this explanation, Prov. xvii. 6, is however of doubtful meaning, although it is remarkable that the expression 'the whole world of wealth' is found with the mention of sins of speech in the immediate context. A clearer parallel may be found in the use in Latin of such words as *mare*, *oceanus*, to express the totality of anything. If we adopt the punctuation of R.V. and W.H. we may render 'the tongue is a fire: the world of iniquity among our members is the tongue,' etc., i.e. among our members, in our microcosm, the tongue represents, or constitutes, the unrighteous world, just as in Luke xvi. 9 we have 'the mammon of unrighteousness' = the unrighteous mammon; and the tongue may well be called 'a world of iniquity,' because it defiles 'the whole body.' If the words are thus explained there does not seem to be any force in the objection that a confusion of metaphors is introduced, inasmuch as there is no world among our members! Moreover, this interpretation would be quite in accordance with the language of St James elsewhere. He tells us here that the tongue, the world of iniquity, 'defiles' the whole body; so in i. 27, 'the world' (the same word in the Greek, cf. iv. 4) is represented as that which 'defiles' a man[1].

An attempt has been made, both in ancient and modern times, to render the word 'world' by another

meaning which sometimes attaches to it, viz. ornament, embellishment; as if the tongue decked out iniquity by its words, and so concealed the real grossness of evil. But in the passage which is often cited for this rendering, 1 Pet. iii. 3, 4, the context supports it, whilst here it cannot be said to do so with the same clearness, and the usage of St James elsewhere (cf. i. 27, iv. 4) points to the meaning adopted both in A. and R.V. Grammatically the word when rendered 'adornment' never expresses that which adorns in an active sense (the meaning required here) but rather that by which a person or thing is adorned[2].

In Jewish literature as indeed in most literatures, the tongue and its words were often likened to a fire, Psalm cxx. 4; Prov. xvi. 27; Ecclus. xxviii. 10–15, 21–23. There is also a striking passage in *Psalms of Solomon*, xii. 2–4 (Ryle and James's trans.): 'The words of the tongue of the evil man are for the accomplishment of frowardness: even as fire in a threshing-floor that burneth up the straw thereof, so is his sojourning among men: that he may set fire to houses with his lying tongue, and cut down the trees of gladness with the flame of his wicked tongue, and put to confusion the houses of the wicked by kindling strife with slanderous lips.' And in a Rabbinical passage, cited amongst others by Spitta, from *Midr. Vayyikra* r. par. 16, we have a very close likeness to the words of St

---

[1] The Syriac Version renders 'the tongue is the fire, the world of iniquity is as the wood,' the forest which the fire consumes; but this is quite inconsistent with the general thought of the passage.

[2] For an able defence of this rendering, which is that of Oecumenius and Wetstein amongst others, see Carr, 'Cambridge Greek Test.' *in loco*. Other commentators, amongst whom Spitta may be mentioned, would dismiss 'the tongue is a fire' etc. as not genuine, but there is no tenable ground for this arbitrary omission of the words.

our members is the tongue, which defileth the whole
body, and setteth on fire the wheel of [1]nature, and is set on

[1] Or, *birth*

James, 'what mighty fires the tongue
kindles!'

is a fire; better perhaps 'maketh
itself a fire'; it was not so 'made'
by God; cf. iv. 4, where the same
verb occurs in the original.

the wheel of nature. If we could
take the word rendered 'nature' in
the sense of 'birth' (cf. i. 23), we might
render 'the wheel of human origin,'
which as soon as men are born begins
to run, i.e. the course of human life;
so apparently R.V. marg., and from
this point of view parallels to the
words of St James have been found
in Greek and Latin literature. Thus
Anacreon, IV. 7, speaks of life rolling
on like the wheel of a chariot, and
Silius Italicus, VI. 120, describes the
wheel of life rolling down the steep
descent. It is not therefore surprising that in what has been called the
earliest extant commentary on this
verse of St James, Isidore of Pelu-
sium, ii. 158, should explain the
words before us of the temporal
course of life which is likened by
St James to a wheel because like a
wheel it revolves in a circle. So again
elsewhere, iv. 1, in commenting on
the same expression, Isidore remarks
that the shape of a circle, of a crown,
of a wheel is the same, and the Scripture speaks in one place of the crown
of the year, and in another passage
of the wheel of life. Others however
would interpret the words of the
endless succession of men as they
are born one after another, an interpretation similar to that of the Syriac
which renders 'the succession of our
generations, which runs as a wheel.'
But this explanation appears to be
foreign to the context in which the

writer speaks of 'the whole body'
as if he had in mind not so much
generations as the individual life.
Another explanation which is perhaps more worthy of consideration
would take the words of the circle
of creation, the orb or totality of
creation; cf. Gen. ii. 4; Wisd. i. 14,
xiii. 3, 5; and also Plato, *Tim.* 29,
where the word is apparently used
of all created things. This rendering
may receive support from the possible translation of the same word
in i. 23, 'the face wherewith he was
created,' and also from the context
here, as in the connecting particle
'for' the writer takes up as it were
the details of creation, arguing that
all are tameable except the tongue.
But, as was pointed out above, the
context seems to be concerned, not
with the details of creation, but
rather with the sphere of the individual human life. Moreover, the
word under discussion need not be
confined in meaning to the inanimate creation, as it is undoubtedly
used in a more general sense. Thus
in Plato, *Rep.* VIII. 525 B, the same
word is used when the philosopher
is bidden to rise above the changing,
and to cling to that which is real.
In Philo the word is of frequent
occurrence, sometimes no doubt as
meaning the creation, but sometimes
as expressing human existence in
general. So in Wisd. vii. 5, the same
word is used of 'life' in general, and
in Judith xii. 18 of the entire life.
With these considerations before us,
the word 'wheel' in this connection
may be used to emphasise the in-
cessantly changing nature of this
human existence, the metaphor be-

7 fire by hell. For every [1]kind of beasts and birds, of creep-

[1] Gr. *nature*.

ing taken from the thought of a wheel in motion; or reference may be made merely to the shape of a wheel at rest, as denoting the circle, the sphere of human life; the tongue would then represent the axle, from which as from a central fire the whole wheel is set in a blaze. But it is perhaps allowable to combine the two thoughts, and to regard human existence with all its constant movement as compared to a revolving wheel set on fire from the axle, i.e. by the tongue[1].

It seems quite fanciful to see in the phrases before us a knowledge of, or a reference to, the Orphic mysteries, and to Orphic views of metempsychosis. The whole context is against any such notion, and it is impossible to trace any connection between the Orphic doctrines and the destroying power of the tongue. Both words were in use in Jewish literature. It has been recently suggested, *Century Bible, in loco,* that the phrase 'the wheel of nature' may possibly be an awkward attempt of St James to represent in Greek some Aramaic phrase for 'natural impulses' or 'passions,' but in view of the use of the words as traced above, it hardly seems necessary to fall back upon this supposition.

setteth on fire...and is set on fire. In each case the *present* participle is used in the original, as of perpetual action. We may note again the characteristic of St James in taking up as it were and repeating the same word. The verb is found only here in the N.T. but it occurs in Exod. ix. 24; Ps. xcvii. 3; Ecclus. iii. 30; 1 Macc. iii. 5; and similarly in classical writers. The word is also used in *Psalms of Solomon,* xii. 3, of the flame of a wicked tongue.

by hell, i.e. by Gehenna; only here outside the Gospels in the N.T. The word and the thought mark a Jewish writer. In Ecclus. xxviii. 10 ff., often referred to in connection with the present passage, and in which the same two similes of fire and water are found in relation to disputes, we read, *v.* 23, 'Such as forsake the Lord shall fall into it (the flame), and it shall burn in them, and not be quenched.' And if we entertain some of the suspicions which have sometimes been raised against this part of the verse in Ecclus., as by Dr Edersheim in the *Speaker's Commentary,* reference may be made to the language of Isaiah lxvi. 24, concerning the unquenchable fire of Gehenna, and to the language of *Psalms of Solomon,* xii. 5, 'let the slanderous tongue perish from among the saints in flaming fire.'

In Ecclus. xxviii. 13 the Syriac has 'Also the third tongue let it be cursed, for it has laid low many corpses,' and Dr Edersheim, in commenting on the verse, points out that the expression 'the third tongue' is of post-Biblical Jewish usage, and that its designation is expressed by

---

[1] It should be noted that in the original the same word may be rendered either *course* or *wheel* according as the accent is placed on the first or second syllable. In the present case there can be no doubt as to the predominance of authorities in favour of the second rendering, but sometimes the two renderings run into one another, as in the former part of the above comment.

ing things and things in the sea, is tamed, and hath been

this, that it kills three, the person who speaks the calumny, the person who listens to it, and the person concerning whom it is spoken. The same writer recalls the Talmudic legend, with which we may compare the language of St James in *v.* 8 below; according to it, in reply to a question by R. Samuel b. Nachman, the serpent explains that if its poisonous bite in one member extends to all the members, a calumnious tongue speaks in one place and its killing stroke falls in Rome, or else it speaks in Rome and its stroke falls in Syria.

It is noteworthy that whilst in the passages from the O.T. and Apocrypha the injury done by the tongue to others is insisted upon, the representation of the tongue as defiling the man himself, his whole body, is peculiar to St James, although he does not forget the other mischievous effects of the felon tongue.

Wetstein tells the story of the servant who was bidden by his master to procure, in the first place, good food from the market, and, in the second place, bad food. On each occasion the servant brought back a tongue. And when his master asked the reason, the servant replied: 'From the tongue both good and evil results to man. If it is good, nothing is better; if it is evil, nothing is worse.'

7. It is perhaps best, and at all events simplest, to see in these words a proof adduced by the writer in support of his statement as to the exceeding mischief emanating from the tongue, a mischief begotten of a more than human agency.

every kind, A.V. and R.V. text; 'kind' in its old meaning, 'nature,'

cf. R.V. marg., and this may well have been intended by our translators. Wycl. had 'kind' in this archaic sense, and A.V. followed him here; other intermediate English Versions rendering 'nature.' So too below, 'by mankind' = 'by the human nature,' R.V. marg. We may compare the expression of the Litany, 'kindly fruits' = natural, and for a similar use of the word 'kind,' Shakespeare, *Tempest*, ii. 1. 167.

For the classification which follows, cf. LXX, Gen. i. 26, ix. 2; 1 Kings iv. 33; and a similar classification of living creatures is given by Philo, M. 2, pp. 352 foll. The nearest parallel is that of Gen. ix. 2, where the same Greek word, which is here rendered 'beasts,' seems to be used for quadrupeds in what evidently purports to be an exhaustive classification. It was to be expected that of the two words commonly translated 'beasts' in A.V. (but not in R.V., cf. Rev. iv. 6–9) St James would use in the present connection the one most expressive of the mischievous and brutal element. With the O.T. passages cf. Ecclus. xvii. 4, 'and he put the fear of man upon all flesh, and gave him dominion over beasts and fowls,' and also Acts x. 12, xi. 6 (but in the latter 'the wild beasts' appear to be distinguished from 'the quadrupeds'); see Trench, *Syn.* II. p. 142.

creeping things, R.V.; this is the literal trans. of the Greek word which through the Latin *serpo* is rendered in A.V. and so in the Vulg. by 'serpents.' In classical Greek the word is no doubt used chiefly of serpents, although also of any sort of animals, but in Biblical Greek it is opposed to quadrupeds

8 tamed [1]by [2]mankind : but the tongue can no man tame ; *it*
9 *is* a restless evil, *it is* full of deadly poison.   Therewith

[1] Or, *unto*   [2] Gr. *the human nature.*

and birds (Acts x. 12, xi. 16 ; Rom. i.
23), and here also to marine animals.

things in the sea; not found in
LXX, and only here in N.T., often in
classical Greek with the same meaning. We may include in this passage
not only fish but all that live in the
waters, and thus it may be joined to
'creeping things,' because some of
these are amphibious, beasts and
birds being coupled together as the
nobler orders.

is tamed; only once elsewhere in
the N.T. of the demoniac, whom no
man had strength to tame, Mark v. 4.
The verb is used of horses in classical
Greek, and so too by Galen, and by
Strabo of elephants. *And hath been
tamed.* The two tenses should be
noted ; man's dominion was no new
fact although it was freshly illustrated day by day.

by mankind, R.V., or better still,
by the human nature, if we may
combine text and marg., i.e. in contrast to the nature of the animal
world (cf. Xen. *Mem.* I. 4. 14, where
the same Greek word is used of man
excelling in nature, in body, in soul).
For this dignity of man's nature in
exercising such control we naturally
refer to Gen. i. 26, ix. 2 ; Psalm
viii. 6–8 : with these we may compare Philo, *De Mund. Opif.* M. I.
p. 20, where we read that all things
whatsoever in the three elements,
earth, water, air, are subjected to
man. From classical writers parallels
are cited in abundance ; the most
striking is that in Soph. *Antig.* 332ff.,
where in one or two verses a verbal
likeness to the passage before us
may be found ; cf. also Seneca, *De
Benef.* II. 29, where the strongest

animals and everything mortal are
described as under the yoke of man ;
and to the same effect Cicero, *De
Nat. Deorum*, II. 60, 61.

8. *but the tongue can no man
tame;* the same verb repeated in
accordance with the characteristic
style of the writer, lit. 'no one of
men can tame, not even one.'

The comment of St Augustine is
to be remembered, 'for he does not
say that no one can tame the tongue,
but no one of men ; so that when it
is tamed we confess that this is
brought about by the pity, the help,
the grace of God,' *De Nat. et Grat.*
c. 15.   The words of St James here
help us to understand more clearly
what is meant in *v.* 2, and on the
other hand the remarkable expression 'the third tongue' quoted above
enables us to realise how the results
of a man's speech cannot be esti-
mated by the man himself, and that
words once uttered pass beyond
human control.

it is a restless evil, R.V.   In A.V.
we have 'an unruly evil,' but this
is a translation of another Greek
word.   The reading 'restless' is now
generally received, and it fits in no
less well with the context, as if the
tongue resembled in its restlessness
an untameable beast ; cf. Vulg. *in-
quietum.* The same adj. is also used
by the writer in i. 8 (and the cognate
noun iii. 16), although somewhat
differently rendered in the translation. In Hermas, *Mand.* ii. 3, the
same word occurs, 'slander is evil;
it is a restless demon, never at peace,
but always having its home among
factions.'

In Isaiah liv. 11, where alone it is

bless we the Lord and Father ; and therewith curse we men,

found in Sept., it is rendered 'tossed
with tempest.'

it is full of deadly poison, R.V.
The adj. 'deadly' only here in N.T.,
lit. 'death-bringing'; it occurs in
Numb. xviii. 22; Job xxxiii. 23
(doubtful meaning); 4 Macc. viii.
18, 26, xv. 26; and so in classical
writers. The comparison used of
the tongue here may be illustrated
from Pss. lviii. 4, cxl. 3 ; Eccles. x. 11 ;
and so too, Philo, *De leg. ad Cai.*
p. 1016 B, it is said of the Egyptians
that they mingled in their tongues
the poison and anger of their native
crocodiles and snakes.

In *Testaments of the xii. Patriarchs*, Gad 6, we have the expression 'the hatred of a diabolical
poison filleth the heart,' and it is of
interest to note that in *Sib. Orac.*
proemium 70, we have a mention of
the worship of snakes and creeping
things as gods, 'out of whose mouth
flows deadly poison,' where the same
adjective is used and the same word
for poison as in St James. *Didache*,
ii. 5, also speaks of the double tongue
as a snare of death. In classical
writers similar thoughts often find
expression, e.g. Lucian, *Fugit.* 19,
speaks of false philosophers as having
their mouths full of poison.

It will be noted that R.V. twice
uses the copula 'it is,' and this is
borne out by the original, where the
change in the gender and the case
in the clause 'full of deadly poison'
make it simpler to understand the
word 'the tongue' as the subject of
both clauses.

9.   *therewith*, lit. 'in it,' signifying
the instrument and means; cf. Matt.
v. 13, '*wherewith* shall it be salted ?'
By the repetition of the expression
in the following clause the contrast

here expressed is accentuated ; and
no contrast could illustrate more
pointedly the inconsistent nature of
the tongue, or the vain 'religion,'
i. 27, of the man who fails to bridle
it.   On the evils of the double tongue
Ecclesiasticus dwells repeatedly; cf.
xxviii. 9, 14, 26, and more especially
perhaps *v.* 12, where the same
twofold simile of fire and water, as
in St James, has been noted ; in the
same book, xxxiv. 24, the same sharp
contrast as in the verse before us
finds a place (although the general
lesson is different), 'when one prayeth
and another curseth, whose voice
will the Lord hear ?' In *Sib. Orac.*
iii. 36, the same woe is pronounced
upon the liars and double-tongued
as upon those guilty of the most
heinous offences, while *Testaments
of the Twelve Patriarchs*, Benj. 6,
describes the good mind as not
having two tongues, one of blessing
and the other of cursing.

bless we ; in relation to God the
word means to praise, to celebrate
Him; cf. Psal. cxlv. 21, where the
same verb is used in LXX.   The
prayer which every Israelite, including even women, slaves, and children, was called upon to repeat three
times a day, was called the Eighteen
Benedictions, in which each 'benediction' ended with 'Blessed art
Thou, O Lord,' etc.   The word then
was a very likely one for St James to
use in reference to God, and more
especially so if we adopt the reading
'the Lord and Father,' since in this
Jewish prayer, God is not only
addressed in each Berachah as
'Lord,' but three times as 'Father.'
The Jewish-Christians whom St
James was addressing might well
retain their Jewish customs of

10 which are made after the likeness of God : out of the same

prayer, as there can be no doubt
that the groundwork of the Eighteen
Benedictions was of very considerable
antiquity; see Schürer, *Jewish
People*, Div. II. vol. II. pp. 85, 87;
Edersheim, *Jewish Nation*, p. 340.
At the same time it must be re-
membered that the Jews on uttering
the name of God always added
'Blessed be He.'

It is noteworthy that St James
in his reproof still associates himself
with his brothers and uses the first
person, not simply with reference to
the teacher, cf. *v.* 1, but quite generally.

the Lord and Father, R.V. (so
W.H. with strong support). For the
language, see above, and in O.T.
1 Chron. xxix. 10; Isaiah lxiii. 16.
We have also in Ecclus. xxiii. 1, 4,
the prayer 'O Lord, Father and
Governor of all my whole life,' where
the writer has just been speaking of
sins of the tongue, and we may
venture to compare the words of the
Divine Teacher, Matt. xi. 25. Here
God is thought of in His sovereignty
and in His love.

curse we men; commonly contrasted in the original with the word
'to bless,' Psalm lxii. 4, cix. 28;
Luke vi. 27; Rom. xii. 13, etc.; and
see also above. The verb need not
be confined in its scope to literal
cursing.

*which are made after the likeness
of God.* The truth was insisted
upon in Jewish literature, both in
and outside the O.T. Cf. Gen. i. 26,
27, v. 1, ix. 6; Ecclus. xvii. 3;
Wisd. ii. 23; 2 Esdras viii. 44. The
same teaching is found in Philo, M. I.
pp. 16, 35, where after referring to
the words that man was made 'after
the image and likeness of God' he

points out that this 'image' con-
sisted not in external form, but in
the possession of 'reason.' But
perhaps the most striking commentary on the words of St James, and
one which helps us to understand
most fully the contrast in the texts,
is to be found not only in the words
of R. Akiba on Gen. ix. 6, 'Whoso
sheddeth blood, they reckon it to
him as if he diminished *the likeness,*'
Bereshith Rabbah xxiv., but also
in the passage in which the same
Rabbi refers to Lev. xix. 18, 'Thou
shalt love thy neighbour as thyself,'
and adds, 'Do not say: after that
I am despised, let my neighbour also
be despised.' R. Tanchuma said,
'If you do so, understand that you
despise him of whom it was written
"in the likeness of God made He
him."' The lesson would therefore
be that he that curseth curseth not
man but God.

This same truth that man is made
in the image of God finds also an
important place elsewhere in the
N.T.; cf. 1 Cor. xi. 7; Col. iii. 10;
Ephes. iv. 24; in each passage there
is apparently an allusion to Gen. i.
26, 27. Moreover, in the *Didache*,
which presents so many points
of similarity to the Epistle before
us, in the stress laid, e.g., upon
the thought of God as the Creator,
we read, v. 2, of those who follow the
way of death as 'not recognising
Him that made them...corrupters
of the image of God.'

But further; it would seem that
Jewish literature was not forgetful
of the additional and most important
truth, implied in the words of St
James, viz. that this Divine likeness
was perpetuated, not destroyed, a
truth emphasised in the oft-quoted

mouth cometh forth blessing and cursing. My brethren,

words of Bengel, 'We have lost the likeness of God, but an imperishable nobility still remains.' Thus in the 'Book of the Generations of Adam' we read: 'God created man in the *likeness* of God....Adam begat a son in his own *likeness* after his image,' Gen. v. 1, 3; and then follow the remarks of Ramban: 'It is known that all that are born of living beings are in the likeness and image of their parents; but because Adam was exalted in his likeness and his image, for it is said of him that in the likeness of God made He him, it says expressly here that his offspring likewise were in that exalted likeness, but it does not say this of Cain and Abel, not wishing to dilate upon them, etc.' (on the whole subject, see Taylor, *Sayings of the Fathers*, pp. 56, 122, 158, 2nd ed.). The honour of humanity could thus have been taught by the N.T. writers as Jews, but as Christians their teaching would be deepened and ennobled by the realisation of a humanity, regenerated by the word of truth, and glorified by the faith of our Lord Jesus Christ (i. 18, ii. 1). If that faith is a reality it says to us to-day, '*Despise none; despair of none.*' 'The Jews would not willingly tread upon the smallest piece of paper in their way, but took it up; for possibly, said they, the name of God may be on it. Though there was a little superstition in this, yet truly there is nothing but good religion in it, if we apply it to man.' 'Trample not on any; there may be some work of grace there that thou knowest not of. The name of God may be written upon that soul thou treadest on; it may be a soul that Christ thought so much of, as to give His

precious blood for it: therefore despise it not': Coleridge, 'Aids to Reflection,' *Aphor*. lxvi. For classical parallels to the assertion of the truth of man's likeness to God we may quote Xen. *Mem.* I. 4. 14, where men in comparison with all other living creatures are said to live as gods: cf. Ovid, *Met.* I. 82; Cicero, *Tusc.* v. 13.

10. *out of the same mouth,* etc. The fatal inconsistency is again emphatically marked. Jewish literature bore constant testimony against the evil inconsistencies of the tongue and their inevitable results; cf. Prov. xviii. 21; *Jalk. Rub.* f. 120, 'whoever has a reviling tongue, his prayers do not ascend to God.' St James bids us lay stress upon the word *the same.* No man could be sincere in praising and blessing God, while he failed to recognise in his fellow-man the image of God; cf. 1 John iv. 20. The Apostle no doubt saw around him in Jerusalem those who claimed to be 'religious' thanking God that they were not as other men, while all the time they regarded those who knew not the law as 'accursed,' St John vii. 49 (see further Introd. p. xxxvii.). And within the fold of Christ St James may have seen the same spirit at work, the spirit which broke out in tones of bitter contempt against those whom Peter had evangelised, Acts xi. 2, 3; the spirit which not only refused to tolerate, but which even excluded from the pale of salvation those who were uncircumcised, Acts xv. 1.

My brethren. The familiar word comes in here with fresh force and fulness of affection—God is the Father, and men made in His

11 these things ought not so to be.　Doth the fountain send
12 forth from the same opening sweet *water* and bitter? can

likeness should remember that they
are also brothers, Mal. ii. 10.

ought not. The Greek word occurs
only here in the N.T. It may be
said to denote fitness or congruity—
it was abnormal that a man should
bless God in his prayers or creed,
and yet should despise or speak
evil of members of his own family,
inasmuch as he and his fellow-men
were the offspring of a common Father. It is significant that in Ps. cxli.,
which was sung every evening by
the early Church, the desire of the
Psalmist that his prayer shall be set
forth in God's sight as the incense,
and that the lifting up of his hands
shall be an evening sacrifice, is
closely followed by the petition 'Set
a watch, O Lord, before my mouth,
and keep the door of my lips.'

11.　*Doth the fountain.*　The
article may be used for vividness,
or to emphatically generalise the
question.

from the same opening, R.V.;
A.V. and Tynd. 'at the same place.'
As in the verse preceding stress
should be laid on the word '*the
same* opening.'

In the N.T. the word occurs only
elsewhere in Heb. xi. 38, where
the heroes of faith wander in caves
and '*holes* of the land.' In dis-
cussing this latter expression Bishop
Westcott has the interesting conjecture that this may be a quotation from some familiar description,
and he points out that the word so
rendered as above occurs again in
James iii. 11, with reference to
another feature of the limestone
rocks of Palestine; see further
Introd. p. xxiv.

sweet water and bitter: in the

original the word for *water* is omitted, and perhaps in this way the
contrast is even more sharply indicated, although for the general
sense of the passage the word may
be fairly understood.

The word rendered 'bitter' is only
found here in the N.T. and in *v.* 14,
but it is found twice in LXX, in the
same sense, of wine and of water,
Isaiah xxiv. 9, Jer. xxiii. 15, and often
in a figurative sense. If St James
is here alluding to the Dead Sea (see
v. 12), its water might be described
as really bitter, and the Greek word
in this verse, as well as the more
usual word in *v.* 12, was sometimes
employed of such water, as in Hero-
dotus VII. 35 of salt water, opposed,
as here, to sweet.

To mark the unnaturalness of
blessing and cursing from the same
mouth St James is illustrating from
monstrosities in nature which could
only occur in the last days, the
days of the sinners, when everything was disordered and ripe for
destruction. Thus we read, 'And
salt waters shall be found in the
sweet,' 2 Esdras v. 9; 'And in those
times the fruits of the earth will be
backward and not grow in their
season, and the fruits of the trees
will be withheld in their season...
and all things on earth will alter
and not appear in their season,'
Enoch, lxxx. 3.

12.　The comparison of the fig-
tree and of the vine will be familiar
to those who thought of every Jewish
home as having its vine and its fig-
tree, and such illustrations would be
quite natural to a man writing in a
country where the fig-tree, the vine,
and the olive abounded.

a fig tree, my brethren, yield olives, or a vine figs? neither
can salt water yield sweet.

13　　Who is wise and understanding among you? let him

But the parallel afforded to our
Lord's own words, Matt. vii. 16 (xii.
33–36), Luke vi. 44, is very striking,
and St James may well have had
these utterances in mind. There is
therefore no reason to suppose that
he is borrowing from some classical
proverbial saying, although no doubt
some close parallels may be found to
this teaching in ancient authors, as
e.g. Arrian, *Epict.* ii. 20; Plut. *Mor.*
492 f. So Seneca, *Epist.* 87, writes
that evil is not derived from good,
any more than a fig-tree from an
olive. It is of course quite possible
that our Lord Himself may have
been employing some proverbial
figure in common use to bring home
His Divine teaching.

can a fig tree? i.e. is it able? It
has sometimes been supposed that
St James, having first expressed
something unnatural, would now
express something impossible. But
the general lesson in each case is
the same, viz. that nothing can
produce anything contrary to its
nature; 'like root, like fruit,' this
was for St James a fundamental
law, as it has been called, of nature
and of grace.

*neither can salt water yield
sweet*, R.V.[1] The sentence reads as
if a negative clause not only in
meaning but in form had preceded.
The words of blessing and of cursing
could proceed out of the same mouth,
but if so, the former would in such a

case be only vain and unmeaning,
while bitterness was nourished in
the heart. Everything in nature
continues this day according to God's
ordinance, and all things serve Him;
man alone would pervert that order
in the endeavour to unite what God
and nature had put asunder.

It is noticeable that the Greek
word rendered 'salt' is frequently
used in the O.T. for the Dead Sea,
which is never so called in the Bible,
but most frequently (nine times) the
'Sea of Salt.'

13. *Who is wise and understanding,* etc. The words might
naturally be referred to the re-
quirements and qualifications of a
teacher, but at the same time the
wisdom to be aimed at is not
regarded as the possession of the
teacher alone but of every true
Christian.

For a similar combination of the
two adjectives see Deut. i. 13, iv. 6;
Hosea xiv. 9.

St James is writing to men who
placed a high value upon wisdom,
while they were in danger of forgetting its true worth and meaning.
More wisdom more scholars, said
Hillel (*Sayings of the Fathers,* ii. 8),
but there are passages in the same
collection which may fairly represent
dangers similar to, if not the same
as, those with which St James was
conversant. Such sayings, e.g., as
'whosesoever fear of sin precedes

---

[1] This more concise reading appears to be that from which other readings
like that of A.V. are derived. It is adopted by nearly all modern editors,
and is supported by Old Latin and Vulgate, as well as by the weight of
Greek mss. But the passage presents such difficulties that Blass regards it
as corrupt.

shew by his good life his works in meekness of wisdom.

his wisdom, his wisdom stands,' or 'whosoever works are in excess of his wisdom, his wisdom stands,' *u. s.* iii. 12–14, show that 'the wise,' to whom reference is so constantly made, might forget the foundation of their wisdom or allow it to become barren and void. But our Lord's own words, Matt. xi. 25 (cf. St Paul's warning in 1 Cor. i. 18), in which He thanks His Father for revealing unto babes what He had hidden from 'the wise and prudent,' are sufficient to show that St James may have been well aware of a danger which Christ so clearly recognised, and the words before us read as an echo of the phrase used by our Lord.

Many attempts have been made to distinguish between the two words 'wise' and 'understanding.' The former word is used of those who are skilled and expert, of those who are wise in the sense of learning, like the Jewish theologians; St James if he has this latter sense in mind, as is probable, explains the word on its practical side, as of one whose life is ruled by the true wisdom: 'understanding' in classical Greek is used of one having the knowledge of an expert, a specialist, so that the former word may relate to the possession of wisdom as such, and the latter to its application to the practical details of life; but it is very doubtful how far any precise distinction can be maintained, or how far it was intended by the writer.

by his good life. The word translated 'life' as in R.V. is in A.V. 'conversation,' a term which in its primary sense meant conduct, manner of life (lit. a turning hither and thither, a turning one's self about, so in Vulg. *conversatio*, from which the A.V. rendering may be derived). The translation 'conversation' is never used in A.V. to express conversation in its limited sense amongst ourselves, but as the wider sense has become archaic the R.V. rendering is fully justified; cf. amongst other passages Ps. l. 23; Job iv. 14; Gal. i. 13; 1 Pet. i. 15. In Bunyan's *Pilgrim's Progress* we have an illustration of the word in its primary sense, 'your conversation gives this your mouth-profession the lye' (Hastings' *B. D.*; see also Smith's *B. D.*[2], 'Conversation.' The word rendered 'good' is rather 'beautiful, noble'; cf. ii. 7, iv. 17; 1 Pet. ii. 12; it is expressive of that which is ideal, perfect, or, at least, attractive to others; cf. John x. 11.

his works in meekness of wisdom, R.V. St James does not say simply, 'let him show his wisdom,' but he introduces two of his favourite terms, 'works'...'meekness,' not words but deeds, and deeds done *in* meekness of wisdom, not as in A.V. '*with* meekness,' as if of some quality inserted over and above, but as of that which is characteristic of true wisdom, and the possession of which is a proof of the existence of such wisdom. St James may well have had in mind Ecclus. xix. 20 (especially as the same passage affords a somewhat close likeness to the teaching of i. 22, 25 *supra*), 'all wisdom is fear of the Lord, and in all wisdom there is doing; and wisdom is not knowledge of wickedness' (the word for 'knowledge' being the cognate noun of the adjective translated 'understanding' in the opening question of this verse). With

14 But if ye have bitter jealousy and faction in your heart,

the teaching of St James here it is interesting to compare Ecclus. iii. 17 ff., *Didache*, iii. 2, 5, 7–9, for some closely similar thoughts.

'Life'...'works,' in the former the general manifestation, and in the latter the particular results.

14. *But if ye have.* Probably St James had in mind members of the Church who showed themselves without wisdom, inasmuch as they were without the meekness which was an inseparable attribute of it.

jealousy. Here as often in the N.T. the Greek word is used in a bad sense (cf. Acts v. 17, xiii. 45; Rom. xiii. 13; Gal. v. 20), although it is capable of a good significance (cf. e.g. 2 Cor. xi. 2), and so generally in classical Greek and sometimes in the O.T. That it is used here in a bad sense is evident from the word 'bitter' joined with it, with reference apparently to *vv.* 11, 12, and also because it is associated with the word 'faction' as in Gal. v. 20; 2 Cor. xii. 20; and also with 'strife' in Rom. xiii. 13; 1 Cor. iii. 3. St James knew well what this zeal and jealousy meant in its bad sense, and what it was working in his own fatherland. There had been from the times of the Maccabees men who made it their aim to defend the Jewish law, 'Zealots' as they were called, but this spirit of zeal and jealousy for the law, which on its good side was characteristic of a Phinehas, 4 Macc. xviii. 13, or of an Elijah, 1 Macc. ii. 58, was liable to be perverted by unrighteous violence and excess.

St Paul describes himself as 'exceedingly zealous' for the traditions of his fathers, Gal. i. 14, and we know to what lengths his 'zeal' carried

him; St James truly described the Jewish-Christians as 'zealous for the law,' Acts xxi. 20, and we know how this zeal took the form of a bitter and fanatical opposition to St Paul. In the political world St James would have known how this same degenerate spirit prompted the formation of the fanatical sect 'the Zealots' under Judas of Galilee, with a certain Pharisee named Sadduk, and he would live to see how this same fanaticism became the instigator of every kind of cruelty and violence, as the pages of Josephus testify. In the *Didache* it is noticeable that we read the following: 'Be not angry, for anger leadeth to murder, nor *jealous* nor *contentious* (where we have the two cognate adjectives of the nouns "jealousy" and "strife" which are associated as above in the N.T.) nor wrathful; for of all these things murders are engendered,' iii. 1. On the word 'zeal' or 'jealousy' see Trench, *Synonyms*, I. 99, and below.

faction, R.V. here and elsewhere. The word is joined sometimes with 'jealousy' as above. It is connected with a noun which means a man working for hire, a hireling, and hence it is used as a political term for the canvassing of hired partisans, and so for the promotion of party spirit, factiousness (Arist. *Pol.* v. 2, 6, III. 9). It is noticeable that it is employed by St Ignatius just as here by St James, *Phil.* viii. 2, 'do ye nothing after a spirit of factiousness, but after the teaching of Christ.'

in your heart, R.V. and W.H. In Vulg. and Syriac we have 'hearts,' but sing. best. 'The heart' (see note on i. 26) was regarded as the source of moral action among the Hebrews;

15 glory not and lie not against the truth. This wisdom is
not *a wisdom* that cometh down from above, but is earthly,

and as our Lord (St Matt. xv. 19)
had taught that no ceremonial clean-
ness could compensate for inward
impurity, so St James would teach
the same principle, and would have
men understand that no loud and
pretentious claim to the possession
of 'wisdom' could avail while 'out
of the heart proceeded evil things.'
On 'Heart' see Art. in Hastings'
B. D. vol. II.

*glory not and lie not against the
truth*, R.V. In this rendering both
the verbs seem to be connected with
the words 'against the truth.' St
James might of course mean that in
thus giving themselves out to be wise,
while strife and bitterness were in
their hearts, there was a manifest
contradiction to the conditions of
the attainment of wisdom, and so a
contradiction of Divine truth; cf.
e.g. Wisd. i. 4, 'for into an ill-devising
soul wisdom shall not enter'; vi. 23,
'neither will I go with consuming
envy; for such a man shall have no
fellowship with wisdom.' But when
we remember his use of the word
'the truth' elsewhere (cf. i. 18, v. 19),
the words gain a still deeper meaning, and men are warned against
expressions and deeds which contra-
dicted 'the faith of our Lord Jesus
Christ,' ii. 1, which knows no respect
of persons, and against the violation
of the law of love, which was imperative upon the heirs of the kingdom

of heaven, ii. 5, 8; cf. i. 12 (see also
1 John i. 6)[1].

15. *This wisdom*, i.e. of the man
who has bitterness and faction in his
heart.

*is not a wisdom that cometh down
from above.* The participle is used
as an adjective, thus marking a
characteristic of the wisdom which
is truly wisdom; cf. i. 5, 17. The
thought expressed in the words would
have been familiar to a Jew: cf. Prov.
viii. 22; Ecclus. i. 1–4, xxiv. 4, 7;
Wisdom vii. 25, ix. 4. Passages to
the same effect may be quoted from
Philo; so too *Enoch*, xlii. 2, 'Wisdom
came to make her dwelling among
the children of men and found no
dwelling-place; thus Wisdom returned to her place and took her
seat among the angels'; cf. lxxxiv. 3.

earthly. The three adjectives
form a climax; the first is in direct
antithesis to the previous words, inasmuch as this false wisdom belongs
not to the heaven above, but to the
earth beneath; and those who possess
it have their wisdom set on 'earthly
things,' Phil. iii. 19; John viii. 23.
The word does not occur in the LXX,
but it is used in classical Greek from
Plato downwards, whilst in Plut.
Mor. 566 D, we have the remarkable
expression 'that which is earthly of
the soul.' In Hermas, *Mand.* ix. 11,
and again in xi. 5, we have expressions which certainly seem to be

---

[1] Mayor and Beyschlag apparently prefer to take the expression 'against
the truth' to mean 'against the facts of the case,' i.e. the claim to a wisdom
apart from gentleness was in reality a claim to a wisdom which was of the
devil, and not of God. It has very recently been urged that 'the truth' here
as in v. 19 means the ideal of regenerate human life. But it is allowed at the
same time that such an ideal is closely related to the words 'the faith of our
Lord Jesus Christ, our glory'; in Him was embodied a fresh revelation of the
glory of man's nature, and a fresh principle of life working within. Parry,
St James, pp. 21 ff.

16 [1]sensual, [2]devilish. For where jealousy and faction are,

[1] Or, *natural* Or, *animal* [2] Gr. *demoniacal.*

reminiscences of the passage before us. In the former, after condemning doublemindedness, the writer proceeds, '"Thou seest thus," saith he, "that faith is from above from the Lord, and hath great power; but doublemindedness is an earthly spirit from the devil, and hath no power."'

sensual, in A.V. and R.V., but the latter in marg. 'natural' or 'animal,' and the former in marg. 'natural.' To understand the word we must remember the trichotomy of 1 Thess. v. 23 (cf. Jos. *Ant.* I. 1, 2, where man is represented as composed of body, soul, spirit), with which we may compare for the use of the adjective before us as connoting opposition to the highest part of man's nature, 'spirit,' 1 Cor. ii. 14, and Jude *v.* 19 (where R.V. renders the word as here with same marg. alternatives). This 'sensual' or 'natural' man may be described as higher than the 'carnal' man (*carnalis,* Vulg.), who is enslaved by his fleshly appetites, yet he is ruled, not by that part of his nature by which the Spirit of God enters into communion with the spirit of man (*spiritalis,* Vulg.), but by that which is in comparison the lower (although not the lowest) part of his nature (*animalis,* Vulg.), the part which is 'unspiritual,' the part where human feeling and human reason reign supreme[1]. It is impossible to express

the Greek adjective by one unambiguous word in English, as the 'soul' is so often used to signify man's spiritual nature, and the distinction between it and 'spirit' is thus lost.

devilish, A.V. and R.V., but latter marg. 'demoniacal.' The latter rendering is best, because in the N.T. as in the O.T. 'demons' are evil spirits, the ministers and messengers of the devil, whereas Satan is never spoken of as a 'demon,' and his ministers are never called by his name 'the devil' or 'a devil,' for the Greek word for the latter is an adjective and not a noun when applied to men. As Dr Plummer points out, it is a misfortune that our R.V. has not taken the opportunity of distinguishing sharply between 'the devil' and 'the demons' which are subject to him, in accordance with the suggested correction of the American Revisers. If we compare ii. 19 (see note) the word here used by St James would seem to describe a fanatical and desperate malignity, like that inspired by the 'demons' in their votaries. No wonder that St James thus characterises this false wisdom after he had written *v.* 6. The editors of the marginal references in our R.V. apparently lay stress upon the lying nature of the pseudo-wisdom, and its false teaching: cf. 1 Kings xxii. 22; 2 Thess. ii. 9, 10; 1 Tim. iv. 1.

---

[1] The term is sometimes taken as almost equivalent to 'carnal' (see Art. 'Psychology,' Hastings' *B. D.* III. p. 167), or at all events to 'fleshly,' 2 Cor. i. 12, 'fleshly wisdom,' and so perhaps here, of a wisdom which depends entirely upon human reason, a wisdom of this world, cf. 1 Cor. ii. 14. Although the word does not occur in the canonical LXX it is used in a philosophical sense in 4 Macc. i. 32, where desires are divided into 'mental' and 'bodily,' while reason reigns over both; see further Trench, *Syn.* II. p. 94, and Plummer *in loco.*

17 there is confusion and every vile deed. But the wisdom
that is from above is first pure, then peaceable, gentle,

16. *confusion.* Cf. *v.* 8 and i. 8.
In the LXX the word is found in Prov.
xxvi. 28, 'a flattering mouth worketh
ruin,' and in Tob. iv. 13, in a sense
similar to that in the passage before
us. In the N.T. God is said to be
the author not of 'confusion' but
of 'peace,' 1 Cor. xiv. 33; with this
the language of St James may be
compared, in which 'the wisdom
which is from above' is characterised
as 'peaceable' and contrasted with
that which comes not from God, but
from those opposed to Him. In
2 Cor. xii. 20 the same word is
joined with jealousy and faction, as
in this passage, with the apparent
meaning of disorders, and in the
same Epistle, 2 Cor. vi. 5, it is found
possibly in the sense of seditions,
but in both these passages R.V. has
'tumult' in the text (cf. also Luke
xxi. 9, of the tumults of war). In
Clem. Rom. *Cor.* xiv. 1, the same word
is joined with jealousy and arrogance
in the sense of unruliness, as marking those in the Church who are
disobedient to God, probably with
this passage in mind. There is no
need to suppose that St James is
referring to any divisions between
Jewish and Gentile Christians; but
he saw plainly enough much in
Jerusalem to justify his warning.
The great Jewish teacher Hillel had
exhorted men to be 'loving peace,
and pursuing peace,' and another
great teacher Rabban Shime'on ben
Gamliel taught 'on three things the
world stands; on Judgment, and on
Truth, and on Peace' (*Sayings of
the Fathers*, p. 25).

and every vile deed, R.V. All
E.VV. have 'work,' but the Greek
implies a thing done, as often in

N.T.; cf. Luke i. 1; Acts v. 4; 2 Cor.
vii. 11; Heb. vi. 18.

vile (cf. John iii. 20, v. 29; 2 Cor.
v. 10; Tit. ii. 8), evil in its good-for-
nothingness, as if no good could ever
come forth from it, and so opposed
both in the N.T. and in classical
Greek to 'good.' Trench, *Synonyms*, II. p. 151. Antithesis, says
Bengel, to 'full of mercy and of good
fruits' (see below).

17. *first pure.* The order has
been called one of thought and not of
time, and the writer evidently places
first the 'pureness' of wisdom, because this 'wisdom from above' had
its origin with God, and came out
of His holy heavens and from the
throne of His glory, Wisdom ix.
4, 9; *Enoch*, lxxxiv. 3, etc.

In the famous passage Wisdom
vii. 7 ff., which was plainly before the
mind of St James, a different adjective in Greek is used to describe
wisdom as 'pure'; cf. vii. 25. But it
is said by Philo, *De Opif. Mund.* 8,
that this word cannot be applied to
any things of sense, so that St James
although by a different word may
here imply, and deepen the same
thought, and denote by 'purity' the
Divine essence of the true wisdom,
as contrasted with the false wisdom
which is 'earthly,' wholly engrossed
in sense and time; the words of the
Lord are 'pure' words, Ps. xii. 6.
God Himself is 'pure,' 1 John iii. 3
(in each case the same word in the
original as in St James).

In this Divine 'purity' the single-
heartedness which has sometimes
been regarded as its equivalent would
be comprised, a sincerity which would
exclude all doublemindedness, the
divided heart, i. 8, iv. 8, the eye not

single, Matt. vi. 22, all hypocrisies
(see Trench, *Syn.* II. 157, 169); which
would proclaim Christ, not of faction
but with pure unsullied motives (see
esp. Phil. i. 17). We note as quite
characteristic that St James in his
picture of wisdom is primarily practical, a contrast, it has well been
noted, with the picture in the Book
of Wisdom, where the interest is
primarily intellectual.

then peaceable. The preceding
epithet characterises wisdom as it
were from within, whilst the epithets which follow regard it as it
were from without. The first three
adjectives employed are opposed to
the jealousy and faction mentioned
above. As impurity is in reality
selfishness, so the temper of the
possessor of the true wisdom, which
is centred not in self but in God, is
peaceable; to see God, as the pure
in heart see Him, is to love God,
and he that loveth God will love
his brother also. On the close connection between love and peace we
may compare Ephes. iv. 3; Col. iii.
14; and in the Talmud Peace is a
Name of God (*Sayings of the Fathers*,
p. 26).

It has been well pointed out that
whilst no less than twenty-one epithets are applied to wisdom in the
famous passage Wisd. vii. 22 ff.
mentioned above, not one of them
makes reference to its peaceable and
placable character. In Prov. iii. 11
we read that 'all her paths are
peace,' but nothing further is said to
develop the thought; but on the
lips of Christ the peacemakers are
reckoned as 'sons of God,' and in
His teaching the temper which loves
peace follows closely upon the purity
which sees God; cf. Matt. v. 8, 9.

In Ecclesiasticus iv. 8, the only
place in which the same adjective

occurs in the Sapiential books of the
Apocrypha, we read, 'Incline thine
eye to the poor, and answer him
peaceful things in meekness,' where
the same word for meekness is also
used as by St James in i. 21 and
iii. 13.

gentle. The adjective employed in
the original is connected primarily
with a word implying what is fit and
reasonable, but in its later meaning
it is evidently associated with a verb
which means 'to yield,' and so the
cognate noun has been taken to
mean a *yieldingness* which does not
insist upon the utmost tittle of one's
rights, which prefers equity to strict
justice, and which can even put up
with injurious treatment. But it
must not be supposed that the virtue
in question is a weak one, since it is
not only described in terms of com-
mendation by Greek philosophers,
but is ascribed to God by Philo, and
in Psalm lxxxvi. 5, also *Psalms of Sol.*
v. 14, 2 Macc. x. 4. Thus too in
Wisdom xii. 18, it is said of God,
'but thou, mastering thy power,
judgest with *equity*' (A.V.), and as
'the archetype and pattern of this
grace is thus found in God,' what
wonder that we should read of the
meekness and *gentleness* of the only-
begotten Son Who declared God to
the world, 2 Cor. x. 1. Perhaps
some rendering such as 'gently-
reasonable' is most suitable here,
as combining the thought of tender
and unselfish, but not weak consideration, of fairness, but not mere
concession.

As compared with the virtue of
'meekness' cf. i. 21, iii. 13. This
'gentleness' belongs rather perhaps
to matters of outward bearing and
action in relation to man, as we can
see by its association with benevo-
lence, humanity; cf. 3 Macc. iii. 15,

easy to be intreated, full of mercy and good fruits, without

vii. 6; whilst 'meekness' belongs rather to a temper of mind, a meekness, primarily in respect of God, although also such in respect of our fellow-men (but it is doubtful how far this distinction can always be maintained). In this 'meekness' we see (1) how the teaching of the N.T. is rooted in the O.T.; the character of the meek often finds a place in the Psalms; meekness in Ecclus. is extolled by the writer throughout the book, cf. i. 27, faith and meekness are God's delight, xlv. 4; Moses is sanctified in his faith and meekness; whilst it has been truly said that the Christian Beatitude, Matt. v. 5, almost literally translates Psalm xxxvii. 11, and in both passages the meek are promised the possession of the earth : (2) how Christianity, as in the case of other 'passive' virtues, not only confers a higher place and dignity upon this virtue than it had ever gained in the scale of pagan ethics, cf. Arist. *Ethic. Nic.* IV. 5, but also reveals the character of an ideal meekness and gentleness and of a Person in Whom that ideal was embodied, and from Whom men could learn and find rest for their souls, Matt. xi. 29; 2 Cor. x. i. See, further, 'Meekness,' Hastings' *B. D.* vol. III., and Trench, *Synonyms*, I. pp. 173 ff.; Lightfoot on Col. iii. 13.

easy to be intreated, i.e. open to persuasion, conciliatory, compliant, ready to be guided. But the word may possibly be active, 'winning its way by gentleness, persuasive.' In the one passage to which reference can be made in the LXX, 4 Macc. xii. 6, there is some doubt as to the reading, but in the same book the noun is used three times of obedience to law.

full of mercy and good fruits. The whole clause contrasts with the *every vile deed* above. St James, as is characteristic of him, insists upon the practical nature of the true wisdom; faith to be of any avail must clothe the naked and feed the hungry, and so too wisdom must concern itself not merely with matters of criticism or with causes of provocation, but with the charities which heal, and soothe, and bless (cf. the fruits Gal. v. 22). In Wisdom vii. 22, 23, Wisdom is described as not only pure and undefiled, but 'as *ready to do good*, loving mankind'; cf. i. 6. With reference to this description Wisdom has been called 'the sole true Euergetes' (cf. Luke xxii. 25); but the full realisation of the virtue which prophets and kings desired to see was only found in the Incarnate Wisdom of God, 'Who went about *doing good*,' Acts x. 38.

without variance, R.V. text, but marg. *doubtfulness*, *partiality*, so A.V. text (but A.V. marg. *wrangling*). The choice seems to lie between *doubtfulness* and *partiality*, as the rendering *variance* is not very intelligible.

If we translate 'without doubtfulness' the Greek word is rendered on the analogy of the corresponding verb as in i. 6, and in contrast to the doubleminded man, the possessor of the true wisdom possesses that which is stedfast and unwavering, a simple, absolute trust in God. St Ignatius twice uses the word in the sense of 'stedfast,' as he writes to the Magnesians (xv.), that they should possess 'a *stedfast* spirit which is Jesus Christ,' and to the Trallians (i. 1) that they had 'a mind unblameable and *stedfast* in pa-

18 [1]variance, without hypocrisy.　And the fruit of righteousness is sown in peace [2]for them that make peace.

[1] Or, *doubtfulness*　Or, *partiality*　　　　　[2] Or, *by*

tience'; so again St Clement of Alex.
speaks of '*stedfast* faith,' *Paed.* II.
iii. p. 100[1]. The thought contained
in the rendering 'without partiality'
would of course befit a stedfast,
singleminded wisdom which would
make no distinction between rich
and poor, but if we adopt this latter
rendering it would seem to confine
us chiefly, if not entirely, to a warning against the danger of respect of
persons, which St James condemns
in ii. 1 ff. (with which compare
Didache, iv. 3), or of the rivalries
which he saw around him.

without hypocrisy.　Cf. i. 22, 26,
ii. 1: of the epithets applied to
wisdom in the passage Wisdom vii.
22, we may compare the epithet
rendered 'plain,' i.e. 'whether in
essence or in undeceiving mani-
festations' (cf. Thuc. I. 22, where the
neuter of the same adjective in
Greek is rendered 'the truth,' and
the verb cognate to it is used often
of truth opposed to falsehood). The
one Greek word rendered 'without
hypocrisy' is found twice in the
same book of Wisdom, but nowhere
else in LXX. But such a characteristic may well have been emphasised
by one who remembered that the
true Wisdom from above had taught
the way of God in truth, not regarding the person of men, Matt. xxii. 16.
It is noteworthy that whilst the same
adjective is applied not only by
St James but by St Paul and St
Peter to some characteristic Christian
virtue, it is not found in pagan
ethics, although the cognate adverb

is used by M. Antoninus, VIII. 5.
Our Lord repeatedly warned His
disciples against the leaven of the
Pharisees, 'which is hypocrisy,' and
in the *Didache* special warnings are
directed against the same fault; cf.
ii. 6, iv. 12, v. 1, viii. 1.

18.　*the fruit of righteousness,*
i.e. the fruit which is righteousness,
that wherein the fruit consists; cf.
Heb. xii. 11 (although it is sometimes taken to mean the fruit which
righteousness produces; cf. Ephes.
v. 9). The verse gives us the result
of the true wisdom, just as *v.* 16
had described the results of the
false wisdom.　There are several
places in the O.T. with which the
present passage may be compared,
e.g. Amos v. 7, where, as here, 'the
fruit of righteousness' is opposed to
'bitterness'; Hos. x. 12; Prov. xi.
21; so too Isaiah xxxii. 16, 17.

is sown; a pregnant expression, for
not the fruit but the seed is sown.
We may compare with the thought
here such passages as Prov. xi. 30,
and *Apocalypse of Baruch,* xxxii. 1,
'but ye, if ye prepare your hearts,
so as to sow in them the fruits of
the law,' etc.

in peace. The words are to be
taken with the verb, and can only
mean 'in peace,' i.e. the spirit in
which, and the conditions under
which, alone the seed sown ripens
to the fruit of righteousness. The
thought and language are quite
characteristic of a man who knew
the Beatitudes, Matt. v. 8, with their
blessing on those who work peace,

---

[1] The passages are referred to by Dr Plummer; see also Mayor *in loco.*

with their stress upon the acquisition of righteousness, not only in a future world, but in the practical daily life of a kingdom in which no evil deed or confusion could have place (cf. 1 Cor. xiv. 33).

for them that make peace; better perhaps 'that work peace,' as the words thus embrace a wider range than that of the mere reconciling of persons at variance. The phrase is found in 2 Macc. i. 4; 3 Macc. ii. 20; and also in Ephes. ii. 15. But the closest parallel is *Psalms of Solomon*, xii. 6, where it occurs closely conjoined with a warning against a slanderous tongue: 'the Lord direct the man that worketh peace in his house.' 'For them,' but R.V. marg. 'by them.' The dative is taken sometimes as a dative of the agent, sometimes as a *dativus commodi*,

but in either case the peacemakers are those who sow the seed and those who reap this fruit of righteousness. The verse has been well described as a characteristic and most suggestive apothegm: 'How are we to get from human life a harvest of righteousness? James answers that this harvest must be sown *in peace*, and it will be reaped by those whose spirit and temper make peace. Not through a fierce and angry temper, by which we ourselves are liable to be betrayed into gross injustice and into many other sins, but by gentleness, kindness, peaceableness, will righteousness at last come to prevail: the wrath of man worketh not the righteousness of God.' Dr Dale, *Epistle of St James*, p. 120.

CHAPTER IV.

1—3. The Divine wisdom produces peace; from whence then come wars, whence come fightings among you? come they not from the pleasures which wage war against all that checks their gratification? you desire, but the desire remains unsatiated; fighting, war, leaves you still lusting, yet not obtaining; even in your prayers you pray amiss, because your heart is set not upon God but upon self. **4—8.** But in so doing you break your vows to God, you choose a love which is enmity against Him, and He is a jealous God, and longs for the whole undivided affection of the heart. If this seems too great a demand, He giveth more grace, and that to those who are humble. The proud are wilful, but the humble seek not their own will, but that of God; resist the devil, who opposes that holy will, and he will flee from you, for temptation comes not from God; by that very act of resistance you are the more fit to draw nigh unto God, Who will Himself draw nigh unto you. But this approach to God must be made with hands cleansed from evil, for how else can they be raised in prayer? and with hearts purified from every debasing desire; and thus in thought and deed, doublemindedness will be put away.

9, 10. This approach to God will teach you to express your repentance both inwardly and by outward signs; your laughter must be turned to mourning and your rejoicing to heaviness, in so far as merriment and joy have been the joy not of the Lord but of the world; but in thus humbling yourself before God you will realise the promise that he that

humbleth himself shall be exalted.　**11, 12.**　But this spirit of humility
could not coexist with the spirit which speaks against the brethren; such
censoriousness in speech leads in itself to one of the worst forms of pride;
the man who is guilty of it sets himself not only against his brethren, but
against the law of love and Him who gave it; to God alone, as the source
of all law, belong the issues of judgment; who art thou that presumest to
judge?　**13—17.**　This same spirit of presumption and self-assurance,
this same want of humility and dependence upon God, is at work on every
side. Instead of reckoning upon time and getting gain, you ought to
consider that your life is fleeting, that you yourselves are a vapour, and
that the truly religious man would say in view of the future 'if God will';
but ye glory in your boastful talk, and so, knowing and not accepting
that good and perfect will of God, ye sin.

IV.　Whence *come* wars and whence *come* fightings among

IV. 1. *Whence come wars and
whence come fightings among you?*
The two words for 'wars' and
'fightings' are sometimes said to be
employed just as we distinguish
between 'war' and 'battle,' the
former denoting the whole course of
hostilities, the latter no more than
the actual encounter of armed forces
(Trench, *Syn.* II. p. 157).

The latter word is frequently used
with a secondary meaning, as e.g. in
Prov. xv. 18; Ecclus. xxviii. 8; 1 Tim.
vi. 4; Tit. iii. 9; and so in classical
Greek. So, though less frequently,
is the former word, not only in
classical Greek, but in *Psalms of
Solomon*, xii. 4, a Psalm which is
entitled 'concerning the tongue of
the wicked' (see above on iii. 6),
we read of the evil man that by
his words he would set fire to
houses with his lying tongue, 'and
put to confusion the houses of the
wicked by kindling strife with slanderous lips,' where 'strife' is the
same word as St James employs and
which is translated here 'wars.' (Cf.
with this 'Psalm of Solomon,' Ps. cxx.
v. 2 and *v.* 7.) See for similar use
Testaments of the Twelve Patri-

archs, Dan 5, Gad 5, Sim. 5,
where in each case 'war' is used in
connection with the results of envy
and hatred as above. No doubt
both words might be used of the
strifes and disputes of the Jewish
sects and Rabbis, the former word
denoting perhaps a lasting state of
hostility, the latter a sharp out-
burst of passion, but as St James
wrote he had before him the state
of society in Jerusalem and Palestine, wherein righteousness had once
dwelt, but now robbers and murder-
ers; cf. Matt. xxi. 13; Luke xiii. 1;
Acts xxi. 38; Jos. *B. J.* II. 1. 3; *Ant.*
xx. 8. 5, xviii. 1.

The repetition of the word
'whence' in R.V. is indicative of
the strong intensity and passion of
the writer. With the language here
and the question, cf. Clem. Rom.
Cor. xlvi. 5, where the similarity
is clear: 'Wherefore are there strifes
and wraths and factions and divisions
and war among you?'

among you. The expression may
indicate that the writer passes as it
were beyond the circle of 'teachers,'
and has in view the community as a
whole.

you? *come they* not hence, *even* of your pleasures that war
2 in your members? Ye lust, and have not: ye kill, and

even of your pleasures, R.V.
The word 'lusts' in A.V. is in the
original simply 'pleasures,' but this
latter word, although seldom used
in the Greek Test., is always found
there in a bad sense: cf. Luke viii.
14; Tit. iii. 3; 2 Pet. ii. 13.

As the German *Lust* so the Greek
word is used of the desire for the
pleasure, and for the pleasure itself.
Sometimes in philosophical language, as in Xen. *Mem.* I. 2. 23, the
Greek word for 'pleasures' is used
for evil desires, and in 4 Macc. i.
20 ff. the same word is used of
different desires of the soul and
body which lead to sin unless
governed by 'pious reason,' and
again, 4 Macc. v. 23, wisdom is said
to teach temperance, so as to control
pleasures and desires; cf. the language of Plato, *Symp.* 196 c, and his
definition of temperance. So Philo
speaks of 'the unreasonable pleasures,' and often joins together
'pleasures and desires' of evil things.
A further parallel may be found in
the Letter of Aristeas, 277, 'Why,'
asks the king, 'do not men receive
virtue?' And the answer is 'because by nature all are incontinent
and are inclined to *pleasures*. From
this results unrighteousness, and an
abundance of selfishness.'

that war in your members.
Carrying on the metaphor these lusts
are described as having their camp
in the members of the body, in the
sensual man; there they encamp,
not for rest, but to make war against
all which interferes with, and against
everyone who crosses, their gratifica-

tion. This seems best on the whole,
and fits in well with the following
verse, so that there is no need to
supply the words 'against the soul'
as is sometimes proposed (cf. Rom.
vii. 23; 1 Pet. ii. 11), although the
very fact that the 'pleasures' thus
war is a proof that they are not
subject to the law of God, or to the
higher nature of the man.

A remarkable passage in Plato,
Phaedo, 66 c, 'wars and factions and
fightings have no other source than
the body and its lusts,' has often
been compared with the words of
St James: but whereas in the words
which follow Plato speaks of getting
rid of the body as that which
prevents us from seeing the truth
and attaining to the heavenly wisdom, St James would teach us that
now, in this life, the wisdom from
above may be enjoyed by the pure
in heart, that now, as peacemakers,
we are the friends and sons of God,
not slaves to the service of the body[1].
From this point of view a striking passage may be quoted from
*Testaments of the Twelve Pa-
triarchs,* Dan 5, 'Keep, my children, the commandments of the
Lord and obey his law...speak the
truth every man to his neighbour,
and ye shall not fall into pleasure
(same word as here used by St James)
and turmoil, but ye shall be in peace,
having the God of peace, and no war
(same word as in St James) shall
overcome you.'

2. The punctuation of R.V. as in
W.H. leaves what has been called
the extraordinary anti-climax '*ye*

---

[1] The passage from Plato is quoted in full by Plummer, p. 218, and the
contrast drawn out between his teaching and that of St James. For parallels
in the language of Philo to the metaphor of St James see Mayor *in loco*.

kill and covet,' marg. R.V. 'are jealous, as the Greek may be used in either sense (cf. iii. 14, 1 Cor. xii. 31); so too A.V. text has 'ye kill and desire *to have.'*

But in A.V. marg. we have 'ye envy' instead of 'ye kill' by the adoption of another reading. This makes very good sense; desire, envy, jealousy insatiate, result in wars and fightings, but it cannot be said that there is the least manuscript authority to support the proposed change[1].

Another suggested change of importance is to place a colon, or a full-stop, after 'ye kill,' and in this way we have two sentences of similar meaning, exactly balancing one another, whilst no violence is done to the Greek. Thus 'ye lust and have not' corresponds with 'ye covet and cannot obtain,' and 'ye kill' with 'ye fight and war,' and thus too the abrupt collocations 'ye kill,' 'ye fight and war,' the abruptness being quite characteristic of St James, express in each case a result of what precedes; so Mayor and W.H. marg.

If therefore we read 'ye kill' it may be fairly urged that there was quite enough of violence and fanaticism in the social life around St James to justify even this charge of murder against his fellow-countrymen, and that in such a state of society murder might often be regarded as an expedient always ready to hand, and not only as a last and final resource. And upon such

fatal violence insatiable covetousness might well follow and fresh deeds of blood ensue.

It has indeed been suggested that the verb translated 'covet' in this verse might be rendered 'ye act as zealots,' as if the writer had in mind the men who called themselves by this name, and gloried in the most atrocious acts. If this technical name was not in existence at the early date to which we may refer the Epistle, yet St James must have seen in the followers of Judas the Gaulonite, in their reckless violation of law and order, in their utter disregard of the value of life, the immediate precursors of the Zealots, whilst he would have known something of the anarchy which prevailed through the country at a still earlier date when Varus was prefect of Syria, in days when deeds of murder were rife amongst the Jews and were committed not only against the Romans but much more frequently against their own countrymen: Jos. *Ant.* XVII. 10. 4, 8, XVIII. 1; *B. J.* II. 8. 1, VII. 8. 1 (see also above, iii. 14).

How atrociously the Jews on occasion could anticipate the decisions of law and judgment we very plainly see in the conspiracy related in Acts xxiii. 12, 13.

Certainly in face of the use of the same verb in *v.* 6, cf. ii. 11, and the striking passage in *Didache*, iii. 2, 'be not angry, for anger leadeth to murder, nor jealous, nor contentious,

---

[1] The reading was adopted by Erasmus and others, and so earlier by Oecumenius in his text but not in his note; so too by Tyndale and Cranmer amongst E. Versions. Mayor supposes that in the Greek the word for 'ye envy' was carelessly written and was then corrupted into a somewhat similar Greek word 'ye murder,' and on this occasion he is in agreement with Spitta. But would a reading which makes the sense more difficult have been introduced from the easier 'ye envy'? and would not the latter easily suggest itself from the frequent collocation of the nouns 'envy' and 'zeal'?

¹covet, and cannot obtain : ye fight and war ; ye have not,
3 because ye ask not.　Ye ask, and receive not, because ye

¹ Gr. *are jealous*.

nor wrathful, for of all these things
murders are engendered,' there can
be no decisive reason against a literal
rendering here, and St James might
well have feared that even Jewish-
Christians might be tempted perhaps
by a perverted view of the Messiah's
kingdom to join in deeds of selfish
extortion and murderous violence.
On the other hand the expression
still presents such difficulties to many
minds that it has been maintained
that there is no alternative but to
take the verb as used to denote that
hatred of his brother which makes a
man a murderer, Matt. v. 22, 1 John
iii. 15¹; but if this interpretation is
admitted it still remains strange
that such a strong word should
precede 'covet,' as we should have
expected a reverse order.

One other explanation, connected
to a certain extent with the foregoing,
may be mentioned. In Ecclus. xxxiv.
21, 22, we read: 'the bread of the
needy is the life of the poor: he that
defraudeth him thereof is a man of
blood. He that taketh away his
neighbour's living slayeth him (the
same word as is used in the passage
before us for "to kill"), and he that
defraudeth the labourer of his hire
is a bloodshedder'; cf. Deut. xxiv. 6.
This meaning, half literal, half metaphorical, as it may be fairly described,
is commended by the fact that St
James so clearly shows his acquaint-

ance with Ecclesiasticus elsewhere,
and also because such an explanation
fits in well with the rest of the
picture of Jewish social life as St
James presents it².

Perhaps, however, the best solution
of the passage is to be found in
adopting the punctuation of W.H.
marg. (see above), and with this
sequence of the clauses the passage
in the *Didache* above is in accordance, where jealousy and wrath en-
gender murder, and so too is the
passage Clem. Rom. *Cor.* iv. 7, 9,
where jealousy and envy are described as working a brother's murder, and causing persecution unto
death ; so too vi. 4, where it is said
of jealousy and strife that they have
overthrown great cities and uprooted
great nations.

*ye fight and war ; ye have not,
because ye ask not.* So R.V. but A.V.
renders 'ye fight and war, yet,' etc.
But 'yet' should be omitted, not
only because it has so little support,
but because even without the punctuation suggested above, it is not
needed³, as the terseness of the
sentence is quite characteristic of
St James.

ye have not. The repetition of a
preceding clause is again characteristic of the writer; cf. i. 6.

ye ask not. It may be observed
that in the original the verb is in
the middle voice, and so too in the

---

¹ So Estius, and amongst recent commentators von Soden and Beyschlag.
² Among recent commentators both Dr Zahn and Dr Plummer favour this
interpretation.
³ It is omitted by W.H. Von Soden retains the word 'and' before 'ye
have not,' for which there is certainly more authority than for the adversative
copula expressed in A.V.

4 ask amiss, that ye may spend *it* in your pleasures. Ye
adulteresses, know ye not that the friendship of the world

second clause of *v.* 3, whereas in the
first clause of the verse the same
verb is used in the active voice.
No very satisfactory explanation of
this is forthcoming, and it is very
doubtful how far we can make any
precise distinction, or how far any
such distinction was in the mind of
the writer. It is indeed contended
that, as in the case of some other
verbs, the active and middle voices
may be used indiscriminately. It is
also very doubtful how far the word
employed here expresses, as many
writers have held, the request of an
inferior to a superior, whereas it
would rather seem that the verb in
question denotes a request for something to be *given, not done,* emphasising the *thing* asked for rather
than the *person* (Grimm-Thayer).

3. *because ye ask amiss;* they
pray, but in vain, because whilst
their words fly up their thoughts
remain below, fixed solely on the
acquisition of some material gain
and pleasure: 'In church thou shalt
confess thy transgressions, and shalt
not betake thyself to prayer with an
evil conscience,' *Didache,* iv. 14. And
so the essential condition of all acceptable prayer was omitted, 1 John
v. 14, 'if we ask anything according
to His will he heareth us.'

The history of Christendom is, alas!
full of instances of the manner in
which men can 'ask amiss,' even
when they retain the formality of
prayer as the outward aid to worship.

St Augustine would ask God to
give him continence and chastity,
but not yet, *Conf.* viii. 17; a Cornish
wrecker could pass from church to
his fiendish work of plunder and

murder; a Russian peasant can turn
the face of his *eikon* to the wall,
whilst he violates some command of
God's law. The words of Seneca,
Epist. x. (the first half of the
passage being quoted by him from
Athenodorus), stand out still as a
rebuke to the failures of Christians:
'Then know that you are freed from
all evil desires, that you ask nothing
of God except what you could ask
openly. So live with men as if God
sees; so speak with God, as if men
hear.'

that ye may spend it, viz. what
you thus dare to ask from God.
'Consume,' A.V., is used for another
word in the original elsewhere. For
the verb here cf. Luke xv. 14. One
important MS. has a compound of
the same verb which expresses even
more strongly the entirety of the
expenditure; it occurs in Wisd. v. 13
of men 'utterly spent' in their own
wickedness: cf. also below, *v.* 5.

in your pleasures; the preposition
marking the realm *in* which (not the
object *on* which) the expenditure is
made, viz. in the kingdom of the
senses, in the lower part of the man's
nature.

4. *Ye adulteresses.* The authorities may be fairly called absolutely
decisive for this reading, and its difficulty is also in its favour. It is very
probable that the masculine was
inserted, as in A.V. 'adulterers and
adulteresses,' because it was thought
that the word was to be taken
literally, and it seemed strange that
St James should refer only to the
weaker sex. But the context in *v.* 5
shows that the language is figurative
(while no doubt the mention of
sensual pleasures in *v.* 3 would natu-

is enmity with God? Whosoever therefore would be a

rally suggest the thought of estrangement from God's love). God is conceived of as in O.T. language—e.g. Ps. lxxiii. 27 ; Isaiah liv. 5 ; Jer. iii. 20 ; Hos. ii. 2—as the husband of Israel which is bound to Him by a marriage tie ; cf. also our Lord's own words, Matt. xii. 39, xvi. 4 ; Mark viii. 38. The American Revisers thus add suitably in the margin after the word 'adulteresses,' 'that is, who break your marriage vow to God.'

It has been sometimes suggested that the feminine noun is used here with a touch of scorn as well as of indignation : cf. Hom. *Iliad*, II. 225, 'women, not men, of Achaia.'

One or two passages from Jewish writings may be cited in connection with the above. In the *Jerusalem Talmud*, in comments on the Ten Words, and amongst them our Seventh Commandment, 'Said R. Levi, It is written (Prov. xxiii. 26), My son, give me thine heart, and let thine eyes observe my ways : the Holy One, blessed is He, saith, If thou hast given me thy heart and thine eye, I know then, thou art MINE.'

In the *Mechilta* it is asked, 'How were the Ten Words given ? five on this Table and five on that... It was written, Thou shalt have no other etc., and it was written opposite to it, Thou shalt not commit adultery. The Scripture shows that whosoever practises strange worship, the Scripture imputes to him as if he committed adultery from God, for it is said (Ezek. xvi. 32), As a wife that committeth adultery, which taketh strangers instead of her husband, and Hos. iii. 1.' It would therefore seem quite plain that the spiritual adultery might be attributed not

only to the Jewish Church, but to each individual member of it.

know ye not. The writer appeals to the Christian consciousness of his readers: cf. 1 Cor. iii. 16, vi. 9, 19 ; Rom. vi. 16.

the friendship of the world. The whole context *vv.* 5 and 6 seems to show that the relationship of the soul to God—'thy Maker is thy husband'—is inconsistent with the introduction of a friendship with that which is opposed to Him. The appeal of St James comes naturally from one who had heard and no doubt enforced our Lord's own warning, Matt. vi. 24; Luke xvi. 13; cf. John xv 19. The word is best taken actively as 'friend' (cf. 'enemy' just below), although it might include the being loved as well as the loving. The noun itself is found only here in the N.T. but it is frequent in LXX. Our Lord's words, referred to above, speak of wealth, Mammon, as that which is loved, or clung to, in preference to God, and so some have taken this word here to mean the love of worldly goods, and others of earthly lusts, Tit. ii. 12, but the word 'friendship' may well include the love of sinful companions as well as of things sinful ; see note on i. 27.

is enmity with God. The Greek word is best taken as a noun, so in A. and R.V. (as an adj. by the Vulgate); and thus the contrast is marked between the two opposites, hatred and friendship. There is no need to suppose that the words are a quotation from some other source unknown to us.

Whosoever therefore would be, R.V., 'will be,' A.V. Stress is sometimes laid upon the verb in the original, as indicating that this

5 friend of the world maketh himself an enemy of God. Or
 think ye that the scripture [1]speaketh in vain? [2]Doth the
 spirit which [3]he made to dwell in us long unto envying?

[1] Or, *saith in vain*,　　　[2] Or, *The spirit which he made to dwell in us he
yearneth for even unto jealous envy*. Or, *That spirit which he made to dwell
in us yearneth* for us *even unto jealous envy*.　　[3] Some ancient authorities
read *dwelleth in us*.

man's choice of friendship is de-
liberately made with all his mind
and will, a choice again emphasised
by the rendering 'maketh himself
the enemy' (see below), or as meaning that where a man cannot from
circumstances be the open enemy
of God, he has yet the wish to be,
and so is equally guilty of enmity
against God.

maketh himself (cf. iii. 6), is thereby constituted, Vulg. *constituitur*,
so in iii. 6; Rom. v. 19 (2 Pet. i. 8)[1].
The words again recall our Lord's
saying, Matt. vi. 24.

5. *Or think ye;* cf. i. 26: he will
show by means of the question how
utterly incompatible the two things
are—love of God and love of the
world.

in vain. Cf. Deut. xxxii. 47; Isaiah
xlix. 4, LXX.

the scripture speaketh; cf. 2 Cor.
vi. 17, as here in R.V. marking a
reference to the general sense rather
than to the actual words. It is
sometimes urged that the word
'scripture' when used in the N.T.
in the singular always refers to a
particular passage of Scripture, and
that in most cases there is no difficulty in fixing the particular passage
referred to[2]. But it cannot be said
that there is no such difficulty in

this verse, and a consideration of it
would rather lead us to refer the
expression here, not to any one
passage, but to the general sense of
several passages; cf. e.g. John vii. 38,
where our Lord Himself apparently
applies the words 'the scripture
hath said' not to any one passage,
but to the thought expressed in
several O.T. passages. The difficulty
was evidently felt so much by the
Revisers that in distinction to A.V.
they break up the sentence into
two questions (cf. W.H. marg.), 'Or
think ye that the scripture speaketh
in vain ? Doth the spirit which he
made to dwell in us long unto envying ?' The difficulty is thus avoided
of regarding the words 'the scripture
saith' (A.V.) as introducing a passage
from the O.T. which does not occur
there. But it is very doubtful
whether the Revisers have adopted
the best explanation by their second
question, if, that is, it is understood as
an inquiry whether the Holy Spirit
so longeth for us as to be an example
of envy and jealousy, the implied
answer being No; He is a Spirit of
gentleness: see further below.

long unto envying? The A.V. by
its rendering 'lusteth to envy,' i.e.
to a degree bordering on envy, gives
even more positively a bad sense to

---

[1] See Mayor's note on the many instances of the verb in the passive voice;
on the other hand Grimm-Thayer take it here and in iii. 6 as middle.
[2] See however Art. 'Scripture,' Hastings' *B. D.*, where Dr Hort (1 Pet. ii. 6)
is quoted as saying that in St Paul and St John the expression 'the Scripture'
'is capable of being understood as approximating to the collective sense.'

the original word, a sense which is by no means necessary. For this verb, rendered 'to long' or 'to yearn,' is frequently used elsewhere in the N.T. and always in a good sense, as also its cognate substantive and adjective; cf. Rom. i. 11, xv. 23; Phil. i. 8, iv. 1: in LXX it also frequently occurs, and rarely with a bad meaning. It seems best therefore to translate, with the second marginal rendering of R.V., 'That spirit which he made to dwell in us yearneth *for us* even unto jealous envy.' The first marginal rendering of the Revisers is not so good, for if *God* is taken as the subject of both verbs He is represented as yearning for His own Spirit in us (a view, however, to which Mr Mayor now inclines), although it is of course possible to take 'the spirit' as meaning the human spirit; cf. Gen. ii. 7; Zech. xii. 1; Eccles. xii. 7. And this makes perfectly good sense[1], the main objection being that the human spirit would scarcely be spoken of as the spirit which God 'made to dwell in us' (see the passages in Hermas quoted below).

If therefore we adopt the second marginal R.V. the thought is in reality a sequel to that which has preceded; no adultery, no alien friendship, can be tolerated by the Spirit, Who claims from us and in us an undivided affection. In adopting this interpretation the Scripture reference is not to any one passage, but rather to a combination of passages, or at any rate to their collective sense, as e.g. Deut. xxxii. 10, 11, where we have the tender care of God for Israel described, and the same verb used as is here rendered 'yearneth,' and 19, 21, where we have the thought of God's jealousy expressed in view of the nation's unfaithfulness; cf. Zech. i. 14, viii. 2; see also Isaiah lxiii. 8–16; Ezek. xxxvi. 17; Gen. vi. 3–5.

It has indeed been further suggested that if the words before us are compared with Gal. v. 17, as affording a parallel to the words there used, 'the Spirit lusteth against the flesh,' so here 'the Spirit lusteth against envy,' there may be a common Hebrew original, a Hebrew gospel now lost to us, behind the two texts[2]. But whilst it is no doubt true that the preposition employed by St James, and in Gal., can well be rendered 'against' (as Luther, Bengel, and others have taken it here), yet such a rendering, allowable if hostility was implied, would be obviously out of place if we attach to the verb 'to yearn' its usual meaning of strong affection. A similar explanation has been attempted for the other part of the verse, 'the spirit *which dwelleth in us,*' by citing as parallels Rom. viii. 9; 1 Cor. iii. 16. But if the difference in reading between the expression used by St James *made to dwell* and that in Rom. and 1 Cor. *dwelleth* might be passed over, the difficulty in the above interpretation of the

---

[1] Amongst recent commentators von Soden and the Romanist Trenkle, and in England Parry, *St James,* pp. 39 ff. The solution proposed by Weiss, viz. to regard the words after 'speaketh in vain' to 'grace' parenthetically, and to regard the interrupted quotation as taken up again in 'wherefore the scripture saith,' seems forced and not very natural. It is equally unsatisfactory to refer the words 'Or think ye......saith in vain' to the latter part of *v.* 4, as not only is there no quotation in that verse, but the formula 'the scripture saith' refers more naturally to what follows than to what precedes.

[2] Resch, *Agrapha,* pp. 131, 256. (For the recent conjecture that the words πρὸς τὸν θεὸν should be substituted for the words rendered 'unto yearning,' πρὸς φθόνον, see *Studien und Kritiken,* 4, 1904.)

6 But he giveth ¹more grace.   Wherefore *the scripture* saith,

¹ Gr. *a greater grace.*

other part of the supposed quotation still remains. With regard to the two readings *made to dwell* (adopted here by nearly all modern editors) and *dwelleth* a striking passage in Hermas, *Mand.* iii. 1, may be quoted in connection with the verse under discussion; 'again he saith to me, "Love truth, and let nothing but truth proceed out of thy mouth, that the Spirit which God *made to dwell* in this flesh may be found true in the sight of all men; and thus shall the Lord who dwelleth in thee be glorified."' Lightfoot apparently takes the word 'the Spirit' as referring here to the Holy Spirit; and in Hermas, *Sim.* v. 6. 5, we have 'the Holy Preexistent Spirit which created the whole creation, God *made to dwell* in flesh that He desired.'

6. *But he giveth more grace,* or R.V. marg. 'a greater grace.' Adopting the interpretation of the previous words as above, the best meaning appears to be that the Spirit of God bestows upon those who submit to the Divine will, and surrender themselves to it entirely, richer supplies of grace to effect that complete surrender to the yearnings of the Divine love, and to count all things as loss in response to it.

The words are sometimes taken as part of the quotation, but as the writer at once supports the statement by a definite passage of Scripture, it is best to regard this sentence in question as a complement to the preceding verse made by the writer, 'the more we surrender, the more He bestows' (cf. Mark x. 29, 30); and the greater our weakness, His grace is still sufficient. In a somewhat

similar manner St Paul after a quotation from Gen. ii. 7, in 1 Cor. xv. 45, adds a complement in his own words.

In advocating the reference of 'spirit' in *v.* 5 to the human spirit, it is suggested that the words before us refer to a greater gift than that spirit, viz. the gift of regeneration, wherefore we should submit ourselves wholly to God, because the danger is greater in neglecting this greater gift.

But this interpretation does not seem fully to recognise that the passage is not entirely one of stern warning: it is also one of expectation; the humble are thought of as well as the proud, and to the humble, as the words are taken above, God gives grace, and that too more abundantly, that they may respond to His affection.

Wherefore the scripture saith, R.V., but the words 'the scripture' are marked as not in the original, so that it is allowable to supply 'God' as the subject; cf. Ephes. iv. 8, or i. 12 above; or the verb may be regarded as impersonal. The quotation is from Prov. iii. 34 in the LXX, with the exception of 'God' for 'Lord'; cf. 1 Pet. v. 5, and for the thought Job xxii. 29. The main object of the quotation is evidently to justify the declaration as to the ungrudging bestowal of God's grace. At the same time we can easily understand how St James would identify the friends of the world with 'the proud'; 'the beginning of pride is when one departeth from God, and his heart is turned away from his Maker,' Ecclus. x. 12; cf. Trench, *Syn.* I. 115 (cf. III. 18). The 'lowly' is set

God resisteth the proud, but giveth grace to the humble.
7 Be subject therefore unto God ; but resist the devil, and

over against the 'proud' as so often
in the Psalms, as e.g. cxxxviii. 6, and
in Ecclesiasticus ; see note on i. 9.
In the *Psalms of Solomon* the same
contrast is also found ; cf. ii. 35, where
the Sadducean princes and their
party are spoken of as the 'proud'
whom God lays low, because they
know Him not, and where, as in
vv. 14 ff., the Psalmist may well be
tacitly contrasting the wealthy Sadducees with the poor and needy
who have taken God alone for their
hope and help, the God Who makes
glad the soul of 'the humble' by
opening His hand in mercy. This
contrast meets us again in a striking
manner in Luke i. 51, 52 (cf. *Didache*, iii. 9) ; and the question has been
asked if St James was acquainted
with the *Magnificat*. In answer it
may at least be said that the thought
expressed both here and there is one
which breathed 'the atmosphere of
religious life in which the Holy
Family lived and which St James
shared.' The pride or haughtiness
here referred to was specially noted
in our Lord's warning, Mark vii.
22, and it finds a place in 'the way of
death,' *Didache*, v. 1, in contrast to
'the way of life' (which is, first of all,
the love of God, i. 2).

resisteth, a word perhaps used to
express, as in the metaphors of warfare so common in St Paul, 'arrayeth
himself against,' but see also below.
The same quotation is found in Clem.
Rom. *Cor*. xxx. 1, and it is probable
that he may have borrowed it from
St James, as it occurs in the same
form, and as, in the context, we read :
'holding ourselves aloof from all
backbiting and evil-speaking (cf. St
James iv. 11), being justified by

works, and not by words.' It is
interesting to note how often this
verse quoted here finds a place in
the *Confessions* of St Augustine.

There seems no sufficient ground
for regarding the words as a saying
of our Lord (as Resch maintains),
although Ephraem Syrus appears to
cite them inexactly as such.

7. *Be subject.* The antithesis in
the original has been noted, although
it can scarcely be pressed in English,
'God setteth himself against the
proud—set yourselves as under God.'
This submission, so hard for the
proud and self-reliant, ought to be
natural for the truly lowly, for they
serve in reality only one Master, even
God ; cf. Col. iii. 22 ; Tit. ii. 9 ; *Didache*,
iv. 11 ; or the thought of warfare
may still be prominent, 'be subject
to God, and not enemies to Him.'
The verb is frequently used in
the Psalms of submission to God :
cf. 2 Macc. ix. 12. The tense
and mood in the Greek denote both
here and in the word 'resist' urgent
entreaty and command.

but resist, R.V. ; cf. 1 Pet. v. 9.
'But' retained not only by R.V. but
by W.H. (perhaps dropped out in
A.V. with the view of giving to the
clause a more independent form).

However submissive, yet as loyal
subjects they must resist the enemy
of the Lord. The verb is not the
same as above, *v.* 6, although both in
A. and R.V. the two verbs are rendered by the same English word,
and may perhaps continue the same
military metaphor ; cf. for use of the
verb in LXX, Wisd. xi. 3, 21 ; Ecclus.
xlvi. 7 ; 1 Esd. ii. 19.

the devil, i.e. the slanderer, who
slanders God to man and man to

8 he will flee from you.   Draw nigh to God, and he will draw
   nigh to you.   Cleanse your hands, ye sinners ; and purify

God, and in whose work men associate themselves by envy, hatred and discord; cf. John viii. 44; no wonder that St James pleads for resistance to such works with the word 'brethren' on his lips, *v.* 11.

and he will flee, perhaps 'shall flee,' not merely an assurance from man to man, but a Divine promise ; *laetum verbum,* 'a gladsome word,' says Bengel; cf. 1 John v. 18. Our Lord's own temptation shows us how submission to the will and appointment of God issues in the defeat and flight of the Evil One. Here again an attempt has been made to refer the words 'Resist the devil' etc. to an unrecorded saying of our Lord, and to refer to the same source the passages 1 Pet. v. 8 ; Ephes. vi. 11, 13 (iv. 27). But it is of course quite possible that such sayings might have formed part of the common stock of Apostolic teaching and exhortation, in fact, a current maxim[1]. A striking parallel to the words of St James is undoubtedly presented by Hermas, *Mand.* xii. 5. 2, where in connection with the devil we read, 'if ye resist him he will be vanquished and will flee from you disgraced'; cf. also xii. 4. 7. But in view of the early date which we assign to the Epistle, Hermas may fairly be supposed to have St James in mind, and there is no need to refer his words also to some lost Hebrew gospel. The second part of the verse also occurs in *Testaments of the xii. Patriarchs,* Napht. 8 (cf. Issach. 7, Dan 5, etc.).

8. *Draw nigh to God;* used in the LXX specially of the priests

offering sacrifices or ministering in the Temple, but also in a wider sense, Isaiah xxix. 13 ; Hos. xii. 6; and in the N.T. Heb. vii. 19. The teaching is similar both in substance and form to several O.T. passages; cf. 2 Chron. xv. 2; Zech. i. 3 ; Mal. iii. 7; and see also Isaiah lvii. 15, to which our Lord refers, Mark vii. 6. It is noticeable that in *Test. xii. Pat.,* Dan 7. 6, we have the exhortation to fear the Lord and beware of Satan and his spirits closely followed by the exhortation, 'Draw nigh to God,' but the context, 'and to the angel who prays for you,' stands out in contrast to the teaching of St James before us. In resisting the devil it may be said that *ipso facto* one draws nigh unto God, or it may be objected that St James does not follow the correct order in placing resistance to the devil before the approach to God, since prayer is the first and best means of resistance ; but it is likely enough that St James was thinking of a man hard pressed by temptation calling upon God in his trouble, and that he wished to assure him of God's gracious response to his need. 'He will draw nigh unto you,' *laetissimum verbum,* 'a most gladsome word,' says Bengel. Here again, in the fuller sense of God's presence, the promise was verified, 'He giveth more grace.'

Cleanse your hands. As the word to draw near was used on occasions in connection with the approach of the priests to the Lord, Exod. xix. 22, and afterwards of spiritual worship, so the washing

---

[1] Ropes, *Die Sprüche Jesu,* p. 41, in answer to Dr Resch.

9 your hearts, ye doubleminded. Be afflicted, and mourn,

and cleansing of hands was connected primarily with ceremonial purity, and then with moral purity; cf. Exod. xxx. 19–21; Ps. xxvi. 6; Isaiah i. 16, etc. It is quite possible that as the writer has spoken of drawing nigh to God, which would no doubt be taken to include at all events the thought of drawing nigh in prayer, he is thinking here of the pure hands raised in prayer to God; cf. 1 Tim. ii. 8; Clem. Rom. *Cor.* xxix. 1, 'let us therefore approach Him in holiness of soul, lifting up pure and undefiled hands unto Him.' It is also quite possible that as the writer had spoken of fightings and murders in Jewish social life, he may have used the expression of the hands as the instruments of action (cf. Isaiah i. 15, lix. 2, 3), and so they are also spoken of by Philo. Men with hands so stained with blood could not draw nigh unto God; cf. Ps. xxiv. 1–4.

ye sinners. The word shows what kind of cleansing is meant, and men guilty of sins such as those described might well be summed up under such a category; the word is in itself a call to repentance, to change of heart and life. It was, we may note, a term characteristic also of a Jewish writer; cf. its frequency not only in the *Book of Enoch,* but in the *Psalms of Solomon,* where it is often used to denote not Romans or heathens but irreligious Jews.

purify your hearts. This clause and the preceding are strikingly combined in Ps. xxiv. 4, lxxiii. 13. The verb is again one used primarily of ceremonial purification, as constantly in LXX, but here it is used of spiritual cleansing: cf. 1 Pet. i. 22; 1 Joh. iii. 3

On the doubleminded, see on i. 8; cf. Hos. x. 2; and Hermas, *Mand.* ix. 7, with an evident reminiscence of the warning of St James, 'cleanse thy heart from doublemindedness,' and Clem. Rom. *Cor.* xi. 2, show how the sin was noted in the early Church as one for special warning. In *Testaments of the Twelve Patriarchs,* Asher 3, we have an interesting passage in the present connection: 'The double-faced serve not God but their own lusts, to please Beliar, and men like to him.' In modern literature we may recall John Bunyan's Mr Facing-both-ways.

We must remember that St James does not address two different classes, but that the sinners and the doubleminded are the same.

It is possible that in the purifying, rendered sometimes 'make chaste,' we have an allusion to the adultery of *v.* 4, but the latter expression may be best explained as above in comment on that verse, and those guilty of acts of lust, envy, murder, are also guilty of this *spiritual* adultery.

The likeness to our Lord's teaching as to the undivided mind and the purity of heart essential to the true service of God is unmistakable; cf. Matt. xxiv. 51, and xv. 1–9.

9. *Be afflicted.* The word may refer to the inward feeling of wretchedness following on the sense of sin, even in a contrite heart; the Romanist commentators for the most part take it of abstinence from comfort and luxury, such outward acts of mortification being regarded as the expression of inward sorrow, and as a help to break the power of sin. St James was himself noted for his ascetic life, and fasting and

and weep : let your laughter be turned to mourning, and

sackcloth were the frequent accompaniments, in Jewish prophetic language, of the call to repentance: Jer. iv. 8; Joel i. 13, 14. It would therefore seem quite natural that he should insist upon the voluntary assumption of hardship and labour, and the word may be used here of the endurance of such labours, as it is used primarily of enduring hardship in classical Greek. But it should be also noted that in the LXX the cognate noun and adjective are often used to denote wretchedness and misery, and so in classical Greek; and the word may be used here much as is the adjective in Rom. vii. 24, Rev. iii. 17, to describe the sense of wretchedness consequent on sin. Clem. Rom. *Cor.* xxiii. 3, after a warning against doublemindedness, adds words of interest in the present connection: 'Let this scripture be far from us where He saith: *Wretched are the doubleminded, which doubt in their soul* and say, These things we did hear in the days of our fathers also, and behold we have grown old, and none of these things hath befallen us.'

and mourn, and weep. If the previous verb expresses the inward grief and pain, the mourning and weeping may denote its outward manifestation. The two verbs are joined together as in 2 Sam. xix. 1; Neh. viii. 9; cf. our Lord's own words, Luke vi. 25 (Mark xvi. 10; Rev. xviii. 15, 19). The grief has sometimes been referred to clothing in sackcloth and other such external evidence of sorrow, and these, as we have seen above, might well be included among the Jews, but in any case a godly sorrow, a change of heart and mind must result. The

cast of St James's language here is very similar to that of the old Hebrew prophets; cf. e.g. Jer. ix. 18; Joel i. 10; Micah iii. 4; Zech. xi. 2.

let your laughter...and your joy, R.V., employing the pronoun with each noun. We may compare again for the language, Amos viii. 10; Prov. xiv. 13; Tobit ii. 6; 1 Macc. ix. 41, etc.; and also our Lord's own prophecy, Luke vi. 25, which St James may have had in mind.

Laughter and joy are not of course evil in themselves; cf. e.g. Job viii. 21, where God filleth the mouth with laughter. It is noticeable however that the noun 'laughter' is only found here in the N.T. and the verb only twice in Luke vi. 21, 25, and this rarity has suggested the remark that so little is heard of 'laughter' in the N.T. because Hebrew laughter was a grave and serious thing; 'it had had no comedy to degrade it.' But in this passage the stress is laid on *your* laughter, *your* joy; it was the unseemly laughter and merriment of the friend of the world, the sport of the fool, which St James reproved; Prov. x. 23.

heaviness; only twice in Biblical Greek, but the cognate adjective occurs Wisd. xvii. 6. The noun is found often in Philo, and it occurs also in classical Greek and in Josephus. Literally it signifies a casting of the eyes downwards, and it is used by Plutarch, *Them.* 9, as a synonym of *despondency, despair.* Here St James calls upon the 'sinners' to adopt as it were the attitude of the publican who could only call himself 'the sinner,' and who 'would not so much as lift up his eyes unto heaven,' Luke xviii. 13.

10 your joy to heaviness. Humble yourselves in the sight of
the Lord, and he shall exalt you.

11   Speak not one against another, brethren. He that
speaketh against a brother, or judgeth his brother, speak-

10. *Humble yourselves.* This may
refer back to the promise of *v.* 6;
or it may be that as the writer has
bidden them to cleanse themselves
and to draw nigh to God, they are
now thought of more specially as
'in the sight of the Lord' (in the
parallel, 1 Pet. v. 6, it is noteworthy
that the expression is different), in
Whose presence the haughtiness of
men shall be brought low, but Who
dwells with the humble and contrite
spirit; cf. also the language of
Ecclus. ii. 17, iii. 18.

the Lord, i.e. God, not Christ in
this passage; cf. *v.* 7.

shall exalt you, R.V. This rendering brings the words more closely
into connection with the words of
our Lord; cf. Matt. xxiii. 12; Luke
xiv. 11.   At the same time the
teaching would be also familiar to
every Jew in the O.T.; cf. Job v. 11;
Ezek. xxi. 26, etc.; so also *Testaments
of the Twelve Patriarchs,* Jos. 18,
'if ye walk in the commandments
of the Lord, he will exalt you.' For
the further bearing of the words
see note on i. 9.

11. *Speak not one against another,
brethren,* R.V. In A.V. 'speak not
evil,' etc.; so in Rom. i. 30, the cognate
adjective = backbiters in both A.V.
and R.V., but the word does not
always contain the idea of secrecy.
Humility before God and the friendship of God would guard from this
sin and love of censoriousness and
fault-finding, not only because the
love of God must mean love of men
as brethren, but also because true
humility would prevent every Chris-

tian from usurping the right of God
to be the sole judge. St James had
already insisted upon the same
urgent necessity of freedom from
this fault, and here the whole
previous context might have well
led him to recur to a similar exhortation. The command seems to be
quite general—cf. 'one another' and
'brethren'—and not to be confined
to the teachers as some have thought,
or to those who may have been
tempted to refuse brotherly love to
the sinners and 'adulterers' who
had vexed them with their lawless
deeds. The verb (although only in
1 Pet. ii. 12, iii. 16, elsewhere in
N.T.) is frequent in LXX, and cf. for
its meaning here Ps. l. 20, ci. 5, and
*Testaments of the Twelve Patri-
archs,* Gad 5. The cognate noun
occurs Wisdom i. 11, where however
it is used of disparagement of God.
The same noun is found 2 Cor. xii.
20, 1 Pet. ii. 1, of evil-speaking
against men, and for the same sense
cf. Clem. Rom. *Cor.* xxx. 1, 3, where
it occurs in a context which reminds
us closely of St James, inasmuch as
the same quotation from Prov. iii. 6
occurs. In Hermas, *Mand.* ii. 2, it
is noteworthy that we have both the
verb and the noun: 'First of all
speak evil of no man...evil-speaking
is evil; it is a restless demon, never
at peace, etc.'

*He that speaketh against a brother,
or judgeth his brother,* R.V., but
A.V. renders '*his* brother' in both
cases, and instead of 'or judgeth'
renders 'and judgeth.' But the
pronoun 'his' is only found in the

eth against the law, and judgeth the law : but if thou
judgest the law, thou art not a doer of the law, but a judge.
12 One *only* is the lawgiver and judge, *even* he who is able to

original in the second clause, where
it intensifies the appeal to brotherhood (the word 'brother' occurs thrice
in this sentence), and in the second
clause the disjunctive 'or' is supported by the highest authorities.

To speak evil presupposes a judgment already formed, but on the other
hand, the act of judgment in the
context may indicate something more
formal and definite than the evil-
speaking, or the two terms may be
practically synonymous ; cf. *v.* 12,
where only the latter verb is used
(Matt. vii. 1). In connection with
the warning here we may read
Didache, ii. 3, 7, 'Thou shalt not
speak evil...thou shalt not hate any
man, but some thou shalt reprove,
and for some thou shalt pray, and
others thou shalt love more than thy
life.'

speaketh against the law, i.e. the
royal law, 'Thou shalt love thy
neighbour as thyself,' ii. 8, a reference which is rightly made plain by
the R.V. reading, *v.* 12, 'who art
thou that judgest *thy neighbour?*'
By speaking against his neighbour
a man speaks against the law of
brotherhood, and practically declares
for the abrogation of the law. As
elsewhere, St James takes up a
previous phrase and repeats it in
the context; cf. note on i. 4.

It is tempting to take the law as
meaning the whole Mosaic law, and
it is no doubt probable that the
question of the observance of that
law had already been mooted. From
the first some Jewish-Christians had
foreseen that it was only transitory,
and perhaps some of these might
have been tempted to speak against

others who were strong in its observance. But St James is not himself
prepared for this, and so he reminds
them that none can change this law
but the only Lawgiver and Judge.
It is, however, best on the whole in
accordance with the general tone of
the passage to interpret the words
as above.

but if thou judgest. By this act of
judgment and setting yourself *ipso
facto* above the law you pass out of
the category of 'doers of the law' and
you arrogate to yourself the position
of a judge to which you have no
right (see next verse); cf. Matt. vii. 1.

12. *One only is the lawgiver
and judge*, R.V. The words 'and
judge' are added by R.V., W.H.
You cannot 'lay down the law' in
the sense of either enactment or
pronouncement, since both enactment and pronouncement are with
Him Who has the power of life and
death; cf. John xix. 11, and the
teaching of St Peter and St Paul,
1 Pet. ii. 13, Rom. xiii. 1.

one, emphatic; not man, but One
Who is the ultimate and only source
of all law. The reference is not to
Christ here, as some have urged from
v. 9, but to God ; see Isaiah xxxiii.
22, where God is spoken of as judge
and lawgiver.

lawgiver, a classical word, only
found here in N.T., but cognate verb
and noun occur in N.T. and in LXX.

even he, R.V., drawing out the
force of the '*One* only' and closely
connected with it.

able to save and to destroy, since
He alone has control over the issues
of life and death: 2 Kings v. 7;
Luke vi. 9; cf. also Matt. x. 28.

save and to destroy : but who art thou that judgest thy neighbour ?

13   Go to now, ye that say, To-day or to-morrow we will

In Hermas, *Mand.* xii. 6. 3, *Sim.* ix. 23. 4, similar expressions are referred to God, a fact which speaks for the reference of the words law-giver and judge to Him as above. (It is to be remembered however that the reference in Matt. x. 28 to God has been keenly disputed, as e.g. by F. D. Maurice ; see also the margin *in loco*.)

With the words and thought we may compare *Sayings of the Fathers,* iv. 31, 32, where God is spoken of as the framer, the creator, and the dis-cerner, and the judge...with Whom is no iniquity, nor forgetfulness, nor respect of persons...*for all is His* : 'Let not thine imagination assume then that the grave is an asylum, for perforce thou wast framed (Jer. xviii. 6), and perforce thou wast born, and perforce thou livest, and perforce thou diest, and perforce thou art about to give account and reckoning before the King of the kings of kings, the Holy One, blessed is He.'

but who art thou that judgest thy neighbour? marking the powerless-ness of man in contrast to the supreme power of God : 'but thou who art thou?' etc. Cf. for the question Rom. ix. 20, xiv. 4. The attitude of men in presence of God is best marked by Clem. Rom. *Cor.* xiii. ff., where, after quoting the words of Christ, 'As ye judge, so shall ye be judged,' he proceeds to exhort to lowliness of mind, and instances Abraham, who in the presence of the Judge of all the earth exclaimed, *I am dust and ashes*; and the law-giver Moses, through whose minis-tration God judged Egypt, who said

at the bush, *Who am I that thou sendest me?*

thy neighbour? So R. V., W.H. and all editors.

'Judge not thy friend,' said Hillel, 'until thou comest into his place'; cf. *Sayings of the Fathers,* ii. 5.

13. *Go to now;* only here and in v. 1 in the N.T.[1] The phrase is used, like an adverb, to arouse attention, and in this case special attention to the warnings which follow.

ye that say. The whole section to ch. v. 6 is sometimes taken to refer not so much to Christians, as to the rich outside the Christian community; cf. ii. 6. But we cannot be sure, in the first place, that the same persons are addressed in iv. 13–17 as in v. 1–6 (see below on v. 1), and it is possible to insist too much upon a parallelism between the two sections on the ground that they both com-mence with the same 'Go to now.'

It is quite true that in the section begun thus, iv. 13–17, the word 'brethren' is wanting, but so it is in iv. 1, while it is scarcely fair to allege that the call to repentance is also wanting, as it may be heard in the language of *vv.* 15, 17. At the same time it is evident that the exhorta-tions and warnings are of such a kind as would be fitly addressed to *Jewish* Christians engaged like so many of their fellow-countrymen in the rest-less activity of commercial enterprise ; men engrossed in business and its gains would be peculiarly liable to a friendship with 'the world' and to the sins of presumption, improvi-dence, and pride (see below).

To-day or to-morrow. So A. and

---

[1] On the phrase and its Biblical use see Hastings' *B.D.* ii. 194.

go into this city, and spend a year there, and trade, and
14 get gain : whereas ye know not what shall be on the

R.V., following the Received Text,
and so in this case Mayor and W.H.
Another reading gives 'to-day *and*
to-morrow,' and it is urged that this
makes the boasting more marked,
inasmuch as a longer journey is thus
intimated, and confidence is assumed
not only with regard to to-morrow,
but also in regard to the day after.
It may also be said that 'to-day and
to-morrow' had become a proverbial
Jewish expression, denoting the
present and the immediate future
(cf. Luke xiii. 32, 33), and thus St
James might naturally employ it
here. Possibly the same phrase may
be found in *Psalms of Solomon*, v.
15[1]. But with either reading, a
warning is plainly directed against
the man who forgets to say 'my times
are in Thy hand,' Psalm xxxi. 15; cf.
also Luke xii. 16 ff.

'If St James rebukes the presumption of those who say, "to-day
or to-morrow we will go," etc., Seneca
in a similar spirit says that the wise
man will "never promise himself anything on the security of fortune, but
will say, I will sail unless anything
happen, and, I will become praetor
unless anything happen, and, my
business will turn out well for me
unless anything happen,"' Lightfoot,
Philippians, p. 287 (and for further
similar instances cf. Wetstein *in loco*).
Philo has an interesting passage,
Leg. Alleg. ii. p. 103 B, 'The husbandman says, "I will cast seeds, I will
plant, the plants will grow, they will
bear fruit,"...but he who made these
calculations did not enjoy them, but
died beforehand; it is best to trust
God, and not uncertain calculations.'

we will go, so A. and R.V., i.e.
'will make our journey,' as if from
this point of view all was mapped
out definitely and securely; cf. note
on the noun in i. 10 rendered 'goings,'
R.V. The future indicative (rather
than the conjunctive which is rendered by some authorities) emphasises
this confidence in their own plans,
and the same presumptuous certainty.

into this city, R.V., i.e. that particular city which each intending
traveller had in his mind, or which
each points out as it were upon the
map. A.V. renders 'into such a city,'
i.e. this or that city, indefinitely, as
if the writer was quite unaware what
city the speakers would name. The
former rendering seems here to fit
in best with the context, as the more
forcible.

and spend a year there, R.V., the
noun being the object of the verb
and not simply accusative of duration. This rendering brings out more
vividly and more correctly than A.V.
the thought that their time was
regarded as in their own power to
measure out as they pleased. The
reading 'one year' is retained by
some authorities (although omitted
by A. and R.V., W.H. and Mayor);
'one year,' 'so they speak,' writes
Bengel, 'as if soon about to deliberate
as to the following years.'

and trade, R.V., 'buy and sell,'
A.V. The verb in the original =
primarily to travel, and then to
travel for traffic or business, to act
as a merchant; so in LXX, Gen. xxxiv.
10, 21.

and get gain. Their hearts were
with their treasures, and so in

---

[1] See James and Ryle's edition, p. 59. The reading 'and' in the verse before
us is supported amongst modern editors by Beyschlag and von Soden.

morrow.   What is your life ?   For ye are a vapour, that

thought they map out each stage of the progress to the goal they had set before them, with no doubt whatever as to the certainty of the issue. The cumulative force of the conjunction 'and' is thus strikingly marked here (cf. i. 24), while the attractive hold of the friendship of the world is witnessed to by the one object of their journey—to get gain. The picture here drawn is quite consistent with what we know at this early period of the trading migratory life of the Jews of the Dispersion : cf. Acts xviii. 2, 18 ; Rom. xvi. 3. (Carr's note in the Cambridge Greek Testament is interesting in its quotations bearing on the commercial life of the Jews.)

14. *whereas ye know not;* in apposition to the preceding nominative: 'seeing that ye belong to a class of persons, to persons whose nature is such that they know not,' etc.

what shall be on the morrow, lit. the thing, the event of to-morrow ; so R.V. or, according to another reading, adopted by W.H. in marg., plural, 'the things, the events of to-morrow'; cf. for similar phrases Luke xx. 25 ; Rom. xiv. 19 ; 2 Cor. xi. 30[1]. In relation to the morrow an almost similar expression meets us in LXX, Prov. xxvii. 1, where we read in the spirit of St James, 'boast not thyself of to-morrow'; and none had emphasised more strongly the folly

of building on to-morrow than our Lord Himself; cf. Luke xii. 16.

In heathen sources the same teaching as to the limit of man's knowledge of the future was very general ; so e.g. Seneca writes, 'No one has gods so propitious that he can promise to himself to-morrow.' Phokylides declares, 'No one knows what shall be on the day after to-morrow, or during the next hour.' The Jews tell how Rabbi Simeon, on returning from a feast at which a man had boasted that he would keep old wine for the joy of his son, was met by the angel of death, who told him that he was appointed to destroy those who boasted that they were able to do this or that, and that accordingly the boaster should die after 30 days (Wetstein, *in loco*). It has been suggested that the words may mean that they are people of such a kind as not to know the one thing which the future of to-morrow must bring ('the thing of to-morrow'), viz. the transitoriness of all that is around them ; but this is rather a strained interpretation of the Greek.

What is your life? So R.V., placing a full-stop after the preceding clause. This would not be unfitting for the abrupt style of St James, but the conjunction 'for' if retained naturally explains and substantiates their lack of knowledge. Perhaps better 'of

---

[1] It should be noted that there is another reading adopted by W.H. and Dr Plummer, and by Dr B. Weiss in Germany, which might be rendered as follows : 'whereas ye know not on the morrow of what kind your life shall be.' But it may be fairly urged that the thought thus expressed is weaker than that of the reading adopted in the text, since it presupposes that they will still live on the following day, whereas even the morrow, in the rendering preferred, is represented as something doubtful. See also Mayor's criticism on the weakening of the passage, and on the harshness of the construction in the proposed alteration.

appeareth for a little time, and then vanisheth away.

what kind is your life,' in a depreciatory sense (cf. 1 Pet. ii. 20), of what a sorry, pitiable nature. Bede would interpret the expression of the life of the ungodly, since the writer says 'your life' not 'our life'; but the thought is more general, and reminds all readers of the fleeting nature of human life (although in Wisdom ii. 4, v. 14, the context refers somewhat similar words to the life of the ungodly).

For ye are a vapour. The (second) 'for' (omitted by W.H. in marg.) continues the same depreciatory note. In A.V. 'it is even a vapour,' but R.V. is strongly supported and also gives a much stronger sense; the *life* is not seen, but *ye*, says St James, are seen, although only for a little while ; cf. what is said of the rich in i. 10. From another point of view indeed, and in so far as men were mindful that they belonged to 'the things unseen eternal,' that the spirit does not mean the breath, they would also know that the true Christian had in his true self an abiding possession although the outward man decayed; cf. esp. Heb. x. 34, R.V. marg.

a vapour; only here in N.T. and in Acts ii. 19 (from Joel ii. 30), translated as here; so in A.V. marg. Wisdom vii. 25. It has in the O.T. and Apoc. more generally the meaning of smoke, as of the altar or furnace. In Clem. Rom. *Cor.* xvii. 6, it is found (in a quotation perhaps from Eldad and Medad) as meaning 'I am smoke from a pot,' or perhaps 'steam from a kettle,' giving the word the signification which it has also in classical Greek, wherever it is used of smoke or steam, Lat. *vapor.* There is some-

thing to be said for rendering it here by 'breath,' as one or two recent commentators urge, on the ground that this rendering would emphasise the comparison which is evidently intended to something of the most fleeting and transient character. It is noteworthy that although we cannot quote LXX in support of this meaning in a context similar to the passage before us, yet in the version of Aquila the word is used to express 'vanity of vanities,' Ecclesiast. xii. 8, whilst Theodotion renders Ps. lxii. 9, 'only vanity are the sons of mankind,' by the same word, meaning 'breath' (cf. the meaning of the Hebrew word used), and so again he renders Ps. cxliv. 4, 'man is like a thing of nought,' by the same Greek word, to translate the Hebrew 'breath.'

that appeareth for a little time, etc. The force of the best supported reading may be expressed even more fully, 'which appeareth for a little while, and afterwards so vanisheth, as it appeared'; appearing, and disappearing as it came. With the imagery of the verse we may compare Ps. cii. 3, cxliv. 4 ; Job viii. 9; Wisdom ii. 4, v. 14; and similar imagery is frequent outside the N.T. Thus Aeschylus speaks of human life as nothing more sure than a shadow of smoke, Horace speaks of men as being simply dust and shade, and parallel expressions meet us in Pindar and Sophocles. St Gregory of Nazianzus thus sums up the different comparisons instituted to enforce the lesson of the uncertainty of human life: 'We are a fleeting dream, a phantom which cannot be grasped, the scud of a passing breeze, a ship that leaves no track upon the sea,

15 [1]For that ye ought to say, If the Lord will, we shall both

[1] Gr. *Instead of your saying.*

dust, a vapour, morning dew, a flower that now springs up and now is done away': see *Speaker's Commentary* on Wisdom ii. 5[1]. One striking passage from one of the best and noblest of the Stoics shows how much the highest ethical teaching outside the N.T. wanted of the sure and certain hope which fortified Christian resignation even in the darkest struggles of life. Marcus Antoninus, II. 17, writes, 'everything which belongs to the body is a stream, and what belongs to the soul is a dream and vapour, and life is a warfare and a stranger's sojourn, and after-fame is oblivion. What then can keep a man straight? one thing and only one, philosophy, and this consists in keeping the divinity within free from violence and unharmed, superior to pains and pleasure; in waiting cheerfully for death, as being nothing else than a dissolution of the elements of which every living being is compounded.... For this is according to nature, and nothing is evil which is according to nature.' The interesting story is well known of the preaching of Christianity at the Court of Edwin of Deira by Paulinus, and what ensued, in consideration of the light thrown by the new faith upon what had preceded and what followed the life of man, 'which appeared for a little time'; see Bede, ii. 13. The pagan priest had already asked that the new religion might be inquired into, and he was followed by a lay noble in words so touching that the poet Wordsworth thought them worthy of his verse (*Eccles. Sonnets*, 16): 'The present life of man, O king, seems to me like to the swift flight of a sparrow through the room, wherein you sit at supper in the winter with your commanders and ministers, and a good fire in the midst, whilst the storms of rain and snow prevail abroad; the sparrow flies in at one door and immediately out at another; while within, he is safe from the wintry storm, but soon he vanishes out of your sight from one winter to another.' 'So,' he added, 'this life of man appears for a short space, but of what went before, or what is to follow, we are wholly ignorant.' 'If therefore,' he concluded, 'this new doctrine contains something more certain, it seems justly to deserve to be followed.' Paulinus was heard, and the conversion of the people ensued.

15. *For that ye ought to say;* but R.V. marg. 'instead of your saying,' plainly referring the words back to 'ye that say' in *v.* 13, *v.* 14 being regarded as parenthetical.

If the Lord will, i.e. God: cf. Acts xviii. 21; 1 Cor. iv. 19, xvi. 7; Heb. vi. 3. Similar sayings may be quoted from classical writers. In *Sayings of the Fathers,* ii. 4, we read, 'Do His will as if it were thy will, that He may do thy will as if it were His will, annul thy will before His will, that He may annul the will of others before thy will'; and in *Didache,* iii. 9, it is part of 'the way of life' to receive the accidents that

---

[1] In the R.V. we have the article expressed in the phrase '*which* appeareth for a little while,' but W.H. omit it. Mayor however defends its retention, and remarks that thus 'the tendency to appear and disappear is made a property of the vapour, and not a mere accidental circumstance.'

16 live, and do this or that.　But now ye glory in your vaunt-

shall befall men as good, knowing that nothing is done without God. So too we may compare the saying of Ben Sira, quoted by Grotius, 'Let a man never say that he will do anything unless he first says, "If God will."' For Jew and Christian alike a living personal Will ruled the universe; the very word 'Lord' used by both of them signified One Who had authority and control.

we shall both live, and do this or that, R.V., making it evident that our life as well as our actions is equally determined by God. The Textus Receptus (but not A.V.) reads the verb 'live' in the subjunctive, and the sense would be 'if the Lord will and we live, we shall do this or that.' But the rendering is not so correct in meaning as above, although it is found in the Syriac and the Vulgate, because it really regards our life as independent of God, and the weight of manuscript authority is undoubtedly against it. Equally forcible objections may be made against reading the verb 'live' as the future indicative, and yet placing it in the protasis, for the incorrect meaning is in this way still retained, and the construction in the original would be considerably strained. It is noteworthy that the repetition of the conjunctions 'both' ...'and' may be compared with the repetition of the same conjunctions in *v*. 13, and may thus bear out the above rendering as being in accord with St James's style.

16. *But now*, i.e. as the case stands, instead of saying what you ought to say: cf. 1 Cor. v. 11, xiv. 6; and Luke xix. 42.

ye glory, R.V. The verb is used

elsewhere of glorying with or without reason; so frequently in LXX.

your vauntings, R.V., i.e. in such speeches as in *v*. 13, 'we will go...we will get gain,' and in their anticipation of time to do all this would be their 'boasting'; cf. Prov. xxvii. 1, 'boast not thyself of to-morrow, for thou knowest not what a day may bring forth.' In classical Greek the word is often associated with braggart and boasting talk, and Plato joins together 'false and boastful words'; in Wisd. ii. 16 the cognate verb is used contemptuously or of vaunting and idle bragging; and St Clement of Rome, *Cor.* xxi. 5, speaks of foolish and senseless men who exalt themselves and boast in the arrogance of their words, using the same noun as, and for 'boast' a verb closely allied to, that employed by St James; see also on *v*. 6 above. But the word may be employed here quite generally of empty presumption and display, which manifest a trust in the stability of earthly things, and it was so interpreted in this verse by the earlier commentators Oecumenius and Theophylact; cf. 1 John ii. 16, and Wisd. v. 8, where we read, 'what hath pride profited us? or what good hath riches with vaunting brought us? all those things are passed away like a shadow'; cf. also 2 Macc. ix. 8, of the braggart vaunting of Antiochus Epiphanes, and see also for further similar use 4 Macc. i. 26. The plural may be used here to mark the various ways in which this display, this pride of life, may assert itself. We have perhaps no word which renders the noun at all so adequately as the German 'Prahlerei,' as Trench points out, and it may be noted that it is so rendered in the German

K.　　　　　　　　　　　　　　　　8

17 ings : all such glorying is evil. To him therefore that knoweth to do good, and doeth it not, to him it is sin.

translation of the passage 4 Macc. i. 26.

all such glorying. There *is* a glorying which is commended (cf. i. 9), but not *such* glorying; the glorying here is merely bragging and boasting: cf. 1 Cor. v. 6.

17. This may be taken either as a conclusion of all that has gone before, reaching back to i. 22, or as referring to the particular sin of presumption, and to such words as those in *v.* 13. But it is not quite easy to see why St James should introduce a general maxim here, where other exhortations are to follow. If we take the words as having a special connection with the verses immediately preceding, the 'doing good' would be the making one's decisions dependent on the will of God; the 'knowing' would be the daily experience of the unreality of human life; the 'not doing' would be the boastful braggart purposing[1]. At the same time we cannot forget how

solemnly our Lord has emphasised this great truth that failure to do right is sin, Matt. xxv. 46.

Another effort has been made in connection with this verse to show that St James may here also go back to a pre-canonical Gospel, and that he may be quoting a saying derived from our Lord. This is supported by a quotation of Luke xii. 47 by Origen *in Jerem.* xvi. 7, where the verb used for 'knowing' His will is the same as is here used by St James for 'knowing' what is good, while St Luke seems to follow another translation of the supposed Gospel in reading another word for 'knowing.' But it is urged by Resch that the general sense in Luke, Origen, James, is the same, and points back to the existence of some old document behind all three. It cannot, however, be said that any reliable force attaches to Resch's contention here.

CHAPTER V.

1—3. From the spirit of commerce and trading, transition is made to the consideration of a spirit more wicked still, a spirit not only of selfishness, but of tyranny and oppression in the employment of wealth. The rich are bidden to weep and howl ; no call to repentance, but a foretelling of the certainty of their coming misery ; the rottenness of their corn, the decay of their garments, the rust of their gold, are symbols of the destruction which is in store for themselves; and yet they have laid up treasures in the last days, when the time was so short and the judge so near. **4—6.** Already the cry of the labourers, whom they had hired and then cheated of their wages, has obtained a hearing from the Lord of Hosts, but they, whilst that exceeding bitter cry went up to heaven, had been taking their pleasure on earth, fattening themselves like sheep for slaughter, sacrificing not their self-will

---

[1] Von Soden, and much to the same effect Plummer ; see too *Century Bible, in loco.*

or their treasures, but the righteous one, who does not resist, because as the Lord's servant he must not strive.   **7—9.**   The brethren therefore must be patient, like the righteous one; the coming of the Lord is sure, and the reward is sure for those who wait for Him, as sure as for the husbandmen of Palestine who wait in patience for the harvest of the earth.   Be on your guard against murmuring and discontent amongst yourselves; ye too no less than your oppressors will be judged; be patient therefore; the Judge is at hand, do not usurp His office.   **10, 11.**   In the prophets of old we have examples of suffering and of patience, and those who patiently endure we call 'blessed.'   Job endured, and we know the issue, how for him mercy gloried over judgment.

Thus St James may be said to work back as it were to the opening Beatitude of his Epistle (cf. i. 12), and all that follows is a kind of postscript suggested by the special circumstances around him.

12, 13.   Above all things, i.e. bearing in mind the different forms of murmuring and impatience to which they might be tempted, the speaking against one another and the forgetfulness of their relationship as brethren, let theirs be the yea, yea, and the nay, nay, and let no further sanction be needed, that they fall not under judgment; but whatever their emotions might be, whether of joy or of sorrow, let them be sanctified by worship, the worship of prayer and praise.   **14, 15.**   One form of suffering is common enough, sickness; if it comes upon anyone, let him send for the elders of the Church, let them pray over the sick and anoint him with oil; if it be God's will the bodily health will be restored, and not only so, but by the prayer of faith, the sins, which may have been the cause of the sickness, shall be forgiven.   **16—18.**   Confess therefore your faults to one another, and pray for one another, that the time of healing may come from the presence of the Lord.   Elijah is an example of the power of prayer and intercession, when offered by a righteous man, and yet by a man of like passions with ourselves.   **19, 20.**   Prayer, remember, may prove to be the first step towards the conversion of one who has wandered from the truth; and this bringing back into the right way will save a soul from death, and confer a blessing upon him who gives, and upon him who accepts, a brother's guidance.

V.   Go to now, ye rich, weep and howl for your miseries

V. 1. *Go to now, ye rich.* It is a difficult question to decide whether the persons addressed in the section before us are the same as those addressed in iv. 13–17. On the one hand it is urged that there is no exhortation to repentance, and no mention of a hope of salvation, which would not have been omitted in the case of Christian believers, and that the return to the word 'brethren,' v. 7, for whom the coming of the Lord is to be a comfort, in contrast to the terror which the same judgment is to bring upon 'the rich,' *v.* 1, indicates that two different classes of persons are intended. The 'rich' here would thus be as the rich in ii. 6, 7, unbelieving Jews. Moreover, it is urged that the words 'go to now' indicate not a parallelism between the two sections, iv. 13–17, v. 1–6, but rather a new beginning. On the other hand, the following points are noted in favour of regarding the persons in both sections as Christians; (1) that it would have been purposeless to address such a denunciation and one dealing so intimately with practical life as that contained in *vv.* 1—6 to unbelieving Jews in a letter not intended for them at all but for Jewish believers; (2) that from this point of view the manifest parallelism between the two sections, both introduced by the same phrase 'go to now,' must be considered; if the merchants of the first section are believers, as may be inferred from iv. 15, it would seem that the rich of the section succeeding must be placed in the same category; (3) that the exhortation to patient endurance, *v.* 7, introduced by the word 'therefore' is evidently based upon the oppression of the rich landowners, and that both oppressor and oppressed belonged to the Christian community : 'murmur not brethren one against another,' *v.* 9 (see however *in loco*)[1]. But it cannot be said that these arguments are convincing, and a further suggestion has been made as a solution of the difficulty (see above, p. xxxix.). If we maintain a very early date for the Epistle, and if we remember that the character of St James for sanctity and piety was widely known amongst his fellow-countrymen, he may have expected that his words would gain a hearing in some circles where his name still carried respect, and where the followers of Jesus of Nazareth would not be regarded as those who had broken away entirely from the Jewish

religion and polity[2]. Closely on the lines of this suggestion is that which would regard St James as here apostrophising after the manner of the O.T. prophets those who belonged neither to hearers nor readers (just as the prophets addressed themselves to heathen towns and people). That the whole section before us reminds us of the stern denunciatory tone of the O.T. cannot be denied, and even in a practical letter such words may well have flowed from the pen of the writer. James the Just, who like another Joel or Amos, possibly in his very dress, most certainly in the stern sanctity of his own life, would find his heart burn within him at the insolent impiety and greed which were eating into the very life of his nation, had caught something of the Spirit of One greater than the greatest prophet in His announcement of the inevitable doom about to follow upon the extortion and excess, which devoured the house of the widow and neglected mercy, judgment, and faith. Nor does it seem difficult to understand how from such a passage as iv. 13-17 a writer might easily pass in thought to the sins of the rich, so closely connected with national and social life : cf. in the O.T. Amos iii. 10-13, viii. 1-10; Hab. ii. 9; Isaiah xxxiii. 1 ff.; Jer. v. 1, etc.

go to now. Cf. for the phrase iv. 13. As the merchantmen of the former section were warned against glorying in their vauntings, so here St James, we may well believe, would have the rich ask the question of Wisdom v. 8, 'what good hath riches with our vaunting brought

---

[1] See especially Zahn and Belser in their N.T. *Introductions.*
[2] Cf. J. V. Bartlet, *Apostolic Age*, pp. 232-236; and see also Stanley, *Sermons on the Apostolic Age*, pp 299-301.

2 that are coming upon you. Your riches are corrupted, and

us?' where the same word is used for 'vaunting' as in iv. 16 (see above, p. 113).

weep and howl (cf. Luke vi. 24, 25); not here in repentance, but in anguish for the impending judgment. The former verb is used of crying, not silently but aloud, and is of frequent occurrence in the O.T. prophets. The second verb is added to intensify the wretchedness of the prospect: cf. Isaiah xv. 3, and so too xiii. 6. In these places it is used as here in close connection with imminent judgment, 'howl ye, for the day of the Lord is at hand.' The verb, an onomatopoetic word, is only found here in the N.T., and whereas in classical Greek it may be used of cries of joy and thanksgiving, in the LXX it is used only of cries of grief. The word 'weep' is in the aorist, not instead of a future tense, but as signifying what ought to be done forthwith.

miseries. See above on iv. 9. The noun is only found here in N.T. and Rom. iii. 16, in a quotation from Isaiah lix. 7, 8. It is frequently found in the LXX with various shades of meaning: cf. e.g. Ps. cxxxix. 10; Amos v. 9, etc.

that are coming upon you, R.V. ('shall come,' A.V.), the present participle denoting that the miseries are close at hand, at the door (cf. Luke xx. 35), or, more abruptly, the words might be rendered, 'your miseries that are coming on' (cf. Ephes. ii. 7, where the same verb is used absolutely), as in the best texts there is no word expressing 'upon you': 'coming on,' i.e. at the Parousia; cf. *vv.* 7, 9. The confusion of the rich in the day of judgment, and the 'woe' pronounced

upon them, are frequently mentioned in the *Book of Enoch*; cf. e.g. xciv. 6, 8, xcvii. 8–10.

2. *Your riches are corrupted.* The three verbs which follow represent in the style of the O.T. prophets that the 'miseries' of the rich are already come upon them. It is a question whether the words are used of wealth in general; cf. the use of the verb in Ecclus. xiv. 19 (the whole passage from *v.* 3 should be compared with the text here), 'every work which is corruptible shall consume away.' But as the same verb is used in connection with the withering of fruit, and of the 'rotting' of the heathen idols, Ezek. xvii. 9, *Epistle of Jeremy, v.* 72, it is suggested that here the word refers to such 'riches' as would be comprised under corn, oil, etc., and might be translated 'rotted.' This meaning would fit in with the context, as gold and silver are separately mentioned just below. If the more general signification of 'riches' is retained, the wealth becomes specialised as garments and treasures. From this point of view a striking passage may be quoted from *Enoch,* xcvii. 8–10, of the 'woe' upon the rich in the day appointed for the judgment of unrighteousness. After speaking in the previous verse of men who will put on more adornments than a woman, who will be poured out as water in royalty and grandeur, in silver and gold, in splendour, and in food, the writer proceeds: 'from henceforth ye know that all your oppression wherewith ye oppressed is written down every day till the day of your judgment ......and now, know ye that ye are prepared for the day of destruction;

3 your garments are moth-eaten.   Your gold and your silver
   are rusted ; and their rust shall be for a testimony ¹against

¹ Or, *unto*

wherefore do not hope to live, ye
sinners, but ye shall depart and die ;
for ye know no ransoms ; for ye
are prepared for the day of the great
judgment and for the day of tribulation, and great shame for your
spirit.'

your garments are moth-eaten, of
which in Oriental countries wealth
was so largely composed : cf. 1 Macc.
xi. 24 ; Acts xx. 33.   In Matt. vi. 19,
of which the expression here very
fitly reminds us, the word moth,
the clothes-moth, clearly indicates
garments as part of the treasure.
The adjective is only found here in
the N.T., but cf. Job xiii. 28 ; Isaiah
li. 8 ; also Ecclus. xlii. 13.   The word
is also used of idol images, *Orac.
Sib.* fragm.

In *Enoch*, xcviii. 1–3, the transitory
glory of gold and silver and purple
and coloured garments is emphatically condemned, and those who give
themselves wholly to such external
possessions are described as finally
losing their personality in them, as
water is lost in the earth.   St James
would have had before his eyes the
picture of the man in fine clothing
whom he had so graphically described in ii. 2.

3.   *are rusted ; and their rust.*
A.V. renders 'are cankered,' but
in the original we have a cognate
verb and noun, so that the R.V. is
justified, and the same rendering is
given by Wycliffe.   The verb might
well be rendered 'are rusted through
and through' or 'are covered with
rust,' as in the original the simple
verb is compounded with an intensi-

fying preposition.   The same verb as
here is found in Ecclus. xii. 11,
in relation to a mirror, where, in the
Speaker's Commentary, Dr Edersheim pleads for the rendering
'tarnished' (although the combination and meaning are difficult),
a rendering which he would also
adopt in the verse of St James before
us.   In Ecclus. xii. 10 and xxix.
10 we have the simple verb, but
nowhere else in the LXX.   The figure
of rusting would be easily transferred
in rhetorical and popular language
from less costly metals, like bronze,
Ecclus. xii. 10, to silver and gold,
of which it could not strictly be used ;
cf. *Epist. of Jer.*, *vv.* 12, 24, where
the cognate noun 'rust' is applied
to the gold and silver of images.
From the testimony of Strabo it
appears that a fuliginous vapour
arose from the Dead Sea which
caused, as he said, brass and silver
and even gold to rust (the same verb
being used as by St James), although
it appears that the rust referred to
was only a change of colour in the
metals caused by the bituminous
exhalation¹.   Dr Edersheim in
Speaker's Commentary, u.s., sees in
this verse another proof of the use
of Ecclesiasticus by St James.   The
figure used by St James of rust
affecting the unused silver and gold
is derived, he thinks, from this
passage in that book.   It is not
found elsewhere in Scripture, and
moreover the noun for 'rust' used
by St James, and by him only in the
same signification in the N.T., is
closely connected with the passage

¹ See Theile's note, where the passage is quoted, and also Mayor *in loco*.

you, and shall eat your flesh as fire.   Ye have laid up your

in Ecclus. where the cognate verb
is employed, whilst the stronger
form of the same verb, which is used
by St James alone in the N.T. in the
verse before us, only occurs elsewhere in Biblical Greek in Ecclus.
xii. 11.

*shall be for a testimony against
you,* R.V. text; so A.V.; 'unto you,'
marg. R.V. The rendering in the
text would support the meaning,
adopted by many from the days of
Oecumenius, that the rust on the
gold and silver shows that these
riches had been hoarded up and not
employed profitably, and would thus
testify against them to their shame
in judgment, and the pronoun in the
dative case may be so used ; cf. Matt.
xxiii. 3. The same phrase occurs
Enoch, xcvi. 4, 'this word shall be
a testimony against you.' But the
preceding words imply that the rust
is the result of the judgment which
had begun, and not the effect of the
want of use of this wealth, and this
consuming of their goods would
rather be a symbol and a testimony
to them of their own impending
destruction; in the destruction of
their treasures they would see that
of themselves. But this process of
judgment might also be described
as a testimony 'against them,' and
the two meanings almost seem to
run into each other. The words have
also been explained as meaning that

when they saw the rust spreading in
place of the lustre and brightness,
in which they had gloried, they
would see for themselves how greatly
they had erred.

shall eat your flesh. The expression was a very natural one for
St James to use, as the same phrase,
with the same verb and noun in the
original, occurs Lev. xxvi. 29 ; 2 Kings
ix. 36 ; Micah iii. 2, 3. In the latter
passage a distinction is made between flesh and bones, the word
'flesh' being in the plural as here, and
signifying as here and elsewhere the
fleshy parts of the body ; cf. Judith
xvi. 17 for a similar use, and so twice
in *Psalms of Solomon,* iv. 21, xiii. 3,
where as in Micah flesh and bones
are distinguished. Although the
word 'flesh' need not imply that St
James regards those of whom he
spoke as being nothing else but
flesh, or as being men who fed their
bodies well, yet it is quite possible
that he would thus wish to emphasise the thought that the chief care
of such men was for the flesh[1].

as fire, i.e. as fire devours[2]. Here
again O.T. expressions, where the
judgment is frequently represented
as a devouring, destroying fire, show
how naturally St James might add
the comparison: cf. Ps. xxi. 10 ; Isaiah
x. 16, 17, xxx. 27 ; Ezek. xv. 7 ;
Amos v. 6. The gradual and certain
corroding by rust is compared in its

---

[1] Both von Soden and the Romanist Trenkle remark that as only the
flesh is mentioned the salvation of the spirit is not excluded; cf. 1 Cor. v. 5
and iii. 16.

[2] Oecumenius (so Grotius) connected this word 'fire' with the following phrase:
'ye have laid up your treasure as fire,' i.e. as a torturing and consuming fire, and
this punctuation is adopted by W.H. But although this is supported by two LXX
(not Hebrew) passages, Prov. xvi. 27, Micah vi. 10, especially the former, the
rendering in the text gives a more natural sense. The Vulgate wrongly
associates the passage with Rom. ii. 5, and renders 'ye have treasured up for
yourselves wrath in the last days.'

4 treasure in the last days.   Behold, the hire of the labourers who mowed your fields, which is of you kept back by fraud,

thoroughness with the utter destruction by fire, which destroys not only the wealth but the possessors of it. It is of course possible that the introduction of the figure of fire may also introduce the thought of 'gnawing pain and swift destruction'; cf. *Enoch,* cii. 1, 'in those days when He brings a grievous fire upon you, whither will ye flee and where will ye find deliverance ?'; but this is not emphasised specially in the text, and the comparison may be quite general.

Ye have laid up your treasure, R.V., expressing the one word in the original: cf. Tob. iv. 9 for the expression. In *Psalms of Solomon* the same verb is connected with the thought of judgment: 'whoso doeth righteousness *layeth up for himself* life at the Lord's hand…for the judgments of the Lord are in righteousness according to each man and his house,' ix. 9, 10.

in the last days, R.V.   In A.V. we have 'for,' not 'in,' but this does not afford a correct rendering of the preposition employed. 'The last days' are those which precede the coming of the Lord, as is evident from the context *vv.* 8, 9; see further on these verses. The phrase or one similar frequently occurs in the O.T., e.g. Isaiah ii. 2, Hos. iii. 5, and cf. Acts ii. 17, *Didache,* xvi. 3. Here it intensifies the irony of the passage, and the senselessness of the conduct which laid up treasures which were so soon to profit nothing. As in the original we have simply 'in last days' it is held by some that the words may be taken more generally as of the last days of life, and not necessarily of the Parousia; cf.

Prov. xxxi. 25. But it is doubtful how far such stress can attach to the absence of the article, since it occurs, e.g. in *Didache,* xvi. 3, where the reference to the Parousia is evident, although it is wanting in 1 Pet. i. 5, to say nothing of perhaps a more general reference in 2 Tim. iii. 1.

4.   *Behold,* occurring four times in this chapter and twice in iii., is Hebraistic, and quite characteristic of the fervent, graphic style of the Epistle and of the intense earnestness of the writer: Introd. p. xxxiii.

of the labourers; in the N.T. usually agricultural labourers, husbandmen, although the word might be used quite generally, Wisdom xvii. 17; Ecclus. xix. 1. In strong contrast to the idle luxury of the rich, who were laying up treasure on earth and not in heaven, St James sees the labourers who have done their work waiting for the pay due to them, and wailing and crying in vain to those who had hired them.

who mowed, R.V. In A.V. 'reaped,' but as the original word here is different from that used for reaping below, the Revisers have distinguished, and this is not perhaps to be wondered at when we remember that the word before us is only found here in N.T., whilst the verb translated 'reaping' occurs more than twenty times. On the other hand, in the LXX the verb before us is found five times, and each time it is translated 'to reap' in R.V., whilst the verb below is found very frequently in the LXX, and is used apparently of both reaping and mowing. It has therefore been urged that no distinction need be made between the two; if we

crieth out : and the cries of them that reaped have entered

look, however, at the probable derivation of the verb before us it
will seem to refer primarily to *cutting*
and secondarily to *gathering in.*
The tense which is used indicates
that the wages were due.

your fields. It may be the sin is
regarded as intensified in the case
of men who owned such large estates
and lands, implied probably by the
word in the original; the fields themselves may in some cases at least
have been added to property by acts
of injustice; cf. Isaiah v. 8 and the
context of the present passage.

*which is of you kept back by
fraud*[1]. So A.V. and R.V. If this
construction of the words is retained
it would seem that ' of ' is equivalent
to ' by,' a common usage in earlier
English (14th—16th centuries) to
express the agent after a passive
verb (Hastings' *Dict.*, Art. 'Of'); or
it might be rendered 'on your part,'
the preposition in the original being
one which might be used to denote
that the fraud proceeds from them,
although they might not be the
direct agents in its perpetration.
But by many of the ablest commentators the words 'of you' are connected with the verb 'crieth,' 'crieth from
you,' i.e. from your coffers, or your
dwellings, the place where the money
was so wrongfully detained. In
support of this reference is made
to Gen. iv. 10; Exod. ii. 23; cf. *Enoch,*
xlvii. 1, 'and in those days the prayer
of the righteous and the blood of
the righteous will have ascended
from the earth before the Lord of
Spirits,' and also lii. 5-7. But even
more to the point perhaps is the

fact that in more than one of the
passages, where the wrong detention
of wages is condemned, we read, 'the
wages of an hired servant shall not
abide with thee all night till the
morning,' Lev. xix. 13, and so again,
'let not the wages of any man that
hath wrought for thee tarry with
thee (abide with thee all night), but
give it him out of hand,' Tob. iv. 14.
This sin of keeping back the reward
of the labourers had been denounced
by the prophets, Mal. iii. 5, Jer. xxii.
13, and its mention both in earlier
and later times seems to mark its
frequent recurrence, Lev. xix. 13;
Deut. xxiv. 14, 15; Job xxiv. 10;
Tob. iv. 14; and when we remember
the other parallels in this Epistle to
passages in Ecclesiasticus, the denunciation in that book against de-
frauding the labourer of his hire,
chap. xxxiv. 21, 22 (cf. iv. 1, xxix.
6), where the same verb is used as
here, may well have been present to
the writer's mind; 'the bread of the
needy is the life of the poor : he that
defraudeth him thereof is a man of
blood. He that taketh away his
neighbour's living slayeth him; and
he that defraudeth the labourer of
his hire is a bloodshedder.'

crieth out; often in LXX of the cry
against wrong and robbery, of crying
to God, to heaven; a vivid and poetic
touch; if men are dumb and silent,
if no just judge appear, the money
cries for vengeance; cf. Hab. ii. 11.
In Hermas, *Vis.* iii. 9. 6, where the
writer is exhorting those who refuse
to share with others to look to the
coming judgment, he adds words
which are an echo, one might well

---

[1] W.H. with Mayor and other editors adopt a different reading, but the verb
which they prefer is very similar in sense to that in our English Version.

5 into the ears of the Lord of Sabaoth. Ye have lived

suppose, of this passage in St James, 'look ye therefore (to the judgment) ye that exult in your wealth, lest they that are in want shall moan, and their moaning shall go up unto the Lord.'

and the cries. The cognate verb is used specially of cries for help, and the noun itself is so used in closely similar expressions, Exod. ii. 23; 1 Sam. ix. 16; frequent in the LXX, but here only in N.T. The thought of the cries of men entering into the ears of God finds frequent expression in the O.T.: cf. Ps. xviii. 6; Isaiah v. 9. In *Enoch,* xcvii. 5, we read concerning those who have acquired silver and gold in unrighteousness, 'in those days the prayer of the righteous will reach unto the Lord, and the days of your judgment will overtake you.'

of them that reaped. The participle shows that their work is done, they have reaped a harvest for others, but nothing for themselves; not even for their hard work in the summer heat and in 'the joy of harvest.'

have entered: see above; the cry is not only uttered but heard; cf. Ps. xxxiv. 15.

into the ears. If the phrase had become a kind of proverbial expression (as von Soden holds), how natural is its use by St James! The ears of the Lord are frequently referred to in the O.T. as open to prayer, especially the prayer of the oppressed; cf. also *Psalms of Solomon,* xviii. 3.

the Lord of Sabaoth. So A.V. and R.V. 'Sabaoth,' i.e. hosts. The question has been asked, what hosts are intended? Originally it may be the armies of Israel, but the word was used also of the angels, who may have been originally denoted by that ex-

pression, and stars and forces of nature, as well as of an army of men. But whatever may have been the *origin* of the title it is used in the prophets (where the genitive *Sabaoth* occurs some 246 times out of 282) as 'the highest and most majestic title' of the God of Israel, expressing not only His majesty and power as creator and ruler of the world, but also as commander of the hosts of heaven. In the LXX the Hebrew title is often rendered by the Lord *Omnipotent,* the Lord *All-sovereign;* cf. 2 Cor. vi. 18, and frequently in Rev. in N.T. The Jewish belief in the Lord Omnipotent as the Lord also of the angels is expressed in a remarkable passage, 3 Macc. vi. 17, where the Jews are represented as crying loudly to heaven, and 'the Lord Omnipotent' opens the celestial gates and sends down to the aid of His people two bright angels terrible to behold! Here the title is used to emphasise the fact that the poor were not those who had no helper, but that they had on their side the Lord of Hosts Who could destroy the tyranny and punish the injustice of the rich oppressors. It is noticeable that the same title occurs frequently in Malachi, and that James may well have it in mind in connection with the oppression of the hireling in his wages; cf. Mal. iii. 5. See Art. 'Lord of Hosts,' Hastings' *B. D.,* and 'Names' in *Encycl. Biblica,* III. 3328. The expression is only used here in the N.T. (for Rom. ix. 29 is a direct quotation), and its use certainly points not only to a Jewish author but also to a Jewish audience. For the curiously wrong manner in which 'Sabaoth' became identified with 'Sabbath' by English classics, Spenser,

delicately on the earth, and taken your pleasure ; ye have

Bacon, Johnson, Scott, see Art. 'Sabaoth,' Smith's *Bibl. Dict.*

5. To injustice was added self-indulgence, and the juxtaposition to the preceding words again emphasises sharply the contrast between the selfish luxury of the rich and the hard lives and bitter wrongs of the poor. *Ye have lived delicately on the earth;* not merely expressing in the last three words their earthly life, but as marking the fact that they lived on regardless of the judgment, far above out of their sight, proceeding against them *in heaven*; regardless that from His throne in heaven the Lord's eyes behold the children of men. Or, the expression 'on the earth' may emphasise the thought that this life of luxury was not lasting, that it ceased when man returned to his dust; cf. Matt. vi. 19. The tense of the verb in the original may here and elsewhere in the verse be fairly rendered by the English perfect, but the standpoint is that of the day of judgment, as if the writer was looking back from that day upon the sinful and luxurious lives of the rich. It has been well noted that we have here the converse of the old Epicurean doctrine; in Tennyson's *Lotos-eaters* the gods in ceaseless enjoyment are 'careless of mankind,' and smile at their woes and lamentations; here men contemn God and say, 'Thou wilt not require it'; yet, in spite of their contempt, 'Thou hast seen it...to take it into thy hand'; cf. *Enoch,* xcviii. 7, 'you do not see that every sin is every day recorded in the presence of the Most High. From henceforth ye know that all your oppression wherewith ye oppressed is written down every day till the day of your judgment.' The verb translated as above in

R.V. is only found here in the N.T., but it is used of a soft and luxurious life, in a bad sense here, and so in Ecclus. xiv. 4, and generally in classical Greek; but in a good sense in Neh. ix. 25, Isaiah lxvi. 11, and so also its compounds, cf. Ps. xxxvi. 4, Isaiah lv. 2. It is derived from a verb which means to break down, and so to enervate, and its cognate noun is found in Luke vii. 25, 2 Pet. ii. 13, and, it should be noted, four times in Ecclus. and once or twice in Wisdom. Another cognate noun is also employed in Ecclus. xxxiv. (xxxi.) 3, in the picture of the rich man filled with delicacies, in contrast, *v.* 4, to the profitless labours of the poor; cf. Luke xii. 18. For a list of Bible passages in which 'delicately' means 'luxuriously,' Art. 'Delicate' in Hastings' *B. D.* may be consulted.

This and the following verb rendered 'have taken your pleasure' in R.V. and 'have been wanton' in A.V. are sometimes regarded as synonymous, but whilst both verbs are used of self-indulgent, dissolute living, the second apparently adds the thought of prodigality, wastefulness: Trench, *Synonyms,* II. 17. It is doubtful whether the R.V. is strong enough to express this. In 1 Tim. v. 6 the participle of the same verb is rendered 'she that giveth herself to pleasure,' and in Ecclus. xxi. 15 'he that is given to pleasure' is contrasted with the man of understanding. It is interesting also to note that in Ezek. xvi. 49 it is found to express the prosperous ease of Sodom, whilst it is added in condemnation of that city, 'neither did she strengthen the hand of the poor and needy.' But the association of the word with the thought of wantonness would cer-

6 nourished your hearts in a day of slaughter. Ye have

tainly seem to be supported by the use of the compound verb in Amos vi. 4, and of the cognate noun in Ecclus. xxvii. 13, and in the passage before us it may be fairly rendered 'ye lived a life of wantonness.' In the explanation of the word given by Clem. Alex. *Strom.* iv. p. 450 both notions of prodigality and wantonness seem to be combined. The verb is found, as usual, in a bad sense, *Epist. of Barnabas*, x. 3, of men living a life of luxury, whilst Hermas, *Sim.* vi. 1, employs the two verbs as here, in close combination, of the sheep led astray by the angel of self-indulgence.

ye have nourished your hearts: cf. Judg. xix. 5; Ps. civ. 15; Luke xxi. 34; Acts xiv. 17. The verb probably implies, as sometimes in classical Greek, to fatten, to satiate with food; cf. LXX, Jer. xxvi. 21, where the same verb is used of fatted calves. 'Hearts' is sometimes taken as = bodies (the heart regarded as the seat and centre of physical life), sometimes as a Hebraism = you, yourselves, but perhaps best explained as signifying not merely the body, but the heart in which the sense of reflection is felt; see also below on *Enoch*, xcviii. 8, 11.

in a day of slaughter, R.V.; so W.H., omitting 'as' A.V.; cf. *v.* 3, 'in the last days.' For the use of a similar expression see Jer. xii. 3, xxv. 34, and of similar imagery Isaiah xxxiv. 2, 6, Ezek. xxi. 15, in describing the day of the Lord's judgment; cf. also *Psalms of Solomon*, viii. 1, where a trumpet proclaims 'slaughter and destruction' in the approaching visitation of the Lord in judgment, and more fully

Enoch, xciv. 9, where of the rich and sinners we read, 'ye have committed blasphemy and unrighteousness and have become ready for the day of slaughter and the day of darkness and of the great judgment,' and xcviii. 8, 11, 'woe to you, ye obstinate of heart......whence have ye good things to eat and drink and to be filled?...know that ye shall be delivered into the hands of the righteous, and they will cut off your necks and slay you.' Like beasts, fattened to be killed, and feasting on the day of their slaughter, so the wicked in their folly were 'nourishing their hearts,' unmindful of the coming doom. In the terrible days of the Roman siege, when the Zealots in their fanatical rage against the rich slew them or left them to die of hunger, when they drank the blood of the populace to one another,' some of those whom he now warned may have recalled the words of St James. See the whole description Josephus, *B. J.* v. 10. 2, XIII. 4[1]. It may well be said that the words of the Jewish historian become here the best commentary on the words of the Christian Apostle.

Other explanations of the phrase are sometimes proposed, as e.g. that reference is made to feasting and banqueting, and the slaying of oxen and fatlings for the same, as if life was one perpetual feast (cf. Isaiah xxii. 13), but the phrase seems more naturally explained by connecting it with the thought of judgment as above. An attempt has been made to exclude all reference to the judgment on the ground that in the original the word 'day' has no article prefixed, so that the ex-

---

[1] See too Plummer *in loco*, and Farrar, *Early Days of Christianity*, pp. 344, 345.

condemned, ye have killed the righteous _one_; he doth not resist you.

pression simply means that a man has killed his higher life through the indulgence of the lower, and has spent his days in that which leads to the loss of his true life; but the question of grammar may be met by such passages as Rom. ii. 5, 1 Pet. ii. 12, and the attempted explanation entirely loses sight of the O.T. and Jewish use of the phrase.

6. _Ye have condemned, ye have killed_, R.V. The omission of 'and' A.V. heightens the effect, and expresses the hastiness with which the murder follows upon the condemnation. The verbs are to be taken literally, cf. iv. 2 above, and there is no need to refer to Ecclus. xxxiv. 21, where the verb used here for killing is also found as follows: 'he that taketh away his neighbour's living slayeth him.' In the condemnation we may see perhaps a reference to the judgment-seats of ii. 6. The verb employed here is found in classical Greek of formal and official condemnation; in the LXX it occurs several times, and four times in Wisdom, notably in ii. 20, 'let us condemn him (the righteous) with a shameful death,' in the famous picture of the poor righteous man, the faithful Israelite, oppressed and condemned to death by his wealthy and luxurious fellow-countrymen (see _v._ 12), a picture strikingly parallel to that before us (see also on ii. 6, above); cf. Amos ii. 6, 7, v. 12.

the righteous one, R.V.; 'the just,' A.V. In Acts iii. 14, vii. 52, xxii. 14 (1 John ii. 1), our Lord is emphatically called 'the Righteous One,' but R.V. makes a distinction between these places and the passage before

us by rendering in Acts 'the Righteous One' and in 1 John ii. 1, where the reference is clear; cf. 1 Pet. iii. 18, 'the righteous.'

In this verse however many able commentators from the time of Oecumenius have referred the title to our Lord, and no doubt it was in early use as a name for the Messiah; cf. _Enoch_, xxxviii. 2, liii. 6. The tense (aorist) used in the preceding verses does not destroy this interpretation, as it might be used of a specific action, as in ii. 21, or of a course of action, as in the verbs of _v._ 5. On the other hand, it is urged that the context does not suit this application of the words, and that 'the righteous _one_' is employed to designate no particular individual but a class in general; cf. the passage in Wisdom above, and the use of the same Greek adjective for a class, Isaiah iii. 10, lvii. 1, and in N.T. Heb. x. 38, 1 Pet. iii. 12, iv. 18, etc. And the spirit against which the prophets had uttered their constant protest, and which they had so sternly condemned, was still alive; St James saw it working all around him, St Stephen had fallen a victim to it, and James the son of Zebedee, and many of the 'saints,' Acts xxvi. 10.

It may be said that in these words the writer seems to anticipate in prophetic spirit his own death, and it has been thought that Hegesippus in his description had this passage in mind when he writes that the scribes and Pharisees said, 'Let us go up and cast him down,' i.e. from the pinnacle of the Temple. 'So they cast down James the Just and began to stone him.' Euseb. _H.E._ II. 23.

7   Be patient therefore, brethren, until the [1]coming of the

[1] Gr. *presence.*

he doth not resist you, i.e. the righteous one. In itself the present tense does not militate against the reference to our Lord. St James might thus vividly picture His patient endurance, and the dramatic effect is intensified by the omission of the connecting 'and' in R.V., although the same tense could of course indicate that the same sufferings and patience were being accomplished in His brethren in the world. The tense expresses in a graphic manner the habitual bearing of the righteous under persecution, especially in face not only of the Jewish picture in Wisdom (cf. *Enoch,* ciii. 15), but also of our Lord's command, Matt. v. 39 (cf. 1 Pet. ii. 23), and of the constant stress laid by St James upon patience. How beautifully St James himself preached in suffering this doctrine of patient endurance we know from the record which tells us how when the cruel hail of the stones beat upon him, he kneeled down, saying, 'My Father, I beseech Thee forgive them, for they know not what they do,' Eusebius, *H. E.* II. 23.

Either of the above interpretations seems preferable to that which would refer the clause to the present patient long-suffering of the Lord. This thought is not in the immediate context, and is rather contained in the verses which immediately follow. Another rendering of the words adopted by W.H. places an interrogative at the end of the verse; 'doth not (the Lord) resist you?' cf.

the same verb as used in iv. 6. But this does not seem so original, or so terse and dramatic as the usual punctuation.

7. *Be patient therefore, brethren.* From utterance of his indignation St James turns again to the thought of his suffering brethren; whatever the wicked might do meanwhile, they are to keep before their eyes the picture of 'the righteous one,' not resisting evil. The curtain falls as it were upon the scene, but it will quickly rise again upon another, upon a more terrible and yet upon a brighter day, when judgment shall return unto righteousness; cf. Ps. xciv. *vv.* 15, 20, 21. The word translated 'be patient' is not the same as is translated 'endureth' i. 12, although this latter verb is sometimes rendered 'to be patient' (cf. Rom. xii. 12; 1 Pet. ii. 20), whilst its cognate noun is three times translated 'patience' in this Epistle, i. 3, 4, v. 11 ('endurance' in margin). A distinction however is drawn between the noun which is cognate to the verb in the verse before us, and the noun just referred to, which may help us here; the former is the self-restraint which does not hastily retaliate a wrong, the latter is the temper which does not easily succumb under suffering, although the distinction is not always true without exception (Lightfoot)[1]. This distinction of meaning, however, is quite in accordance with the context in the present passage, and also with what follows in *vv.* 10, 11 (see

---

[1] See further Trench, *Syn.* II. 10; Westcott, *Hebrews,* p. 157. The two nouns rendered 'endurance' and 'long-suffering' occur together in 2 Cor. vi. 4, 6; Col. i. 11; 2 Tim. iii. 10; and the contrast between the two cognate verbs is well marked in 1 Cor. xiii. 4, 7, 'Love suffereth long......endureth all things.'

below). The verb in our verse with its corresponding noun is used of God, as He bears with man, Rom. ii. 4, 1 Pet. iii. 20 (so too in the O.T., and Apoc., Wisd. xv. 1; Ecclus. xviii. 11), and men strive to imitate this Divine long-suffering, Gal. v. 22; Col. iii. 12.

With the language of St James we may also compare the frequent exhortation to the righteous in *Enoch* to persist in their cry for judgment, and to be hopeful and believing in the face of their rich oppressors; cf. xcvii. 1 ff., civ. 3 ff.

until the coming of the Lord, 'presence' in R.V. marg. The word is the same which our Lord Himself used of His coming, three times in St Matthew's account of the discourse on the Mt of Olives; cf. xxiv. 27, 37, 39, and see also *v.* 3. We can see the impression which the word made upon the Apostolic writers, since it is used by St Peter, St Paul, and St John, and by all of them of the coming of the Lord Jesus in glory. Here we believe that it is used by St James with the same reference, and it is noticeable that the whole passage before us has three points of contact with the discourse of Jesus to which reference has just been made; cf. e.g. Matt. xxiv. 9, 13, with *v.* 11 below, and xxiv. 33 with *v.* 9. No doubt with the other N.T. writers St James conceived of the coming as near at hand, and not only may the current Jewish expectancy of the nearness of the end have contributed to this conception, but our Lord's own words would have intensified the expectancy in Christian circles.

It is indeed maintained by Spitta that this word 'presence' need not be used here of Christ, as it occurs in Jewish writings, e.g. *Testaments of the xii. Patriarchs*, Judah 22, 'until the "presence" of the God of righteousness' (the words are not found in the Armenian translation); so again in *Test. Abr.* xiii., 'until the great and glorious "presence" of God,' and also 'at the second presence' or 'coming[1]'; while the cognate verb is used of the day of judgment, Deut. xxxii. 35; Joel ii. 1. But St James had already assigned a Divine attribute to Jesus, and had spoken of Him as the Lord of glory, ii. 1, and there is no difficulty in supposing that with our Lord's words before him St James should have assigned to the Christ the further Divine prerogative of judgeship. No doubt in Jewish apocalyptic and pseudepigraphical literature we have to take into account two judgments, the Messiah's, and the final; the former executed by the Messiah or the saints, and the latter, except in *Enoch*, xxxvii–lxx., by God alone. But the N.T. writers and our Lord's own words represent Him, as in the most sublime conception of *Enoch*, as a supernatural being and as the universal Judge at the last day. When we consider the lowliness of Jesus of Nazareth and the extreme ignominy of His death, it would have been marvellous enough if men like the Apostles, Hebrews of the Hebrews, had associated Him at such an early date with the conception of a Judge such as that given in the *Psalms of Solomon*, xvii., xviii., where

---

[1] This identical expression is also used by Christian ecclesiastical writers of the 'second coming' of Christ as opposed to His 'first coming,' which took place in His Incarnation and earthly life. And there can be no doubt that the occurrence of the phrase in the *Testament of Abraham* is one of the Christian elements in that document (see Introd. p. xliii.). This Spitta forgets. Moreover, his other references only help to show us that a term which was used of God could also be used by Christ and of Christ.

Lord.   Behold, the husbandman waiteth for the precious
fruit of the earth, being patient over it, until ¹it receive the

¹ Or, *he*

the Messiah appears as a judge, but
not as a pre-existent being, a sub-
ordinate to God in the judgment.
But the marvellousness is increased
when we remember that to this Jesus
of Nazareth is assigned the tremendous office of the Judge of quick
and dead, an office which even in the
O.T. is not assigned to the Messiah,
although in some prophetic passages
He is associated with Jehovah as
His agent in 'the day of the Lord.'
Certainly St James tells us less
than some of the other N.T. writers
as to the details of Christ's coming,
but this silence not only offers a
marked contrast to the fantastic
elaborations of Jewish theology in
dealing with such subjects, but it is
quite natural in a letter so brief in
itself, and in which much would be
no doubt assumed as already known.
See on the whole subject *Encycl.
Bibl.* II., Art. 'Eschatology,' by Dr
Charles; Hastings' *B. D.* I. 749, 751;
and *Psalms of Solomon*, Ryle and
James, pp. li. ff.

*Behold, the husbandman waiteth
for.* See on iii. 5, and v. 4. The
language of the verse and the comparison are very natural from a
native of Palestine (see below, and
Introduction), and in this particular
passage they would fall in well with
the previous mention of the labourers
and the reapers. There is a close
likeness to Ecclus. vi. 19, where it
is said of Wisdom, 'Come unto her
as one that ploweth and soweth, and
wait for her good fruits,' although
the verb for 'wait for' is not the
same as in the present passage (cf.
however 1 Thess. i. 10, where it is
used of a waiting in patience and

trust), and the same lesson is familiar
to us in our Lord's own parables.

In 1 Pet. iii. 20 a cognate if not
an exactly similar verb is used of
the long-suffering of God, and in
Heb. x. 13 the same verb is used of
the 'waiting' of Christ for His final
triumph.

precious, everywhere, and nowhere more so than in Palestine ; the
epithet marks the justification of the
patient waiting.

being patient over it, i.e. over the
fruit ; the participial clause gives
more definition to the preceding
verb, a watchful and constant expectancy. 'Over it'; the prep. in the
original is often so used after verbs
which signify a mental affection or
emotion, as in English we often use
the word 'over' (Grimm-Thayer);
cf. Ecclus. xviii. 11, xxix. 8, xxxv.
(xxxii.) 18 ; Matt. xviii. 26, 29.

until it receive, R.V., but 'he' in
marg., and good authorities may be
quoted for either. Most probably
the subject should be found in the
nearest object 'fruit.' The thought
of the fruit receiving the early and
latter rain would be very natural to
an inhabitant of Palestine; cf. Deut.
xi. 14, Joel ii. 23, Jer. v. 24, Zech. x.
1, for the thought of God giving, or
raining down, the early and latter
rain. The majority of moderns take
this view, but a few still follow Luther
in regarding 'the husbandman' as
the subject, on the ground that a
change of subject is not warranted,
and that attention is fixed primarily
and chiefly on the husbandman himself. Of course if we adopt for the
following words the rendering 'early
and latter fruit' the same word can-

8 early and latter rain.　Be ye also patient; stablish your

not be taken as the subject of the verb 'receive.' This rendering 'early and latter fruit' is justified on the ground that the clause 'until *he* receive the early and latter fruit' is thus constituted a precise parallel to the words 'until the coming of the Lord,' but this parallel cannot fairly be found, nor is it needed (see below). There seems little doubt that the better rendering is 'the early and latter rain,' as A. and R.V.

In some good authorities, e.g. W.H., the reading is simply 'the early and latter,' but in their text the phrase is marked by W.H. as a quotation, and it is to be remembered that in the LXX the complementary noun in the same phrase is always 'rain.' Its omission would of course account for the two variations 'fruit' and 'rain,' and its addition is certainly far more probable than its erasure.

'The early and latter rain' was a common phrase in the LXX, and would have been understood by every inhabitant of Palestine, although it is true that the former adjective is used with reference to early figs, Jer. xxiv. 2, Hos. ix. 10, and the latter with reference to wheat and rye, Exod. ix. 32.

The early and the latter rain were both needful for the harvest of the precious fruit, and both tried the patience and skill of the husbandman. 'Towards the end of October heavy rains begin to fall, at intervals, for a day or several days at a time. These are what the English Bible calls the *early* or *former* rain, literally the *Pourer*. It opens the agricultural year; the soil hardened and cracked by the long summer is

loosened, and the farmer begins ploughing......The *latter rains* of Scripture are the heavy showers of March and April. Coming as they do before the harvest and the long summer drought, they are of far more importance to the country than all the rains of the winter months, and that is why these are passed over in Scripture, and emphasis is laid alone on *the early and the latter rains.*' G. A. Smith, *Historical Geography of the Holy Land*, p. 63.

8. *also*, i.e. after the example of the husbandman; 'the point of the simile lies in the patient waiting, not in that which is waited for.'

stablish your hearts, for the due exercise of patience, and also no doubt with the thought that this patience would not be of long duration. For the expression cf. Judg. xix. 5, 8, Ecclus. xxii. 16, etc., and in N.T. 1 Thess. iii. 13, 1 Pet. v. 10, where, as generally elsewhere, it is the Divine power which stablishes; cf. Ecclus. vi. 37; *Psalms of Solomon*, xvi. 12. From the frequent combination of this verb and noun in Jewish literature it may be fairly said that the writer is using a regular Hebrew mode of expression. This stablishing the heart would be the best preservation against the sin of doublemindedness. With St James's thought here and his remedy against the sin just named, it is interesting to compare Clem. Rom. *Cor.* xxiii. 3, where the doubleminded are exhorted to hope and to consider that as in nature the fruit of the tree soon attaineth unto mellowness, so the Lord whom they expect will come quickly, and will not tarry.

9 hearts : for the [1]coming of the Lord is at hand.　Murmur not, brethren, one against another, that ye be not judged :

[1] Gr. *presence.*

for the coming of the Lord is at hand. The verb in the original is in the perfect tense, 'has come nigh,' and so, is at hand. With the expression we may compare similar language, Luke xxi. 31 ; 1 Pet. iv. 7 ; Phil. iv. 5 ; Heb. x. 25 ; and in the O.T. Joel ii. 1, 'for the day of the Lord cometh, for it is nigh at hand.'

The words have sometimes been classed as a Christian watchword, the Aramaic form of which occurs in 1 Cor. xvi. 22, *Didache,* x. 6, but it is very doubtful whether the expression Maranatha can be interpreted to mean that our Lord cometh (see R.V. marg.), is at hand, will come, or even 'has come'; and whether it may not be best explained as an ejaculation in a supplicatory sense, 'Our Lord come!'; cf. Rev. xxii. 20 ; see Art. 'Maranatha,' J. H. Thayer in Hastings' *B. D.*, and also Art. on same in *Encycl. Biblica.*

The N.T. writers it would seem all expected the Parousia quickly, having respect to our Lord's words, Mark xiii. 30, Matt. xxiv. 34, Luke xxi. 32, and it may be justly said that this expectation was fulfilled, not indeed in the visible return of Jesus, but in the overthrow of Jerusalem ; and in this connection we do well to remember that our Lord Himself had said, 'Henceforth ye shall see the Son of Man sitting at the right hand of power, and coming on the clouds of heaven'; He thus intimates His claim to judge not only hereafter but 'henceforth,' and His coming to judgment is rightly seen in all the great moral catastrophes of the world's history. Voltaire could make merry at the

earthquake of Lisbon, 'How absurd to talk about divine judgments ! Lisbon is overwhelmed, whilst at the same moment in Paris, a city equally guilty, people were dancing!' But it has been well pointed out that if Voltaire had lived on a few years longer, and witnessed the first great French Revolution and the streets of Paris red with blood, he might have seen another illustration of the Lord's parable, 'Wheresoever the carcase is, there will the eagles be gathered together'; he might have been constrained to exclaim with the Psalmist, 'Verily there is a God that judgeth the earth.'

9. *Murmur not,* R.V., i.e. complain not, lit. groan not. A.V. has 'grudge not,' but the word, whatever may have been its former meaning, now rather denotes 'a suppressed feeling of ill-will'; in Psalm lix. 15 however the same verb is used as an equivalent of 'murmur' (complain) (see Driver's *Parallel Psalter*); cf. Shakespeare, *Much Ado*, iii. 4. 90; and Langland, *Piers Plowman*, 6. 219. See further on verse 1 for the reference of the words here, and so also of 'brethren' in the immediate context.

one against another. If the reference is to the Christian brother, and not to the wealthy oppressors just mentioned, we must remember that St James was a keen judge of human nature, and was well aware that the temptation to impatience towards those with whom they were most closely associated would often make itself felt in the irritation produced by continuous oppression.

that ye be not judged, R.V.,

10 behold, the judge standeth before the doors.   Take, brethren,
  for an example of suffering and of patience, the prophets

'condemned,' A.V., but authority
is overwhelming for the reading in
text: cf. Matt. vii. 1; Luke vi. 37
(Rom. ii. 1; 1 Cor. iv. 5). It is urged
that there is no need to suppose
a reference to our Lord's words on
account of the difference of context,
but in St Matthew at all events the
thought of 'the day' of the Lord is
not far removed from the exhortation
in question: cf. Matt. vii. 22; see also
below on *v.* 12.

behold, the judge, i.e. the Lord
Christ, Who is judge both of you
and of those from whom you differ;
the words are thus a warning as well
as an encouragement: cf. ii. 13. The
language here has a striking parallel
in *Apocalypse of Baruch,* xlviii. 39:
'for the judge will come, and will
not tarry.'

standeth before the doors; signifying the imminent nearness: cf. Matt.
xxiv. 33; Mark xiii. 29. There is
thus no need to find an allusion to
Isaiah xxvi. 20 or to the figurative
language which is there employed;
the reference to our Lord's own
words with respect to His coming
seems far more natural. This nearness of the Judge should prevent
the brethren from anticipating His
judgment of their complaints against
their neighbours, and so taking upon
themselves the office of judge, as
was the case with the friends of Job.
The noun which A.V. renders 'door'
(R.V. 'doors') is in the plural as in
the passages cited from the Gospels.
The striking scene in the martyrdom
of St James, Eusebius, *H. E.* II. 23,
as given by Hegesippus, describes
the scribes and Pharisees as setting
him on a pinnacle of the Temple
and asking, 'What is the door of

Jesus?': and the Just answers, 'Why
do ye ask me concerning Jesus the
Son of Man? He is both seated in
heaven on the right hand of Power,
and will come on the clouds of
heaven.' The expression is sometimes referred to our Lord's words
John x. 7–9.

10. *brethren,* R.V., is better at-
tested than *my brethren.* But either
form of expression was, as we have
seen, characteristic of the writer.

for an example. The word is
used of the example of Enoch,
Ecclus. xliv. 16, of the example
of the brave old scribe Eleazar,
2 Macc. vi. 31, of the example of the
seven brethren who would not trans-
gress the law of their fathers, 4
Macc. xvii. 23. In the N.T. it is
used of our Lord's own example,
John xiii. 15.

of suffering, R.V. The noun is
used only here in the N.T., but
the cognate verb is found below
in *v.* 11, 2 Tim. ii. 3, 9, iv. 5. It
is found elsewhere, Mal. i. 13, 2
Macc. ii. 26, 27, and in 4 Macc. ix. 8,
where it is used, as is the word
'example' above, in connection with
the same brethren who answer the
tyrant Antiochus, saying, 'for we
shall receive the rewards of virtue
through this suffering and endurance,' the latter noun being also the
same noun which occurs thrice in
the Epistle (cf. i. 3, 4, v. 13). Deissmann, *Bibelstudien,* II. 91, apparently
takes the word on the evidence of
inscriptions to signify the endurance
of suffering or affliction.

When we read in the next verse
that 'we call them blessed which
endured,' it is most natural to associate such words with our Lord's

11 who spake in the name of the Lord.   Behold, we call them
blessed which endured : ye have heard of the ¹patience of

¹ Or, *endurance*

own Beatitudes, Matt. v. 11, 12. At
the same time the blessedness of
those who endured martyrdom
under the tyrant Antiochus was
often celebrated, as e.g. in 4 Macc. i.
10, vii. 22, x. 15, xii. 1. *patience;* see
on *v.* 7.

the prophets. It is best to refer the
words to the O.T. prophets ; but it
has sometimes been maintained that
prophets in the Christian Church
may also have been included, who
suffered like things with them of
old times.

in the name, i.e. with the power,
and as the representatives of Him
Who sent them ; cf. for this same
formula Isaiah l. 10, Jer. xi. 21,
Micah iv. 5, and see also Matt. vii.
22, x. 41, and see further *v.* 14
below ; cf. Deissmann, *Bibelstudien*,
I. 26¹, and Hastings' *B. D.*, Art.
'Name.'

The words are no doubt meant
to cheer the suffering Christians,
and would help to remind them that
even if the prophets who were so
holy that God spoke through them
endured persecution and suffering,
they must not wonder if a fiery trial
was theirs also ; Bede's comment to
this effect is interesting, and he instances not only the prophets who
were so free from fault that the
Holy Spirit spake through them
God's mysteries to men, but also
the Maccabean martyrs.

The example of the prophets was
often appealed to : cf. e.g. Matt. xxiii.
34 ; Acts vii. 52 ; Heb. xi. So too

Abraham, Isaac, David, and 'the
three children' were cited as examples of those who endured,
4 Macc. xvi. 21.

If we ask why St James appealed
to the old prophets, and not to the
example of Jesus Christ, the great
ensample of godly life, it may be that
he wished to keep before the eyes of
his converts Jesus as the Lord of
glory, as the Lord Whose coming
drew nigh, and that his readers
were not quite prepared for the
preaching of the Person of the Messiah as an example of human virtue ;
if the Epistle was written at a very
early date it is quite possible that the
details of the life of Jesus would be
far less familiar to the readers than
the old and oft-repeated stories of
the sufferings and patience of the
prophets, and it may also be added
that St James may have already
alluded to Christ when he spoke
of the unresisting 'righteous *one*,'
v. 6.

11. *Behold, we call them blessed
which endured,* R.V. This translation brings out more distinctly than
A.V. 'happy' the connection between
the verb 'to call blessed' and the
adjective 'blessed' found, not only in
i. 12, but also used by our Lord in
the Beatitudes ; cf. especially Matt.
v. 12 with the verse before us .
it is also based upon what seems
to be undoubtedly the correct
reading (adopted by W.H. as by
R.V.), the aorist part. 'which endured' instead of the present 'which

¹ For those who study German, reference should also be made to Heitmüller's
exhaustive volume, *Im Namen Jesu*, p. 86 (1903).

Job, and have seen the end of the Lord, how that the Lord
is full of pity, and merciful.

endure.' The same verb rendered
'we call blessed' is applied to
Daniel and his endurance in the den
of lions, 4 Macc. xviii. 13.

ye have heard of the patience, but
in R.V. marg. 'endurance,' because
the word in the original is the
cognate noun of the verb employed
at the end of the preceding clause;
possibly R.V. retained 'patience' in
the text on account of the common
proverbial expression. Here the
reference may only be to that per-
sistent trust in God which Job manifested in his troubles and amidst
the calumniations of his friends. In
Psalms of Solomon, xvi. 15, we read,
'the righteous man if he continue
stedfast shall therein find mercy of
the Lord,' a sentiment strikingly in
agreement with the words of St
James (see also below), and rendered
all the more so not only by the
fact that the verb 'continue stedfast'
is the cognate verb of the noun
rendered here 'endurance,' but also
because the writer of the *Psalms*
evidently had Job in his mind, for
he remarks in the previous verse,
'thou dost prove a man in his flesh,
and in the affliction of poverty.'
The well-known passage in Ezek.
xiv. 14, 20, where Job is mentioned
with Noah and Daniel as an example
of true righteousness, is sufficient to
show how important a place Job
occupied in Jewish thought, and the
Vulg. of Tob. ii. 12–15 contains an
explicit reference to the patience of
Job. A reference may also be made
to *Test. Abr.* xv., where Michael
says of Abraham, 'and there is no
man like him upon the earth, not
even Job, that marvellous man,' a
reference which shows how Abra-

ham and Job stood out in marked
prominence in Jewish thought, just
as in the Epistle of St James the
former appears as the example of
faith, and the latter of endurance.

heard. The word is sometimes
taken to refer to the public reading
in the synagogues, but there is no
need to restrict the reference to
this. It is noticeable that this is
the only reference to Job in the N.T.
and that the Book of Job is only
once quoted, 1 Cor. iii. 19 = Job v.
13. Philo has a quotation from Job
xiv. 4. In *Tanchuma,* 29. 4, we have
a quotation of Job xlii. 10, where we
read that Job in this world was
tried much, but God has rewarded
him double, as it is said, 'and the
Lord gave Job twice as much as he
had before.' Amongst early Christian
writers St Clement of Rome frequently refers to Job. Thus in *Cor.*
xvii. 1, 3 he exhorts his fellow-Christians to be imitators of the prophets,
of Abraham, and of Job, of whom it
is written that he was righteous and
unblameable, and further quotations
from Job are found in xx. 7, xxvi. 3,
xxxix. 3, lvi. 6.

and have seen. So A. and R.V.
and W.H. I.e. like a drama unfolds
itself scene by scene. This is best,
but by some editors a more abrupt
reading is adopted, viz. the imperative, with a full-stop after 'Job':
'See ye also,' etc.

the end of the Lord, i.e. the end
which the Lord makes, and gives;
ye have seen how all things work
together for good (cf. Job xlii. 12).
It is quite possible that St James
has before him the Rabbinical phrase
which corresponds to the explanation
of the words as above; so too the

12   But above all things, my brethren, swear not, neither

Syriac renders 'the end which the Lord made for him.' Job is thus rightly spoken of as blessed. It is sometimes urged that the words may be specially referred to the appearance of the Lord at the end of the Book of Job as settling the controversy, and that this sense well fits in with the idea of the Parousia as the final scene which Christians anticipated; this sequence of thought is possible with the alternative reading mentioned above, but certainly not otherwise, and even then it is not supported by the context.

It should also be mentioned that the words under consideration have been sometimes taken as by St Augustine to refer to the death of Christ, 'the end of the Lord' (cf. *Sermo ad Catechumenos,* x.). The same interpretation of the words was adopted by Bede and by Wetstein.

The latter comments, 'He understands the death which the Lord Jesus endured for our salvation, and which is represented in the Holy Supper,' apparently referring in the last clause to the words 'ye have seen the end, i.e. the death, of the Lord.' But this interpretation however tempting cannot be said to be borne out by the context.

how that, R.V.; explanatory of the preceding, showing and describing the nature of 'the end of the Lord.'

the Lord, i.e. the Lord of the O.T., and so the words just preceding refer evidently to the same Lord.

full of pity. The exact word is not found elsewhere except Hermas, *Mand.* iv. 3. 5, *Sim.* v. 7. 4, used each time of the Lord of the O.T., but

the LXX has a very similar expression, 'plenteous in mercy,' cf. Exod. xxxiv. 6. In the 'Prayer of Manasses' we have a word somewhat similarly compounded, joined with two other adjectives, 'long-suffering' and 'plenteous in mercy,' as in Exod. *u.s.,* 'for thou art the most high Lord, of great compassion, long-suffering, very merciful'; cf., for a somewhat similar combination, Ps. ciii. 8. With the expression here, and the two adjectives, in the original, cf. Col. iii. 12.

merciful; only found once elsewhere in N.T., Luke vi. 36, where it is used as here of God; cf. Clem. Rom. *Cor.* xxiii. 1; but frequent in LXX; cf. esp. Ecclus. ii. 11, 'for the Lord is full of compassion and mercy, long-suffering, and very pitiful, and forgiveth sins and saveth in time of affliction,' a passage which may well have been in the mind of St James, especially when we compare *v.* 12 with James i. 8 above. In *Psalms of Solomon* similar attributes are also ascribed to God; cf. passage quoted above.

This reference to the sure mercy and pity of the Lord would encourage Christian endurance to the end; cf. Matt. x. 22, xxiv. 13.

12. *above all things.* It is interesting to find this phrase quoted from the papyri at the end of a letter. Two instances of its use in this way are given in the *Oxyrhynchus Papyri* from letters dating 22 and 25 A.D.[1]

In the passage before us it is of course quite possible that this emphatic phrase may be limited to what has just preceded, and then it may be regarded as introducing a special

---

[1] Dean of Westminster, *Ephesians,* p. 279.

by the heaven, nor by the earth, nor by any other oath :

warning for those who might be led by suffering to impatience and murmuring, and so to hasty oaths and asseverations. But it is perhaps better to regard the precepts thus emphatically introduced as a kind of postscript to the letter, and in the first instance to find the need of such an extreme warning in the prevalence amongst the Jews of heedless and false swearing, an evil and dangerous habit into which those engaged like the Jews of the Diaspora in commerce and merchandise were very liable to fall ; cf., for its notoriety amongst the Jews in Rome, Martial, *Epig.* XI. 94.

my brethren ; marking here as elsewhere (cf. i. 16) the earnestness and yet tenderness of the writer.

swear not. To swear by the heaven or by the earth was to employ recognised Jewish formulae, and on more than one occasion our Lord refers to the use or rather abuse of such and similar formulae, Matt. v. 34, xxiii. 16, and points out not only the liability of this usage to lead men into irreverence and untruthfulness, but also its real meaning as involving, however men might seek to disguise it, an oath by God Himself.

In any consideration of this verse it should be carefully noted that the reference of the words to contemporary Jewish habits as to the use or non-use of oaths does not exclude a reference to our Lord's words, Matt. v. 34 ff., as has been often maintained. St James employs two formulae to which reference is made by our Lord Himself, Matt. v. 34, 35, and to his words, 'not by any other oath,' we may fairly find a parallel in our Lord's command, 'Swear not at all.'

Von Soden and Spitta (see also

Encycl. Bibl. II. 1825) deny any reference by St James to our Lord's saying, and see in this expression 'the yea yea' etc. only reference to a common every-day formula. But whilst we admit this commonness of the formula, we have still to remember the context in which it is here placed by our Lord and by St James, and the solemn use which they both make of it.

nor by any other oath ; it has indeed been maintained that in the omission of the words 'neither by Jerusalem nor by the temple' we may see an indication that St James's Epistle was not written till after the fall of Jerusalem, and this is urged by Schmiedel (*Encycl. Bibl.* II. 1892), but it is much more to the point to observe that St James may possibly have referred to our Lord's command in Matt. v. in some shortened form, or that his words 'nor by any other oath' fairly include any other usual formulae in vogue in taking an oath. On the miserable subterfuges by which the Jews avoided the obligation of oaths by maintaining that they were not binding unless the Sacred Name of God was introduced, see further p. 153, and Wetstein on Matt. v. 37, with Dalman, *Die Worte Jesu,* p. 168, and E.T., pp. 206, 228.

let your yea be yea. It has been said that the likeness in this verse is closer than in any other in this Epistle to the words of the Sermon on the Mount (cf. R.V. marg.), and St James may well have recalled his Master's words in enforcing his Master's principle. For the words contain no mere prohibition against falsehood ; the sphere of perfect truthfulness was that in which all communication between man and

but [1]let your yea be yea, and your nay, nay; that ye fall
not under judgement.

13   Is any among you suffering? let him pray. Is any

[1] Or, *let yours be the yea, yea, and the nay, nay* Compare Matt. v. 37.

man should be conducted; in a Christian society, where men are truly
brethren in Christian affection, there
should be no need of oaths in the
daily intercourse of social life; cf.
Clem. Alex. *Strom.* vii. 8, where he
says that no true Christian will ever
perjure himself; he will not even
swear, and for him to be put upon
his oath is an indignity. See Additional Note on the Use of Oaths,
p. 153.

that ye fall not under judgement.
For the phrase here cf. Ps. i. 5;
Ecclus. xxix. 19; = 'that ye be not
judged' in *v.* 9; cf. iii. 1, and Matt.
v. 21; John v. 24.

Our Lord in the parallel passage,
Matt. v. 37, says, 'and whatsoever is
more than these is of the evil one,'
R.V., as if He would warn men that
their unscrupulous use of the so-
lemnity of an oath must be referred
not to the God of truth but to the
father of lies. So St James also
warns men against the Divine judgment which would follow upon this
participation in what every true
Christian would condemn as evil,
even as Christ his Lord had condemned it, together with every 'idle
word' for which account would be
given in the day of judgment, Matt.
xii. 36; and even now the judgment was at hand; cf. *v.* 9 above.

This thought of judgment following as a condemnation of vain and
needless swearing, a thought so intensified for the Christian con-

science by the words of Christ and
His nearness as Judge, had been
expressed by the writer of Ecclus.
xxiii. 11, 'and if he swear in vain
(without cause) he shall not be
justified[1].'

13. *Is any among you suffering?
let him pray.* Cf. rendering of cognate noun in *v.* 10, 'suffering,' R.V.

It is doubtful whether the words
have any very close connection with
what has just preceded, and the
various exhortations may be only of
a general character. But on the
other hand it is quite possible to
find some reference to the immediate
context. Thus in the Sermon on the
Mount our Lord, after saying, 'Swear
not at all,' proceeds to enjoin, not
retaliation against, but love towards,
our neighbour. St James inculcates
long-suffering under injury or adversity before a similar injunction
'swear not at all,' and then again
treats of the right attitude under
suffering, the calm attitude of prayer,
not the petulant hastiness which
finds vent in oaths. Or again it is
plausible to connect the first case with
v. 10 above, or the second with iv. 9,
but even if this is admitted as
accounting for the primary application of the words, they may bear a
much wider reference, and the
remedy in the wider as in the more
limited application is to be found in
bringing everything before God.
For the verb see 2 Tim. ii. 3, 9, iv. 5,
and for the cognate noun *v.* 10 above.

[1] The reading 'lest ye fall into hypocrisy' in the clause before us is very
weakly supported, although adopted by Oecumenius, Grotius, and Wetstein. It
may easily have arisen from reading the two words 'under judgment' as the
Greek word meaning 'hypocrisy.'

14 cheerful? let him sing praise.   Is any among you sick? let

The word may include, but is too
general in its signification (so R.V.)
to be identified with, the verb 'to be
sick' in *v.* 14.   It is quite beside the
mark to regard the exhortation to
pray as a bidding to prayer for
vengeance, and to compare *Enoch*,
xlvii. 2, xcvii. 3, civ. 3.   The interrogative form of the sentence, as
also in the succeeding clauses, is
quite in harmony with the vivid
style of St James.

Is any cheerful? R.V.   The A.V.
'merry' refers rather to outward
hilarity than to the universal cheer-
fulness indicated by the original.
The verb is not found in the LXX,
but it is used by Symmachus, Ps.
xxxii. 11, and Prov. xv. 15, 'all the
days of the afflicted are evil, but he
that is of a cheerful heart hath a
continual feast,' and the cognate
adjective is used 2 Macc. xi. 26 of
those who 'go cheerfully about their
own affairs.'

let him sing praise, R.V.; 'let him
sing psalms,' A.V., but not necessarily
so restricted as to imply only 'Psalms
of David'; Ephes. v. 19, Col. iii. 16.
The word 'psalm' is derived from the
verb here employed in the original
Greek.   This verb meant primarily
to touch or strike a chord, to twang
the strings, and hence it is used
absolutely as meaning to play the
harp, etc., and in LXX to play on
some stringed instrument, and also
to sing to the music of the harp,
often in honour of God (but see also
Ecclus. ix. 4).

In *Psalms of Solomon*, iii. 2 (a
Psalm entitled 'concerning the
righteous'), the writer in the opening
verse gives the summons to sing a
new song unto God, and in xv. 5 we
have a point of contact with the
verse before us in the words wherein

'a psalm and praise with a song in
gladness of heart' are described as
a means for preserving the safety of
the righteous.   In the N.T. the same
verb is used of singing of hymns, of
celebrating the praise of God, Rom.
xv. 9; 1 Cor. xiv. 15; Ephes. v. 19
(cf. LXX, Judg. v. 3).   Here the words
may refer primarily to private devotion and worship, but they evidently have a wider application; cf.
Hooker, *E. P.* v. 38, on the power of
melody in public prayer, melody
both vocal and instrumental, for the
raising up of men's hearts, and the
sweetening of their affection towards
God.   Luther wished to see all the
arts employed in the service of Him
Who gave them, and he writes, 'The
devil is a sad spirit and makes folks
sad, hence he cannot bear cheerful-
ness; and therefore gets as far off
from music as possible, and never
stays where men are singing, especially spiritual songs.'   William Law
devotes a whole chapter (xv.) in his
Serious Call to the benefit of chant-
ing psalms in our private devotions,
and he writes: 'He therefore that
saith he wants a voice, or an ear, to
sing a psalm, mistakes the case: he
wants the spirit that really rejoices
in God; the dulness is in his heart
and not in his ear; and when his
heart feels a true joy in God, when
it has a full relish of what is expressed in the psalms, he will find it
very pleasant to make the motions
of his voice express the motions of
his heart.'

The two injunctions here given
to prayer and praise practically teach
us that all our feelings of sorrow or
of joy should be sanctified.   On all
occasions our joy should be the 'joy
in the Holy Ghost'; on all occasions
our sufferings should be met 'ac-

him call for the elders of the church ; and let them pray

cording to the will of God'; joy or sorrow being received with the worship of praise or prayer. At the same time it has been thoughtfully observed that we may with equal truth transpose the two precepts : 'Is any among you suffering? let him praise. Is any cheerful? let him pray': as thanksgiving sweetens sorrow, so supplication sanctifies joy (Plummer). It is interesting to note that in *Testaments of the xii. Pat.* Benj. 4, it is mentioned as one of the general characteristics of the good man that he praises God in song (or, hymn).

14. *Is any among you sick?* The mention of suffering in the wider sense leads to the mention of a common instance of suffering, viz. that of sickness. The verb is used of weakness in means, i.e. poverty, of weakness in convictions, and specially of weakness in bodily health ; so the participle of the same verb is used for 'the sick.'

In connection with the present passage, Ecclus. xxxviii. 1–15 is of interest, especially *v.* 9, 'My son, in thy sickness be not negligent, but pray unto the Lord, and he will make thee whole.'

let him call for the elders. There seems to be no reason why the mention of a body of presbyters in an official capacity should be regarded as indicating a late date, if we consider such passages as Acts xi. 30, xv. 6, xxi. 18, and in the light of such an admittedly early statement as in 1 Thess. v. 12, 13. This latter passage joined with such passages as 1 Pet. v. 1–4, Heb. xiii. 17, may fairly justify the description

of the presbyters as the representatives of the domestic religious life of the Church in every place ; that is to say, any local body of the Christian brethren, as locally constituted and organised (Moberly, *Ministerial Priesthood*, p. 144); see further below.

of the church. It is sometimes said that the word used here for 'church,' and the word translated 'synagogue,' ii. 2, are convertible terms not only in the LXX but in early Christian literature, but such a general statement should be received with some qualification in its reference to the latter[1]. In the verse before us the word 'church' as indicating the Christian community differs from the word 'synagogue,' ii. 2, inasmuch as the latter denotes the *place* of assembly. Eusebius emphasises the fact, *Theoph.* (Syr.) IV. 12, that Jesus called His Church not a synagogue but an Ecclesia, the word used here by St James. In the Gospels this word is used on two occasions, and on each by St Matthew, xvi. 18, xviii. 17. In the first passage our Lord speaks of 'My church,' evidently in the widest sense of the word, and in the second He uses the same word in a manner which might lead us to regard it as a title of the ruling body of the Ecclesia, or congregation, almost in the sense of 'the elders' here. And from this fact that our Lord thus used the term once no doubt of the whole Church which He founded, and once it may be of the Christian community in any city or village[2], the term would very possibly have become familiar

---

[1] See above on ii. 2, and the full examination in Zahn, *Einleitung*, I. 69.
[2] The term is thus understood in Matt. xviii. 17 by Grimm-Thayer, and Dr Hort, *Ecclesia*, p. 9, argues for its application there to a Jewish community.

over him, [1]anointing him with oil in the name of the Lord :

[1] Or, *having anointed*

to St James, to say nothing of its further local use in St Paul's Epistles and in the earlier portions of Acts.

Moreover, it would seem that our Lord, by this use of the word *Ecclesia* in Matt. xvi. 18, claimed for His own Church a term which had been used in the O.T. of the Jewish Church, the Church of God. And in the same way it is not difficult to understand that other terms may have been easily taken over as it were from the Jewish to the Christian Church, as is the case with 'presbyters,' 'elders' (cf. again Ecclus. xxx. 18 (xxxiii. 18) with Hebrews xiii. 17), although we must not hastily conclude that identity of name involves identity of function. Dr Schmiedel contends that the term 'presbyters' in St James is not necessarily of Jewish origin, but to support this he dates the Epistle before us at the same date as St Clement's Epistle to the Corinthians, or even as 1 Pet. which he places about 112 A.D., Art. 'Ministry,' *Encycl. Bibl.* III. 3120.

let them pray. There is evidence to show that amongst the Jews it was customary for the holiest of the Rabbis to go to a sick neighbour's house and to pray for him (see also on *v.* 16)[1]; it would thus be only natural that the elders of the Christian local community should be called upon, especially in the case of Jewish-Christians, for a similar spiritual office. At a later date in the Christian Church we find the presbyters

exhorted to visit all those who are infirm, Polycarp, *Phil.* vi. 1.

over him; not simply 'for him.' It is quite possible that the words mean 'let them pray (stretching their hands) over him,' in accordance with the interpretation given to the words by Origen, *Hom. in Lev.* ii. 4, and this rendering would be quite in accordance with the force of the original[2]. Otherwise, it is taken to mean that the elders come and stand over him, or with reference to him, 'as if their intent, in praying, went out towards him,' i.e. for his healing.

anointing him ('having anointed' R.V. marg.)[3]. The use of oil in anointing the sick for a remedial purpose receives illustration from the O.T. ; cf. Isaiah i. 6 (Jer. viii. 22, xlvi. 11): and there is evidence that it was customary to make a mixture of oil, wine, and water for a similar purpose, the preparation of which was permitted even during the rest of the Sabbath, *Jer. Ber.* II. 2 (Edersheim, *Jewish Social Life*, p. 167). In the N.T. reference is made to a similar use in Luke x. 34 (cf. vii. 46), and oil is frequently mentioned as a medicinal agent amongst the remedies of the ancient world for all kinds of diseases; see Art. 'Medicine,' Hastings' *B. D.* The belief in the same efficacious use is mentioned by Philo, Pliny, Galen, Dion Cassius; cf. also Jos. *Ant.* XVII. 6. 5, and *B. J.* I. 33. 5. For St James, moreover, such use would have received the highest sanction by the

---

[1] See the information given by Dr Schechter in Mr Fulford's *St James,* p. 117.

[2] So Grimm-Thayer explains the preposition 'with hands extended over him.' See also the remarks of Dr Hort, *Ecclesia,* p. 215.

[3] On the force of this aorist participle see Carr's note *in loco*; it may simply express an action contemporaneous with the principal verb.

15 and the prayer of faith shall save him that is sick, and the

practice of the first disciples, Mark vi. 13 ; and if we cannot definitely say that in this passage of St James our Lord's command is presupposed, it certainly intimates to us that His sanction was not withheld[1].

For instances of cures wrought by anointing with oil, see *Dict. of Christ. Ant.*, Arts. 'Oil' and 'Unction,' and also *Journal of Theological Studies*, 2, p. 60, in the case of St Pachomius, St Macarius of Alexandria, Benjamin of Nitria, Ammon, etc.

The subject is further discussed in Additional Note on Anointing with Oil.

in the name of the Lord. The position of the words seems to connect them with the act of anointing, and to intimate that this should be done in trustful dependence upon the power and authority of Christ. If it be said that no express command of Christ had been given for the anointing, it may be fairly alleged in reply that in Mark vi. 13 such a command is presupposed (see also above). On the force of the expression cf. also *v.* 10. And as in that verse the true and the false prophets are contrasted, the true being those who spoke in the name of the Lord, so here it may be that a contrast is marked between those who healed in the name of the Lord and those who claimed to perform their cures by all sorts of magical formulae (cf. Deissmann, *Bibelstudien*, pp. 5 ff.). That cures were wrought in the name of Jesus Christ is the testimony of the N.T. ; cf. e.g. Mark iii. 15 ; Luke x. 17 ; Acts iii. 6, xix. 13. At the same time it

may be fairly maintained that it would be quite permissible to connect the phrase with both prayer and anointing, and if with the former, the words of St John xiv. 13, xv. 16, xvi. 23 bear out the reference of them to prayer in the name of Jesus.

The phrase gains in significance, and the probability of its reference to Christ becomes assured, if we read simply 'in the Name' (omitting with B the words 'of the Lord,' which are placed in brackets by W.H.). For a similar emphatic reference to 'the Name,' i.e. of Christ, cf. Acts v. 41, R.V., 3 John 7, and so too in the early Church, Ignatius, *Ephes.* iii. 1, vii. 1.

15. *and the prayer of faith* (cf. i. 6), faith not as restricted to the particular case, but as the condition of a heart devoted to God. The prayer is that of the presbyters, but the fact that the sick man sends for them is in itself a proof that he is regarded as a sharer in their faith and prayer. If we compare Acts iii. 16 we note that there faith is spoken of as faith in the Name of Jesus, i.e. in the power of Him Who makes a lame man whole, and the prayer of faith here, as the context seems to suggest, may well be an exercise of faith in the same Divine Person and power. In this Name St Peter takes the lame man by the hand and 'raises him up,' Acts iii. 6, 7, where we have the same verb as in the sentence before us ; cf. Matt. ix. 5 ; Mark i. 31 ; John v. 8. See also below.

shall save him that is sick, i.e. from his bodily sickness ; cf. Matt. ix. 22 ; Mark v. 23 ; John xi. 12 ; and so

---

[1] See the stress laid upon this by B. Weiss, *Neue kirchliche Zeitschrift*, June, 1904, p. 438.

Lord shall raise him up ; and if he have committed sins, it

often in the LXX of safety from sickness or death, the same usage being found several times in the *Psalms of Solomon*; cf. the cognate noun in Isaiah xxxviii. 20. An attempt has sometimes been made to take the verb in an eschatological sense, i.e. as if it related here to eternal salvation, and reference is made in support of this to the meaning of the verb in *v.* 20. But the whole context before us is widely different, and points primarily at least to a different meaning. Further support is sometimes found for the same view in restricting the use of the verb in the phrase 'him that is sick' to the dying. But the verb is by no means always employed in this restricted sense, either in Biblical or classical Greek: cf. Job x. 1; 4 Macc. iii. 8; Heb. xii. 3. So in Herod. I. 197 the present participle of the verb is used as here describing 'the sick'.[1]

The Romanist commentators take the saving to be that of the soul, and they also refer the 'raising up' to spiritual comfort and strengthening; see further below. But it is admitted by one of the most recent of them in commenting on this passage that the latter expression may often refer to bodily healing, and that as a result of the spiritual refreshment a recovery of bodily health may often follow. Interesting cases may be cited from Jewish literature, in which special efficacy

attached to the prayer of faith, the prayer of the righteous, for the recovery of health, the restoration being regarded as a proof that sins had been forgiven.

and the Lord shall raise him up, i.e. Christ, bearing in mind the interpretation given to the words 'in the Name of the Lord,' and such passages as Mark i. 31, Acts ix. 34. Although parted from His Church, all power is given unto Christ both in heaven and on earth[2]. The fact that all power belongeth unto Christ, as also the fact that the anointing is in His Name, reminds us that although nothing conditional is expressed in the text, yet the one condition of all faithful prayer is understood (John xiv. 14), so that it may well be said that such a prayer for recovery even if unanswered might truly result in a higher 'salvation' than that of bodily health. But although the thought of a spiritual healing would thus be not altogether absent, as the following clauses 'and if he has committed,' etc., may lead us to infer, and although the verb translated 'to save' is used in i. 21 and ii. 14 of the salvation of the Lord, yet its meaning, as has been maintained above, must be decided by the context, and it seems to be here associated mainly with the thought of bodily health; it would therefore seem very unnatural to refer the expression 'shall raise him up' to the resurrection.

---

[1] The same verb is used twice, it would seem, in Wisdom iv. 16, and xv. 9, once of the dead and once of the sick or dying. This is of interest in connection with its employment here by St James. The more usual word for sickness is found in the previous verse.

[2] ' "I applied the remedies, the Lord was the healer" is the translation of a striking inscription in the ward of a French hospital, possibly suggested by these words of St James'; see Note on this passage in *Expositor*, Aug. 1904, by the Rev. J. H. Dudley Matthews.

16 shall be forgiven him.　Confess therefore your sins one to

*and if he have committed sins, it
shall be forgiven him.*　So A. and
R.V.　It is often urged that the
force of the original is 'even if,' but
although in some cases the same
conjunction and particle in combination may be rightly so rendered,
there are others in which the rendering of A. and R.V. is fully justified.
The clause is sometimes taken to
refer to the sins which the sickness
may have brought home to the man's
conscience, and not necessarily to
mean that the actual sickness in
question had been occasioned by
sin.　But it is best interpreted as
referring to the common connection
in the Jewish mind between sin and
disease : 'No sick man is healed
until all his sins are forgiven him,'
Nedarim, f. 41. 1 ; see also Art.
'Confess' and the connection of
moral and physical troubles, *Encycl.
Bibl.* I. 884.

Some striking instances of the
prevalence of the common Jewish
notion will be found in the *Testaments of the xii. Patriarchs*, Sim. 2,
Gad 5, where Simeon and Gad both
refer their bodily sickness to their
treatment of Joseph, and interesting
notices are given by Dr Edersheim,
Jewish Social Life, p. 163.　In the
N.T. we may refer to such passages
as Matt. ix. 2, 5, John v. 14, ix. 2.
Bede cites 1 Cor. xi. 30, and the
R.V. in marginal references compares the language of Isaiah xxxiii.
24.　But 'the prayer of faith' would
include by its very name a supplication not only for bodily recovery and
strength, but also for repentance

and forgiveness ; cf. Ecclus. xxxviii.
9, 10 ; and St James assures us that
the same Divine power which granted
the former would also bestow the
still greater and spiritual blessings of
the latter : 'My son, in thy sickness
be not negligent : but pray unto the
Lord, and he will make thee whole.
Leave off from sin, and order thine
hands aright, and cleanse thy heart
from all wickedness,' Ecclus. *u. s.*

it shall be forgiven.　The same
impersonal construction is found in
Matt. xii. 32. But the forgiveness is of
course conditional ; see previous note,
and cf. Matt. ix. 2, 5, Mark ii. 1-12.

16.　*Confess therefore your sins
one to another.*　So R.V., adding
the conjunction 'therefore' on good
authority (see W.H. and Mayor's
text), and also reading 'sins' instead
of 'faults' with W.H. (see further
below), the former word which
occurs in the immediate context, *v.*
15, including sins towards God,
while the latter word might refer
rather to offences towards one's
neighbour, although the distinction
cannot always be pressed.　The
addition 'therefore' is important
because it shows that the exhortation to mutual confession is associated
here at all events primarily with the
consideration of the case of the sick
man ; cf. also the words 'that ye may
be healed.'　The terms employed
are no doubt quite general, 'confess
your faults one to another,' but the
context may be fairly held to imply
that the confession had already been
made to the elders who had been
summoned[1] ; otherwise 'the prayer

---

[1] This is admitted by Dean Alford, see note *in loco*, and we may compare
the words of the Bishop of Worcester on the same passage, where he points out
that the general admonition to confess sins mutually one to another probably
implies that the sick man would have confessed his sins to the presbyters whom he
had summoned ; *Church and the Ministry*, p. 253.

of faith' could hardly have found place or mention.

The word translated 'confess' might simply imply that the confession was made from the heart, or that it was made openly in public. With regard to the latter meaning, which it is maintained on the high authority of Bishop Westcott (see note on 1 John i. 9) that the word always has in the N.T., support may be claimed for it in the two interesting uses of the *Didache*, iv. 14, xiv. 1, where in each case the context would imply that public confession was intended, as mention is made in the first instance of the Church, and in the second of the gathering together on the Lord's Day. 'In church thou shalt confess thy transgressions, and shalt not betake thyself to prayer with an evil conscience' (iv. 14); 'And on the Lord's own day gather yourselves together and break bread and give thanks, first confessing your transgressions, that your sacrifice may be pure' (xiv. 1).

The usage of the Jewish synagogue throws light upon these passages in the *Didache*, and no doubt such usage was known to St James. Before the Day of Atonement, mutual forgiveness was sought for sins committed against one another, and the men were to go apart and confess one to the other. Moreover, in a death-bed confession it is interesting to note that while one form of confession was made directly to God, another form was sometimes recited before the persons summoned for the purpose. The great Jewish

authority Dr Hamburger gives from Talmudic literature many instances of forms of confession of sin for domestic use, as well as in public in the synagogue, as e.g. in case of sickness, or when a man has offended against his neighbour. He also points out that in the O.T. confession of sins in private is enjoined on certain occasions, as well as in public. In case of a dangerous illness it seems that it was customary for the holiest of the local Rabbis to go to the house, and pray for God's mercy on the sick man and exhort him to confess his sins, and to set his affairs in order; cf. 2 Kings xx. 1.

These Jewish illustrations, which might be easily multiplied, enable us to see how natural it would be for St James to exhort that in case of illness the local presbyters of the Christian Church should be summoned, and that confession of sins should be made, and how arbitrary it is to maintain that such directions point to a late date for the Epistle[1].

your sins. Mr Mayor with Alford retains the reading 'faults' instead of 'sins' (although it would seem that this retention is against the authority of the best MS.), on the ground that it is more in agreement with the sense of the passage if we take it as referring to our Lord's commands in Matt. v. 23, vi. 14, and he also notes that this same word for 'faults' is used in the two passages of the *Didache* referred to above. He further understands the precept as of general application, and that St James is recommending the habit

---

[1] For the instances above see Buxtorf's *Jewish Synagogue*, ch. xx. pp. 363, 428 (see *Confession and Absolution, Fulham Conference*, p. 15); Hamburger, *Real-Encyclopädie des Judentums*, ii. 8, 1139 ff.; and the extracts given on Dr Schechter's information by Mr Fulford, *Epistle of St James*, p. 117.

another, and pray one for another, that ye may be healed.

of mutual confession between friends[1]; in this interpretation the words 'that ye may be healed' receive a metaphorical meaning, and we do not confine them to the case of the sick man. But whilst advocating this interpretation of the words, and pointing out the benefits arising from such mutual confidences, he rightly urges that no one should be better fitted than the parish priest, if he is wise with the heavenly wisdom of St James, to receive such confidences and to give in return spiritual help and counsel. See further, Additional Note on Confession of Sins.

and pray one for another. Mutual and frank confession would lead to sincerity in prayer, for a man could not pray whilst he was cherishing self-righteous thoughts, and also to sympathy in prayer, whether bodily or spiritual health was in question : cf. Ecclus. xxviii. 3–5, 'One man beareth hatred against another, and doth he seek pardon from the Lord? he showeth no mercy to a man which is like himself, and doth he ask forgiveness of his own sins? if he that is but flesh nourish hatred, who will intreat for pardon of his sins?'

that ye may be healed. The context points primarily at all events to bodily healing; cf. *vv.* 14, 15, and also the reference made to the miraculous power of Elijah's prayer. The verb is no doubt also used of diseases of the soul, although in the cases usually cited the context shows that this and not the literal sense is intended. See e.g. Heb. xii. 13;

1 Pet. ii. 24; and also Isaiah vi. 10; Ecclus. iii. 28. So too in the remarkable saying of Epictetus, 'It is more necessary to heal the soul than the body, for death is better than a bad life,' there can be no doubt of the meaning; and so too in the saying of Arrian that 'healing of sin' is evidently only thorough when a man confesses and repents of his sin.

The tenses used indicate that St James is thinking of continuous action, and thus from the particular case he enforces a general rule for similar practice in all cases of sickness. At the same time it is quite possible that St James might use the word, well remembering its double meaning, and with reference to disease of the soul as well as of the body; in *v.* 19, 20, he speaks of sin and conversion in a manner which shows us that the thought of healing in a spiritual sense may have been present in his mind, as it was in the days of old to the mind of the Hebrew prophet; cf. Isaiah vi. 10. At all events it is noticeable that in *v.* 19 we have the same word used for 'convert' as is used by Isaiah *u.s.* in close connection with the same verb for 'heal' as in the passage before us.

The supplication of a righteous man availeth much in its working, R.V. The words are best taken as strengthening the previous injunction to pray, and they are illustrated by the instance of Elijah. Their introduction without any definite word of connection is quite in the style of

---

1 On the monastic rule to tell to the common body any thought of things forbidden, or inadmissible words, or remissness in prayer, or desire of the ordinary life, that through the common prayers the evil might be cured, see *D.C.A.* I. pp. 647, 648. In modern days reference is made to the Moravian Societies, and to the Methodist Classes which J. Wesley appears to have derived from them.

The supplication of a righteous man availeth much in its

St James. In A.V. the one Greek word rendered by the Revisers 'in its working' is removed from its emphatic position at the end of the sentence in the original, and resolved into two adjectives, but the rendering 'effectual fervent prayer......availeth much' seems to be tautological and adds little; a prayer which is 'effectual' already 'availeth much.' Bishop Lightfoot, *On a Fresh Revision of the N.T.* p. 182, has some interesting remarks on this rendering and its admission into the A.V., which he is disposed to ascribe to carelessness in the correction of the copy of the Bishops' Bible, used by the revisers of 1611 for the press. Others, who are still inclined to think that the R.V. rendering is not sufficiently strong, would translate 'in its earnestness'; cf. Acts xii. 5, and the name which St James himself bore, 'righteous,' and his own practice of always kneeling, in the intensity of his prayer, in the Temple, asking forgiveness for the people (Eusebius, *H. E.* II. 23).

It is maintained on high authority (Lightfoot, *Gal.* v. 6) that the verb in the original is never used by St Paul as passive but as middle, and so, as the passage before us is the only other place in the N.T. in which any doubt could arise, it is best to render the word here as middle, and in his rendering of the passage before us a similar view is taken by the German editor Dr B. Weiss. On the other hand Mayor *in loco* argues at length

for the passive signification, and explains it here as of prayer 'actuated, or inspired by the Spirit[1].' It is interesting to note that in the early Church those who were 'acted or worked on by an evil spirit' bore the name of *Energumeni*, a title which might support a passive meaning of the Greek participle before us, although here of course the word would refer to a prayer inspired by God; cf. Rom. viii. 26. Some of the older commentators interpret the word of the way in which a good man's prayer is 'energised' by his good deeds and efforts; see Euthymius Zigabenus *in loco*.

supplication. The word is different from that rendered 'prayer' in *v.* 15 (and only there so rendered in the N.T.); it is petitionary, and gives expression to the thought of personal need; it is also used of requests to men, but both in the LXX and in the N.T. of petition to God; cf. Psalm liv. 1, and so too *Psalms of Solomon*, v. 7, it is appropriately used as expressing petition to God for the relief of material wants.

of a righteous man. This thought of a special efficacy attaching to the prayers of a righteous man would be quite characteristic of a teacher with the Jewish antecedents of St James, and it may be fairly added to the many links which connect the Epistle with a Jewish writer. Such passages as Isaiah xxxvii. 4 = 2 Kings xix. 4, and so too 1 Kings xviii. 36, in relation to the prayer of Elijah, or Jer.

---

[1] The Dean of Westminster, *Ephesians*, p. 247, also maintains the passive usage by St Paul, but the sense of the passive is not of things to be done, but of powers to be set in operation, and he thinks that in this notoriously difficult passage of St James it is at least possible that the verb in question may mean 'set in operation by Divine agency.'

xv. 1, and Ps. xcix. 6, of the prayer of
Moses and Aaron, 2 Esdras vii. 36 ff.,
may be quoted in this connection,
and also the remarkable passage in
Judith viii. 31, in which the people
ask Judith to pray for rain, 'therefore now pray thou for us, because
thou art a godly woman, and the
Lord will send us rain to fill our
cisterns, and we shall faint no more'
(for these and other references see
Art. 'Prayer,' *Encycl. Biblica*). In the
N.T. as in the O.T. and Apocrypha
this title 'righteous' is used of the
ideally just man: cf. Gen. vi. 9; Wisd.
x. 4. So too it is used of Abel,
Heb. xi. 4; of Lot, 2 Pet. ii. 7; and
our Lord Himself speaks of righteous
Abel, Matt. xxiii. 35, and also of the
'many prophets and righteous men'
who had desired to see what His
own generation saw, Matt. xiii. 17.
But the word might also be taken in
a wider sense, and as 'the poor' and
'the lowly,' so too 'the righteous'
were doubtless familiar figures to
St James as to every typical pious
Hebrew.

Throughout the O.T. 'the righteous' were set over against 'the
sinners, the impious, the ungodly';
cf. Psalm i. 5, xxxvii. 12, 32; Prov.
xiv. 19; Hab. i. 4, 13; Wisd. x. 6, 20:
and with this we may compare the
marked contrast between the same
two classes which pervades the *Book
of Enoch* and the *Psalms of Solomon* (cf. Prov. xi. 31 and 1 Pet. iv.
18). In connection with the passage
before us the emphasis laid upon
repentance in the character of the
'righteous' man in *Psalms of Sol.*
ix. 15, is important: 'the righteous
thou wilt bless, and wilt not correct
them for the sins that they have
committed; and thy kindness is
towards them that sin if so be they
repent.' No doubt the character

had fallen short in many ways of
the ideal set forth, e.g. in Ezekiel
xviii. 5–9, but St James would have
known of 'die Stillen im Lande,'
quiet, righteous men, like Symeon
and Joseph and John the Baptist,
Luke ii. 25, Matt. i. 19, Mark vi. 20,
who were waiting for the salvation of
God. But the need of forgiveness and
repentance was by no means, as we
have seen above, excluded from the
character of the righteous, and there
was no contradiction in St James
classing as 'righteous' those who
were most conscious that their own
sins must be confessed and forgiven.
St James would doubtless have said
with St Peter, 'and if *the righteous
is scarcely saved*, where shall the
ungodly and sinner appear?' 1 Pet.
iv. 18. There is thus no occasion to
suppose that there is any reference
to the thought of a righteous man
appearing before God above for
those confessing their sins, and it is
altogether foreign to the context; Elijah prays on earth, not in
heaven.

On the constant identification in
Old Testament thought of the poor
with 'the righteous' see Art. 'Poor,'
Hastings' *B. D.* iv.

It is interesting and important to
note how Hooker, *E. P.* vi. 4. 7
(see also above, p. 143) connects
this verse with the exhortation to
mutual confession: 'The greatest
thing which made men forward and
willing upon their knees to confess
whatsoever they had committed
against God......was their fervent
desire to be helped and assisted
with the prayers of God's saints.'
And he adds that St James exhorts
to mutual confession, 'alleging this
only for a reason that just men's
devout prayers are of great avail
with God.'

17 working. Elijah was a man of like ¹passions with us, and

¹ Or, *nature*

17. *Elijah.* The important place
which Elijah held in Jewish thought
is witnessed to by such references as
Mal. iv. 6; Ecclus. xlviii. 1–12; 1
Macc. ii. 58. All kinds of traditions
surrounded his name. Thus his
coming would precede by three days
the advent of the Messiah, and it
was customary to open the door
during certain prayers, that Elijah
might enter and proclaim that the
Messiah was at hand ; when a child
was circumcised a chair was always
left vacant for Elijah as the messenger
of the 'covenant'; and often as a
Rabbi was at prayer in the wilder-
ness, or was on a journey, the great
prophet would make himself known
to him (see Smith's *B. D.* 2nd edit.
p. 913). But we do not need the
evidence of Jewish tradition to assure us of an influence which is so
often patent in the records of the
Evangelists.

As this Epistle of St James presents so many points of contact with
Ecclesiasticus, it is quite probable
that the stress laid here upon Elijah
may also be partly accounted for
by the fulness with which that book
dwells upon the prophet's history.
The opening words of chap. xlviii.
in Ecclus. may at all events be
brought into connection with the
passage before us, 'then stood up
Elijah the prophet as fire and his
words burned like a lamp......by
the word of the Lord he shut up the
heaven......O Elias, how wast thou
honoured in thy wondrous deeds !
and who may glory like unto
thee !'

of like passions with us, or 'of
like *nature,*' R.V. marg., and so in
Acts xiv. 15, the only other N.T.

passage in which the Greek adjective
occurs. Primarily the word seems
to mean those of like feelings or
affections, suffering the like with
another, sympathising with them,
and thus it is used quite generally of
those of like nature. Both senses are
found in classical Greek, e.g. in
Plato. The phrase stands here
emphatically to show that no dis-
couragement should be caused by
this reference to the example of
Elijah, for great prophet as he was,
he was also a man of flesh and blood,
liable to human weakness, of which
reminder perhaps St James's readers
stood specially in need, as the power
and greatness of Elijah had been so
enhanced in popular report. There
is no occasion therefore to take the
word as referring specially to sufferings or to connect it with *v.* 10.
A good instance of the use of the
word may be cited from 4 Macc. xii.
13, where it is alleged against the
tyrant Antiochus that he cut out
the tongues of those of like feelings
and nature with himself.

and he prayed fervently, R.V.;
'prayed with prayer,' R.V. marg.: the
reduplication in the wording gives an
intensifying force, and many similar
instances may be quoted from both
Old and New T. of a Hebraism
which was in common use in the
LXX; cf. e.g. Gen. xxxi. 30; Jonah i.
10; Luke xxii. 15; Acts v. 28.
Others take the expression simply
to mean that he prayed with prayer,
and that nothing else but prayer
brought about the lengthy drought.
But how could he pray except in
prayer ? It would seem therefore
that the explanation first given is
thus more natural.

he prayed [1]fervently that it might not rain ; and it rained
18 not on the earth for three years and six months.　And he

[1] Gr. *with prayer.*

that it might not rain. The O.T.
does not tell us in so many words
that Elijah prayed for the drought,
or for the rain which ended it,
although we are told that he
prophesied both ; cf. 1 Kings xvii. 1,
xviii. 1[1]. But even if the words
'before whom I stand' in the former
passage are not taken here as
equivalent to 'stand in prayer' (cf.
Gen. xviii. 22 ; Jer. xv. 1), yet if we
read the passage 1 Kings xviii. 42,
it is evident that Elijah is described
as in an attitude of intense prayer
before the rain was given : 'and he
cast himself down upon the earth,
and put his face between his knees'
(it is said that the attitude itself is
still retained in modern days by
some of the Dervishes).　It would
therefore not be strange if St James
inferred the prayer, or he may have
been following some definite Jewish
tradition (cf. note on ii. 23).　The
words in Ecclus. xlviii. 3 would
seem to refer rather to the prophecy
than to the prayers of the prophet.

*and he prayed that it might not
rain, and it rained not:* the diction
is remarkable, and in itself emphasises the thought of the certain
and immediate avail of the prayer.
Jewish tradition undoubtedly regarded Elijah's prayer as a type
of successful prayer : ' "And Elijah
the Tishbite said that there should
not be dew or rain."　R. Berachiah
said R. Josa and the Rabbonin
dispute about this ; one said that
God accepted his prayer concerning
the rain but not concerning the dew,

and the other that he was heard
both concerning the rain and the
dew' : *Jalk. Sim.* on 1 Kings xvii.
(cf. the *Expository Times*, April,
1904).

on the earth. Although it may be
said that these words merely fill up
the idea of the verb connected with
them, yet it may be noted that the
phrase is characteristically Hebraic :
cf. Gen. ii. 5, vii. 12 ; *Psalms of
Solomon*, xvii. 20, 'for the heaven
ceased to drop rain upon the earth.'
Here as in Luke iv. 25 it seems
quite unnecessary to suppose that
anything more than 'the land of
Israel' was implied.

three years and six months. For
the same duration of time see Luke
iv. 25, and many commentators refer
to the Jewish tradition to the same
effect contained in *Jalkut Simeoni*
on 1 Kings xvi. : see Rabbinical
Illustrations of this Epistle in the
Expository Times, April, 1904.　But
others see a reference to the period
which seems to have become of
traditional duration as marking times
of distress and calamity : Daniel vii.
25, xii. 7 ; cf. Rev. xi. 2, xiii. 5 (cf.
Century Bible).

The expression 1 Kings xviii. 1,
'in the third year,' might well be
taken by the Jews to cover three
years, and the duration of the
famine would not cease with the
rain, but would continue at least for
a time[2].

18.　*And he prayed again ;* cf. 2
Esdras vii. 39, 'and Elijah prayed
for those who received rain.'　There

---

[1] Dean Stanley has some interesting remarks, *Jewish Church*, ii. p. 264.
[2] See Plummer on Luke iv. 25, and Schegg, *Der katholische Brief des Jakobus,*
in loco.

prayed again; and the heaven gave rain, and the earth brought forth her fruit.

19   My brethren, if any among you do err from the truth,

is no force in the objection that the attitude of Elijah in 1 Kings xviii. 42 does not of necessity betoken prayer, as standing, not kneeling, was and *is* the usual attitude for prayer, but cf. Dan. vi. 10; Neh. viii. 6 ('Kneel,' Hastings' *B. D.* III.). Elijah's attitude marks rather the intensity of his prayer.

and the heaven gave rain; a popular and poetical mode of expression; God is said to give rain, 1 Sam. xii. 17; Job v. 10; Acts xiv. 17. 'Heaven' and 'earth' are both spoken of as obeying the prayer of the prophet or rather the will of God; cf. Isaiah v. 6. It is of interest to note how St James by his own prayers was said to have called down rain amidst the droughts of Palestine, 'and when there was no rain he lifted up his hands to heaven and prayed, and straightway *the heaven gave rain*' (same phrase as above in the Greek), Epiphanius (p. 104 *b*).

In Josephus, *Ant.* XIV. 2. 1, and XVIII. 8. 6, we have two remarkable instances of the gift of rain in answer to prayer, one the prayer of Onias, B.C. 64, 'a righteous man who prayed for rain and God rained,' the other the prayer of the Jewish people for rain, and probably of Christians also, in one of the years of drought which preceded the great famine, *Ant.* XX. 5. 2. But this would be too early to be brought into close connection with our Epistle, unless we adopt a very early date indeed (see however Plumptre *in loco*). In early Church history both Tertullian, *Apol.* c. 5, and Eusebius, *H. E.* v. 5, refer to an instance of

a similar kind in answer to the prayers of the Thundering Legion for rain. See further, Additional Note on Prayer.

and the earth brought forth her fruit, a supernatural cause but a natural result, her own fruit, i.e. the fruits which she was wont to bear. For 'brought forth' cf. Gen. i. 11, Ecclus. xxiv. 17, where the verb is used transitively as often in later Greek; but in the other instances of its use in the N.T. it is intransitive.

19. *My brethren.* The best authorities support R.V.; St James's phrase is thus more emphatic and sympathetic than the single word 'brethren' of A.V. He is still plainly mindful of the fellowship which binds both himself and the Christian community to the erring brother: 'if any *among you.*' The verse is closely connected with what had been said in *v.* 16; the thought of mutual confession and brotherly charity, as well as that of mutual prayer, might naturally lead on to the thought of conversion and restoration. No words reveal more fully the tenderness of St James than this closing exhortation of the Epistle, and in them we may see an indication of his close following of the great Overseer and Shepherd of souls. St James, we may also note, does not speak of the conversion of many, but of one; with all his social teaching he thus never forgets to recognise, as the Gospel of Christ has always recognised, the infinite value of the individual soul.

do err. The verb is used primarily of going astray, as e.g. of a sheep,

20 and one convert him ; [1]let him know, that he which con-

Matt. xviii. 12, 13, 1 Pet. ii. 25, and so metaphorically of going astray from the path of rectitude, cf. Heb. v. 2; 2 Pet. ii. 15; 2 Tim. iii. 13. In Wisdom v. 6 we have a remarkable parallel use of the verb 'we have erred from the way of truth.' The presbyters in the early Church are exhorted by St Polycarp, *Phil.* vi. 1, not to neglect the widows, the orphans, and the poor, and also 'to turn back the sheep that are gone astray,' where we have the same verb which is here used of erring joined with the same verb which is rendered here to convert, i.e. to turn, or to turn back.

from the truth. The words have been described as marking a practical and not a theoretical error, but we must not forget that Christian practice for St James depended upon the recognition of the faith of our Lord Jesus Christ, ii. 1. It is best therefore to regard 'the truth' here as meaning the sum and substance of the Apostolic teaching and preaching as it was delivered, the revelation of Christ; and it is evident that the Apostle is not thinking of conversion from Judaism or paganism, but of 'the truth' acknowledged in common by Christians, 'if any among you.' It has been carefully pointed out that this use of the expression 'the truth,' although characteristic of St John, is found also in each group of the Epistles ; cf. Westcott on Heb. x. 26, and Art. 'Truth' in Hastings' *B. D.* No doubt 'the truth' expresses the ideal of human or Christian conduct, the true reality for man, but the revelation of Christ, it is to be remembered, would include not only

the revelation of man to himself, but a fresh revelation, a new power implanted in human nature, enabling a man to walk henceforth in newness of life.

and one convert him; cf. Gal. vi. 1. The verb is frequent both in LXX and N.T. In the LXX it is used both transitively and intransitively; cf. Lam. v. 21 for an instance of the first, and Isaiah vi. 10 of the second. But in the N.T. it is always intransitive except in these two verses of St James and in Luke i. 16, 17. The word may of course simply mean 'to turn back,' i.e. to the truth, but as it is so often used of turning to the Lord, it may be taken so here. It has this meaning both in LXX and N.T., and it may be noted that the same use of the cognate noun is found in *Psalms of Solomon,* ix. 19, xvi. 11. The indefiniteness of the expression 'and one convert him' shows us that the work was not regarded as confined to the presbyters.

20. *let him know.* So A.V. and R.V. text; 'know ye,' R.V. marg. and W.H. text, but the other reading is retained in their margin. So far as the Greek is concerned the 'know ye' might also be indicative, 'ye know'; cf. a similar case of doubtful interpretation in i. 19. If we adopt the imperative, either in the singular or the plural, it is introduced as a word of encouragement, and a motive to effect the work of restoration; if we render the marginal reading as indicative 'ye know,' the well-known truth is emphasised that to convert is to bring into the way of salvation.

he which converteth a sinner. To

verteth a sinner from the error of his way shall save a soul
from death, and shall cover a multitude of sins.

emphasise the fact is the best reason for the repetition, and it is quite characteristic of St James thus to repeat a word; cf. i. 6.

from the error of his way; cf. Wisd. v. 6 (see above). The expression means that the converter does not only turn the sinner back from, but out of, his erring way into the right path, i.e. the path of truth from which he is represented as having wandered, and in the same way 'truth' is opposed to 'error' by St John, cf. 1 John iv. 6. In 2 Pet. ii. 2 we have the striking phrase 'the way of the truth,' R.V., where 'the truth' seems used very much as in *v.* 19 here, and in *v.* 21 of the same chapter we have the phrase 'the way of righteousness,' where evidently the same metaphorical use of the term 'the way' is employed as in the verse before us, and often in the O.T.

shall save a soul. So A. and R.V. The words refer to the converted, not to the converter. It is no doubt quite true that some Jewish writings, e.g. Ecclus. iii. 3, 30, v. 14, Tobit iv. 10, xii. 9 (Dan. iv. 27, with which we may compare *Didache*, iv. 6), are often mentioned as in favour of referring the words to the converter: 'Almsgiving saves from death and purges away all sin,' says Raphael, Tob. xii. 9, and with these and similar remarks in the Apocryphal books quoted, we may compare the following: 'Whosoever makes the many righteous, sin prevails not over him; and whosoever makes the many to sin, they grant him not the faculty

to repent. Moses was righteous, and made the many righteous, and the righteousness of the many was laid upon him': *Sayings of the Jewish Fathers,* v. 26, 27, Dr Taylor, 2nd edit.; so again *Joma,* f. 87. 1, 'who brings many to righteousness, God lets no sin be done by his hand.' But in spite of these expressions of Jewish belief, which might be easily multiplied, it does not at all follow that St James is here maintaining that if a man makes a convert his own sins shall be forgiven him. The whole context 'shall save a soul' and 'a multitude of sins' points much rather here to the 'sinner,' and to the sin which bringeth forth death, i. 15; the converter would scarcely be thought of as needing restoration from death or relief from the weight of unforgiven sin.

from death. For the expression 'shall save a soul' cf. i. 21[1]. The whole phrase is sometimes taken as referring to the day of judgment, but a man may be in the death of which St James speaks, i. 15, here and now, and he may pass out of it into the true life here and now; cf. the striking parallel John v. 24, where we have precisely the same phrase 'out of death,' which is expressed in the original, with the thought of the human agency as saving the soul (cf. 1 John v. 16, R.V. marg.), and there is nothing unscriptural in the thought that the believer does that which God does through him; cf. Rom. xi. 14; 1 Cor. vii. 16.

---

[1] If we adopt the reading 'shall save his soul' with W.H., Weiss, von Soden (Mayor doubtful), the pronoun refers to the converted, not to the converter. On the phrase 'to save out of death' see Westcott's note, Heb. v. 7.

and shall cover a multitude of sins. Cf. Prov. x. 12, 'love covereth all transgressions,' Heb., a passage even more closely related to all appearance with 1 Pet. iv. 8, 'love covereth a multitude of sins.' The verb used in the Hebrew sometimes means to cover sin, i.e. to pardon, forgive; cf. its use in Psalm xxxii. 1, lxxxv. 3, Neh. iv. 5 (iii. 37), with reference to the pardon and forgiveness of God. But it is remarkable that in the LXX of Prov. x. 12, although the same Greek verb is found for 'cover' as in the other verses just cited, the passage runs, 'friendship covers all those that are not contentious.' As St Peter commonly quotes from the LXX he has in this instance preferred the Hebrew, or it is quite possible that both he and St James may be referring to some proverbial saying, and not consciously to Proverbs. Or it is possible that both writers may have in mind an *Agraphon* of Christ Himself[1]. It is noticeable that the words as given in St Peter are often found in patristic writings, cf. Clem. Rom. *Cor.* xlix. 5, *Clem. Hom.* ii. 16, and undoubtedly in several of these instances we may have a quotation from St Peter's Epistle. But in *Didascalia*, ii. 3, we read, 'because the Lord saith, *Love covers a multitude of sins.*' This is the strongest reference in support of the view before us, and in addition it may be noted that Clem. Alex. *Paedag.* iii. 12, 91, couples the passage in question with a canonical

saying of our Lord, Luke xii. 25, but there is much room for doubt as to whether he regarded both sayings as spoken by Christ. But, as in the previous clause, the question arises as to whether the reference is to the sins of the converter or of the converted. There seems no doubt that passages may be cited both from Jewish (see previous note) and from early Christian writers in support of a reference to the sins of the converter. Perhaps the most notable passage from Christian writers is that in which Origen, *Hom. in Lev.* ii. 4, places the conversion of a sinner amongst the different ways in which forgiveness of sins may be obtained in the Gospel[2]. This interpretation however hardly commends itself, not only on account of the difficulties already referred to (see previous note), but also because St James as a Christian teacher has already spoken in very definite terms as to how the soul may be saved. There is a third view strongly supported, which would see in such words a reference to the truth that the work of conversion is twice blessed, blessing both the converter and the converted. It may well be that such a thought may fairly be connected with the words before us, and such a connection is of course very different from the idea that a man could be supposed to set to work to atone for his own sins by effecting the conversion of another. With this whole passage, *vv.* 19, 20, our Lord's own words may be fitly

---

[1] Resch, *Agrapha*, pp. 248, 253; but cf. also Mayor's criticism *in loco*, and Ropes, *Die Sprüche Jesu*, p. 75.

[2] Mayor quotes this and other passages *in loco*; cf. Mr Fulford's valuable note, *Epistle of St James*, pp. 93–95. The majority of modern commentators, with the exception of Spitta and von Soden, adopt the view taken in the text. The Romanist commentators have as a rule regarded the sins to be covered as those of the converter, but Trenkle is a recent noteworthy exception. Reference may also be made to Art. 'Sin,' Hastings' *B. D.* IV. 534.

compared : 'If thy brother sin (a-gainst thee), go, show him his fault between thee and him alone ; if he hear thee, thou hast gained thy brother,' Matt. xviii. 15.

The clause under consideration has sometimes been regarded as mere tautology, but this is to ignore the truth that the soul is not only saved out of death, not merely rescued from peril, but blessed, Ps. xxxii. 1. And so the stern Epistle ends with a message of blessing, with an exhortation to consideration and love, perhaps emphasising in the very abruptness of its conclusion the greatness of the Christian duty and privilege so earnestly commended. St James himself had known the blessedness of being converted to the truth, and of converting others by his words (Euseb. *H. E.* ii. 23). St James had known the blessedness

and privilege of prayer, and the Epistle closes, as it began, with a call to prayer, prayer for the sick and suffering, for self, and for sinners (Parry, *St James*, p. 10).

It is of course quite possible that the Epistle ends as it does because it was meant as a general exhorta-tion and was not addressed to any particular individuals or to any one Church.

It has been pointed out that both the books to which St James most frequently refers, Ecclesiasticus and Wisdom, have a similar abruptness in their conclusion, but there is no need to suppose that St James was consciously imitating the writers of those books in this respect, although we may perhaps agree with Theile that he concludes more powerfully than with a series of salutations.

ADDITIONAL NOTE.—THE USE OF OATHS.

The oath, we have been reminded, played a great part among the Israel-ites in ordinary social life, and no sin was more severely condemned by the prophets than perjury ; cf. Ezek. xvi. 59, xvii. 13–18 (Ps. xv. 4, xxiv. 4), Zeph. i. 5 ; while such passages as Ecclesiastes ix. 2 and Ecclus. xxiii. 9–11 show what a grievous sin the use of vain and reckless swearing was considered. It is therefore perhaps not surprising to find that men like the Essenes regarded the taking an oath in the ordinary concerns of daily life in a worse light than perjury, Jos. *B. J.* ii. 8. 6. The words of Philo too are often quoted in which he judges it best to abstain from swearing altogether, since an oath indicates not confidence but want of trust, although elsewhere he counsels that if a man must swear, he should not swear by God, but by the earth, the sun, the moon, the stars, the heaven (Philo, *Spec. Legg.* M. 2, p. 271). But there is no reason to suppose that in this injunction St James would forbid the use of oaths at all times and in all places. If he had meant that the words were to be so taken it is difficult to believe that he would not have given some further reason for such an absolute injunction. The Essenes, in spite of their strong dislike of oaths, obliged those who desired to join their community to take 'terrific oaths,' Jos. *B. J.* ii. 8. 6 ; *Ant.* xv. 10. 4. But further than this : appeal is rightly made to the practice of St Paul, Rom. ix. 1, 2 Cor. xi. 31, Phil. i. 8, in his frequent calling upon God to witness, and in his use of strong asseverations, and, above all, to the fact that our Lord Himself, although He so severely condemned light and false swearing, so constantly used the solemn asseveration 'Amen' (Dalman, *Words of Jesus*, p. 229, E.T.), and allowed Himself to be put on oath before the high-priest (Matt. xxvi. 63, 64).

In view of the whole evidence the language of our Article admirably expresses the Christian view of the use of an oath (see Smith and Cheetham, *Dict. of Christ. Ant.* II. 1416; and for Jewish and other literature, Hastings' *B. D.*, 'Oath,' and *Encycl. Bibl.* III. 3452). According to Article XXXIX., while vain and rash swearing is forbidden to Christian men by our Lord Jesus Christ and James his Apostle, yet the Christian religion does not prohibit the use of an oath, as in a court of justice, provided that the occasion be in accordance with the three conditions of the prophet's teaching : 'in truth, in judgment, and in righteousness' (Jer. iv. 2). In an ideal society, in which men realised that bond of holiest brotherhood, which St James so often enforces, in a society in which the royal law was fulfilled, *Thou shalt love thy neighbour as thyself,* there would be no need of anything more binding than a man's word, but 'for the hardness of men's hearts' the use of oaths is not merely allowable but often necessary (see also note *in loco*).

No doubt the early Christians had serious scruples about the matter, but these scruples naturally became intensified at a time when the taking of an oath before a heathen magistrate became an act of idolatry. But on some occasions and by always guarding themselves against the adoption of idolatrous formulae the early Christians were willing to be put on oath; cf. e.g. Tertullian, *Apol.* c. 32 (but see Mayor's note *in loco*), and Constantine's general law, *Cod. Theod.* II. xxxix. 3, that in a court of justice all witnesses were to be bound by oath, although there was always the feeling expressed by St Clement of Alexandria that it was an indignity for a Christian to be placed on oath, and by St Augustine who, while urging from Scripture the lawfulness of oaths, desired that they should be employed as little as possible ; cf. *Ep.* clvii., and his remarks on this verse, *Serm.* 180 (quoted by Mayor). St Augustine was apparently much puzzled by the words 'above all things swear not,' but, as we have seen, the expression 'above all things' may be connected with the immediately preceding injunctions, and there was every reason why St James should emphasise singleness of word and deed in social life.

ADDITIONAL NOTE.—ANOINTING WITH OIL.

Whilst presbyters are here specially mentioned, perhaps as the representatives of the whole Church, perhaps as possessing the gifts of healing in the fullest measure, many instances may be cited to prove that in the early Church liberty was granted to all Christians to *use* the anointing oil for themselves and for their friends. Thus in the third century the Emperor Septimius Severus was healed by a Christian steward, Proculus Torpacion, who anointed him with oil, Tert. *Ad Scap.* iv., and even when it was provided that the consecrator should be a bishop or presbyter, as in *Apost. Const.* viii. 28, and as is apparently assumed in the Sacramentary of Serapion, the application of the oil was permitted to any Christian. In the important letter of Innocent I. to Decentius of Gubbio, *Ep.* xxv. 11, in 416 A.D., whilst the consecrator of the oil for the sick is a bishop, any of the faithful might administer it, and so we read, 'it is lawful not for the priests only, but for all Christians, to use it, for assisting in their own need and in the need of members of their household[1].' Again, in the eighth century we find Bede referring to these words of Innocent, and in accordance with them holding that the oil for the sick could be administered by any Christian in his own or another's necessity. It would seem that it is not until early in the ninth

---

[1] Caesarius of Arles, 502 A.D., in an epidemic of sickness advises the head of a household to anoint his family with oil that had been blessed.

century that we come across any definite formulation of the theory that by
the anointing of the sick not only bodily health but remission of sins may be
conveyed[1], although no doubt it is true that the theory would have been
spreading some time before its authoritative definition.   In the tenth
century it would seem that the administration, as well as the blessing of
the oil, was much more, if not entirely, restricted to the priest.   And this
restriction led to further and momentous consequences, although it is not
until the twelfth century that we meet with such terms as 'extreme unction'
or 'sacrament of the dying,' expressions clearly showing that the unction is
no longer intended, as originally, for the healing of the body, but it had
become restricted to a time when the sickness was regarded as practically
beyond all human means of recovery[2].   But the words of St James plainly
show that he was not considering the case only of those sick unto death, but
of the sick generally, and this fact has evidently weighed with some of the
ablest Roman Catholic writers, e.g. Cajetan and Baronius, not to draw from
this passage any sanction for what the Roman Church calls the Sacrament
of Extreme Unction.

In the Eastern Church this latter term finds no place, while the anointing
with oil is employed with a view to bodily cure as well as a means of spiritual
help.   Nor in the East has the rule ever obtained that the sacred oil must
be 'made by the bishop'; presbyters might make the chrism for the sick,
as we learn from Theodore of Canterbury, born at Tarsus, in the seventh
century; and although at present it is deemed desirable that seven priests
shall be brought together for the consecration of the oil, yet the act of one
priest is regarded as sufficient.

In the First Prayer Book of Edward VI., 1549, unction was still allowed,
but in a simpler and more discretionary form than in the older offices for the
Visitation of the Sick, the words being 'if the sick person desire it.'   The
words of the accompanying prayer regard the 'visible oil' as an outward
visible sign of an inward spiritual grace, the anointing with the Holy Ghost,
for the bestowal of which supplication is offered, while the latter part of the
prayer supplicates for a restoration to bodily health and strength[3].   Earnest
pleas have been made in recent days for a revival of the anointing of the

---

[1] This and other important points are duly emphasised by Mr Puller in his
valuable lectures on the Unction of the Sick, *Guardian*, Dec. 10th, and following
weeks, 1902.   He maintains that in the second benedictory prayer for the Oil of
the Sick in the Sacramentary of Serapion, the clause that the oil may be to
those who use it 'for good grace and the remission of sins,' is an interpolation,
and certainly no such clause is found in the prayer concerning the oil which
forms part of the Eucharistic liturgy in the same Sacramentary.   But at all
events it is evident that this ancient prayer places first the medicinal use of the
oil, and that there is nothing in it to justify later Roman usage and restriction.
So far as liturgical evidence is concerned, it may be added that in the Gelasian
and Gregorian Sacramentaries the form of consecrating the oil shows that it
was used as a means of restoring bodily health (cf. Dr Swete, *Services and
Service-Books*, p. 158), and that in the East, Egypt and Syria employed in the
fourth century what we may call the non-sacramental unction.   These lectures
are now expanded and published as a book, *The Anointing of the Sick*, S.P.C.K.
1904.

[2] On the groundless distinction which the language used by the Council of
Trent attempts to draw between the *promulgation* of what the Council terms
the Sacrament of Extreme Unction by St James and its *insinuation* by St Mark,
see the first of the lectures referred to, *Guardian*, Dec. 10, 1902, and Plummer,
Epistle of St James, p. 332.

[3] No provision, however, was made for the benediction of the oil; 'even
extreme unction,' the Romanists complained in 1551, 'is administered with
unconsecrated oil'; Dr Swete, *Services and Service-Books*, p. 161.

sick in the English Church, and it is of interest to remember that in the eighteenth century the Non-jurors retained the use, while in the same century one of the Scottish bishops is said to have kept by him the oils of confirmation and of the sick. But even those who most strongly advocate the revival are not unmindful that it must of necessity be safeguarded by authoritative regulations of the bishops, lest the practice should again suffer from the superstition and error which became associated with it in early and later ages of the Church[1].

ADDITIONAL NOTE.—CONFESSION.

The words of Mr Mayor, to which reference is made in p. 144, remind us of similar advice emphasised by Hooker. After pointing out, in connection with the verse before us, that St James doth exhort unto mutual confession, alleging this only for a reason that just men's devout prayers are of great avail with God, and that on this account penitents had been wont to unburden their minds even to private persons, and to crave their prayers, and after quoting the allusions of Cassian and Gregory of Nyssa to the help afforded by the sympathy and prayers of others, he adds that of all men there is, or should be, none in this respect more fit for troubled and distracted minds to repair unto than God's ministers, *E. P.* VI. ch. iv. 7.

In the same chapter of his sixth book Hooker makes another reference (sec. 5) to the same passage in St James. In *v.* 14 he sees a relation to that gift of healing which our Saviour promised His Church, Mark xvi. 18, adding, with reference to *v.* 15, 'and of the other member of the exhortation which toucheth mutual confession, do not some of themselves, as namely Cajetan, deny that any other confession is meant than only that which seeketh either association of prayer, or reconciliation, and pardon of wrongs[2]?'

But it is very interesting to note that in this same chapter we have Hooker's question, ' Were the Fathers then without use of private confession as long as public was in use?' to which he answers, ' I affirm no such thing,' and he quotes passages from Origen, 'the first and ancientest that mentioneth this confession,' and Gregory of Nyssa. But it will be observed that this confession is regarded by Hooker as not in any way implying that the Fathers 'for many hundred years after Christ' taught sacramental confession : 'public confession,' he says, 'they thought necessary by way of discipline, not private confession as in the nature of a sacrament, necessary.'

It would seem therefore that the early Fathers, whilst they referred to private confession, connected it more or less directly with public discipline[3].

---

[1] See the lectures in the *Guardian* as above, 'The Unction of the Sick'; and note on preceding page.

[2] The famous Cardinal, so well known for his conference with Luther at Augsburg in 1518, remarks on James v. 16 that 'nothing is here said as to sacramental confession, as is plain from the words "confess one to another," for sacramental confession is not made mutually but only to priests.' The passage is quoted by Hooker in his note *u. s., Works,* Oxford, Clarendon Press.

[3] One of the most candid of modern Romanist writers, Pierre Batiffol, has recently discussed very fully the question of public and private confession from an historical point of view. According to him the power to restore penitents was deputed in the fourth and fifth centuries to the priests, and the question which they had to decide was whether the penitent shall be obliged to submit to public confession before the Church. For this a preliminary or private instruction and confession was necessary, and it is easy to see how many persons would gladly avail themselves of this means of escaping from the shame and

But the famous letter of Leo to the Campanian bishops (6th May, 459 A.D.) is justly regarded as marking an era in the history of Confession in the Latin Church; by its terms secret confession to the priest was substituted for open confession before the Church, and the intercession of the priest for the intercession of the Church; the door thus opened for escaping the shame of public confession was never afterwards closed, and secret confession became the rule of the Church[1]. The Lateran Council, A.D. 1215, saw this obligation become binding, as henceforth it was ordered that all of each sex should confess at least once a year to their parish priest (4 Conc. Lateran. c. 21).

It was this rule of compulsory confession, as enjoined by this Council, which, as all schools of thought in the Anglican Church are agreed, our Reformers desired to abrogate.

But English Churchmen of all schools of thought are also agreed that our formularies, as e.g. the Exhortation to Communion and the Visitation of the Sick[2], permit private confession and absolution in certain circumstances[3], although how far this permission is encouraged by the formularies, or how far it should extend in practical life, are matters upon which such general agreement is apparently unattainable[4].

It is of interest to note that the Homily 'Of Repentance' expressly denies that any authority in support of auricular confession can be derived from James v. 16, and concludes that it is against true Christian liberty that any man should be bound to the numbering of his sins, while it practically repeats and enlarges upon the invitation given by the Minister in the warning for the Celebration of Holy Communion. In Canon 113 of 1603, the caution given to Ministers not to reveal 'secret and hidden sins' such as may have been confessed to them 'for the unburdening of anyone's conscience and to receive spiritual consolation and ease of mind' certainly seems to imply that 'the confession of secret and hidden sin' is one form in which the 'opening of grief' may be made (see *Fulham Conference*, pp. 57, 67).

---

humiliation of public confession, so that by degrees the latter dropped more and more into abeyance, whilst private confession more and more developed. Batiffol's examination extends more or less through four chapters of his book, *Études d'Histoire et de Théologie Positive*, 2nd edit. 1902, in the essay entitled *Les Origines de la Pénitence* ; see e.g. pp. 106, 146, 158, 165, 200 ff., 212, 217, for his own views and the criticism of those of others.

[1] Art. 'Exomologesis,' *Dict. of Christian Antiquities*, I. p. 647. For some valuable points in the history of Confession in East and West see Plummer's *St James*, p. 340. See also Dr Swete, 'Penitential Discipline in the first three Centuries' in *Journal of Theol. Studies*, April 1903 (with special reference on p. 322 to *St James*, ch. v. 16).

[2] On the changes made in the different revisions of the Prayer Book see *Fulham Conference on Confession and Absolution*, pp. 55, 62.

[3] On following the Church's counsel in this respect see the practical remarks of George Herbert in the chapter on 'The Parson Comforting' in *A Priest to the Temple*.

[4] In the Introduction to *Fulham Conference*, p. 8, the Bishop of London marks as a most valuable point the acknowledgment of the Conference that Confession and Absolution are permitted in certain circumstances, and he adds, 'the frank agreement that private confession and absolution are in certain circumstances allowed is all that the great majority of the parish priests of the Church of England who ever make use of it wish to maintain.' For practical considerations as to the relation of Confession and Absolution to the spiritual and moral life of men and women, the pages of the *Fulham Conference*, 85–108, are full of interest. Amongst recent biographies some striking remarks will be found in that of *Felicia Skrine of Oxford*, p. 355.

ADDITIONAL NOTE.—PRAYER.

Two remarks may here be made upon prayer and its relation to modern thought. (1) It is interesting to note that the same Epistle which encourages us to pray for the recovery of the sick, or for changes of weather, is also the Epistle which lays stress upon the unchangeableness of God, 'the Father of lights, with whom can be no variation, neither shadow that is cast by turning,' i. 17. If we turn to recent scientific utterances upon the subject of prayer it is noteworthy, first of all, that the same utterance which demands that both science and faith should accept as a truth the reign of law, sometimes called the uniformity of nature, also tells us that 'if we have instinct for prayer, for communion with saints or with Deity, let us trust that instinct, for there lies the true realm of religion,' and again, 'religious people seem to be losing some of their faith in prayer; they think it scientific not to pray in the sense of simple petition. They may be right; it may be the highest attitude never to ask for anything specific, only for acquiescence. If saints feel it so they are doubtless right, but, so far as ordinary science has anything to say to the contrary, a more childlike attitude might turn out to be more in accordance with the total scheme. Prayer for a fancied good that might really be an injury would be foolish; prayer for breach of law would be not foolish only but profane; but who are we to dogmatise too positively concerning law?......Prayer, we have been told, is a mighty engine of achievement, but we have ceased to believe it. Why should we be so incredulous? Even in medicine, for instance, it is not really absurd to suggest that drugs and no prayer may be almost as foolish as prayer and no drugs. Mental and physical are interlocked.' Sir Oliver Lodge, *Hibbert Journal*, Jan. 1903, pp. 210, 224, 225.

We turn from such utterances to another recent pronouncement in the field, not of physical but of psychical science, and there also we find stress laid upon the reality of the religious life and its accompaniments of prayer and trust: 'in prayer, spiritual energy, which otherwise would slumber, does become active, and spiritual work of some kind is effected really' (although we are not told, whether this work is subjective or objective), James, *The Varieties of Religious Experiences*, p. 477. All this is very far removed from the dogmatic assertion that there is no place in the universe for prayer, or that prayer at its best is useless and its very attitude degrading.

(2) But all true prayer is conditioned also by the words of this same Epistle of St James, 'If the Lord will,' iv. 15 (cf. i. 6), yet that will is the will not of a capricious tyrant but of a righteous Father; and when we pray we pray indeed according to law, but according to the law of a Father, the law of the paternal relation; and just as in the earthly family there are relations between parent and child which no science has ever yet been able strictly to analyse or define, so the Father of spirits may answer His children, may enter into communion with them, now in one way and now in another, because He *is* the Father, and because His love is not the breaking but the fulfilling of law.

But, further, if we thus believe in a personal God, many of the objections urged against prayer would seem to be deprived of their plausibility. It is said, e.g., that to pray for a shower of rain is to ask for a violation of the law of the conservation of force. But is this the right way of putting it? ought not a distinction to be drawn between creation of force and distribution of force? and may not a personal God change by His intervention a whole series of physical phenomena without creating new energy? (See further Jellett's *Donnellan Lectures*, p. 154; Worlledge, *Prayer*, pp. 50 ff.; Matheson, 'Scientific Basis of Prayer,' *Expositor*, 1901.)

INDEX.

CAMBRIDGE: PRINTED BY JOHN CLAY, M.A. AT THE UNIVERSITY PRESS.

A SELECTION OF BOOKS
PUBLISHED BY METHUEN
AND CO. LTD., LONDON
36 ESSEX STREET
W.C.

CONTENTS

A SELECTION OF

Messrs. Methuen's

PUBLICATIONS

In this Catalogue the order is according to authors. An asterisk denotes that the book is in the press.

Colonial Editions are published of all Messrs. Methuen's Novels issued at a price above 2s. 6d., and similar editions are published of some works of General Literature. Colonial Editions are only for circulation in the British Colonies and India.

All books marked net are not subject to discount, and cannot be bought at less than the published price. Books not marked net are subject to the discount which the bookseller allows.

Messrs. Methuen's books are kept in stock by all good booksellers. If there is any difficulty in seeing copies, Messrs. Methuen will be very glad to have early information, and specimen copies of any books will be sent on receipt of the published price *plus* postage for net books, and of the published price for ordinary books.

This Catalogue contains only a selection of the more important books published by Messrs. Methuen. A complete and illustrated catalogue of their publications may be obtained on application.

Abraham (G. D.). MOTOR WAYS IN LAKELAND. Illustrated. *Second Edition. Demy 8vo.* 7s. 6d. net.

Adcock (A. St. John). THE BOOK-LOVER'S LONDON. Illustrated. *Cr. 8vo.* 6s. net.

*Ady (Cecilia M.). PIUS II.: The Humanist Pope. Illustrated. *Demy 8vo.* 10s. 6d. net.

Andrewes (Lancelot). PRECES PRIVATAE. Translated and edited, with Notes, by F. E. Brightman. *Cr. 8vo.* 6s.

Aristotle. THE ETHICS. Edited, with an Introduction and Notes, by John Burnet. *Demy 8vo.* 10s. 6d. net.

Atkinson (C. T.). A HISTORY OF GERMANY, 1715-1815. *Demy 8vo.* 12s. 6d. net.

Atkinson (T. D.). ENGLISH ARCHITECTURE. Illustrated. *Third Edition. Fcap. 8vo.* 3s. 6d. net.

A GLOSSARY OF TERMS USED IN ENGLISH ARCHITECTURE. Illustrated. *Second Edition. Fcap. 8vo.* 3s. 6d. net.

ENGLISH AND WELSH CATHEDRALS. Illustrated. *Demy 8vo.* 10s. 6d. net.

Bain (F. W.). A DIGIT OF THE MOON: A Hindoo Love Story. *Tenth Edition. Fcap. 8vo.* 3s. 6d. net.

THE DESCENT OF THE SUN : A Cycle of Birth. *Fifth Edition. Fcap. 8vo.* 3s. 6d. net.

A HEIFER OF THE DAWN. *Seventh Edition. Fcap. 8vo.* 2s. 6d. net.

IN THE GREAT GOD'S HAIR. *Fifth Edition. Fcap. 8vo.* 2s. 6d. net.

A DRAUGHT OF THE BLUE. *Fifth Edition Fcap. 8vo.* 2s. 6d. net.

AN ESSENCE OF THE DUSK. *Third Edition. Fcap. 8vo.* 2s. 6d. net.

AN INCARNATION OF THE SNOW. *Third Edition. Fcap. 8vo.* 3s. 6d. net.

A MINE OF FAULTS. *Third Edition. Fcap. 8vo.* 3s. 6d. net.

THE ASHES OF A GOD. *Second Edition. Fcap. 8vo.* 3s. 6d. net.

BUBBLES OF THE FOAM. *Second Edition. Fcap. 4to.* 5s. net. *Also Fcap. 8vo.* 3s. 6d. net.

Balfour (Graham). THE LIFE OF ROBERT LOUIS STEVENSON. Illustrated. *Eleventh Edition. In one Volume. Cr. 8vo.* Buckram, 6s. *Also Fcap. 8vo.* 1s. net.

Baring (Hon. Maurice). LANDMARKS IN RUSSIAN LITERATURE. *Second Edition. Cr. 8vo.* 6s. net.

RUSSIAN ESSAYS AND STORIES. *Second Edition. Cr. 8vo.* 5s. net.

THE RUSSIAN PEOPLE. *Demy 8vo.* 15s. net.

Baring-Gould (S.). THE LIFE OF NAPOLEON BONAPARTE. Illustrated. *Second Edition. Royal 8vo. 10s. 6d. net.*
THE TRAGEDY OF THE CÆSARS: A STUDY OF THE CHARACTERS OF THE CÆSARS OF THE JULIAN AND CLAUDIAN HOUSES. Illustrated. *Seventh Edition. Royal 8vo. 10s. 6d. net.*
THE VICAR OF MORWENSTOW. With a Portrait. *Third Edition. Cr. 8vo. 3s. 6d. Also Fcap. 8vo. 1s. net.*
OLD COUNTRY LIFE. Illustrated. *Fifth Edition. Large Cr. 8vo. 6s. Also Fcap. 8vo. 1s. net.*
A BOOK OF CORNWALL. Illustrated. *Third Edition Cr. 8vo. 6s.*
A BOOK OF DARTMOOR. Illustrated. *Second Edition. Cr. 8vo. 6s.*
A BOOK OF DEVON. Illustrated. *Third Edition. Cr. 8vo. 6s.*

Baring-Gould (S.) and Sheppard (H. Fleetwood). A GARLAND OF COUNTRY SONG. English Folk Songs with their Traditional Melodies. *Demy 4to. 6s.*
SONGS OF THE WEST. Folk Songs of Devon and Cornwall. Collected from the Mouths of the People. New and Revised Edition, under the musical editorship of CECIL J. SHARP. *Large Imperial 8vo. 5s. net.*

Barker (E.). THE POLITICAL THOUGHT OF PLATO AND ARISTOTLE. *Demy 8vo. 10s. 6d. net.*

Bastable (C. F.). THE COMMERCE OF NATIONS. *Sixth Edition. Cr. 8vo. 2s. 6d.*

Beckford (Peter). THOUGHTS ON HUNTING. Edited by J. OTHO PAGET. Illustrated. *Third Edition. Demy 8vo. 6s.*

Belloc (H.). PARIS. Illustrated *Third Edition. Cr. 8vo. 6s.*
HILLS AND THE SEA. *Fourth Edition. Fcap. 8vo. 5s. Also Fcap. 8vo. 1s. net.*
ON NOTHING AND KINDRED SUBJECTS. *Fourth Edition. Fcap. 8vo. 5s.*
ON EVERYTHING. *Third Edition. Fcap. 8vo. 5s.*
ON SOMETHING. *Second Edition. Fcap. 8vo. 5s.*
FIRST AND LAST. *Second Edition. Fcap. 8vo. 5s*
THIS AND THAT AND THE OTHER. *Second Edition. Fcap. 8vo. 5s.*
MARIE ANTOINETTE. Illustrated. *Third Edition. Demy 8vo. 15s. net.*
THE PYRENEES. Illustrated. *Second Edition. Demy 8vo. 7s. 6d. net.*

Bennett (Arnold). THE TRUTH ABOUT AN AUTHOR. *Crown 8vo. 6s.*

Bennett (W. H.). A PRIMER OF THE BIBLE. *Fifth Edition Cr. 8vo. 2s. 6d.*

Bennett (W. H.) and Adeney (W. F.). A BIBLICAL INTRODUCTION. With a concise Bibliography. *Sixth Edition. Cr. 8vo. 7s. 6d. Also in Two Volumes. Cr. 8vo. Each 3s. 6d. net.*

Benson (Archbishop). GOD'S BOARD. Communion Addresses. *Second Edition. Fcap. 8vo. 3s. 6d. net.*

***Berriman (Algernon E.).** AVIATION. Illustrated. *Cr. 8vo. 10s. 6d. net.*

Bicknell (Ethel E.). PARIS AND HER TREASURES. Illustrated. *Fcap. 8vo. Round corners. 5s. net.*

Blake (William). ILLUSTRATIONS OF THE BOOK OF JOB. With a General Introduction by LAURENCE BINYON. Illustrated. *Quarto. 21s. net.*

Bloemfontein (Bishop of). ARA CŒLI: AN ESSAY IN MYSTICAL THEOLOGY. *Fifth Edition. Cr. 8vo. 3s. 6d. net.*
FAITH AND EXPERIENCE. *Second Edition. Cr. 8vo. 3s. 6d. net.*

***Boulenger (G. A.).** THE SNAKES OF EUROPE. Illustrated. *Cr. 8vo. 6s.*

Bowden (E. M.). THE IMITATION OF BUDDHA. Quotations from Buddhist Literature for each Day in the Year. *Sixth Edition. Cr. 16mo. 2s. 6d.*

Brabant (F. G.). RAMBLES IN SUSSEX. Illustrated. *Cr. 8vo. 6s.*

Bradley (A. G.). THE ROMANCE OF NORTHUMBERLAND. Illustrated. *Third Edition. Demy 8vo. 7s. 6d. net.*

Braid (James). ADVANCED GOLF. Illustrated. *Seventh Edition. Demy 8vo. 10s. 6d. net.*

Bridger (A. E.). MINDS IN DISTRESS. A Psychological Study of the Masculine and Feminine Minds in Health and in Disorder. *Second Edition. Cr. 8vo. 2s. 6d. net.*

Brodrick (Mary) and Morton (A. Anderson). A CONCISE DICTIONARY OF EGYPTIAN ARCHÆOLOGY. A Handbook for Students and Travellers. Illustrated. *Cr. 8vo. 3s. 6d.*

Browning (Robert). PARACELSUS. Edited with an Introduction, Notes, and Bibliography by MARGARET L. LEE and KATHARINE B. LOCOCK. *Fcap. 8vo. 3s. 6d. net.*

Buckton (A. M.). EAGER HEART: A CHRISTMAS MYSTERY-PLAY. *Eleventh Edition. Cr. 8vo. 1s. net.*

Bull (Paul). GOD AND OUR SOLDIERS. *Second Edition. Cr. 8vo. 6s.*

Burns (Robert). THE POEMS AND SONGS. Edited by ANDREW LANG and W. A. CRAIGIE. With Portrait. *Third Edition. Wide Demy 8vo. 6s.*

Calman (W. T.). THE LIFE OF CRUSTACEA. Illustrated. *Cr. 8vo.* 6s.

Carlyle (Thomas). THE FRENCH REVOLUTION. Edited by C. R. L. FLETCHER. *Three Volumes. Cr. 8vo.* 18s.

THE LETTERS AND SPEECHES OF OLIVER CROMWELL. With an Introduction by C. H. FIRTH, and Notes and Appendices by S. C. LOMAS. *Three Volumes. Demy 8vo.* 18s. net.

Chambers (Mrs. Lambert). LAWN TENNIS FOR LADIES. Illustrated. *Second Edition. Cr. 8vo.* 2s. 6d. net.

Chesser (Elizabeth Sloan). PERFECT HEALTH FOR WOMEN AND CHILDREN. *Cr. 8vo.* 3s. 6d. net.

Chesterfield (Lord). THE LETTERS OF THE EARL OF CHESTERFIELD TO HIS SON. Edited, with an Introduction by C. STRACHEY, and Notes by A. CALTHROP. *Two Volumes. Cr. 8vo.* 12s.

Chesterton (G. K.). CHARLES DICKENS. With two Portraits in Photogravure. *Eighth Edition. Cr. 8vo.* 6s.
Also *Fcap. 8vo.* 1s. net.

THE BALLAD OF THE WHITE HORSE. *Fourth Edition. Fcap. 8vo.* 5s.

ALL THINGS CONSIDERED. *Seventh Edition. Fcap. 8vo.* 5s.

TREMENDOUS TRIFLES. *Fifth Edition. Fcap. 8vo.* 5s.

ALARMS AND DISCURSIONS. *Second Edition. Fcap. 8vo.* 5s.

A MISCELLANY OF MEN. *Second Edition. Fcap. 8vo.* 5s.

*****Clausen (George).** ROYAL ACADEMY LECTURES ON PAINTING. Illustrated. *Cr. 8vo.* 5s. net.

Conrad (Joseph). THE MIRROR OF THE SEA: Memories and Impressions. *Fourth Edition. Fcap. 8vo.* 5s.

Coolidge (W. A. B.). THE ALPS: IN NATURE AND HISTORY. Illustrated. *Demy 8vo.* 7s. 6d. net.

Correvon (H.). ALPINE FLORA. Translated and enlarged by E. W. CLAYFORTH. Illustrated. *Square Demy 8vo.* 16s. net.

Coulton (G. G.). CHAUCER AND HIS ENGLAND. Illustrated. *Second Edition. Demy 8vo.* 10s. 6d. net.

Cowper (William). POEMS. Edited, with an Introduction and Notes, by J. C. BAILEY. Illustrated. *Demy 8vo.* 10s. 6d. net.

Cox (J. C.). RAMBLES IN SURREY. Illustrated. *Second Edition. Cr. 8vo.* 6s.
RAMBLES IN KENT. Illustrated. *Cr. 8vo.* 6s.

Crawley (A. E.). THE BOOK OF THE BALL: AN ACCOUNT OF WHAT IT DOES AND WHY. Illustrated. *Cr. 8vo.* 3s. 6d. net.

Crowley (H. Ralph). THE HYGIENE OF SCHOOL LIFE. Illustrated. *Cr. 8vo.* 3s. 6d. net.

Davis (H. W. C.). ENGLAND UNDER THE NORMANS AND ANGEVINS: 1066–1272. *Third Edition. Demy 8vo.* 10s. 6d. net.

Dawbarn (Charles). FRANCE AND THE FRENCH. Illustrated. *Demy 8vo.* 10s. 6d. net.

Dearmer (Mabel). A CHILD'S LIFE OF CHRIST. Illustrated. *Large Cr. 8vo.* 6s.

Deffand (Madame du). LETTRES DE LA MARQUISE DU DEFFAND A HORACE WALPOLE. Edited, with Introduction, Notes, and Index, by Mrs. PAGET TOYNBEE. *Three Volumes. Demy 8vo.* £3 3s. net.

Dickinson (G. L.). THE GREEK VIEW OF LIFE. *Eighth Edition. Cr. 8vo.* 2s. 6d. net.

Ditchfield (P. H.). THE OLD-TIME PARSON. Illustrated. *Second Edition. Demy 8vo.* 7s. 6d. net.

THE OLD ENGLISH COUNTRY SQUIRE. Illustrated. *Demy 8vo.* 10s. 6d. net.

Dowden (J.). FURTHER STUDIES IN THE PRAYER BOOK. *Cr. 8vo.* 6s.

Driver (S. R.). SERMONS ON SUBJECTS CONNECTED WITH THE OLD TESTAMENT. *Cr. 8vo.* 6s.

Dumas (Alexandre). THE CRIMES OF THE BORGIAS AND OTHERS. With an Introduction by R. S. GARNETT. Illustrated. *Second Edition. Cr. 8vo.* 6s.

THE CRIMES OF URBAIN GRANDIER AND OTHERS. Illustrated. *Cr. 8vo.* 6s.

THE CRIMES OF THE MARQUISE DE BRINVILLIERS AND OTHERS. Illustrated. *Cr. 8vo.* 6s.

THE CRIMES OF ALI PACHA AND OTHERS. Illustrated. *Cr. 8vo.* 6s.

MY PETS. Newly translated by A. R. ALLINSON. Illustrated. *Cr. 8vo.* 6s.

Dunn-Pattison (R. P.). NAPOLEON'S MARSHALS. Illustrated. *Second Edition. Demy 8vo.* 12s. 6d. net.

THE BLACK PRINCE. Illustrated. *Second Edition. Demy 8vo. 7s. 6d. net.*

Durham (The Earl of). THE REPORT ON CANADA. With an Introductory Note. *Demy 8vo. 4s. 6d. net.*

Egerton (H. E.). A SHORT HISTORY OF BRITISH COLONIAL POLICY. *Fourth Edition. Demy 8vo. 7s. 6d. net.*

Evans (Herbert A.). CASTLES OF ENGLAND AND WALES. Illustrated. *Demy 8vo. 12s. 6d. net.*

Exeter (Bishop of). REGNUM DEI. (The Bampton Lectures of 1901.) *A Cheaper Edition. Demy 8vo. 7s. 6d. net.*

Ewald (Carl). MY LITTLE BOY. Translated by ALEXANDER TEIXEIRA DE MATTOS. Illustrated. *Fcap. 8vo. 5s.*

Fairbrother (W. H.). THE PHILO-SOPHY OF T. H. GREEN. *Second Edition. Cr. 8vo. 3s. 6d.*

ffoulkes (Charles). THE ARMOURER AND HIS CRAFT. Illustrated. *Royal 4to. £2 2s. net.*

*DECORATIVE IRONWORK. From the xith to the xviiith Century. Illustrated. *Royal 4to. £2 2s. net.*

Firth (C. H.). CROMWELL'S ARMY. A History of the English Soldier during the Civil Wars, the Commonwealth, and the Protectorate. Illustrated. *Second Edition. Cr. 8vo. 6s.*

Fisher (H. A. L.). THE REPUBLICAN TRADITION IN EUROPE. *Cr. 8vo. 6s. net.*

FitzGerald (Edward). THE RUBA'IYÁT OF OMAR KHAYYÁM. Printed from the Fifth and last Edition. With a Commentary by H. M. BATSON, and a Biographical Introduction by E. D. ROSS. *Cr. 8vo. 6s.*

*Also Illustrated by E. J. SULLIVAN. *Cr. 4to. 15s. net.*

Flux (A. W.). ECONOMIC PRINCIPLES. *Demy 8vo. 7s. 6d. net.*

Fraser (E.). THE SOLDIERS WHOM WELLINGTON LED. Deeds of Daring, Chivalry, and Renown. Illustrated. *Cr. 8vo. 5s. net.*

*THE SAILORS WHOM NELSON LED. Their Doings Described by Themselves. Illustrated. *Cr. 8vo. 5s. net.*

Fraser (J. F.). ROUND THE WORLD ON A WHEEL. Illustrated. *Fifth Edition. Cr. 8vo. 6s.*

Galton (Sir Francis). MEMORIES OF MY LIFE. Illustrated. *Third Edition. Demy 8vo. 10s. 6d. net.*

Gibbins (H. de B.). INDUSTRY IN ENGLAND: HISTORICAL OUT-LINES. With Maps and Plans. *Eighth Edition. Demy 8vo. 10s. 6d.*

THE INDUSTRIAL HISTORY OF ENGLAND. With 5 Maps and a Plan. *Twentieth Edition. Cr. 8vo. 3s.*

ENGLISH SOCIAL REFORMERS. *Third Edition. Cr. 8vo. 2s. 6d.*

Gibbon (Edward). THE MEMOIRS OF THE LIFE OF EDWARD GIBBON. Edited by G. BIRKBECK HILL. *Cr. 8vo. 6s.*

THE DECLINE AND FALL OF THE ROMAN EMPIRE. Edited, with Notes, Appendices, and Maps, by J. B. BURY. Illustrated. *Seven Volumes. Demy 8vo. Illustrated. Each 10s. 6d. net. Also in Seven Volumes. Cr. 8vo. 6s. each.*

Glover (T. R.). THE CONFLICT OF RELIGIONS IN THE EARLY ROMAN EMPIRE. *Fourth Edition. Demy 8vo. 7s. 6d. net.*

VIRGIL. *Second Edition. Demy 8vo. 7s. 6d. net.*

THE CHRISTIAN TRADITION AND ITS VERIFICATION. (The Angus Lecture for 1912.) *Cr. 8vo. 3s. 6d. net.*

Godley (A. D.). LYRA FRIVOLA. *Fourth Edition. Fcap. 8vo. 2s. 6d.*

VERSES TO ORDER. *Second Edition. Fcap. 8vo. 2s. 6d.*

SECOND STRINGS. *Fcap. 8vo. 2s. 6d.*

Gostling (Frances M.). AUVERGNE AND ITS PEOPLE. Illustrated. *Demy 8vo. 10s. 6d. net.*

Gray (Arthur). CAMBRIDGE. Illustrated. *Demy 8vo. 10s. 6d. net.*

Grahame (Kenneth). THE WIND IN THE WILLOWS. *Seventh Edition. Cr. 8vo. 6s.*
*Also Illustrated. *Cr. 4to. 7s. 6d. net.*

Granger (Frank). HISTORICAL SOCI-OLOGY: A TEXT-BOOK OF POLITICS. *Cr. 8vo. 3s. 6d. net.*

*Gretton (M. Sturge).** A CORNER OF THE COTSWOLDS. Illustrated. *Demy 8vo. 7s. 6d. net.*

Grew (Edwin Sharpe). THE GROWTH OF A PLANET. Illustrated. *Cr. 8vo. 6s*

Griffin (W. Hall) and Minchin (H. C.). THE LIFE OF ROBERT BROWNING. Illustrated. *Second Edition. Demy 8vo 12s. 6d. net.*

Haig (K. G.). HEALTH THROUGH DIET. *Second Edition. Cr. 8vo. 3s. 6d. net.*

Hale (J. R.). FAMOUS SEA FIGHTS: FROM SALAMIS TO TSU-SHIMA. Illustrated. *Second Edition. Cr. 8vo. 6s. net.*

Hall (H. R.). THE ANCIENT HISTORY OF THE NEAR EAST FROM THE EARLIEST TIMES TO THE BATTLE OF SALAMIS Illustrated. *Second Edition. Demy 8vo. 15s. net.*

Hannay (D.). A SHORT HISTORY OF THE ROYAL NAVY. Vol. I., 1217-1688. Vol. II., 1689-1815. *Demy 8vo. Each 7s. 6d.*

Hare (B.). THE GOLFING SWING SIMPLIFIED AND ITS MECHANISM CORRECTLY EXPLAINED. *Third Edition. Fcap. 8vo. 1s. net.*

Harper (Charles G.). THE AUTOCAR ROAD-BOOK. With Maps. *Four Volumes. Cr. 8vo. Each 7s. 6d. net.*

   Vol. I.—SOUTH OF THE THAMES.

   Vol. II.—NORTH AND SOUTH WALES AND WEST MIDLANDS.

   Vol. III.—EAST ANGLIA AND EAST MIDLANDS.

   *Vol. IV.—THE NORTH OF ENGLAND AND SOUTH OF SCOTLAND.

Harris (Frank). THE WOMEN OF SHAKESPEARE. *Demy 8vo. 7s. 6d. net.*

Hassall (Arthur). THE LIFE OF NAPOLEON. Illustrated. *Demy 8vo. 7s. 6d. net.*

Headley (F. W.). DARWINISM AND MODERN SOCIALISM. *Second Edition. Cr. 8vo. 5s. net.*

Henderson (M. Sturge). GEORGE MEREDITH: NOVELIST, POET, REFORMER. With a Portrait. *Second Edition. Cr. 8vo. 6s.*

Henley (W. E.). ENGLISH LYRICS: CHAUCER TO POE. *Second Edition. Cr. 8vo. 2s. 6d. net.*

Hill (George Francis). ONE HUNDRED MASTERPIECES OF SCULPTURE. Illustrated. *Demy 8vo. 10s. 6d. net.*

Hind (C. Lewis). DAYS IN CORNWALL. Illustrated. *Third Edition. Cr. 8vo. 6s.*

Hobhouse (L. T.). THE THEORY OF KNOWLEDGE. *Demy 8vo. 10s. 6d. net.*

Hobson (J. A.). INTERNATIONAL TRADE: AN APPLICATION OF ECONOMIC THEORY. *Cr. 8vo. 2s. 6d. net.*

PROBLEMS OF POVERTY: AN INQUIRY INTO THE INDUSTRIAL CONDITION OF THE POOR. *Eighth Edition. Cr. 8vo. 2s. 6d.*

THE PROBLEM OF THE UN-EMPLOYED: AN INQUIRY AND AN ECONOMIC POLICY. *Fifth Edition. Cr. 8vo. 2s. 6d.*

GOLD, PRICES AND WAGES: WITH AN EXAMINATION OF THE QUANTITY THEORY. *Second Edition. Cr. 8vo. 3s. 6d. net.*

Hodgson (Mrs. W.). HOW TO IDENTIFY OLD CHINESE PORCELAIN. Illustrated. *Third Edition. Post 8vo. 6s.*

Holdich (Sir T. H.). THE INDIAN BORDERLAND, 1880-1900. Illustrated. *Second Edition. Demy 8vo. 10s. 6d. net.*

Holdsworth (W. S.). A HISTORY OF ENGLISH LAW. *Four Volumes. Vols. I., II., III. Demy 8vo. Each 10s. 6d. net.*

Holland (Clive). TYROL AND ITS PEOPLE. Illustrated. *Demy 8vo. 10s. 6d. net.*

Horsburgh (E. L. S.). WATERLOO: A NARRATIVE AND A CRITICISM. With Plans. *Second Edition. Cr. 8vo. 5s.*

THE LIFE OF SAVONAROLA. Illustrated. *Cr. 8vo. 5s. net.*

Hosie (Alexander). MANCHURIA. Illustrated. *Second Edition. Demy 8vo. 7s. 6d. net.*

*Howell (A. G. Ferrers).** ST. BERNARDINO OF SIENA. Illustrated. *Demy 8vo. 10s. 6d. net.*

Hudson (W. H.). A SHEPHERD'S LIFE: IMPRESSIONS OF THE SOUTH WILTSHIRE DOWNS. Illustrated. *Third Edition. Demy 8vo. 7s. 6d. net.*

Humphreys (John H.). PROPORTIONAL REPRESENTATION. *Cr. 8vo. 5s. net.*

Hutton (Edward). THE CITIES OF SPAIN. Illustrated. *Fourth Edition. Cr. 8vo. 6s.*

THE CITIES OF UMBRIA. Illustrated. *Fifth Edition. Cr. 8vo. 6s.*

THE CITIES OF LOMBARDY. Illustrated. *Cr. 8vo. 6s.*

*THE CITIES OF ROMAGNA AND THE MARCHES. Illustrated. *Cr. 8vo. 6s.*

FLORENCE AND NORTHERN TUSCANY WITH GENOA. Illustrated. *Second Edition. Cr. 8vo. 6s.*

SIENA AND SOUTHERN TUSCANY Illustrated. *Second Edition. Cr. 8vo. 6s.*

VENICE AND VENETIA. Illustrated. *Cr. 8vo.* 6s.

ROME. Illustrated. *Third Edition. Cr. 8vo.* 6s.

COUNTRY WALKS ABOUT FLORENCE. Illustrated. *Second Edition. Fcap. 8vo.* 5s. *net.*

A BOOK OF THE WYE. Illustrated. *Demy 8vo.* 7s. 6d. *net.*

Ibsen (Henrik). BRAND. A Dramatic Poem, translated by WILLIAM WILSON. *Fourth Edition. Cr. 8vo.* 3s. 6d.

Inge (W. R.). CHRISTIAN MYSTICISM. (The Bampton Lectures of 1899.) *Third Edition. Cr. 8vo.* 5s. *net.*

Innes (A. D.). A HISTORY OF THE BRITISH IN INDIA. With Maps and Plans. *Cr. 8vo.* 6s.

ENGLAND UNDER THE TUDORS. With Maps. *Fourth Edition. Demy 8vo.* 10s. 6d. *net.*

Innes (Mary). SCHOOLS OF PAINTING. Illustrated. *Second Edition. Cr. 8vo.* 5s. *net.*

Jenks (E.). AN OUTLINE OF ENGLISH LOCAL GOVERNMENT. *Second Edition.* Revised by R. C. K. ENSOR *Cr. 8vo.* 2s. 6d. *net.*

A SHORT HISTORY OF ENGLISH LAW: FROM THE EARLIEST TIMES TO THE END OF THE YEAR 1911. *Demy 8vo.* 10s. 6d. *net.*

Jerningham (Charles Edward). THE MAXIMS OF MARMADUKE. *Second Edition. Fcap. 8vo.* 5s.

Jevons (F. B.). PERSONALITY. *Cr. 8vo.* 2s. 6d. *net.*

Johnston (Sir H. H.). BRITISH CENTRAL AFRICA. Illustrated. *Third Edition. Cr. 4to.* 18s. *net.*

THE NEGRO IN THE NEW WORLD. Illustrated. *Demy 8vo.* 21s. *net.*

Julian (Lady) of Norwich. REVELATIONS OF DIVINE LOVE. Edited by GRACE WARRACK. *Fourth Edition. Cr. 8vo.* 3s. 6d.

Keats (John). POEMS. Edited, with Introduction and Notes, by E. de SÉLINCOURT. With a Frontispiece in Photogravure. *Third Edition. Demy 8vo.* 7s. 6d. *net.*

Keble (John). THE CHRISTIAN YEAR. With an Introduction and Notes by W. LOCK. Illustrated. *Third Edition. Fcap. 8vo.* 3s. 6d.

Kempis (Thomas à). THE IMITATION OF CHRIST. From the Latin, with an Introduction by DEAN FARRAR. Illustrated. *Fourth Edition. Fcap. 8vo.* 3s. 6d.

*THOMAE HEMERKEN A KEMPIS DE IMITATIONE CHRISTI. Edited by ADRIAN FORTESCUE. *Cr. 4to.* £1 1s. *net.*

Kipling (Rudyard). BARRACK-ROOM BALLADS. 119th *Thousand. Thirty-sixth Edition. Cr. 8vo.* Buckram, 6s. Also *Fcap. 8vo.* Cloth, 4s. 6d. *net* ; leather, 5s. *net.*

THE SEVEN SEAS. 99th *Thousand. Twenty-third Edition. Cr. 8vo.* Buckram, 6s. Also *Fcap. 8vo.* Cloth, 4s. 6d. *net*; leather, 5s. *net.*

THE FIVE NATIONS. 82nd *Thousand. Thirteenth Edition. Cr. 8vo.* Buckram, 6s. Also *Fcap. 8vo.* Cloth, 4s. 6d. *net* ; leather, 5s. *net.*

DEPARTMENTAL DITTIES. *Twenty-Fourth Edition. Cr. 8vo.* Buckram, 6s. Also *Fcap. 8vo.* Cloth, 4s. 6d. *net*; leather, 5s. *net.*

Lamb (Charles and Mary). THE COMPLETE WORKS. Edited, with an Introduction and Notes, by E. V. LUCAS. A New and Revised Edition in Six Volumes. With Frontispiece. *Fcap. 8vo.* 5s. each.
The volumes are :—
I. MISCELLANEOUS PROSE. II. ELIA AND THE LAST ESSAYS OF ELIA. III. BOOKS FOR CHILDREN. IV. PLAYS AND POEMS. V. and VI. LETTERS.

Lane-Poole (Stanley). A HISTORY OF EGYPT IN THE MIDDLE AGES. Illustrated. *Cr. 8vo.* 6s.

Lankester (Sir Ray). SCIENCE FROM AN EASY CHAIR. Illustrated. *Seventh Edition. Cr. 8vo.* 6s.

Lee (Gerald Stanley). INSPIRED MILLIONAIRES. *Cr. 8vo.* 3s. 6d. *net.*
CROWDS : A STUDY OF THE GENIUS OF DEMOCRACY, AND OF THE FEARS, DESIRES, AND EXPECTATIONS OF THE PEOPLE. *Cr. 8vo.* 6s.

Lock (Walter). ST. PAUL, THE MASTER BUILDER. *Third Edition. Cr. 8vo.* 3s. 6d.
THE BIBLE AND CHRISTIAN LIFE. *Cr. 8vo.* 6s.

Lodge (Sir Oliver). THE SUBSTANCE OF FAITH, ALLIED WITH SCIENCE : A CATECHISM FOR PARENTS AND TEACHERS *Eleventh Edition. Cr. 8vo.* 2s. *net.*
MAN AND THE UNIVERSE : A STUDY OF THE INFLUENCE OF THE ADVANCE IN SCIENTIFIC KNOWLEDGE UPON OUR UNDERSTANDING OF CHRISTIANITY. *Ninth Edition. Demy 8vo.* 5s. *net.* Also *Fcap. 8vo.* 1s. *net.*

THE SURVIVAL OF MAN : A STUDY IN UNRECOGNISED HUMAN FACULTY. *Fifth Edition. Wide Cr. 8vo. 5s. net.*

REASON AND BELIEF. *Fifth Edition. Cr. 8vo. 3s. 6d. net.*

MODERN PROBLEMS. *Cr. 8vo. 5s. net.*

Loreburn (Earl). CAPTURE AT SEA. *Cr. 8vo. 2s. 6d. net.*

Lorimer (George Horace). LETTERS FROM A SELF-MADE MERCHANT TO HIS SON. Illustrated. *Twenty-fourth Edition. Cr. 8vo. 3s. 6d. Also Fcap. 8vo. 1s. net.*

OLD GORGON GRAHAM. Illustrated. *Second Edition. Cr. 8vo. 6s. Also Cr. 8vo. 2s. net.*

Lucas (E. V.). THE LIFE OF CHARLES LAMB. Illustrated. *Fifth Edition. Demy 8vo. 7s. 6d. net.*

A WANDERER IN HOLLAND. Illustrated. *Fifteenth Edition. Cr. 8vo. 6s.*

A WANDERER IN LONDON. Illustrated. *Fifteenth Edition, Revised. Cr. 8vo. 6s.*

A WANDERER IN PARIS. Illustrated. *Eleventh Edition. Cr. 8vo. 6s. Also Fcap. 8vo. 5s.*

A WANDERER IN FLORENCE. Illustrated. *Fourth Edition. Cr. 8vo. 6s.*

THE OPEN ROAD : A LITTLE BOOK FOR WAYFARERS. *Twenty-second Edition. Fcap. 8vo. 5s. India Paper, 7s. 6d. Also Illustrated. Cr. 4to. 15s. net.*

THE FRIENDLY TOWN : A LITTLE BOOK FOR THE URBANE. *Seventh Edition. Fcap. 8vo. 5s.*

FIRESIDE AND SUNSHINE. *Seventh Edition. Fcap. 8vo. 5s.*

CHARACTER AND COMEDY. *Sixth Edition. Fcap. 8vo. 5s.*

THE GENTLEST ART : A CHOICE OF LETTERS BY ENTERTAINING HANDS. *Seventh Edition. Fcap. 8vo. 5s.*

THE SECOND POST. *Third Edition. Fcap. 8vo. 5s.*

HER INFINITE VARIETY : A FEMININE PORTRAIT GALLERY. *Sixth Edition. Fcap. 8vo. 5s.*

GOOD COMPANY : A RALLY OF MEN. *Second Edition. Fcap. 8vo. 5s.*

ONE DAY AND ANOTHER. *Fifth Edition. Fcap. 8vo. 5s.*

OLD LAMPS FOR NEW. *Fourth Edition. Fcap. 8vo. 5s.*

*LOITERER'S HARVEST. *Fcap. 8vo. 5s.*

LISTENER'S LURE : AN OBLIQUE NARRATION. *Tenth Edition. Fcap. 8vo. 5s.*

OVER BEMERTON'S : AN EASY-GOING CHRONICLE. *Eleventh Edition. Fcap. 8vo. 5s.*

MR. INGLESIDE. *Tenth Edition. Fcap. 8vo. 5s.*

*LONDON LAVENDER. *Fcap. 8vo. 5s.*

THE BRITISH SCHOOL : AN ANECDOTAL GUIDE TO THE BRITISH PAINTERS AND PAINTINGS IN THE NATIONAL GALLERY. *Fcap. 8vo. 2s. 6d. net.*

HARVEST HOME. *Fcap. 8vo. 1s. net.*

A LITTLE OF EVERYTHING. *Third Edition. Fcap. 8vo. 1s. net.*
See also Lamb (Charles).

Lydekker (R.). THE OX AND ITS KINDRED. Illustrated. *Cr. 8vo. 6s.*

Lydekker (R.) and Others. REPTILES, AMPHIBIA, FISHES, AND LOWER CHORDATA. Edited by J. C. CUNNINGHAM. Illustrated. *Demy 8vo. 10s. 6d. net.*

Macaulay (Lord). CRITICAL AND HISTORICAL ESSAYS. Edited by F. C. MONTAGUE. *Three Volumes. Cr. 8vo. 18s.*

McCabe (Joseph). THE EMPRESSES OF ROME. Illustrated. *Demy 8vo. 12s. 6d. net.*

THE EMPRESSES OF CONSTANTINOPLE. Illustrated. *Demy 8vo. 10s. 6d. net.*

MacCarthy (Desmond) and Russell (Agatha). LADY JOHN RUSSELL : A MEMOIR. Illustrated. *Fourth Edition. Demy 8vo. 10s. 6d. net.*

McDougall (William). AN INTRODUCTION TO SOCIAL PSYCHOLOGY. *Seventh Edition. Cr. 8vo. 5s. net.*

BODY AND MIND : A HISTORY AND A DEFENCE OF ANIMISM. *Second Edition. Demy 8vo. 10s. 6d. net.*

Maeterlinck (Maurice). THE BLUE BIRD : A FAIRY PLAY IN SIX ACTS. Translated by ALEXANDER TEIXEIRA DE MATTOS. *Fcap. 8vo. Deckle Edges. 3s. 6d. net. Also Fcap. 8vo. 1s. net.* An Edition, illustrated in colour by F. CAYLEY ROBINSON, is also published. *Cr. 4to. 21s. net.* Of the above book Thirty-three Editions in all have been issued.

MARY MAGDALENE : A PLAY IN THREE ACTS. Translated by ALEXANDER TEIXEIRA DE MATTOS. *Third Edition. Fcap. 8vo. Deckle Edges. 3s. 6d. net. Also Fcap. 8vo. 1s. net.*

*OUR ETERNITY. Translated by ALEXANDER TEIXEIRA DE MATTOS. *Fcap. 8vo. 5s. net.*

*Maeterlinck (Mme. M.) (Georgette Leblanc). THE CHILDREN'S BLUEBIRD. Translated by ALEXANDER TEIXEIRA DE MATTOS. Illustrated. *Fcap 8vo. 5s. net.*

Mahaffy (J. P.). A HISTORY OF EGYPT UNDER THE PTOLEMAIC DYNASTY. Illustrated. *Cr. 8vo. 6s.*

Maitland (F. W.). ROMAN CANON LAW IN THE CHURCH OF ENGLAND. *Royal 8vo. 7s. 6d.*

Marett (R. R.). THE THRESHOLD OF RELIGION. *New and Revised Edition. Cr. 8vo. 5s. net.*

Marriott (Charles). A SPANISH HOLIDAY. Illustrated. *Demy 8vo. 7s. 6d. net.*
THE ROMANCE OF THE RHINE. Illustrated. *Demy 8vo. 10s. 6d. net.*

Marriott (J. A. R.). ENGLAND SINCE WATERLOO. With Maps. *Demy 8vo. 10s. 6d. net.*

Masefield (John). SEA LIFE IN NELSON'S TIME. Illustrated. *Cr. 8vo. 3s. 6d. net.*
A SAILOR'S GARLAND. Selected and Edited. *Second Edition. Cr. 8vo. 3s. 6d. net.*

Masterman (C. F. G.). TENNYSON AS A RELIGIOUS TEACHER. *Second Edition. Cr. 8vo. 6s.*
THE CONDITION OF ENGLAND. *Fourth Edition. Cr. 8vo. 6s. Also Fcap. 8vo. 1s net.*
Also Fcap. 8vo. 1s. net.

Mayne (Ethel Colburn). BYRON. Illustrated. *Two Volumes. Demy 8vo. 21s. net.*

Medley (D. J.). ORIGINAL ILLUSTRATIONS OF ENGLISH CONSTITUTIONAL HISTORY. *Cr. 8vo. 7s. 6d. net.*

Methuen (A. M. S.). ENGLAND'S RUIN: DISCUSSED IN FOURTEEN LETTERS TO A PROTECTIONIST. *Ninth Edition. Cr. 8vo. 3d. net.*

Miles (Eustace). LIFE AFTER LIFE; OR, THE THEORY OF REINCARNATION. *Cr. 8vo. 2s. 6d. net.*
THE POWER OF CONCENTRATION: HOW TO ACQUIRE IT. *Fourth Edition. Cr. 8vo. 3s. 6d. net.*

Millais (J. G.). THE LIFE AND LETTERS OF SIR JOHN EVERETT MILLAIS. Illustrated. *New Edition. Demy 8vo. 7s. 6d. net.*

Milne (J. G.). A HISTORY OF EGYPT UNDER ROMAN RULE. Illustrated. *Second Edition. Cr. 8vo. 6s.*

Mitchell (P. Chalmers). THOMAS HENRY HUXLEY. *Fcap. 8vo. 1s. net.*

Moffat (Mary M.). QUEEN LOUISA OF PRUSSIA. Illustrated. *Fourth Edition. Cr. 8vo. 6s.*
MARIA THERESA. Illustrated. *Demy 8vo. 10s. 6d. net.*

Money (L. G. Chiozza). RICHES AND POVERTY. *New and Revised Issue. Cr. 8vo. 1s. net.*
MONEY'S FISCAL DICTIONARY, 1910. *Second Edition. Demy 8vo. 5s. net.*
THINGS THAT MATTER: PAPERS ON SUBJECTS WHICH ARE, OR OUGHT TO BE, UNDER DISCUSSION. *Demy 8vo. 5s. net.*

Montague (C. E.). DRAMATIC VALUES. *Second Edition. Fcap. 8vo. 5s.*

Moorhouse (E. Hallam). NELSON'S LADY HAMILTON. Illustrated. *Third Edition. Demy 8vo. 7s. 6d. net.*

Morgan (C. Lloyd). INSTINCT AND EXPERIENCE. *Second Edition. Cr. 8vo. 5s. net.*

Nevill (Lady Dorothy). MY OWN TIMES. Edited by her Son. *Second Edition. Demy 8vo. 15s. net.*

O'Donnell (Elliot). WERWOLVES. *Cr. 8vo. 5s. net.*

Oman (C. W. C.). A HISTORY OF THE ART OF WAR IN THE MIDDLE AGES. Illustrated. *Demy 8vo. 10s. 6d. net.*
ENGLAND BEFORE THE NORMAN CONQUEST. With Maps. *Third Edition, Revised. Demy 8vo. 10s. 6d. net.*

Oxford (M. N.). A HANDBOOK OF NURSING. *Sixth Edition, Revised. Cr. 8vo. 3s. 6d. net.*

Pakes (W. C. C.). THE SCIENCE OF HYGIENE. Illustrated. *Second and Cheaper Edition.* Revised by A. T. NANKIVELL. *Cr. 8vo. 5s. net.*

Parker (Eric). A BOOK OF THE ZOO. Illustrated. *Second Edition. Cr. 8vo. 6s.*

Pears (Sir Edwin). TURKEY AND ITS PEOPLE. *Second Edition. Demy 8vo. 12s. 6d. net.*

Petrie (W. M. Flinders.) A HISTORY OF EGYPT. Illustrated. *Six Volumes. Cr. 8vo. 6s. each.*
VOL. I. FROM THE 1ST TO THE XVITH DYNASTY. *Seventh Edition.*
VOL. II. THE XVIITH AND XVIIITH DYNASTIES. *Fifth Edition.*
VOL. III. XIXTH TO XXXTH DYNASTIES.
VOL. IV. EGYPT UNDER THE PTOLEMAIC DYNASTY. J. P. MAHAFFY.
VOL V. EGYPT UNDER ROMAN RULE. J. G MILNE. *Second Edition.*
VOL. VI. EGYPT IN THE MIDDLE AGES. STANLEY LANE-POOLE.

RELIGION AND CONSCIENCE IN ANCIENT EGYPT. Illustrated. *Cr. 8vo.* 2s. 6d.

SYRIA AND EGYPT, FROM THE TELL EL AMARNA LETTERS. *Cr. 8vo.* 2s. 6d.

EGYPTIAN TALES. Translated from the Papyri. First Series, ivth to xiith Dynasty. Illustrated. *Second Edition. Cr. 8vo.* 3s. 6d.

EGYPTIAN TALES. Translated from the Papyri. Second Series, xviiith to xixth Dynasty. Illustrated. *Second Edition. Cr. 8vo.* 3s. 6d.

EGYPTIAN DECORATIVE ART. Illustrated. *Cr. 8vo* 3s. 6d.

Pollard (Alfred W.). SHAKESPEARE FOLIOS AND QUARTOS. A Study in the Bibliography of Shakespeare's Plays, 1594–1685. Illustrated. *Folio.* £1 1s. net.

Porter (G. R.). THE PROGRESS OF THE NATION. A New Edition. Edited by F. W. HIRST. *Demy 8vo.* £1 1s. net.

Power (J. O'Connor). THE MAKING OF AN ORATOR. *Cr. 8vo.* 6s.

Price (L. L.). A SHORT HISTORY OF POLITICAL ECONOMY IN ENGLAND FROM ADAM SMITH TO ARNOLD TOYNBEE. *Seventh Edition. Cr. 8vo.* 2s. 6d.

Pycraft (W. P.). A HISTORY OF BIRDS. Illustrated. *Demy 8vo.* 10s. 6d. net.

Rawlings (Gertrude B.). COINS AND HOW TO KNOW THEM. Illustrated. *Third Edition. Cr. 8vo.* 6s.

Regan (C. Tait). THE FRESHWATER FISHES OF THE BRITISH ISLES. Illustrated. *Cr. 8vo.* 6s.

Reid (Archdall). THE LAWS OF HEREDITY. *Second Edition. Demy 8vo.* £1 1s. net.

Robertson (C. Grant). SELECT STATUTES, CASES, AND DOCUMENTS, 1660–1832. *Second, Revised and Enlarged Edition. Demy 8vo.* 10s. 6d. net.

ENGLAND UNDER THE HANOVERIANS. Illustrated. *Second Edition. Demy 8vo.* 10s. 6d. net.

Roe (Fred). OLD OAK FURNITURE. Illustrated. *Second Edition. Demy 8vo.* 10s. 6d net.

*Rolle (Richard). THE FIRE OF LOVE and THE MENDING OF LIFE. Edited by FRANCES M. COMPER. *Cr. 8vo.* 3s. 6d. net.

Ryan (P. F. W.). STUART LIFE AND MANNERS: A SOCIAL HISTORY. Illustrated. *Demy 8vo.* 10s. 6d. net.

*Ryley (A. Beresford). OLD PASTE. Illustrated. *Royal 8vo.* £2 2s. net.

St. Francis of Assisi. THE LITTLE FLOWERS OF THE GLORIOUS MESSER, AND OF HIS FRIARS. Done into English, with Notes by WILLIAM HEYWOOD. Illustrated. *Demy 8vo.* 5s. net.

'Saki' (H. H. Munro). REGINALD. *Third Edition. Fcap. 8vo.* 2s. 6d. net.

REGINALD IN RUSSIA. *Fcap. 8vo.* 2s. 6d. net.

Sandeman (G. A. C.). METTERNICH. Illustrated. *Demy 8vo.* 10s. 6d. net.

Schidrowitz (Philip). RUBBER. Illustrated. *Demy 8vo.* 10s. 6d. net.

Schloesser (H. H.). TRADE UNIONISM. *Cr. 8vo.* 2s. 6d.

Selous (Edmund). TOMMY SMITH'S ANIMALS. Illustrated. *Twelfth Edition. Fcap. 8vo.* 2s. 6d.

TOMMY SMITH'S OTHER ANIMALS. Illustrated. *Sixth Edition. Fcap. 8vo.* 2s. 6d.

JACK'S INSECTS. Illustrated. *Cr. 8vo.* 6s.

Shakespeare (William).
THE FOUR FOLIOS, 1623; 1632; 1664; 1685. Each £4 4s. net, or a complete set, £12 12s. net.

THE POEMS OF WILLIAM SHAKESPEARE. With an Introduction and Notes by GEORGE WYNDHAM. *Demy 8vo. Buckram,* 10s. 6d.

Shaw (Stanley). WILLIAM OF GERMANY. *Demy 8vo.* 7s. 6d. net.

Shelley (Percy Bysshe). POEMS. With an Introduction by A. CLUTTON-BROCK and notes by C. D. LOCOCK. *Two Volumes. Demy 8vo.* £1 1s. net.

Smith (Adam). THE WEALTH OF NATIONS. Edited by EDWIN CANNAN. *Two Volumes. Demy 8vo.* £1 1s. net.

Smith (G. F. Herbert). GEM-STONES AND THEIR DISTINCTIVE CHARACTERS. Illustrated. *Second Edition. Cr. 8vo.* 6s. net.

Snell (F. J.). A BOOK OF EXMOOR. Illustrated. *Cr. 8vo. 6s.*
THE CUSTOMS OF OLD ENGLAND. Illustrated. *Cr. 8vo. 6s.*

'Stancliffe.' GOLF DO'S AND DONT'S. *Fifth Edition. Fcap. 8vo. 1s. net.*

Stevenson (R. L.). THE LETTERS OF ROBERT LOUIS STEVENSON. Edited by Sir SIDNEY COLVIN. *A New and Enlarged Edition in four volumes. Fourth Edition. Fcap. 8vo. Each 5s. Leather, each 5s. net.*

Storr (Vernon F.). DEVELOPMENT AND DIVINE PURPOSE. *Cr. 8vo. 5s. net.*

Streatfeild (R. A.). MODERN MUSIC AND MUSICIANS. Illustrated. *Second Edition. Demy 8vo. 7s. 6d. net.*

Surtees (R. S.). HANDLEY CROSS. Illustrated. *Fcap. 8vo. Gilt top. 3s. 6d. net.*
MR. SPONGE'S SPORTING TOUR. Illustrated. *Fcap. 8vo. Gilt top. 3s. 6d. net.*
ASK MAMMA; OR, THE RICHEST COMMONER IN ENGLAND. Illustrated. *Fcap. 8vo. Gilt top. 3s. 6d. net.*
JORROCKS'S JAUNTS AND JOLLITIES. Illustrated. *Fourth Edition. Fcap. 8vo. Gilt top. 3s. 6d. net.*
MR. FACEY ROMFORD'S HOUNDS. Illustrated. *Fcap. 8vo. Gilt top. 3s. 6d. net.*
HAWBUCK GRANGE; OR, THE SPORTING ADVENTURES OF THOMAS SCOTT, ESQ. Illustrated. *Fcap. 8vo. Gilt top. 3s. 6d. net.*

*Suso (Henry). THE LIFE OF THE BLESSED HENRY SUSO. By HIMSELF. Translated by T. F. Knox. With an Introduction by DEAN INGE. *Cr. 8vo. 3s. 6d. net.*

Swanton (E. W.). FUNGI AND HOW TO KNOW THEM. Illustrated. *Cr. 8vo. 6s. net.*
BRITISH PLANT - GALLS. *Cr. 8vo. 7s. 6d. net.*

Symes (J. E.). THE FRENCH REVOLUTION. *Second Edition. Cr. 8vo. 2s. 6d.*

Tabor (Margaret E.). THE SAINTS IN ART. With their Attributes and Symbols Alphabetically Arranged. Illustrated. *Third Edition. Fcap. 8vo. 3s. 6d. net.*

Taylor (A. E.). ELEMENTS OF METAPHYSICS. *Second Edition. Demy 8vo. 10s. 6d. net.*

Taylor (Mrs. Basil) (Harriet Osgood). JAPANESE GARDENS. Illustrated. *Cr. 4to. £1 1s. net.*

Thibaudeau (A. C.). BONAPARTE AND THE CONSULATE. Translated and Edited by G. K. FORTESCUE. Illustrated. *Demy 8vo. 10s. 6d. net.*

Thomas (Edward). MAURICE MAETERLINCK. Illustrated. *Second Edition. Cr. 8vo. 5s. net.*

Thompson (Francis). SELECTED POEMS OF FRANCIS THOMPSON. With a Biographical Note by WILFRID MEYNELL. With a Portrait in Photogravure *Twentieth Thousand. Fcap. 8vo. 5s. net.*

Tileston (Mary W.). DAILY STRENGTH FOR DAILY NEEDS. *Twentieth Edition. Medium 16mo. 2s. 6d. net.* Also an edition in superior binding, *6s.*
THE STRONGHOLD OF HOPE. *Medium 16mo. 2s. 6d. net.*

Toynbee (Paget). DANTE ALIGHIERI. HIS LIFE AND WORKS. With 16 Illustrations. *Fourth and Enlarged Edition. Cr. 8vo. 5s. net.*

Trevelyan (G. M.). ENGLAND UNDER THE STUARTS. With Maps and Plans. *Fifth Edition. Demy 8vo. 10s. 6d. net.*

Triggs (H. Inigo). TOWN PLANNING: PAST, PRESENT, AND POSSIBLE. Illustrated. *Second Edition. Wide Royal 8vo. 15s. net.*

Turner (Sir Alfred E.). SIXTY YEARS OF A SOLDIER'S LIFE. *Demy 8vo. 12s. 6d. net.*

Underhill (Evelyn). MYSTICISM. A Study in the Nature and Development of Man's Spiritual Consciousness. *Fourth Edition. Demy 8vo. 15s. net.*

Urwick (E. J.). A PHILOSOPHY OF SOCIAL PROGRESS. *Cr. 8vo. 6s.*

Vardon (Harry). HOW TO PLAY GOLF. Illustrated. *Fifth Edition. Cr. 8vo. 2s. 6d. net.*

Vernon (Hon. W. Warren). READINGS ON THE INFERNO OF DANTE. With an Introduction by the Rev. Dr. MOORE. *Two Volumes. Second Edition. Cr. 8vo. 15s. net.*
READINGS ON THE PURGATORIO OF DANTE. With an Introduction by the late DEAN CHURCH. *Two Volumes. Third Edition. Cr. 8vo. 15s. net.*

READINGS ON THE PARADISO OF DANTE. With an Introduction by the BISHOP OF RIPON. *Two Volumes. Second Edition. Cr. 8vo. 15s. net.*

Vickers (Kenneth H.). ENGLAND IN THE LATER MIDDLE AGES. With Maps. *Demy 8vo. 10s. 6d. net.*

Wade (G. W. and J. H.). RAMBLES IN SOMERSET. Illustrated. *Cr. 8vo. 6s.*

Waddell (L. A.). LHASA AND ITS MYSTERIES. With a Record of the Expedition of 1903-1904. Illustrated. *Third and Cheaper Edition. Medium 8vo. 7s. 6d. net.*

Wagner (Richard). RICHARD WAGNER'S MUSIC DRAMAS. Interpretations, embodying Wagner's own explanations. By ALICE LEIGHTON CLEATHER and BASIL CRUMP. *Fcap. 8vo. 2s. 6d. each.*
THE RING OF THE NIBELUNG.
Fifth Edition.
LOHENGRIN AND PARSIFAL.
Second Edition, rewritten and enlarged.
TRISTAN AND ISOLDE.
TANNHÄUSER AND THE MASTERSINGERS OF NUREMBURG.

Waterhouse (Elizabeth). WITH THE SIMPLE-HEARTED. Little Homilies to Women in Country Places. *Third Edition. Small Pott 8vo. 2s. net.*
THE HOUSE BY THE CHERRY TREE. A Second Series of Little Homilies to Women in Country Places. *Small Pott 8vo. 2s. net.*
COMPANIONS OF THE WAY. Being Selections for Morning and Evening Reading. Chosen and arranged by ELIZABETH WATERHOUSE. *Large Cr. 8vo. 5s. net.*
THOUGHTS OF A TERTIARY. *Small Pott 8vo. 1s. net.*
VERSES. A New Edition. *Fcap. 8vo. 2s. net.*

Waters (W. G.). ITALIAN SCULPTORS. Illustrated. *Cr. 8vo. 7s. 6d. net.*

Watt (Francis). EDINBURGH AND THE LOTHIANS. Illustrated. *Second Edition. Cr. 8vo. 10s. 6d. net.*

*R. L. S. *Cr. 8vo. 6s.*

Wedmore (Sir Frederick). MEMORIES. *Second Edition. Demy 8vo. 7s. 6d. net.*

Weigall (Arthur E. P.). A GUIDE TO THE ANTIQUITIES OF UPPER EGYPT: FROM ABYDOS TO THE SUDAN FRONTIER. Illustrated. *Second Edition. Cr. 8vo. 7s. 6d. net.*

Wells (J.). OXFORD AND OXFORD LIFE. *Third Edition. Cr. 8vo. 3s. 6d.*
A SHORT HISTORY OF ROME. *Twelfth Edition.* With 3 Maps. *Cr. 8vo. 3s. 6d.*

Whitten (Wilfred). A LONDONER'S LONDON. Illustrated. *Second Edition. Cr. 8vo. 6s.*

Wilde (Oscar). THE WORKS OF OSCAR WILDE. *Twelve Volumes. Fcap. 8vo. 5s. net each volume.*
I. LORD ARTHUR SAVILE'S CRIME AND THE PORTRAIT OF MR. W. H. II. THE DUCHESS OF PADUA. III. POEMS. IV. LADY WINDERMERE'S FAN. V. A WOMAN OF NO IMPORTANCE. VI. AN IDEAL HUSBAND. VII. THE IMPORTANCE OF BEING EARNEST. VIII. A HOUSE OF POMEGRANATES. IX. INTENTIONS. X. DE PROFUNDIS AND PRISON LETTERS. XI. ESSAYS. XII. SALOMÉ, A FLORENTINE TRAGEDY, and LA SAINTE COURTISANE.

Williams (H. Noel). A ROSE OF SAVOY: MARIE ADÉLAIDE OF SAVOY, DUCHESSE DE BOURGOGNE, MOTHER OF LOUIS XV. Illustrated. *Second Edition. Demy 8vo. 15s. net.*
THE FASCINATING DUC DE RICHELIEU: LOUIS FRANÇOIS ARMAND DU PLESSIS (1696-1788). Illustrated. *Demy 8vo. 15s. net.*
A PRINCESS OF ADVENTURE: MARIE CAROLINE, DUCHESSE DE BERRY (1798-1870). Illustrated. *Demy 8vo. 15s. net.*
THE LOVE AFFAIRS OF THE CONDÉS (1530-1740). Illustrated. *Demy 8vo. 15s. net.*

*Wilson (Ernest H.). A NATURALIST IN WESTERN CHINA. Illustrated. *Demy 8vo. £1 10s. net.*

Wood (Sir Evelyn). FROM MIDSHIPMAN TO FIELD-MARSHAL. Illustrated. *Fifth Edition. Demy 8vo. 7s. 6d. net.*
Also Fcap. 8vo. 1s. net.
THE REVOLT IN HINDUSTAN (1857-59). Illustrated. *Second Edition. Cr. 8vo. 6s.*

Wood (W. Birkbeck) and Edmonds (Col. J. E.). A HISTORY OF THE CIVIL WAR IN THE UNITED STATES (1861-65). With an Introduction by SPENSER WILKINSON. With 24 Maps and Plans. *Third Edition. Demy 8vo. 12s. 6d. net.*

Wordsworth (W.). POEMS. With an Introduction and Notes by NOWELL C. SMITH. *Three Volumes. Demy 8vo. 15s. net.*

Yeats (W. B.). A BOOK OF IRISH VERSE. *Third Edition. Cr. 8vo. 3s. 6d.*

PART II.—A SELECTION OF SERIES

Ancient Cities

General Editor, SIR B. C. A. WINDLE

Cr. 8vo. 4s. 6d. net each volume

With Illustrations by E. H. NEW, and other Artists

BRISTOL. Alfred Harvey.

CANTERBURY. J. C. Cox.

CHESTER. Sir B. C. A. Windle.

DUBLIN. S. A. O. Fitzpatrick.

EDINBURGH. M. G. Williamson.

LINCOLN. E. Mansel Sympson.

SHREWSBURY. T. Auden.

WELLS and GLASTONBURY. T. S. Holmes.

The Antiquary's Books

General Editor, J. CHARLES COX

Demy 8vo. 7s. 6d. net each volume

With Numerous Illustrations

*ANCIENT PAINTED GLASS IN ENGLAND. Philip Nelson.

ARCHÆOLOGY AND FALSE ANTIQUITIES. R. Munro.

BELLS OF ENGLAND, THE. Canon J. J. Raven. *Second Edition.*

BRASSES OF ENGLAND, THE. Herbert W. Macklin. *Third Edition.*

CELTIC ART IN PAGAN AND CHRISTIAN TIMES. J. Romilly Allen. *Second Edition.*

CASTLES AND WALLED TOWNS OF ENGLAND, THE. A. Harvey.

CHURCHWARDEN'S ACCOUNTS FROM THE FOURTEENTH CENTURY TO THE CLOSE OF THE SEVENTEENTH CENTURY.

DOMESDAY INQUEST, THE. Adolphus Ballard.

ENGLISH CHURCH FURNITURE. J. C. Cox and A. Harvey. *Second Edition.*

ENGLISH COSTUME. From Prehistoric Times to the End of the Eighteenth Century. George Clinch.

ENGLISH MONASTIC LIFE. Abbot Gasquet. *Fourth Edition.*

ENGLISH SEALS. J. Harvey Bloom.

FOLK-LORE AS AN HISTORICAL SCIENCE. Sir G. L. Gomme.

GILDS AND COMPANIES OF LONDON, THE. George Unwin.

*HERMITS AND ANCHORITES OF ENGLAND, THE. Rotha Mary Clay.

MANOR AND MANORIAL RECORDS, THE. Nathaniel J. Hone. *Second Edition.*

MEDIÆVAL HOSPITALS OF ENGLAND, THE. Rotha Mary Clay.

OLD ENGLISH INSTRUMENTS OF MUSIC. F. W. Galpin. *Second Edition.*

The Antiquary's Books—continued

OLD ENGLISH LIBRARIES. James Hutt.

OLD SERVICE BOOKS OF THE ENGLISH CHURCH. Christopher Wordsworth, and Henry Littlehales. *Second Edition.*

PARISH LIFE IN MEDIÆVAL ENGLAND. Abbot Gasquet. *Third Edition.*

PARISH REGISTERS OF ENGLAND, THE. J. C. Cox.

REMAINS OF THE PREHISTORIC AGE IN ENGLAND. Sir B. C. A. Windle. *Second Edition.*

ROMAN ERA IN BRITAIN, THE. J. Ward.

ROMANO-BRITISH BUILDINGS AND EARTH-WORKS. J. Ward.

ROYAL FORESTS OF ENGLAND, THE. J. C. Cox.

SHRINES OF BRITISH SAINTS. J. C. Wall.

The Arden Shakespeare.

Demy 8vo. 2s. 6d. net each volume

An edition of Shakespeare in Single Plays; each edited with a full Introduction, Textual Notes, and a Commentary at the foot of the page

ALL'S WELL THAT ENDS WELL.

ANTONY AND CLEOPATRA. *Second Edition.*

AS YOU LIKE IT.

CYMBELINE.

COMEDY OF ERRORS, THE

HAMLET. *Third Edition.*

JULIUS CAESAR.

*KING HENRY IV. PT. I.

KING HENRY V.

KING HENRY VI. PT. I.

KING HENRY VI. PT. II.

KING HENRY VI. PT. III.

KING LEAR.

KING RICHARD II.

KING RICHARD III.

LIFE AND DEATH OF KING JOHN, THE.

LOVE'S LABOUR'S LOST. *Second Edition.*

MACBETH.

MEASURE FOR MEASURE.

MERCHANT OF VENICE, THE *Second Edition.*

MERRY WIVES OF WINDSOR, THE.

MIDSUMMER NIGHT'S DREAM, A.

OTHELLO.

PERICLES.

ROMEO AND JULIET.

TAMING OF THE SHREW, THE.

TEMPEST, THE.

TIMON OF ATHENS.

TITUS ANDRONICUS.

TROILUS AND CRESSIDA.

TWO GENTLEMEN OF VERONA, THE.

TWELFTH NIGHT.

VENUS AND ADONIS.

WINTER'S TALE, THE.

Classics of Art

Edited by DR. J. H. W. LAING

With numerous Illustrations. Wide Royal 8vo

ART OF THE GREEKS, THE. H. B. Walters. 12s. 6d. net.

ART OF THE ROMANS, THE. H. B. Walters. 15s. net.

CHARDIN. H. E. A. Furst. 12s. 6d. net.

DONATELLO. Maud Cruttwell. 15s. net.

FLORENTINE SCULPTORS OF THE RENAIS-SANCE. Wilhelm Bode. Translated by Jessie Haynes. 12s. 6d. net.

GEORGE ROMNEY. Arthur B. Chamberlain. 12s. 6d. net.

Classics of Art—*continued*

GHIRLANDAIO. Gerald S. Davies. *Second Edition.* 10s. 6d. *net.*

LAWRENCE. Sir Walter Armstrong. £1 1s. *net.*

MICHELANGELO. Gerald S. Davies. 12s. 6d. *net.*

RAPHAEL. A. P. Oppé. 12s. 6d. *net.*

REMBRANDT'S ETCHINGS. A. M. Hind. Two Volumes. 21s. *net.*

RUBENS. Edward Dillon. 25s. *net.*

TINTORETTO. Evelyn March Phillipps. 15s. *net.*

TITIAN. Charles Ricketts. 15s. *net.*

TURNER'S SKETCHES AND DRAWINGS. A. J. Finberg. *Second Edition.* 12s. 6d. *net.*

VELAZQUEZ. A. de Beruete. 10s. 6d. *net.*

The 'Complete' Series.

Fully Illustrated. Demy 8vo

THE COMPLETE ASSOCIATION FOOTBALLER. B. S. Evers and C. E. Hughes-Davies. 5s. *net.*

THE COMPLETE ATHLETIC TRAINER. S. A. Mussabini. 5s. *net.*

THE COMPLETE BILLIARD PLAYER. Charles Roberts. 10s. 6d. *net.*

THE COMPLETE BOXER. J. G. Bohun Lynch. 5s. *net.*

THE COMPLETE COOK. Lilian Whitling. 7s. 6d. *net.*

THE COMPLETE CRICKETER. Albert E Knight. 7s. 6d. *net. Second Edition.*

THE COMPLETE FOXHUNTER. Charles Richardson. 12s. 6d. *net. Second Edition.*

THE COMPLETE GOLFER. Harry Vardon. 10s. 6d. *net. Thirteenth Edition.*

THE COMPLETE HOCKEY-PLAYER. Eustace E. White. 5s. *net. Second Edition.*

THE COMPLETE HORSEMAN. W. Scarth Dixon. *Second Edition.* 10s. 6d. *net.*

THE COMPLETE LAWN TENNIS PLAYER. A. Wallis Myers. 10s. 6d. *net. Third Edition, Revised.*

THE COMPLETE MOTORIST. Filson Young. 12s. 6d. *net. New Edition (Seventh).*

THE COMPLETE MOUNTAINEER. G. D. Abraham. 15s. *net. Second Edition.*

THE COMPLETE OARSMAN. R. C. Lehmann. 10s. 6d. *net.*

THE COMPLETE PHOTOGRAPHER. R. Child Bayley. 10s. 6d. *net. Fourth Edition.*

THE COMPLETE RUGBY FOOTBALLER, ON THE NEW ZEALAND SYSTEM. D. Gallaher and W. J. Stead. 10s. 6d. *net. Second Edition.*

THE COMPLETE SHOT. G. T. Teasdale-Buckell. 12s. 6d. *net. Third Edition.*

THE COMPLETE SWIMMER. F. Sachs. 7s. 6d. *net.*

THE COMPLETE YACHTSMAN. B. Heckstall-Smith and E. du Boulay. *Second Edition, Revised.* 15s. *net.*

The Connoisseur's Library

With numerous Illustrations. Wide Royal 8vo. 25s. *net each volume*

ENGLISH FURNITURE. F. S. Robinson.

ENGLISH COLOURED BOOKS. Martin Hardie.

ETCHINGS. Sir F. Wedmore *Second Edition.*

EUROPEAN ENAMELS. Henry H. Cunynghame.

GLASS. Edward Dillon.

GOLDSMITHS' AND SILVERSMITHS' WORK. Nelson Dawson. *Second Edition.*

ILLUMINATED MANUSCRIPTS. J. A. Herbert. *Second Edition.*

IVORIES. Alfred Maskell.

JEWELLERY. H. Clifford Smith. *Second Edition.*

MEZZOTINTS. Cyril Davenport.

MINIATURES. Dudley Heath.

PORCELAIN. Edward Dillon.

FINE BOOKS. A. W. Pollard.

SEALS. Walter de Gray Birch.

WOOD SCULPTURE. Alfred Maskell. *Second Edition.*

Handbooks of English Church History

Edited by J. H. BURN. *Crown 8vo. 2s. 6d. net each volume*

THE FOUNDATIONS OF THE ENGLISH CHURCH. J. H. Maude.

THE SAXON CHURCH AND THE NORMAN CONQUEST. C. T. Cruttwell.

THE MEDIÆVAL CHURCH AND THE PAPACY. A. C. Jennings.

THE REFORMATION PERIOD. Henry Gee.

THE STRUGGLE WITH PURITANISM. Bruce Blaxland.

THE CHURCH OF ENGLAND IN THE EIGHTEENTH CENTURY. Alfred Plummer.

Handbooks of Theology

THE DOCTRINE OF THE INCARNATION. R. L. Ottley. *Fifth Edition, Revised. Demy 8vo. 12s. 6d.*

A HISTORY OF EARLY CHRISTIAN DOCTRINE. J. F. Bethune-Baker. *Demy 8vo. 10s. 6d.*

AN INTRODUCTION TO THE HISTORY OF RELIGION. F. B. Jevons. *Fifth Edition. Demy 8vo. 10s. 6d.*

AN INTRODUCTION TO THE HISTORY OF THE CREEDS. A. E. Burn. *Demy 8vo. 10s. 6d.*

THE PHILOSOPHY OF RELIGION IN ENGLAND AND AMERICA. Alfred Caldecott. *Demy 8vo. 10s. 6d.*

THE XXXIX ARTICLES OF THE CHURCH OF ENGLAND. Edited by E. C. S. Gibson. *Seventh Edition. Demy 8vo. 12s. 6d*

The 'Home Life' Series

Illustrated. Demy 8vo. 6s. to 10s. 6d. net

HOME LIFE IN AMERICA. Katherine G. Busbey. *Second Edition.*

HOME LIFE IN FRANCE. Miss Betham-Edwards. *Sixth Edition.*

HOME LIFE IN GERMANY. Mrs. A. Sidgwick. *Second Edition.*

HOME LIFE IN HOLLAND. D. S. Meldrum. *Second Edition.*

HOME LIFE IN ITALY. Lina Duff Gordon. *Second Edition.*

HOME LIFE IN NORWAY. H. K. Daniels. *Second Edition.*

HOME LIFE IN RUSSIA. A. S. Rappoport.

HOME LIFE IN SPAIN. S. L. Bensusan. *Second Edition.*

The Illustrated Pocket Library of Plain and Coloured Books

Fcap. 8vo. 3s. 6d. net each volume

WITH COLOURED ILLUSTRATIONS

THE LIFE AND DEATH OF JOHN MYTTON, ESQ. Nimrod. *Fifth Edition.*

THE LIFE OF A SPORTSMAN. Nimrod.

HANDLEY CROSS. R. S. Surtees. *Fourth Edition.*

MR. SPONGE'S SPORTING TOUR. R. S. Surtees. *Second Edition.*

JORROCKS'S JAUNTS AND JOLLITIES. R. S. Surtees. *Third Edition.*

ASK MAMMA. R. S. Surtees.

THE ANALYSIS OF THE HUNTING FIELD. R. S. Surtees.

THE TOUR OF DR. SYNTAX IN SEARCH OF THE PICTURESQUE. William Combe.

THE TOUR OF DR. SYNTAX IN SEARCH OF CONSOLATION. William Combe.

THE THIRD TOUR OF DR. SYNTAX IN SEARCH OF A WIFE. William Combe.

LIFE IN LONDON. Pierce Egan.

WITH PLAIN ILLUSTRATIONS

THE GRAVE: A Poem. Robert Blair.

ILLUSTRATIONS OF THE BOOK OF JOB. Invented and Engraved by William Blake.

Leaders of Religion

Edited by H. C. BEECHING. *With Portraits*

Crown 8vo. 2s. net each volume

CARDINAL NEWMAN. R. H. Hutton.

JOHN WESLEY. J. H. Overton.

BISHOP WILBERFORCE. G. W. Daniell.

CARDINAL MANNING. A. W. Hutton.

CHARLES SIMEON. H. C. G. Moule.

JOHN KNOX. F. MacCunn. *Second Edition.*

JOHN HOWE. R. F. Horton.

THOMAS KEN. F. A. Clarke.

GEORGE FOX, THE QUAKER. T. Hodgkin. *Third Edition.*

JOHN KEBLE. Walter Lock.

THOMAS CHALMERS. Mrs. Oliphant. *Second Edition.*

LANCELOT ANDREWES. R. L. Ottley. *Second Edition.*

AUGUSTINE OF CANTERBURY. E. L. Cutts.

WILLIAM LAUD. W. H. Hutton. *Fourth Edition.*

JOHN DONNE. Augustus Jessop.

THOMAS CRANMER. A. J. Mason.

LATIMER. R. M. and A. J. Carlyle.

BISHOP BUTLER. W. A. Spooner.

The Library of Devotion

With Introductions and (where necessary) Notes

Small Pott 8vo, cloth, 2s.; leather, 2s. 6d. net each volume

THE CONFESSIONS OF ST. AUGUSTINE. *Eighth Edition.*

THE IMITATION OF CHRIST. *Sixth Edition.*

THE CHRISTIAN YEAR. *Fifth Edition.*

LYRA INNOCENTIUM. *Third Edition.*

THE TEMPLE. *Second Edition.*

A BOOK OF DEVOTIONS. *Second Edition.*

A SERIOUS CALL TO A DEVOUT AND HOLY LIFE. *Fifth Edition.*

A GUIDE TO ETERNITY.

THE INNER WAY. *Second Edition.*

ON THE LOVE OF GOD.

THE PSALMS OF DAVID.

LYRA APOSTOLICA.

THE SONG OF SONGS.

THE THOUGHTS OF PASCAL. *Second Edition.*

A MANUAL OF CONSOLATION FROM THE SAINTS AND FATHERS.

DEVOTIONS FROM THE APOCRYPHA.

THE SPIRITUAL COMBAT.

THE DEVOTIONS OF ST. ANSELM.

BISHOP WILSON'S SACRA PRIVATA.

GRACE ABOUNDING TO THE CHIEF OF SINNERS.

LYRA SACRA. A Book of Sacred Verse. *Second Edition.*

A DAY BOOK FROM THE SAINTS AND FATHERS.

A LITTLE BOOK OF HEAVENLY WISDOM. A Selection from the English Mystics.

LIGHT, LIFE, and LOVE. A Selection from the German Mystics.

AN INTRODUCTION TO THE DEVOUT LIFE.

THE LITTLE FLOWERS OF THE GLORIOUS MESSER ST. FRANCIS AND OF HIS FRIARS.

DEATH AND IMMORTALITY.

THE SPIRITUAL GUIDE. *Second Edition.*

DEVOTIONS FOR EVERY DAY IN THE WEEK AND THE GREAT FESTIVALS.

PRECES PRIVATAE.

HORAE MYSTICAE. A Day Book from the Writings of Mystics of Many Nations.

Little Books on Art

With many Illustrations. Demy 16mo. 2s. 6d. net each volume

Each volume consists of about 200 pages, and contains from 30 to 40 Illustrations, including a Frontispiece in Photogravure

ALBRECHT DÜRER. L. J. Allen.

ARTS OF JAPAN, THE. E. Dillon. *Third Edition.*

BOOKPLATES. E. Almack.

BOTTICELLI. Mary L. Bonnor.

BURNE-JONES. F. de Lisle.

CELLINI. R. H. H. Cust.

CHRISTIAN SYMBOLISM. Mrs. H. Jenner.

CHRIST IN ART. Mrs. H. Jenner.

CLAUDE. E. Dillon.

CONSTABLE. H. W. Tompkins. *Second Edition.*

COROT. A. Pollard and E. Birnstingl.

EARLY ENGLISH WATER-COLOUR. C. E. Hughes.

ENAMELS. Mrs. N. Dawson. *Second Edition.*

FREDERIC LEIGHTON. A. Corkran.

GEORGE ROMNEY. G. Paston.

GREEK ART. H. B. Walters. *Fourth Edition.*

GREUZE AND BOUCHER. E. F. Pollard.

HOLBEIN. Mrs. G. Fortescue.

ILLUMINATED MANUSCRIPTS. J. W. Bradley.

JEWELLERY. C. Davenport. *Second Edition.*

JOHN HOPPNER. H. P. K. Skipton.

SIR JOSHUA REYNOLDS. J. Sime. *Second Edition.*

MILLET. N. Peacock. *Second Edition.*

MINIATURES. C. Davenport, V.D., F.S.A. *Second Edition.*

OUR LADY IN ART. Mrs. H. Jenner.

RAPHAEL. A. R. Dryhurst.

RODIN. Muriel Ciolkowska.

TURNER. F. Tyrrell-Gill.

VANDYCK. M. G. Smallwood.

VELAZQUEZ. W. Wilberforce and A. R. Gilbert.

WATTS. R. E. D. Sketchley. *Second Edition.*

The Little Galleries

Demy 16mo. 2s. 6d. net each volume

Each volume contains 20 plates in Photogravure, together with a short outline the life and work of the master to whom the book is devoted

A LITTLE GALLERY OF REYNOLDS.

A LITTLE GALLERY OF ROMNEY.

A LITTLE GALLERY OF HOPPNER.

A LITTLE GALLERY OF MILLAIS.

The Little Guides

With many Illustrations by E. H. NEW and other artists, and from photographs

Small Pott 8vo. Cloth, 2s. 6d. net; leather, 3s. 6d. net each volume

The main features of these Guides are (1) a handy and charming form ; (2) illustrations from photographs and by well-known artists ; (3) good plans and maps ; (4) an adequate but compact presentation of everything that is interesting in the natural features, history, archæology, and architecture of the town or district treated

CAMBRIDGE AND ITS COLLEGES. A. H. Thompson. *Third Edition, Revised.*

CHANNEL ISLANDS, THE. E. E. Bicknell.

ENGLISH LAKES, THE. F. G. Brabant.

ISLE OF WIGHT, THE. G. Clinch.

LONDON. G. Clinch.

MALVERN COUNTRY, THE. Sir B.C.A.Windle.

NORTH WALES. A. T. Story.

The Little Guides—*continued*

OXFORD AND ITS COLLEGES. J. Wells. *Ninth Edition.*

ST. PAUL'S CATHEDRAL. G. Clinch.

SHAKESPEARE'S COUNTRY. Sir B. C. A. Windle. *Fifth Edition.*

SOUTH WALES. G. W. and J. H. Wade.

WESTMINSTER ABBEY. G. E. Troutbeck. *Second Edition.*

———

BERKSHIRE. F. G. Brabant.

BUCKINGHAMSHIRE. E. S. Roscoe.

CHESHIRE. W. M. Gallichan.

CORNWALL. A. L. Salmon. *Second Edition.*

DERBYSHIRE. J. C. Cox.

DEVON. S. Baring-Gould. *Third Edition.*

DORSET. F. R. Heath. *Third Edition.*

DURHAM. J. E. Hodgkin.

ESSEX. J. C. Cox.

HAMPSHIRE. J. C. Cox. *Second Edition.*

HERTFORDSHIRE. H. W. Tompkins.

KENT. G. Clinch.

KERRY. C. P. Crane. *Second Edition.*

LEICESTERSHIRE AND RUTLAND. A. Harvey and V. B. Crowther-Beynon.

MIDDLESEX. J. B. Firth.

MONMOUTHSHIRE. G. W. and J. H. Wade.

NORFOLK. W. A. Dutt. *Third Edition, Revised.*

NORTHAMPTONSHIRE. W. Dry. *New and Revised Edition.*

NORTHUMBERLAND. J. E. Morris.

NOTTINGHAMSHIRE. L. Guilford.

OXFORDSHIRE. F. G. Brabant.

SHROPSHIRE. J. E. Auden.

SOMERSET. G. W. and J. H. Wade. *Second Edition.*

STAFFORDSHIRE. C. Masefield.

SUFFOLK. W. A. Dutt.

SURREY. J. C. Cox.

SUSSEX. F. G. Brabant. *Third Edition.*

WILTSHIRE. F. R. Heath.

YORKSHIRE, THE EAST RIDING. J. E. Morris.

YORKSHIRE, THE NORTH RIDING. J. E. Morris.

YORKSHIRE, THE WEST RIDING. J. E. Morris. *Cloth, 3s. 6d. net; leather, 4s. 6d. net.*

———

BRITTANY. S. Baring-Gould.

NORMANDY. C. Scudamore.

ROME. C. G. Ellaby.

SICILY. F. H. Jackson.

The Little Library

With Introduction, Notes, and Photogravure Frontispieces

Small Pott 8vo.   Each Volume, cloth, 1s. 6d. net

Anon. A LITTLE BOOK OF ENGLISH LYRICS. *Second Edition.*

Austen (Jane). PRIDE AND PREJUDICE. *Two Volumes.*
NORTHANGER ABBEY.

Bacon (Francis). THE ESSAYS OF LORD BACON.

Barham (R. H.). THE INGOLDSBY LEGENDS. *Two Volumes.*

Barnett (Annie). A LITTLE BOOK OF ENGLISH PROSE.

Beckford (William). THE HISTORY OF THE CALIPH VATHEK.

Blake (William). SELECTIONS FROM THE WORKS OF WILLIAM BLAKE.

Borrow (George). LAVENGRO. *Two Volumes.*
THE ROMANY RYE.

Browning (Robert). SELECTIONS FROM THE EARLY POEMS OF ROBERT BROWNING.

Canning (George). SELECTIONS FROM THE ANTI-JACOBIN : With some later Poems by GEORGE CANNING.

Cowley (Abraham). THE ESSAYS OF ABRAHAM COWLEY.

The Little Library—_continued_

Crabbe (George). SELECTIONS FROM THE POEMS OF GEORGE CRABBE.

Craik (Mrs.). JOHN HALIFAX, GENTLEMAN. _Two Volumes._

Crashaw (Richard). THE ENGLISH POEMS OF RICHARD CRASHAW.

Dante Alighieri. THE INFERNO OF DANTE. Translated by H. F. CARY.
THE PURGATORIO OF DANTE. Translated by H. F. CARY.
THE PARADISO OF DANTE. Translated by H. F. CARY.

Darley (George). SELECTIONS FROM THE POEMS OF GEORGE DARLEY.

Dickens(Charles). CHRISTMAS BOOKS. _Two Volumes._

Ferrier (Susan). MARRIAGE. _Two Volumes._
THE INHERITANCE. _Two Volumes._

Gaskell (Mrs.). CRANFORD. _Second Edition._

Hawthorne (Nathaniel). THE SCARLET LETTER.

Henderson (T. F.). A LITTLE BOOK OF SCOTTISH VERSE.

Kinglake (A. W.). EOTHEN. _Second Edition._

Lamb (Charles). ELIA, AND THE LAST ESSAYS OF ELIA.

Locker (F.). LONDON LYRICS.

Marvell (Andrew). THE POEMS OF ANDREW MARVELL.

Milton (John). THE MINOR POEMS OF JOHN MILTON.

Moir (D. M.). MANSIE WAUCH.

Nichols (Bowyer). A LITTLE BOOK OF ENGLISH SONNETS.

Smith (Horace and James). REJECTED ADDRESSES.

Sterne (Laurence). A SENTIMENTAL JOURNEY.

Tennyson (Alfred, Lord). THE EARLY POEMS OF ALFRED, LORD TENNYSON.
IN MEMORIAM.
THE PRINCESS.
MAUD.

Thackeray (W. M.). VANITY FAIR. _Three Volumes._
PENDENNIS. _Three Volumes._
HENRY ESMOND.
CHRISTMAS BOOKS.

Vaughan (Henry). THE POEMS OF HENRY VAUGHAN.

Waterhouse (Elizabeth). A LITTLE BOOK OF LIFE AND DEATH. _Fourteenth Edition._

Wordsworth (W.). SELECTIONS FROM THE POEMS OF WILLIAM WORDSWORTH.

Wordsworth (W.) and Coleridge (S. T.). LYRICAL BALLADS. _Second Edition._

The Little Quarto Shakespeare

Edited by W. J. CRAIG. With Introductions and Notes

Pott 16_mo._ 40 _Volumes._ _Leather, price_ 1_s. net each volume_

Mahogany Revolving Book Case. 10_s. net_

Miniature Library

Demy 32_mo._ _Leather,_ 1_s. net each volume_

EUPHRANOR: A Dialogue on Youth. Edward FitzGerald.

THE LIFE OF EDWARD, LORD HERBERT OF CHERBURY. Written by himself.

POLONIUS; or, Wise Saws and Modern Instances. Edward FitzGerald.

THE RUBÁIYÁT OF OMAR KHAYYÁM. Edward FitzGerald. _Fourth Edition._

The New Library of Medicine

Edited by C. W. SALEEBY. *Demy 8vo*

CARE OF THE BODY, THE. F. Cavanagh. *Second Edition.* 7s. 6d. net.

CHILDREN OF THE NATION, THE. The Right Hon. Sir John Gorst. *Second Edition.* 7s. 6d. net.

DISEASES OF OCCUPATION. Sir Thos. Oliver. 10s. 6d. net. *Second Edition.*

DRINK PROBLEM, in its Medico-Sociological Aspects, The. Edited by T. N. Kelynack. 7s. 6d. net.

DRUGS AND THE DRUG HABIT. H. Sainsbury.

FUNCTIONAL NERVE DISEASES. A. T. Schofield. 7s. 6d. net.

HYGIENE OF MIND, THE. T. S. Clouston. *Sixth Edition.* 7s. 6d. net.

INFANT MORTALITY. Sir George Newman. 7s. 6d. net.

PREVENTION OF TUBERCULOSIS (CONSUMPTION), THE. Arthur Newsholme. 10s. 6d. net. *Second Edition.*

AIR AND HEALTH. Ronald C. Macfie. 7s. 6d. net. *Second Edition.*

The New Library of Music

Edited by ERNEST NEWMAN. *Illustrated. Demy 8vo.* 7s. 6d. net

BRAHMS. J. A. Fuller-Maitland. *Second Edition.*

HANDEL. R. A. Streatfeild. *Second Edition.*

HUGO WOLF. Ernest Newman.

Oxford Biographies

Illustrated. Fcap. 8vo. Each volume, cloth, 2s. 6d. net; leather, 3s. 6d. net

DANTE ALIGHIERI. Paget Toynbee. *Third Edition.*

GIROLAMO SAVONAROLA. E. L. S. Horsburgh. *Sixth Edition.*

JOHN HOWARD. E. C. S. Gibson.

ALFRED TENNYSON. A. C. Benson. *Second Edition.*

SIR WALTER RALEIGH. I. A. Taylor.

ERASMUS. E. F. H. Capey.

ROBERT BURNS. T. F. Henderson.

CHATHAM. A. S. McDowall.

CANNING. W. Alison Phillips.

BEACONSFIELD. Walter Sichel.

JOHANN WOLFGANG GOETHE. H. G. Atkins.

FRANÇOIS DE FÉNELON. Viscount St. Cyres.

Four Plays

Fcap. 8vo. 2s. net

THE HONEYMOON. A Comedy in Three Acts. Arnold Bennett. *Second Edition.*

THE GREAT ADVENTURE. A Play of Fancy in Four Acts. Arnold Bennett. *Second Edition.*

MILESTONES. Arnold Bennett and Edward Knoblauch. *Sixth Edition.*

KISMET. Edward Knoblauch. *Third Edition.*

TYPHOON. A Play in Four Acts. Melchior Lengyel. English Version by Laurence Irving. *Second Edition.*

The States of Italy

Edited by E. ARMSTRONG and R. LANGTON DOUGLAS

Illustrated. Demy 8vo

A HISTORY OF MILAN UNDER THE SFORZA. Cecilia M. Ady. 10s. 6d. net.

A HISTORY OF PERUGIA. W. Heywood. 12s. 6d. net.

A HISTORY OF VERONA. A. M. Allen. 12s. 6d. net.

The Westminster Commentaries

General Editor, WALTER LOCK

Demy 8vo

THE ACTS OF THE APOSTLES. Edited by R. B. Rackham. *Sixth Edition.* 10s. 6d.

THE FIRST EPISTLE OF PAUL THE APOSTLE TO THE CORINTHIANS. Edited by H. L. Goudge. *Third Edition.* 6s.

THE BOOK OF EXODUS. Edited by A. H. M'Neile. With a Map and 3 Plans. 10s. 6d.

THE BOOK OF EZEKIEL. Edited by H. A. Redpath. 10s. 6d.

THE BOOK OF GENESIS. Edited, with Introduction and Notes, by S. R. Driver. *Ninth Edition.* 10s. 6d.

ADDITIONS AND CORRECTIONS IN THE SEVENTH AND EIGHTH EDITIONS OF THE BOOK OF GENESIS. S. R. Driver. 1s.

THE BOOK OF THE PROPHET ISAIAH. Edited by G. W. Wade. 10s. 6d.

THE BOOK OF JOB. Edited by E. C. S. Gibson. *Second Edition.* 6s.

THE EPISTLE OF ST. JAMES. Edited, with Introduction and Notes, by R. J. Knowling. *Second Edition.* 6s.

The 'Young' Series

Illustrated. Crown 8vo

THE YOUNG BOTANIST. W. P. Westell and C. S. Cooper. 3s. 6d. net.

THE YOUNG CARPENTER. Cyril Hall. 5s.

THE YOUNG ELECTRICIAN. Hammond Hall. 5s.

THE YOUNG ENGINEER. Hammond Hall. *Third Edition.* 5s.

THE YOUNG NATURALIST. W. P. Westell. *Second Edition.* 6s.

THE YOUNG ORNITHOLOGIST. W. P. Westell. 5s.

Methuen's Shilling Library

Fcap. 8vo. 1s. net

BLUE BIRD, THE. Maurice Maeterlinck.

*CHARLES DICKENS. G. K. Chesterton.

*CHARMIDES, AND OTHER POEMS. Oscar Wilde.

CHITRÀL: The Story of a Minor Siege. Sir G. S. Robertson.

CONDITION OF ENGLAND, THE. G. F. G. Masterman.

DE PROFUNDIS. Oscar Wilde.

FROM MIDSHIPMAN TO FIELD-MARSHAL. Sir Evelyn Wood, F.M., V.C.

HARVEST HOME. E. V. Lucas.

HILLS AND THE SEA. Hilaire Belloc.

HUXLEY, THOMAS HENRY. P. Chalmers-Mitchell.

IDEAL HUSBAND, AN. Oscar Wilde.

INTENTIONS. Oscar Wilde.

JIMMY GLOVER, HIS BOOK. James M. Glover.

JOHN BOYES, KING OF THE WA-KIKUYU. John Boyes.

LADY WINDERMERE'S FAN. Oscar Wilde.

LETTERS FROM A SELF-MADE MERCHANT TO HIS SON. George Horace Lorimer.

LIFE OF JOHN RUSKIN, THE. W. G. Collingwood.

LIFE OF ROBERT LOUIS STEVENSON, THE. Graham Balfour.

LIFE OF TENNYSON, THE. A. C. Benson.

LITTLE OF EVERYTHING, A. E. V. Lucas.

LORD ARTHUR SAVILE'S CRIME. Oscar Wilde.

LORE OF THE HONEY-BEE, THE. Tickner Edwardes.

MAN AND THE UNIVERSE. Sir Oliver Lodge.

MARY MAGDALENE. Maurice Maeterlinck.

OLD COUNTRY LIFE. S. Baring-Gould.

OSCAR WILDE: A Critical Study. Arthur Ransome.

PARISH CLERK, THE. P. H. Ditchfield.

SELECTED POEMS. Oscar Wilde.

SEVASTOPOL, AND OTHER STORIES. Leo Tolstoy.

TWO ADMIRALS. Admiral John Moresby.

UNDER FIVE REIGNS. Lady Dorothy Nevill.

VAILIMA LETTERS. Robert Louis Stevenson.

VICAR OF MORWENSTOW, THE. S. Baring-Gould.

Books for Travellers

Crown 8vo. 6s. each

Each volume contains a number of Illustrations in Colour

AVON AND SHAKESPEARE'S COUNTRY, THE. A. G. Bradley.

BLACK FOREST, A BOOK OF THE. C. E. Hughes.

BRETONS AT HOME, THE. F. M. Gostling.

CITIES OF LOMBARDY, THE. Edward Hutton.

CITIES OF ROMAGNA AND THE MARCHES, THE. Edward Hutton.

CITIES OF SPAIN, THE. Edward Hutton.

CITIES OF UMBRIA, THE. Edward Hutton.

DAYS IN CORNWALL. C. Lewis Hind.

FLORENCE AND NORTHERN TUSCANY, WITH GENOA. Edward Hutton.

LAND OF PARDONS, THE (Brittany). Anatole Le Braz.

NAPLES. Arthur H. Norway.

NAPLES RIVIERA, THE. H. M. Vaughan.

NEW FOREST, THE. Horace G. Hutchinson.

NORFOLK BROADS, THE. W. A. Dutt.

NORWAY AND ITS FJORDS. M. A. Wyllie.

RHINE, A BOOK OF THE. S. Baring-Gould.

ROME. Edward Hutton.

ROUND ABOUT WILTSHIRE. A. G. Bradley.

SCOTLAND OF TO-DAY. T. F. Henderson and Francis Watt.

SIENA AND SOUTHERN TUSCANY. Edward Hutton.

SKIRTS OF THE GREAT CITY, THE. Mrs. A. G. Bell.

THROUGH EAST ANGLIA IN A MOTOR CAR. J. E. Vincent.

VENICE AND VENETIA. Edward Hutton.

WANDERER IN FLORENCE, A. E. V. Lucas.

WANDERER IN PARIS, A. E. V. Lucas.

WANDERER IN HOLLAND, A. E. V. Lucas.

WANDERER IN LONDON, A. E. V. Lucas.

Some Books on Art

ARMOURER AND HIS CRAFT, THE. Charles ffoulkes. Illustrated. *Royal 4to.* £2 2s. net.

ART AND LIFE. T. Sturge Moore. Illustrated. *Cr. 8vo.* 5s. net.

BRITISH SCHOOL, THE. An Anecdotal Guide to the British Painters and Paintings in the National Gallery. E. V. Lucas. Illustrated. *Fcap. 8vo.* 2s. 6d. net.

*DECORATIVE IRON WORK. From the XIth to the XVIIIth Century. Charles ffoulkes. *Royal 4to.* £2 2s. net.

FRANCESCO GUARDI, 1712–1793. G. A. Simonson. Illustrated. *Imperial 4to.* £2 2s. net.

ILLUSTRATIONS OF THE BOOK OF JOB. William Blake. *Quarto.* £1 1s. net.

JOHN LUCAS, PORTRAIT PAINTER, 1828–1874. Arthur Lucas. Illustrated. *Imperial 4to.* £3 3s net.

OLD PASTE. A. Beresford Ryley. Illustrated. *Royal 4to.* £2 2s. net.

ONE HUNDRED MASTERPIECES OF PAINTING. With an Introduction by R. C. Witt. Illustrated. *Second Edition. Demy 8vo.* 10s. 6d. net.

ONE HUNDRED MASTERPIECES OF SCULPTURE. With an Introduction by G. F. Hill. Illustrated. *Demy 8vo.* 10s. 6d. net.

ROMNEY FOLIO, A. With an Essay by A. B. Chamberlain. *Imperial Folio.* £15 15s. net.

*ROYAL ACADEMY LECTURES ON PAINTING. George Clausen. Illustrated. *Crown 8vo.* 5s. net.

SAINTS IN ART, THE. Margaret E. Tabor. Illustrated. *Second Edition, Revised. Fcap. 8vo.* 3s. 6d. net.

SCHOOLS OF PAINTING. Mary Innes. Illustrated. *Cr. 8vo.* 5s. net.

CELTIC ART IN PAGAN AND CHRISTIAN TIMES. J. R. Allen. Illustrated. *Second Edition. Demy 8vo.* 7s. 6d. net.

'CLASSICS OF ART.' See page 14.

'THE CONNOISSEUR'S LIBRARY.' See page 15.

'LITTLE BOOKS ON ART.' See page 18.

'THE LITTLE GALLERIES.' See page 18.

Some Books on Italy

ETRURIA AND MODERN TUSCANY, OLD. Mary L. Cameron. Illustrated. *Second Edition. Cr. 8vo. 6s. net.*

FLORENCE: Her History and Art to the Fall of the Republic. F. A. Hyett. *Demy 8vo. 7s. 6d. net.*

FLORENCE, A WANDERER IN. E. V. Lucas. Illustrated. *Fourth Edition. Cr. 8vo. 6s.*

FLORENCE AND HER TREASURES. H. M. Vaughan. Illustrated. *Fcap. 8vo. 5s. net.*

FLORENCE, COUNTRY WALKS ABOUT. Edward Hutton. Illustrated. *Second Edition. Fcap. 8vo. 5s. net.*

FLORENCE AND THE CITIES OF NORTHERN TUSCANY, WITH GENOA. Edward Hutton. Illustrated. *Second Edition. Cr. 8vo. 6s.*

LOMBARDY, THE CITIES OF. Edward Hutton. Illustrated. *Cr. 8vo. 6s.*

MILAN UNDER THE SFORZA, A HISTORY OF. Cecilia M. Ady. Illustrated. *Demy 8vo. 10s. 6d. net.*

NAPLES: Past and Present. A. H. Norway. Illustrated. *Third Edition. Cr. 8vo. 6s.*

NAPLES RIVIERA, THE. H. M. Vaughan. Illustrated. *Second Edition. Cr. 8vo. 6s.*

PERUGIA, A HISTORY OF. William Heywood. Illustrated. *Demy 8vo. 12s. 6d. net.*

ROME. Edward Hutton. Illustrated. *Third Edition. Cr. 8vo. 6s.*

ROMAGNA AND THE MARCHES, THE CITIES OF. Edward Hutton. *Cr. 8vo. 6s.*

ROMAN PILGRIMAGE, A. R. E. Roberts. Illustrated. *Demy 8vo. 10s. 6d. net.*

ROME OF THE PILGRIMS AND MARTYRS. Ethel Ross Barker. *Demy 8vo. 12s. 6d. net.*

ROME. C. G. Ellaby. Illustrated. *Small Pott 8vo. Cloth, 2s. 6d. net; leather, 3s. 6d. net.*

SICILY. F. H. Jackson. Illustrated. *Small Pott 8vo. Cloth, 2s. 6d. net; leather, 3s. 6d. net.*

SICILY: The New Winter Resort. Douglas Sladen. Illustrated. *Second Edition. Cr. 8vo. 5s. net.*

SIENA AND SOUTHERN TUSCANY. Edward Hutton. Illustrated. *Second Edition. Cr. 8vo. 6s.*

UMBRIA, THE CITIES OF. Edward Hutton. Illustrated. *Fifth Edition. Cr. 8vo. 6s.*

VENICE AND VENETIA. Edward Hutton. Illustrated. *Cr. 8vo. 6s.*

VENICE ON FOOT. H. A. Douglas. Illustrated. *Second Edition. Fcap. 8vo. 5s. net.*

VENICE AND HER TREASURES. H. A. Douglas. Illustrated. *Fcap. 8vo. 5s. net.*

VERONA, A HISTORY OF. A. M. Allen. Illustrated. *Demy 8vo. 12s. 6d. net.*

DANTE AND HIS ITALY. Lonsdale Ragg. Illustrated. *Demy 8vo. 12s. 6d. net.*

DANTE ALIGHIERI: His Life and Works. Paget Toynbee. Illustrated. *Cr. 8vo. 5s. net.*

HOME LIFE IN ITALY. Lina Duff Gordon. Illustrated. *Third Edition. Demy 8vo. 10s. 6d. net.*

LAKES OF NORTHERN ITALY, THE. Richard Bagot. Illustrated. *Fcap. 8vo. 5s. net.*

LORENZO THE MAGNIFICENT. E. L. S. Horsburgh. Illustrated. *Second Edition. Demy 8vo. 15s. net.*

MEDICI POPES, THE. H. M. Vaughan. Illustrated. *Demy 8vo. 15s. net.*

ST. CATHERINE OF SIENA AND HER TIMES. By the Author of 'Mdlle. Mori.' Illustrated. *Second Edition. Demy 8vo. 7s. 6d. net.*

S. FRANCIS OF ASSISI, THE LIVES OF. Brother Thomas of Celano. *Cr. 8vo. 5s. net.*

SAVONAROLA, GIROLAMO. E. L. S. Horsburgh. Illustrated. *Cr. 8vo. 5s. net.*

SHELLEY AND HIS FRIENDS IN ITALY. Helen R. Angeli. Illustrated. *Demy 8vo. 10s. 6d. net.*

SKIES ITALIAN: A Little Breviary for Travellers in Italy. Ruth S. Phelps. *Fcap. 8vo. 5s. net.*

UNITED ITALY. F. M. Underwood. *Demy 8vo. 10s. 6d. net.*

WOMAN IN ITALY. W. Boulting. Illustrated. *Demy 8vo. 10s. 6d. net.*

PART III.—A SELECTION OF WORKS OF FICTION

Albanesi (E. Maria). SUSANNAH AND ONE OTHER. *Fourth Edition.* Cr. 8vo. 6s.

THE BROWN EYES OF MARY. *Third Edition.* Cr. 8vo. 6s.

I KNOW A MAIDEN. *Third Edition.* Cr. 8vo. 6s.

THE INVINCIBLE AMELIA; OR, THE POLITE ADVENTURESS. *Third Edition.* Cr. 8vo. 3s. 6d.

THE GLAD HEART. *Fifth Edition.* Cr. 8vo. 6s.

OLIVIA MARY. *Fourth Edition.* Cr. 8vo. 6s.

THE BELOVED ENEMY. *Second Edition.* Cr. 8vo. 6s

Bagot (Richard). A ROMAN MYSTERY. *Third Edition* Cr. 8vo. 6s.

THE PASSPORT. *Fourth Edition.* Cr. 8vo. 6s.

ANTHONY CUTHBERT. *Fourth Edition.* Cr. 8vo. 6s.

LOVE'S PROXY. Cr. 8vo. 6s.

DONNA DIANA. *Second Edition.* Cr. 8vo. 6s.

CASTING OF NETS. *Twelfth Edition.* Cr. 8vo. 6s.

THE HOUSE OF SERRAVALLE. *Third Edition.* Cr. 8vo. 6s.

DARNELEY PLACE. *Second Edition.* Cr. 8vo. 6s.

Bailey (H. C.). STORM AND TREASURE. *Third Edition.* Cr. 8vo. 6s.

THE LONELY QUEEN. *Third Edition.* Cr. 8vo. 6s.

THE SEA CAPTAIN. Cr. 8vo. 6s.

Baring-Gould (S.). IN THE ROAR OF THE SEA. *Eighth Edition.* Cr. 8vo. 6s.

MARGERY OF QUETHER. *Second Edition.* Cr. 8vo. 6s.

THE QUEEN OF LOVE. *Fifth Edition.* Cr. 8vo. 6s.

JACQUETTA. *Third Edition.* Cr. 8vo. 6s.

KITTY ALONE. *Fifth Edition.* Cr. 8vo. 6s.

NOÉMI. Illustrated. *Fourth Edition.* Cr. 8vo. 6s.

THE BROOM-SQUIRE. Illustrated. *Fifth Edition.* Cr. 8vo. 6s.

BLADYS OF THE STEWPONEY. Illustrated. *Second Edition.* Cr. 8vo. 6s.

PABO THE PRIEST. Cr. 8vo. 6s.

WINEFRED. Illustrated. *Second Edition.* Cr. 8vo. 6s.

ROYAL GEORGIE. Illustrated. Cr. 8vo. 6s.

IN DEWISLAND. *Second Edition.* Cr. 8vo. 6s.

MRS. CURGENVEN OF CURGENVEN. *Fifth Edition.* Cr. 8vo. 6s.

Barr (Robert). IN THE MIDST OF ALARMS. *Third Edition.* Cr. 8vo. 6s.

THE COUNTESS TEKLA. *Fifth Edition.* Cr. 8vo. 6s.

THE MUTABLE MANY. *Third Edition.* Cr. 8vo. 6s.

Begbie (Harold). THE CURIOUS AND DIVERTING ADVENTURES OF SIR JOHN SPARROW, BART.; OR, THE PROGRESS OF AN OPEN MIND. *Second Edition.* Cr. 8vo. 6s.

Belloc (H.). EMMANUEL BURDEN, MERCHANT. Illustrated. *Second Edition.* Cr. 8vo. 6s.

A CHANGE IN THE CABINET. *Third Edition.* Cr. 8vo. 6s.

Bennett (Arnold). CLAYHANGER. *Eleventh Edition.* Cr. 8vo. 6s.

THE CARD. *Sixth Edition.* Cr. 8vo. 6s.

HILDA LESSWAYS. *Eighth Edition.* Cr. 8vo. 6s.

BURIED ALIVE. *Third Edition.* Cr. 8vo. 6s.

A MAN FROM THE NORTH. *Third Edition.* Cr. 8vo. 6s.

THE MATADOR OF THE FIVE TOWNS. *Second Edition.* Cr. 8vo. 6s.

THE REGENT: A FIVE TOWNS STORY OF ADVENTURE IN LONDON. *Third Edition.* Cr. 8vo. 6s.

ANNA OF THE FIVE TOWNS. *Fcap.* 8vo. 1s. net.

TERESA OF WATLING STREET. *Fcap.* 8vo. 1s. net.

Benson (E. F.). DODO: A DETAIL OF THE DAY. *Sixteenth Edition.* Cr. 8vo. 6s.

Birmingham (George A.). SPANISH GOLD. *Seventeenth Edition. Cr 8vo. 6s.*
Also Fcap. 8vo. 1s. net.
THE SEARCH PARTY. *Sixth Edition. Cr. 8vo. 6s.*
Also Fcap. 8vo. 1s. net.
LALAGE'S LOVERS. *Third Edition. Cr. 8vo. 6s.*
THE ADVENTURES OF DR. WHITTY. *Fourth Edition. Cr. 8vo. 6s.*

Bowen (Marjorie). I WILL MAINTAIN *Ninth Edition. Cr. 8vo. 6s.*
DEFENDER OF THE FAITH. *Seventh Edition. Cr. 8vo. 6s.*
A KNIGHT OF SPAIN. *Third Edition. Cr. 8vo. 6s.*
THE QUEST OF GLORY. *Third Edition. Cr. 8vo. 6s.*
GOD AND THE KING. *Fifth Edition. Cr. 8vo. 6s.*
THE GOVERNOR OF ENGLAND. *Second Edition. Cr. 8vo. 6s.*

Castle (Agnes and Egerton). THE GOLDEN BARRIER. *Cr. 8vo. 6s.*

*Chesterton (G. K.). THE FLYING INN. *Cr. 8vo. 6s.*

Clifford (Mrs. W. K.). THE GETTING WELL OF DOROTHY. Illustrated. *Third Edition. Cr. 8vo. 3s. 6d.*

Conrad (Joseph). THE SECRET AGENT: A SIMPLE TALE. *Fourth Edition. Cr. 8vo. 6s.*
A SET OF SIX. *Fourth Edition. Cr. 8vo. 6s.*
UNDER WESTERN EYES. *Second Edition. Cr. 8vo. 6s.*
CHANCE. *Cr. 8vo. 6s.*

Conyers (Dorothea). SALLY. *Fourth Edition. Cr. 8vo. 6s.*
SANDY MARRIED. *Third Edition. Cr. 8vo. 6s.*

Corelli (Marie). A ROMANCE OF TWO WORLDS. *Thirty-Second Edition. Cr. 8vo. 6s.*
VENDETTA; OR, THE STORY OF ONE FORGOTTEN. *Thirtieth Edition. Cr. 8vo. 6s.*
THELMA: A NORWEGIAN PRINCESS. *Forty-third Edition. Cr. 8vo. 6s.*
ARDATH: THE STORY OF A DEAD SELF. *Twenty-first Edition. Cr. 8vo. 6s.*
THE SOUL OF LILITH. *Seventeenth Edition. Cr. 8vo. 6s.*
WORMWOOD: A DRAMA OF PARIS. *Nineteenth Edition. Cr. 8vo. 6s.*
BARABBAS: A DREAM OF THE WORLD'S TRAGEDY. *Forty-sixth Edition. Cr. 8vo. 6s.*
THE SORROWS OF SATAN. *Fifty-eighth Edition. Cr. 8vo. 6s.*
THE MASTER-CHRISTIAN. *Fourteenth Edition. 179th Thousand. Cr. 8vo. 6s.*
TEMPORAL POWER: A STUDY IN SUPREMACY. *Second Edition. 150th Thousand. Cr. 8vo. 6s.*

GOD'S GOOD MAN: A SIMPLE LOVE STORY. *Sixteenth Edition. 154th Thousand. Cr. 8vo. 6s.*
HOLY ORDERS: THE TRAGEDY OF A QUIET LIFE. *Second Edition. 120th Thousand. Cr. 8vo. 6s.*
THE MIGHTY ATOM. *Twenty-ninth Edition. Cr. 8vo. 6s.*
Also Fcap. 8vo. 1s. net.
BOY: A SKETCH. *Thirteenth Edition. Cr. 8vo. 6s.*
Also Fcap. 8vo. 1s. net.
CAMEOS. *Fourteenth Edition. Cr. 8vo. 6s.*
THE LIFE EVERLASTING. *Sixth Edition. Cr. 8vo. 6s.*
JANE: A SOCIAL INCIDENT. *Fcap. 8vo. 1s. net.*

Crockett (S. R.). LOCHINVAR. Illustrated. *Third Edition. Cr. 8vo. 6s.*
THE STANDARD BEARER. *Second Edition. Cr. 8vo. 6s.*

Croker (B. M.). THE OLD CANTONMENT. *Second Edition. Cr. 8vo. 6s.*
JOHANNA. *Second Edition. Cr. 8vo. 6s.*
THE HAPPY VALLEY. *Fourth Edition. Cr. 8vo. 6s.*
A NINE DAYS' WONDER. *Fifth Edition. Cr. 8vo. 6s.*
ANGEL. *Fifth Edition. Cr. 8vo. 6s.*
KATHERINE THE ARROGANT. *Seventh Edition. Cr. 8vo. 6s.*
BABES IN THE WOOD. *Fourth Edition. Cr. 8vo. 6s.*

*Danby (Frank). JOSEPH IN JEOPARDY. *Fcap. 8vo. 1s. net.*

Doyle (Sir A. Conan). ROUND THE RED LAMP. *Twelfth Edition. Cr. 8vo. 6s.*
Also Fcap. 8vo. 1s. net.

Drake (Maurice). WO₂. *Fifth Edition. Cr. 8vo. 6s.*

Findlater (J. H.). THE GREEN GRAVES OF BALGOWRIE. *Fifth Edition. Cr. 8vo. 6s.*
THE LADDER TO THE STARS. *Second Edition. Cr. 8vo. 6s.*

Findlater (Mary). A NARROW WAY. *Fourth Edition. Cr. 8vo. 6s.*
THE ROSE OF JOY. *Third Edition. Cr. 8vo. 6s.*
A BLIND BIRD'S NEST. Illustrated. *Second Edition. Cr. 8vo. 6s.*

Fry (B. and C. B.). A MOTHER'S SON. *Fifth Edition. Cr. 8vo. 6s.*

Harraden (Beatrice). IN VARYING MOODS. *Fourteenth Edition. Cr. 8vo. 6s.*
HILDA STRAFFORD and THE REMITTANCE MAN. *Twelfth Edition. Cr. 8vo. 6s.*
INTERPLAY. *Fifth Edition. Cr. 8vo. 6s.*

Hauptmann (Gerhart). THE FOOL IN
CHRIST : EMMANUEL QUINT. Translated
by THOMAS SELTZER. *Cr. 8vo. 6s.*

Hichens (Robert). THE PROPHET OF
BERKELEY SQUARE. *Second Edition.
Cr. 8vo. 6s.*
TONGUES OF CONSCIENCE. *Third
Edition. Cr. 8vo. 6s.*
FELIX : THREE YEARS IN A LIFE. *Tenth
Edition. Cr. 8vo. 6s.*
THE WOMAN WITH THE FAN. *Eighth
Edition. Cr. 8vo. 6s.
Also Fcap. 8vo. 1s. net.*
BYEWAYS. *Cr. 8vo. 6s.*
THE GARDEN OF ALLAH. *Twenty-
third Edition. Cr. 8vo. 6s.*
THE BLACK SPANIEL. *Cr. 8vo. 6s.*
THE CALL OF THE BLOOD. *Ninth
Edition. Cr. 8vo. 6s.*
BARBARY SHEEP. *Second Edition. Cr.
8vo. 3s. 6d.
Also Fcap. 8vo. 1s. net.*
THE DWELLER ON THE THRESHOLD.
Cr. 8vo. 6s.
THE WAY OF AMBITION. *Fourth Edi-
tion. Cr. 8vo. 6s.*

Hope (Anthony). THE GOD IN THE
CAR. *Eleventh Edition. Cr. 8vo. 6s.*
A CHANGE OF AIR. *Sixth Edition. Cr.
8vo. 6s.*
A MAN OF MARK. *Seventh Edition. Cr.
8vo. 6s.*
THE CHRONICLES OF COUNT AN-
TONIO. *Sixth Edition. Cr. 8vo. 6s.*
PHROSO. Illustrated. *Ninth Edition. Cr.
8vo. 6s.*
SIMON DALE. Illustrated. *Ninth Edition.
Cr. 8vo. 6s.*
THE KING'S MIRROR. *Fifth Edition.
Cr. 8vo. 6s.*
QUISANTÉ. *Fourth Edition. Cr. 8vo. 6s.*
THE DOLLY DIALOGUES. *Cr. 8vo. 6s.*
TALES OF TWO PEOPLE. *Third Edi-
tion. Cr. 8vo. 6s.*
A SERVANT OF THE PUBLIC. Illus-
trated. *Sixth Edition. Cr. 8vo. 6s.*
THE GREAT MISS DRIVER. *Fourth
Edition. Cr. 8vo. 6s.*
MRS. MAXON PROTESTS. *Third Edi-
tion. Cr. 8vo. 6s.*

Hutten (Baroness von). THE HALO.
*Fifth Edition. Cr. 8vo. 6s.
Also Fcap. 8vo. 1s. net.*

'The Inner Shrine' (Author of). THE
WILD OLIVE. *Third Edition. Cr. 8vo.
6s.*
THE STREET CALLED STRAIGHT.
Fourth Edition. Cr. 8vo. 6s.
THE WAY HOME. *Second Edition. Cr.
8vo. 6s.*

Jacobs (W. W.). MANY CARGOES.
Thirty-third Edition. Cr. 8vo. 3s. 6d.
Also Illustrated in colour. *Demy 8vo.
7s. 6d. net.*
SEA URCHINS. *Seventeenth Edition. Cr.
8vo. 3s. 6d.*
A MASTER OF CRAFT. Illustrated.
Tenth Edition. Cr. 8vo. 3s. 6d.
LIGHT FREIGHTS. Illustrated. *Eleventh
Edition. Cr. 8vo. 3s. 6d.
Also Fcap. 8vo. 1s. net.*
THE SKIPPER'S WOOING. *Eleventh
Edition. Cr. 8vo. 3s. 6d.*
AT SUNWICH PORT. Illustrated. *Tenth
Edition. Cr. 8vo. 3s. 6d.*
DIALSTONE LANE. Illustrated. *Eighth
Edition. Cr. 8vo. 3s. 6d.*
ODD CRAFT. Illustrated. *Fifth Edition.
Cr. 8vo. 3s. 6d.*
THE LADY OF THE BARGE. Illustrated.
Ninth Edition. Cr. 8vo. 3s. 6d.
SALTHAVEN. Illustrated. *Third Edition.
Cr. 8vo. 3s. 6d.*
SAILORS' KNOTS. Illustrated. *Fifth
Edition. Cr. 8vo. 3s. 6d.*
SHORT CRUISES. *Third Edition. Cr.
8vo. 3s. 6d.*

James (Henry). THE GOLDEN BOWL.
Third Edition. Cr. 8vo. 6s.

Le Queux (William). THE HUNCHBACK
OF WESTMINSTER. *Third Edition.
Cr. 8vo. 6s.*
THE CLOSED BOOK. *Third Edition.
Cr. 8vo. 6s.*
THE VALLEY OF THE SHADOW.
Illustrated. *Third Edition. Cr. 8vo. 6s.*
BEHIND THE THRONE. *Third Edition.
Cr. 8vo. 6s.*

London (Jack). WHITE FANG. *Ninth
Edition. Cr. 8vo. 6s.*

Lowndes (Mrs. Belloc). THE CHINK
IN THE ARMOUR. *Fourth Edition.
Cr. 8vo. 6s. net.*
MARY PECHELL. *Second Edition. Cr.
8vo. 6s.*
STUDIES IN LOVE AND IN TERROR.
Second Edition. Cr. 8vo. 6s.
THE LODGER. *Crown 8vo. 6s.*

Lucas (E. V.). LISTENER'S LURE : AN
OBLIQUE NARRATION. *Tenth Edition.
Fcap. 8vo. 5s.*
OVER BEMERTON'S : AN EASY-GOING
CHRONICLE. *Eleventh Edition. Fcap. 8vo.
5s.*
MR. INGLESIDE. *Tenth Edition. Fcap.
8vo. 5s.*
LONDON LAVENDER. *Sixth Edition.
Fcap. 8vo. 5s.*

Lyall (Edna). DERRICK VAUGHAN, NOVELIST. *44th Thousand. Cr. 8vo.* 3s. 6d.

Macnaughtan (S.). THE FORTUNE OF CHRISTINA M‘NAB. *Sixth Edition. Cr. 8vo.* 2s. net.
PETER AND JANE. *Fourth Edition. Cr. 8vo.* 6s.

Malet (Lucas). A COUNSEL OF PER-FECTION. *Second Edition. Cr. 8vo.* 6s.
COLONEL ENDERBY'S WIFE. *Sixth Edition. Cr. 8vo.* 6s.
THE HISTORY OF SIR RICHARD CALMADY: A ROMANCE. *Ninth Edition. Cr. 8vo.* 6s.
THE WAGES OF SIN. *Sixteenth Edition. Cr. 8vo.* 6s.
THE CARISSIMA. *Fifth Edition. Cr. 8vo.* 6s.
THE GATELESS BARRIER. *Fifth Edition. Cr. 8vo.* 6s.

Mason (A. E. W.). CLEMENTINA. Illustrated. *Eighth Edition. Cr. 8vo.* 6s.

Maxwell (W. B.). THE RAGGED MES-SENGER. *Third Edition. Cr. 8vo.* 6s.
VIVIEN. *Twelfth Edition. Cr. 8vo.* 6s.
THE GUARDED FLAME. *Seventh Edition. Cr. 8vo.* 6s.
Also Fcap. 8vo. 1s. net.
ODD LENGTHS. *Second Edition. Cr. 8vo.* 6s.
HILL RISE. *Fourth Edition. Cr. 8vo.* 6s.
Also Fcap. 8vo. 1s. net.
THE COUNTESS OF MAYBURY: BE-TWEEN YOU AND I. *Fourth Edition. Cr. 8vo.* 6s.
THE REST CURE. *Fourth Edition. Cr. 8vo.* 6s.

Milne (A. A.). THE DAY'S PLAY. *Fifth Edition. Cr. 8vo.* 6s.
THE HOLIDAY ROUND. *Second Edition. Cr. 8vo.* 6s.

Montague (C. E.). A HIND LET LOOSE. *Third Edition. Cr. 8vo.* 6s.
THE MORNING'S WAR. *Second Edition. Cr. 8vo.* 6s.

Morrison (Arthur). TALES OF MEAN STREETS. *Seventh Edition. Cr. 8vo.* 6s.
Also Fcap. 8vo. 1s. net.
A CHILD OF THE JAGO. *Sixth Edition. Cr. 8vo.* 6s.
THE HOLE IN THE WALL. *Fourth Edition. Cr. 8vo.* 6s.
DIVERS VANITIES. *Cr. 8vo.* 6s.

Ollivant (Alfred). OWD BOB, THE GREY DOG OF KENMUIR. With a Frontispiece. *Twelfth Edition. Cr. 8vo.* 6s.

THE TAMING OF JOHN BLUNT. *Second Edition. Cr. 8vo.* 6s.
THE ROYAL ROAD. *Second Edition. Cr. 8vo.* 6s.

Onions (Oliver). GOOD BOY SELDOM: A ROMANCE OF ADVERTISEMENT. *Second Edition. Cr. 8vo.* 6s.
THE TWO KISSES. *Cr. 8vo.* 6s.

Oppenheim (E. Phillips). MASTER OF MEN. *Fifth Edition. Cr. 8vo.* 6s.
THE MISSING DELORA. Illustrated. *Fourth Edition. Cr. 8vo.* 6s.
Also Fcap. 8vo. 1s. net.

Orczy (Baroness). FIRE IN STUBBLE. *Fifth Edition. Cr. 8vo.* 6s.
Also Fcap. 8vo. 1s. net.

Oxenham (John). A WEAVER OF WEBS. Illustrated. *Fifth Edition. Cr. 8vo.* 6s.
THE GATE OF THE DESERT. *Eighth Edition. Cr. 8vo.* 6s.
Also Fcap. 8vo. 1s. net.
PROFIT AND LOSS. *Fourth Edition. Cr. 8vo.* 6s.
THE LONG ROAD. *Fourth Edition. Cr. 8vo.* 6s.
Also Fcap. 8vo. 1s. net.
THE SONG OF HYACINTH, AND OTHER STORIES. *Second Edition. Cr. 8vo.* 6s.
MY LADY OF SHADOWS. *Fourth Edition. Cr. 8vo.* 6s.
LAURISTONS. *Fourth Edition. Cr. 8vo.* 6s.
THE COIL OF CARNE. *Sixth Edition. Cr. 8vo.* 6s.
THE QUEST OF THE GOLDEN ROSE. *Fourth Edition. Cr. 8vo.* 6s.
MARY ALL-ALONE. *Third Edition. Cr. 8vo.* 6s.

Parker (Gilbert). PIERRE AND HIS PEOPLE. *Seventh Edition. Cr. 8vo.* 6s.
MRS. FALCHION. *Fifth Edition. Cr. 8vo.* 6s.
THE TRANSLATION OF A SAVAGE. *Fourth Edition. Cr. 8vo.* 6s.
THE TRAIL OF THE SWORD. Illus-trated. *Tenth Edition. Cr. 8vo.* 6s.
WHEN VALMOND CAME TO PONTIAC: THE STORY OF A LOST NAPOLEON. *Seventh Edition. Cr. 8vo.* 6s.
AN ADVENTURER OF THE NORTH: THE LAST ADVENTURES OF 'PRETTY PIERRE.' *Fifth Edition. Cr. 8vo.* 6s.
THE SEATS OF THE MIGHTY. Illus-trated. *Nineteenth Edition. Cr. 8vo.* 6s.
THE BATTLE OF THE STRONG: A ROMANCE OF TWO KINGDOMS. Illustrated. *Seventh Edition. Cr. 8vo.* 6s.

THE POMP OF THE LAVILETTES.
Third Edition. Cr. 8vo. 3s. 6d.
NORTHERN LIGHTS. *Fourth Edition.
Cr. 8vo. 6s.*
THE JUDGMENT HOUSE. *Cr. 8vo. 6s.*

Pasture (Mrs. Henry de la). THE
TYRANT. *Fourth Edition. Cr. 8vo. 6s.
Also Fcap. 8vo. 1s. net.*

Pemberton (Max). THE FOOTSTEPS
OF A THRONE. Illustrated. *Fourth
Edition. Cr. 8vo. 6s.*
I CROWN THEE KING. Illustrated. *Cr.
8vo. 6s.*
LOVE THE HARVESTER: A STORY OF
THE SHIRES. Illustrated. *Third Edition.
Cr. 8vo. 3s. 6d.*
THE MYSTERY OF THE GREEN
HEART. *Fifth Edition. Cr. 8vo. 2s. net*

Perrin (Alice). THE CHARM. *Fifth
Edition. Cr. 8vo. 6s.
Also Fcap. 8vo. 1s. net.*
THE ANGLO-INDIANS. *Sixth Edition.
Cr. 8vo. 6s.*

Phillpotts (Eden). LYING PROPHETS.
Third Edition. Cr. 8vo. 6s.
CHILDREN OF THE MIST. *Sixth
Edition. Cr. 8vo. 6s.*
THE HUMAN BOY. With a Frontispiece.
Seventh Edition. Cr. 8vo. 6s.
SONS OF THE MORNING. *Second Edi-
tion. Cr. 8vo. 6s.*
THE RIVER. *Fourth Edition. Cr. 8vo. 6s.*
THE AMERICAN PRISONER. *Fourth
Edition. Cr. 8vo. 6s.*
KNOCK AT A VENTURE. *Third Edition.
Cr. 8vo. 6s.*
THE PORTREEVE. *Fourth Edition. Cr.
8vo. 6s.*
THE POACHER'S WIFE. *Second Edition.
Cr. 8vo. 6s.*
THE STRIKING HOURS. *Second Edition.
Cr. 8vo. 6s.*
DEMETER'S DAUGHTER. *Third Edi-
tion. Cr. 8vo. 6s.*
THE SECRET WOMAN. *Fcap. 8vo. 1s.
net.*

Pickthall (Marmaduke). SAÏD, THE
FISHERMAN. *Tenth Edition. Cr. 8vo.
6s.*
Also Fcap. 8vo. 1s. net.

'Q' (A. T. Quiller-Couch). THE MAYOR
OF TROY. *Fourth Edition. Cr. 8vo. 6s.*
MERRY-GARDEN AND OTHER STORIES.
Cr. 8vo. 6s.
MAJOR VIGOUREUX. *Third Edition.
Cr. 8vo. 6s.*

Ridge (W. Pett). ERB. *Second Edition.
Cr. 8vo. 6s.*
A SON OF THE STATE. *Third Edition.
Cr. 8vo. 3s. 6d.*
A BREAKER OF LAWS. *A New Edition.
Cr. 8vo. 3s. 6d.*
MRS. GALER'S BUSINESS. Illustrated.
Second Edition. Cr. 8vo. 6s.
THE WICKHAMSES. *Fourth Edition.
Cr. 8vo. 6s.*
SPLENDID BROTHER. *Fourth Edition.
Cr. 8vo. 6s.
Also Fcap. 8vo. 1s. net.*
NINE TO SIX-THIRTY. *Third Edition.
Cr. 8vo. 6s.*
THANKS TO SANDERSON. *Second
Edition. Cr. 8vo. 6s.*
DEVOTED SPARKES. *Second Edition.
Cr. 8vo. 6s.*
THE REMINGTON SENTENCE. *Third
Edition. Cr. 8vo. 6s.*

Russell (W. Clark). MASTER ROCKA-
FELLAR'S VOYAGE. Illustrated.
Fifth Edition. Cr. 8vo. 3s. 6d.

Sidgwick (Mrs. Alfred). THE KINS-
MAN. Illustrated. *Third Edition. Cr.
8vo. 6s.*
THE LANTERN-BEARERS. *Third Edi-
tion. Cr. 8vo. 6s.*
THE SEVERINS. *Sixth Edition. Cr. 8vo.
6s.*
Also Fcap. 8vo. 1s. net.
ANTHEA'S GUEST. *Fourth Edition. Cr.
8vo. 6s.*
LAMORNA. *Third Edition. Cr. 8vo. 6s.*
BELOW STAIRS. *Second Edition. Cr.
8vo. 6s.*

Snaith (J. C.). THE PRINCIPAL GIRL.
Second Edition. Cr. 8vo. 6s.
AN AFFAIR OF STATE. *Second Edition.
Cr. 8vo. 6s.*

Somerville (E. Œ.) and Ross (Martin).
DAN RUSSEL THE FOX. Illustrated.
*Seventh Edition. Cr. 8vo. 6s.
Also Fcap. 8vo. 1s. net.*

Thurston (E. Temple). MIRAGE. *Fourth
Edition. Cr. 8vo. 6s.
Also Fcap. 8vo. 1s. net.*

Watson (H. B. Marriott). ALISE OF
ASTRA. *Third Edition. Cr. 8vo. 6s.*
THE BIG FISH. *Third Edition. Cr. 8vo,
6s.*

Webling (Peggy). THE STORY OF
VIRGINIA PERFECT. *Third Edition.
Cr. 8vo. 6s.
Also Fcap. 8vo. 1s. net.*

THE SPIRIT OF MIRTH. *Sixth Edition.*
Cr. 8vo. 6s.

FELIX CHRISTIE. *Third Edition. Cr.
8vo.* 6s.

THE PEARL STRINGER. *Third Edition. Cr. 8vo.* 6s.

**Westrup (Margaret) (Mrs. W. Sydney
Stacey).** TIDE MARKS. *Third Edition.
Cr. 8vo.* 6s.

Weyman (Stanley). UNDER THE RED
ROBE. Illustrated. *Twenty-third Edition. Cr. 8vo.* 6s.
Also Fcap. 8vo. 1s. net.

Whitby (Beatrice). ROSAMUND. *Second
Edition. Cr. 8vo.* 6s.

Williamson (C. N. and A. M.). THE
LIGHTNING CONDUCTOR: The
Strange Adventures of a Motor Car. Illustrated. *Twenty-first Edition. Cr. 8vo.* 6s.
Also Cr. 8vo. 1s. net.

THE PRINCESS PASSES: A ROMANCE
OF A MOTOR. Illustrated. *Ninth Edition.
Cr. 8vo.* 6s.

LADY BETTY ACROSS THE WATER.
Eleventh Edition. Cr. 8vo. 6s.
Also Fcap. 8vo. 1s. net.

THE BOTOR CHAPERON. Illustrated.
Tenth Edition. Cr. 8vo. 6s.
Also Fcap. 8vo. 1s. net.

THE CAR OF DESTINY. Illustrated.
Seventh Edition. Cr. 8vo. 6s.

MY FRIEND THE CHAUFFEUR. Illustrated. *Thirteenth Edition. Cr. 8vo.* 6s

SCARLET RUNNER. Illustrated. *Third
Edition. Cr. 8vo.* 6s.

SET IN SILVER. Illustrated. *Fourth
Edition. Cr. 8vo.* 6s.

LORD LOVELAND DISCOVERS
AMERICA. *Second Edition. Cr. 8vo.* 6s.

THE GOLDEN SILENCE. *Sixth Edition.
Cr. 8vo.* 6s.

THE GUESTS OF HERCULES. *Third
Edition. Cr. 8vo.* 6s.

THE HEATHER MOON. *Fifth Edition.
Cr. 8vo.* 6s.

THE LOVE PIRATE. Illustrated. *Second
Edition. Cr. 8vo.* 6s.

THE DEMON. *Fcap. 8vo.* 1s. net.

Wyllarde (Dolf). THE PATHWAY OF
THE PIONEER (Nous Autres). *Sixth
Edition. Cr. 8vo.* 6s.

Books for Boys and Girls

Illustrated. Crown 8vo. 3s. 6d.

GETTING WELL OF DOROTHY, THE. Mrs.
W. K. Clifford.

GIRL OF THE PEOPLE, A. L. T. Meade.

HONOURABLE MISS, THE. L. T. Meade.

MASTER ROCKAFELLAR'S VOYAGE. W. Clark
Russell.

ONLY A GUARD-ROOM DOG. Edith E.
Cuthell.

RED GRANGE, THE. Mrs. Molesworth.

SYD BELTON: The Boy who would not go
to Sea. G. Manville Fenn.

THERE WAS ONCE A PRINCE. Mrs. M. E
Mann.

Methuen's Shilling Novels

Fcap. 8vo. 1s. net

ANNA OF THE FIVE TOWNS. Arnold Bennett.

BARBARY SHEEP. Robert Hichens.

*BOTOR CHAPERON, THE. C. N. & A. M.
Williamson.

BOY. Marie Corelli.

CHARM, THE. Alice Perrin.

DAN RUSSEL THE FOX. E. Œ. Somerville
and Martin Ross.

DEMON, THE. C. N. and A. M. Williamson.

FIRE IN STUBBLE. Baroness Orczy.

*GATE OF DESERT, THE. John Oxenham.

GUARDED FLAME, THE. W. B. Maxwell.

HALO, THE. Baroness von Hutten.

HILL RISE. W. B. Maxwell.

JANE. Marie Corelli.

Methuen's Shilling Novels—*continued.*

*JOSEPH IN JEOPARDY. Frank Danby.

LADY BETTY ACROSS THE WATER. C. N. and A. M. Williamson.

LIGHT FREIGHTS. W. W. Jacobs.

LONG ROAD, THE. John Oxenham.

MIGHTY ATOM, THE. Marie Corelli.

MIRAGE. E. Temple Thurston.

MISSING DELORA, THE. E. Phillips Oppenheim.

ROUND THE RED LAMP. Sir A. Conan Doyle.

SAÏD, THE FISHERMAN. Marmaduke Pickthall.

SEARCH PARTY, THE. G. A. Birmingham.

SECRET WOMAN, THE. Eden Phillpotts.

SEVERINS, THE. Mrs. Alfred Sidgwick.

SPANISH GOLD. G. A. Birmingham

SPLENDID BROTHER. W. Pett Ridge.

TALES OF MEAN STREETS. Arthur Morrison.

TERESA OF WATLING STREET. Arnold Bennett.

TYRANT, THE. Mrs. Henry de la Pasture.

UNDER THE RED ROBE. Stanley J. Weyman.

VIRGINIA PERFECT. Peggy Webling.

WOMAN WITH THE FAN, THE. Robert Hichens.

Methuen's Sevenpenny Novels

Fcap. 8vo. 7d. net

ANGEL. B. M. Croker.

BROOM SQUIRE, THE. S. Baring-Gould

BY STROKE OF SWORD. Andrew Balfour.

*HOUSE OF WHISPERS, THE. William L Queux.

HUMAN BOY, THE. Eden Phillpotts.

I CROWN THEE KING. Max Pemberton.

*LATE IN LIFE. Alice Perrin.

LONE PINE. R. B. Townshend.

MASTER OF MEN. E. Phillips Oppenheim.

MIXED MARRIAGE A Mrs. F. E. Penny.

PETER, A PARASITE. E. Maria Albanesi.

POMP OF THE LAVILETTES, THE. Sir Gilbert Parker.

PRINCE RUPERT THE BUCCANEER. C. J. Cutcliffe Hyne.

*PRINCESS VIRGINIA, THE. C. N. & A. M. Williamson.

PROFIT AND LOSS. John Oxenham.

RED HOUSE, THE. E. Nesbit.

SIGN OF THE SPIDER, THE. Bertram Mitford.

SON OF THE STATE, A. W. Pett Ridge.

Printed by MORRISON & GIBB LIMITED, *Edinburgh*

25/10/13